Reading Parfit

p 262 –
Adams makes
my point about
consequentialism
wrongness, and
blameworthiness.

Get *Ethics* 96 (1986) [No.?]

Symposium on
R & P – Adams'
discusses it.

Non teleological
practical reasoning –
Adams p259

pp 265-266 – Adams'
argument against
science fiction examples
(he's following Susan
Wolf).

Reading Parfit

Edited by
Jonathan Dancy

BLACKWELL
Publishers

Copyright © Blackwell Publishers, Ltd, 1997

First published 1997

2 4 6 8 10 9 7 5 3 1

Blackwell Publishers Ltd
108 Cowley Road
Oxford OX4 1JF
UK

Blackwell Publishers Inc
350 Main Street
Malden, Massachusetts 02148,
USA

All rights reserved. Except for the quotation of short passages for the purposes of criticism
and review, no part of this publication may be reproduced, stored in a retrieval system, or
transmitted, in any form or by any means, electronic, mechanical, photocopying, recording
or otherwise, without the prior permission of the publisher.

Except in the United States of America, this book is sold subject to the condition that it
shall not, by way of trade or otherwise, be lent, resold, hired out, or otherwise circulated
without the publisher's prior consent in any form of binding or cover other than that in
which it is published and without a similar condition including this condition being imposed
on the subsequent purchaser.

British Library Cataloging in Publication Data

A CIP catalogue record for this book is available from the
British Library.

Library of Congress Cataloging-in-Publication Data

Reading Parfit / edited by Jonathan Dancy.
    p. cm.
  Includes bibliographical references and index.
  ISBN 0-631-16871-0 (alk. paper). – ISBN 0-631-19726-5 (pbk.: alk. paper)
  1. Parfit, Derek. Reasons and persons. 2. Ethics. 3. Rationalism.
4. Self. I. Dancy, Jonathan.
BJ1012.P393R43 1997
170–dc21   96-37737
                                                                                                   CIP

Typeset in 10 on 12 pt Times
by Best-set Typesetter Ltd., Hong Kong
Printed in Great Britain by Hartnolls Ltd, Bodmin, Cornwall

This book is printed on acid-free paper

Contents

Preface   vii

1   *Jonathan Dancy*
Parfit and Indirectly Self-defeating Theories   1

2   *David Gauthier*
Rationality and The Rational Aim   24

3   *Frank Jackson*
Which Effects?   42

4   *Michael Stocker*
Parfit and the Time of Value   54

5   *Philip Pettit and Michael Smith*
Parfit's P   71

6   *David O. Brink*
Rational Egoism and the Separateness of Persons   96

7   *Sydney Shoemaker*
Parfit on Identity   135

8   *Mark Johnston*
Human Concerns without Superlative Selves   149

9   *Simon Blackburn*
Has Kant Refuted Parfit?   180

10   *Judith Jarvis Thomson*
People and their Bodies   202

11   *John McDowell*
Reductionism and the First Person   230

12 *Robert Merrihew Adams*
Should Ethics Be More Impersonal? 251

13 *Larry S. Temkin*
Rethinking the Good, Moral Ideals and the Nature of
Practical Reasoning 290

Notes on Contributors 346

Index of Names 349

Index of Examples, Positions, Theories etc., originally from
Reasons and Persons 351

Preface

This collection of essays on Derek Parfit's *Reasons and Persons* (Clarendon Press, Oxford, 1984) was first conceived in 1987, and most of the papers that it contains were written by 1990. My original intention, in proposing such a volume and in inviting contributions, was to promote discussion and understanding of the complex material in *Reasons and Persons*, and also to give those who wanted to teach classes on the book something in the way of a series of papers that might help them and their students to find their way through it. The second of those purposes is no less relevant now, nearly ten years later, than it was then. Matters have changed somewhat in respect of the first; to judge by the constant stream of enquiries that I have received about what was happening to my collection, interest in Parfit's work is growing just as I wanted it to. I hope that the publication of the collection, better late than never, will further encourage this tendency.

All the essays printed here appear for the first time, apart from the two Critical Notices by Sydney Shoemaker and Robert Adams, which appeared in *Mind* and the *Philosophical Review* respectively. I am grateful to the editors of those journals for permission to reprint these two pieces.

Essays are printed in the order in which the topics they treat occur in *Reasons and Persons*. (This, and nothing else, explains why my own paper comes first.) This rule has been hard to apply to the papers on Part 3: that is, those concerned with the metaphysics of the self. Here I confess that my ordering is a little arbitrary. Otherwise unattributed references are throughout to *Reasons and Persons*. Readers should be warned that though there is as yet no second edition of that book, its reprinting of 1987 contained a few significant alterations (summarized on page x there). Like myself, my contributors will have been working from copies printed before 1987.

It is galling now to recognize that the collection could have been published in its present form five or six years ago. The reason for the delay was my desire to include responses that Derek Parfit had agreed to write to the suggestions and criticisms of the contributors. These responses rapidly grew to such a size that the whole could no longer be contained in a single volume. The plan then was to divide the one volume into two: one on *Reasons* and one on *Persons*, roughly. But even that plan failed. Parfit has now written so much new material that it will itself make three new books, which will eventually be published under the titles of *Practical Realism*, *The Metaphysics of the Self* and *On What Matters*. I greatly regret the delay in publication. But I have at least the consolation of knowing the quality of the new work that Parfit is producing in response to the papers in this volume. On several occasions I have delivered a contributor's paper to him, thinking silently that he would have a lot of trouble dealing with this one; and on each I have been proved, if not wrong, then at least greatly over-confident.

One consequence of the delay has been that many of the essays in *Reading Parfit* have become well known, and there have even been responses to some of them published in the journals. My contributors have sometimes asked me whether they can make changes to their essays, either as a result of this or just because they have changed their minds about something. I have been deaf to all such appeals, for the reason that Parfit's new work, though it is not confined to the essays in this volume, still stands in some degree as a direct response to them, and he has been working on the original versions. So readers should bear in mind that what is contained in *Reading Parfit* was written between five and ten years ago, and no change has been permitted since.

I end by apologizing to all my contributors, and to a frustrated readership, for my failure to get this collection published in proper time.

Jonathan Dancy
Reading, Sept. 1996

1

Parfit and Indirectly Self-defeating Theories

Jonathan Dancy

In this essay I examine the arguments at the very beginning of *Reasons and Persons*. Here Parfit accepts that two theories, one a theory of rationality and the other a theory of moral value, are indirectly self-defeating. A theory is indirectly self-defeating when it is true that, if we try to achieve the aims that it gives us, these aims will be worse achieved.[1] Parfit argues that though his two theories are like this, this does not amount to a refutation of them. I want to suggest that the sort of self-defeat at issue is more damaging than Parfit allows, and in effect amounts to self-refutation.

I start by laying out some of the theoretical substructure of the arguments in this chapter. Parfit allows these elements to emerge gradually, in response to progressive difficulties. But for my own purposes I need to lay them out in a more formal style. So the elements I now mention are (in a sense) argued for in Parfit, but I shall offer them without argument.

I

There are two distinctions in play: between act and agent and between the objective and the subjective. Let us see how these distinctions emerge with respect to the first theory, that of rationality. This theory is the Self-interest Theory, or S. Parfit says: 'This is a theory about rationality. S gives to each person this aim: the outcomes that would be best for himself, and that would make his life go, for him, as well as possible' (p. 3). Parfit unpacks this theory as follows: S's *central claim* is:

(S1)   For each person, there is one supremely rational ultimate aim: that his life go, for him, as well as possible. (p. 4)

'When applied to acts', Parfit says, S claims both

(S2)   What each of us has most reason to do is whatever would be
       best for himself, and
(S3)   It is irrational for anyone to do what he believes will be worse
       for himself. (p. 8)

This can be tidied up in the following way, for S3 is not about the
rationality of agents but about the subjective rationality of acts:

An *act* is *objectively rational* if no available alternative would be better
for the agent.

An *act* is *subjectively rational* if the agent believes that no available
alternative would be better for him.

What is it for an agent to be rational? Agent rationality is defined in
terms of motives (i.e. desires and dispositions). We call a set of motives
'S-approved' if having that set would promote one's S-given aim as well
as having any alternative set of motives.[2] (The aim which S gives each of
us is: the outcomes that would be best for himself, and that would make
his life go, for him, as well as possible.) Such a set is one which it would
be rational (in S's terms) for an agent to get if he could, and irrational for
him to lose. So we can say:

An *agent* is *objectively rational* (here[3]) if his motive is a member of an
S-approved set of motives.

An *agent* is *subjectively rational* (here) if his motive is a member of a
set of motives which he believes to be S-approved.

Notice that our assessment of an individual motive depends on what
other motives are present with it. Motives are assessed not individually,
but in sets which are up for S's approval as a whole. As a result, there
may well be more than one set of motives which is S-approved. One
crucial point for Parfit is that S itself should not amount to the specification of any recommended motive or set of motives. He holds that S
specifies aims but not motives; S leaves it open which motives would best
realize S-given aims.

I will make some comments on the distinction between subjective and
objective, and of the use to which it may be put, after looking at the
second theory, to which I now turn. This is Consequentialism, or C. Parfit
writes that C's central claim is (p. 24):

(C1)   There is one ultimate moral aim: that outcomes be as good as
       possible.

What does this tell us about acts and agents? Parfit says that 'applied to acts, C claims both:

(C2) What each of us ought to do is whatever would make the outcome best, and

(C3) If someone does what he believes will make the outcome worse, he is acting wrongly.' (ibid.)

Remember that these remarks are both about the worth or rightness of *acts*. We could re-express them as follows, in order to make them explicitly analogous to similar claims of S:

An *act* is *objectively right* if its outcome is the best possible.

An *act* is *subjectively right* if the agent believes that its outcome will be the best possible.

What about agents? Again, the worth of agents is defined in terms of that of motives or sets of motives. We call a set of motives 'C-approved' if having that set of motives would lead to outcomes at least as good as the outcomes of any alternative set of motives. Such a set of motives is one which it would be right in C's terms for an agent to cause himself to have and wrong in C's terms for him to cause himself to lose. We can then define the worth of agents, as opposed to that of acts, as follows:

An *agent* is *objectively blameless* (here) if his motive is a member of a C-approved set of motives.

An *agent* is *subjectively blameless* (here) if he believes his motive to be a member of a C-approved set of motives.[4]

It should be said that in these formulations I have to some extent tidied up the suggestions in Parfit's text.

We now have two distinctions, which combine to yield four definitions for each of S and C. In the case of S, both acts and agents may be either objectively or subjectively rational. Note that there is a clear distinction between the (subjective or objective) rationality of the agent and the subjective rationality of the act (and similarly with C); we must be careful, therefore, not to confuse the two. However, the objective/subjective distinction turns out, perhaps rather surprisingly, not to make any difference. For it only comes into play when the agent is either ignorant of or mistaken about some relevant fact. And none of Parfit's examples are of this form. So despite the potential complications introduced by the objective/subjective distinction, all the real work in Parfit's defence of

4 *Jonathan Dancy*

the claim that S and C are only indirectly self-defeating is done by the distinction between act and agent. I now turn to argue that this defence is unsuccessful.

II

I start with Parfit's attempt to show that S is only indirectly self-defeating. He accepts without qualms the claim that S is, in the case of most people, at least indirectly self-defeating. We call people 'never self-denying' if they never do what would be worse for them in S's terms.[5] S is indirectly self-defeating if it would be worse in S's terms for a person to be never self-denying than to have some other disposition. A hedonist version of S would probably be indirectly self-defeating. As Parfit says, 'Hedonists have long known that happiness, when aimed at, is harder to achieve. If my strongest desire is that I be happy, I may be less happy than I would be if I had other desires that were stronger' (p. 6). A non-hedonist proof of the same point involves the example of someone stranded in a desert, who wants to persuade a reluctant motorist to give him a lift into town. Suppose that this person is unable to lie convincingly. Now, though he will perhaps promise to reward the driver on arrival, he knows that he will not in fact keep his promise. For to do so would be worse for him (in S's terms), once he has got back to safety. So his promise will be a lying promise, and the driver will detect his lie and drive on without him. In this case, then, it is worse for him (in S's terms) to be never self-denying – that is, to be someone who always tries to achieve his S-given aim.

So S is indirectly individually self-defeating. What we learn from this is that our S-given aim is one thing, and the motives which we should have are another. For if our motive is simply to achieve our S-given aim, we will fail to achieve it, or at least achieve it less completely than if we had had some other set of motives. And this shows us that S itself tells us to adopt (or have) some other set of motives. But S is a theory of *rationality*, and its central claim is a specification of a single supremely rational ultimate aim (p. 8). It looks then as if S holds that there is a single rational aim, but that it would not be rational to aim at this aim because the very aiming at it reduces one's chances of achieving it. So we seem to have here a rational aim which it would be irrational to aim at. Is this a proof that S is worse than indirectly self-defeating?

One might think that there is no genuine problem here. We are used to cases where we are told to aim at something else if we want to achieve our aim – that is, the outcome we hope for. For instance, if there is a wind, I may need to aim to the left of my target (to 'aim off') if I want to hit what I am aiming to hit: namely the centre. It is important to see that examples like this one fail to dissolve the difficulty I am trying to bring out. They play on the distinction between *aims* and *outcomes*. They tell us that our best hope of achieving a certain outcome is not to aim directly at it. But S is a theory not about outcomes but about aims. It specifies a rational aim, not a rational outcome. It does not say: 'Here is an outcome you (should) want and you will best achieve it if you aim off a little.' It says: 'Here is an outcome you (should) want and you will best achieve it if you do not want it.'[6] The difference between the derived aim of the archer and the motives of which S can approve is that if the archer hits what he is (for derivative reasons) aiming at, he will be (and should be) disappointed. But if we achieve the outcomes which S can approve our aiming for, we should by S's lights be satisfied, even though we will not even have been aiming at the target which S, in specifying a single supremely rational ultimate aim, sets us.

Parfit considers an objection which is at least closely related to the one I am trying to bring out here. He asks: 'If . . . a person believes S, it tells him to cause himself to be disposed to act in a way that S claims to be irrational. Is this a damaging implication? Does it give us any reason to reject S?' (p. 12). I say that this *may* be the same objection, because Parfit expresses his version as arising only in the case where the person *believes* S. It looks then as if the objection, in Parfit's hands, is going to concern subjective rationality rather than objective rationality; whereas the objection I outlined in the previous two paragraphs showed no signs of being circumscribed in the same way. But as this unfolds, it becomes clear that this is a misconception. Nothing in the objection or in the reply to it turns on the question of whether the person believes S.

The general drift of Parfit's discussion here is unclear. But as I understand it, he argues against the objection just mentioned as a route to arguing against the objection with which I am principally concerned: namely, that there is an aim which S holds to be both rational and irrational. The argument is conducted around two examples. The first is called 'Schelling's answer to armed robbery'. An armed robber breaks into my house. I just have time to call the police, who are going to take 15 minutes to arrive, before he threatens to kill my children one by one if I don't tell him where my gold is. I believe that if I do tell him, he will kill us all anyway, in order to prevent us describing him and his get-away car to the police. But I have a special drug, which 'causes one to be, for a brief period, very irrational' (p. 13). I take the drug, and become irrational. I say to the man: 'I love my children. So please kill them.' He tortures me, and I cry: 'This is agony. So please don't stop.' Although this method of self-defence is not guaranteed to succeed, it at least improves the chances that the robber will retire baffled, since his threats will no longer work on me, and in my present state I am unlikely to be able eventually to describe him or to record the number of his car.

Parfit argues first that in this case it is rational of me to cause myself to be disposed to act irrationally. My act of taking the drug is a rational one, even though its effect is that I behave irrationally. In assessing this claim, I shall impose on the discussion the act/agent distinction, which in Parfit's text does not appear until the next section; in fact he ignores it completely in the discussion of Schelling's answer to armed robbery, claiming at one point that after taking the drug I am very irrational, and at another that my acts become very irrational. Let us start with his original description of the case, according to which the drug caused *me* to become irrational. If we were to take this description seriously, we would have to describe the drug as causing me to have a set of motives that are not S-approved. But this would be wrong. In S's terms, my motives after taking the drug are S-approved, since having that set of motives is as likely to promote my S-given aims as having any other set – more likely, if Schelling's answer is sound. So it is rational of me to acquire those motives if I can, and irrational of me to lose them. After taking the drug, I remain rational in S's terms. Is the suggestion rather that 'during this period, my acts are very irrational' (p. 13), so that the irrationality belongs not to me but to my acts? In S's terms this is not true. Acts are rational in S's terms if no available alternative would be better for the agent (i.e. would more effectively promote the agent's S-given aims). And after taking the drug, my acts are just like this. It is true that in some sense we want to describe either me or my acts as irrational during this period. But in S's terms this is not true. In S's terms this is not a case where it is rational of me to cause myself to act irrationally.

What is going on here is that Parfit is appealing to an intuitive sense of 'rational' in order to establish that it can be rational to cause oneself to be disposed to act irrationally, intending to use this in defence of S. But the intuitive senses of 'rational' and 'irrational' are not available to S; so this defence fails. Parfit's conclusion that it can be rational to cause oneself to act irrationally is not one with which S can agree, and therefore it is not one which S is entitled to use in its own defence. And even if the conclusion that Parfit wishes to draw from the case of Schelling's answer to armed robbery could be drawn, it would still not provide an answer to the paradox with which I am primarily concerned. In the Schelling case, there are two acts (or sets of acts) and two sets of motives; after taking the drug, I suppose that I have a new set of motives, though I have no idea what they could possibly be like. All that the case is intended to establish, in the first instance, is that the first, rational act can have an irrational act as its intended consequence. But my later irrational acts are not the intentional objects of my first motive. In taking the drug,

I have only the vaguest idea of what my subsequent acts will be. We could not describe me as acting irrationally on purpose because that is the wisest choice in the circumstances. This means that the case of Schelling's answer to armed robbery does not by itself resolve our paradox. It does not give us a *single* action which is irrational but which the agent is rational in doing.

But Parfit moves from that case in a rather indirect way. He considers a certain principle:

(G1) If there is some motive that it would be both (a) rational for someone to cause himself to have, and (b) irrational for him to cause himself to lose, then (c) it cannot be irrational for him to act upon this motive.

Parfit comments that Schelling's answer to armed robbery disproves this principle. But it should be clear that the conclusion (c) is multiply ambiguous. There are three possible readings:

(c1) acts done on this motive cannot be irrational, or
(c2) a person who acts on that motive cannot be irrational, or
(c3) it cannot be irrational to cause oneself to act on that motive.

Let us take these in order. The Schelling case is supposed to provide a counter-example to (G1). Is this an example of an irrational act done on an S-approved set of motives? No: in S's terms, my acts are rational while under the drug. Is it an example of an irrational agent: that is, one who has a set of motives which is not S-approved? Again, no: the motives on which I am acting are ones which in S's terms it is rational of me to acquire if I can, and irrational of me to cause myself to lose. Is it an example of an act–motive combination which it is irrational of me to cause myself to have? Again, no. On Parfit's own showing, it is eminently rational of me to cause myself to act in this way; indeed, that was the main point of the example. I conclude that (G1) is unimpugned by Schelling's answer to armed robbery.

Parfit, however, takes himself to have shown that (G1) is false, and describes the Schelling case as one of rational irrationality. Even if this were an acceptable description, it would amount only to the claim that it can be rational to cause oneself to become irrational. The notion of rational irrationality has a different sense in his second example, which is nearer to my concerns here. This is the contorted case of Kate. Kate is a writer whose strongest desire is that her books be as good as possible. This leads her to work enormously hard, and to suffer fits of extreme depression. Notably, since we are supposed to be discussing the question whether S is indirectly self-defeating, Parfit does not say that this has the result that her books are worse than they would otherwise have been. Instead, he says that if Kate worked less hard, her books would be only slightly worse, and she would be happier. She would find her work just as rewarding, and she would not suffer fits of depression. The peculiarity of Kate is that, as things are with her, she would only work less hard if her desire that her books be as good as possible were much less strong. And in such a case she *would* find her work boring, and this would mean that things would be worse for her overall than they are now, since it is worse (in S's terms) to be uniformly bored than to suffer occasional fits of depression.

Parfit draws two conclusions from the case of Kate. The first is that Kate is further proof (from a hedonist point of view) that it can be worse for us in S's terms to be never self-denying, and hence that S is indirectly self-defeating. Later Kate reappears, and the question is raised whether it is rational for Kate to work as hard as she does. There is the danger for S that this is both rational and irrational. Encouraged by his diagnosis of the Schelling case as an acceptable example of rational irrationality, Parfit wants to say similar things here. But this time he introduces the act/agent distinction to argue that while Kate's actions are irrational, she herself is rational. This is rational irrationality of a new sort.

In S's terms, Kate is rational. For she has and acts on an S-approved set of motives. As things are, there is no alternative set of motives that she could have which would make her life go, for her, any better. (This holds both for objective and for subjective rationality, since Kate is neither ignorant of nor in error about any relevant fact.) So as far as this goes, Parfit's diagnosis is correct. What about the acts? Here matters are more complicated. According to S, an act is rational if no available alternative would be better for the agent. How do things stand for Kate? From one point of view, there is an available alternative which would be better for her: namely, that she should work a little less hard on her books. If she did this, her books would be only slightly worse, and she would be much happier. Kate could do this. But as things stand, the only way she could get herself to do it would be to begin to care much less about her books, and if she did that, she would find her life boring. So the question is whether the action of working less hard is one whose availability shows that what Kate actually does is irrational. The impression that this is so is given by concentrating on what one might think of as simple actions, uncomplicated by any consideration of the motives which might generate them or of the more general plans and projects of which this action might be a part and to which it might contribute.

In considering the rationality of an action, according to S, one compares that action to others. The question is: 'Which others?' That is, what is the comparison class within which the rationality of an action is to be determined? In order to establish the irrationality of Kate's acts in his example, Parfit is constrained to evaluate those acts in isolation from any motive and from any more general considerations. This approach rules out the following argument. If Kate were to work less hard, her life would go, for her, less well (because she would only work less hard if she cared much less about her books, which would make her life very boring). An action is rational if doing it makes one's life go better for one than would any available alternative. Therefore her action of working less hard would be irrational, and her action of overworking herself so that she suffers from fits of depression emerges as rational. This argument, which seems to me to be perfectly consistent with the general thrust of S, is ruled out, apparently, because its first premiss (that if Kate were to work less hard her life would go, for her, less well) is contradicted by the truth that if Kate were to work less hard, her books would be not much worse and she would be happier – that is, that if Kate were to work less hard her life would go, for her, as well as possible. We have here two opposing subjunctive conditionals: if it were the case that p, it would be the case that q, and if it were the case that p, it would not be the case that q. We know that in general we cannot infer from two such conditionals the contradictory consequence that if it were the case that p, it both would and would not be the case that q. This is because each of the two original conditionals has its own comparison class. Returning to Kate, the question then is which of the two competing conditionals should be held to determine the rationality of her acts. We can choose the first comparison class, which gives us the conclusion that her act of overworking herself is irrational, or we can choose the second class, which would give us the conclusion that her act is rational.

Our choice here can be expressed in terms of possible worlds. Both approaches, of course, start from the actual world, and move out in search of the nearest world in which the antecedent of the relevant subjunctive conditional is true. How things are in other respects in that world (or group of worlds) determines the truth of the conditional. The first approach, which is Parfit's, starts from here, and asks simply whether there is a world in which Kate works less hard on her books and is happier. There is such a world; so Parfit announces that this world establishes that this course of action is available to Kate, and shows that what she actually does is irrational. The second approach, which is mine, starts from here, including the story of Kate's present motivational structure, and asks whether in the nearest world in which Kate works less hard she is happier. It turns out that the nearest world in which, with something like that pattern, she can get herself to work less hard is one in which she gets very bored and unhappy. So what she actually does is rational.

In arguing that Kate's action, according to S, is irrational, Parfit implicitly assumes that the proper comparison class is the first of the two. This can only be because Parfit takes the nature of S itself to pre-empt our choice. Acts are to be considered not as parts of wider plans, nor in relation to the motives which generate them, because S says not. In this sense S, in Parfit's hands, is a doctrine which takes an atomistic view of actions. But there is, so far as we have yet seen, no intrinsic reason why S should not take a different, broader view of actions, one which sees them in relation to the motives from which they spring. Indeed, the broader view seems to make S much more plausible. But if S does take the broader view, we lose the conclusion which Parfit needs to defend S against the charge that it contradicts itself by saying that there is an aim which it is both rational and irrational to adopt: namely, that one's life go, for one, as well as possible. For we lose the conclusion, in the case of Kate, that her action of overworking herself is irrational. On this broader approach, she is rational, and so is her action.

It is not just that there are two ways of approaching this matter, and that S has a free choice between them. I want to argue that my way is far better, far more natural, than Parfit's. For the worlds which I am looking at to see if Kate would be happier if she worked less hard are much nearer than the world to which Parfit appeals to show that she could have worked less hard and been happier, and the appeal to them seems to me a far more natural appeal. There is a further, *ad hominem* point here. The account of personal identity which emerges in Part 3 of *Reasons and Persons* has it that the less strong the relations of continuity and connectedness between two person-stages, the less they are the same person. The world in which Kate, working less hard, is happier than she is here is one in which her cares and concerns are very different from those here. That Kate is not very closely related to this one. But we should also remember that the example of Kate is run from a hedonist point of view, and for hedonists it is important that the pleasure or happiness in prospect, and which determines the rationality of one's acts, be *one's own* pleasure or happiness, not that of some distant relation of oneself. (Kate's question is: 'Is this action something which *I* could do and which would make *my* life go better?') My approach sustains this general demand, while Parfit's does not, and this is further evidence that mine is the right one to take in the case of Kate.[7]

My conclusion, then, is that the most plausible version of S cannot be defended against the charge of contradiction by appeal either to Schelling's answer to armed robbery or to the case of Kate. There remains one further manoeuvre by which Parfit might claim to escape this conclusion. This concerns the distinction between formal and substantive theories. He writes: 'In its central claim, S gives to each person one substantive aim: that his life go, for him, as well as possible. Does S give to each person *another* substantive aim: to be rational, and to act rationally? It does not. According to S, our formal aim is not a substantive aim' (p. 9).

This fails to extricate Parfit from the problem with which I have been concerned. For that problem did not concern the contrast between two potentially competing aims: that of being rational and that of getting one's life to go as well as possible. It concerned only S's claim that there is a single rational aim which it is not rational to aim at. The charge that this is a contradiction is not evaded by saying that one use of 'rational' in that sentence is a formal use and the other a substantive use. If it is rational to aim for one's life to go, for oneself, as well as possible, this is a substantive matter. And if it is not rational to make this one's aim, this also is for substantive reasons.

III

The question now is whether similar remarks can be made about C. The difficulties for S, as we originally expressed them, concerned the fact that S specified a certain *aim*, which it seemed to say that it was both rational and irrational to pursue. It was not a theory about outcomes, since there is no such thing as a rational outcome. But C is also a theory about aims, in Parfit's hands. C's central claim is that there is one ultimate moral aim: that outcomes be as good as possible (p. 24). This makes room for the charge that it both recommends and forbids a certain aim.

Like S, C is indirectly self-defeating.[8] Parfit considers various ways in which outcomes will be worse if we are 'pure do-gooders' – that is, if our only motive is that outcomes be as good as possible. For instance, we would have to cease to care especially for our family and friends, and to suppress many of our other strongest desires. He suggests that there would be an enormous cost in this, so great that the world would probably go worse overall if we acted in this way.

Parfit's response to the fact that C is indirectly self-defeating is the same as his response in the case of S: this does not matter, because there is no aim which C recommends us both to have and to avoid. Instead, our C-given aim is one thing, and the motives from which we should act are another. If our motive is simply to achieve our C-given aim, we will fail to achieve it, or at least achieve it less completely than if we had some other set of motives. And this shows that C itself tells us to adopt (or have) some other set of motives, a C-approved set whose adoption will further as much as any our C-given aim.

But again, it seems that we have a theory, C, which specifies a single ultimate aim for us, an aim which we *ought* to pursue, and then tells us that we ought not to pursue it because the very pursuit of it reduces our chances of achieving it. We have here a moral aim which in some sense it would be immoral to aim at, since there is available to us a better alternative practice. The question is whether Parfit succeeds in showing that this is better than self-contradictory, leaving C in the intermediate position of being undamagingly self-defeating. The problem arises, as with S, because we have here a theory which is silent on outcomes. If C specified a desirable outcome, it could hope to distinguish between what it says about outcomes and what it says about motives. It could say: 'Things go best if such and such outcomes occur, but you should not try to make those outcomes occur.' But in Parfit's hands C does not specify a desirable *outcome*;[9] it gives us an *aim*, that outcomes be as good as possible. It then tells us not to aim at this aim. Can this be coherent?

Parfit's reply to this is effectively that the notion of a C-given aim is ambiguous. There are aims we ought to have in the sense of motives which we should adopt, and there are aims we ought to have in the sense of outcomes whose nature determines how well the world is going and how well we have acted. The appearance of contradiction in the idea that there are ultimate moral aims which it would be wrong of us to pursue derives from failing to keep apart these two senses of 'aim'. Since the worth of agents is determined by the motives from which they act, this resolution can be expressed in terms of the act/agent distinction. A case in which we act from a set of motives which we ought to have, though our action does not lead to the best outcome, is not one in which what we did was both right and wrong, but one in which *we* should not be blamed for doing an *action* which is forbidden.

Parfit describes this as 'blameless wrongdoing'. He does not say that we are to be commended if we act in this way, only that we should not be blamed. But I think that the most natural way of describing this sort of situation is the say that it is one in which though what we did was wrong, we were right to do it. This description implies positive approval rather than merely the absence of blame. But I don't think that Parfit can object to that. For once we have the distinction between act and agent in place, how can we avoid approving of agents whose motives are what C says they should be? So this description is the one I shall mostly use in what follows. What I want to argue is that though that description itself is not contradictory, it is in fact impossible for C to keep our evaluation of act and agent apart in the way that it suggests.[10] C cannot commend us for doing an action which it forbids.

Parfit offers two examples to persuade us that the idea of blameless wrongdoing is coherent. The first is that of Clare. Clare loves her child, and her love for her child is a C-approved motive – or, better, a member of a C-approved set of motives which Clare has. She could either give her child some benefit, or give much greater benefits to some unfortunate stranger. Because she loves her child, she benefits him rather than the stranger. This action makes the outcome worse, as Clare recognizes. But the set of motives of which Clare's love for her child is a part is a set which it would be wrong (in C's terms) for Clare to lose and right for her to get. So it would be wrong of Clare to change her motives (even if she could) unless there is some other set of motives which is more C-approved than hers and which she could without serious loss have adopted. There is no such set of motives. So Clare is blameless in benefiting her child because of her love for him, even though her act in so doing is wrong (in C's terms) because its outcome is worse than the outcome of some available alternative act.

Though Parfit puts the case of Clare first, it is in fact analogous in the structure of his argument to the case of Kate. In Kate's case Parfit prepared the way for what he wanted to say by his discussion of Schelling's answer to armed robbery. Analogous to the latter, in the discussion of C, is the example of 'My Moral Corruption'. In this example I am a politician who has an enemy who wants to corrupt me – that is, to make me against my will into an accomplice to his crimes. He threatens to kill my children unless I allow him to take a film of me engaging in obscene acts. Later he will ask me to help in his criminal activities, on pain of publication of the film and the ruination of my career. I know that I will accede to these requests, so as to protect my career; my enemy has assured me that once I have made the film, there will be no further threat to my children unless I abandon my career. So I will have a choice between being exposed and engaging in criminal acts, and I will make the wrong choice. (It would be the right choice if there was any continuing threat to my children.)

Given the choice presented to me, I ought to let my enemy make the film. But once I have done this, I shall have a motive to engage in criminal acts. So, in C's terms, there is an action which I ought to do but which will have the effect of causing me to acquire a set of motives which will cause me to do what in C's terms is wrong. I ought to cause it to be true that I shall later act wrongly.

In this case, like that of Schelling's answer to armed robbery, there are two actions and two sets of motives: the first set causes me to allow the film to be made and the second causes me to commit criminal acts to protect my good name and career. My first act is right, and I am right to do it, because it stems from a C-approved set of motives; but the second act is wrong, and I am wrong to do it, since it stems from a set of motives which is not C-approved. The peculiarity of my moral corruption is that the second set of motives, with its attendant actions, is a predictable consequence of the first, right act. So the wrong act springs indirectly but predictably from a C-approved set of motives. The right choice for me, once the film has been made, is to allow myself to be exposed, and so have my career ruined. I will not made this choice, because I care too much about my career.[11] This shows that my criminal acts are wrong, and that I am wrong to do them.[12] Now what Parfit is using the case of my moral corruption to show is that it is possible for an acceptable moral theory to tell us to cause ourselves to do what the theory tells us is wrong. This may be intended to back up the conclusion that Clare is someone who is told by C to do acts which are wrong in C's terms, without this being an objection to C. But the case of my moral corruption cannot be used in this way, for the simple reason that it offers no *one* action which (1) is wrong and (2) I am right to do (blameless in doing). The claim for Clare was that she was involved in blameless wrongdoing, but nothing in my moral corruption can help us to see how this is possible. (These remarks mirror those I made earlier about Kate and Schelling.)

Let us then return directly to Clare. If my moral corruption offers no help, our only other resource in dissolving the appearance of contradiction is the act/agent distinction. We are trying to make sense of the idea that Clare is blameless in doing – that is, right in C's terms to do – an act which is wrong in C's terms. Should we accept this description of the situation? Note that Clare is not facing the choice we face every day between spending money on our family and sending it to Oxfam; she is in an unusual situation in which there is a particular stranger whom she could help by giving him the money she was going to spend on taking her child to the Heritage Theme Park. Let us take it that Clare's motives are a C-approved set, and hence that she is right to give (blameless in giving) her child this small benefit rather than give the stranger the much greater benefit. So much for Clare as agent. Should we also agree that Clare's *act* is wrong? An act is wrong if there is an available alternative which would produce a better outcome. Is there such an act available? This depends on our approach. We might say that Clare could give the money to the stranger, and if she did, outcomes would be better. So that action constitutes a better available alternative. But there is a different approach. Clare defended herself at one point by saying: 'I could have acted differently. But this only means that I *would* have done so if my motives had been different. Given my actual motives, it is causally impossible that I act differently. And, if my motives had been different, this would have made the outcome, on the whole, worse. Since my actual motives are one of the best possible sets, in Consequentialist terms, the bad effects *are*, in the relevant sense, part of one of the best possible sets of effects' (pp. 32–3). Her point is that an act is not a better available alternative if she would need to have some less C-approved set of motives to do it. For if she needs another set of motives to do it, and if her having that set would be worse in C's terms, her doing that action would in fact be worse in C's terms. If she did it, outcomes would be worse than if she didn't. To put the matter in possible world talk, for an intuitive check on her argument:

> In the nearest group of worlds in which she does the alternative act, her motives are not her actual set Ma, but a different set M1.
>
> The nearest group of worlds in which her set of motives is M1 are worse in C's terms, contain worse outcomes, than the nearest group of worlds in which her set of motives is Ma.
>
> So the nearest group of worlds in which she does the alternative act is a group in which outcomes are worse in C's terms.
>
> So (unpacking the possible worlds metaphor) if she were to do the alternative act, outcomes would be worse in C's terms.
>
> So this alternative act, at least, is not one which would lead to an improvement in outcomes.
>
> So her act of benefiting her child in preference to the stranger is not shown to be wrong in C's terms by the existence of this 'available alternative'.

What this shows is that Clare's defence of herself can be turned into a defence of her act, so that, instead of having an agent rightly doing a wrong act, we have a right act which the agent is right to do. As I said, then, there are two approaches to Clare. The choice between them is a choice between a broader and a narrower interpretation of the consequentialist criterion for acts. C's central claim was that there is one ultimate moral aim: that outcomes be as good as possible. Parfit extracts from this the following criterion for act-rightness:

(1)   An act is right if its outcome is better than that of any available alternative.

But there is a different criterion available:

(2)   An act is right if outcomes would be better if it was done than if any alternative were done.

With this broader criterion we do not restrict our attention to the effects of *this* action. Instead we look to see in general what the world would be like if this action were done; in possible world terms, we look to the differences between this world and the nearest world in which the action is done. Though not purely causal, (2) is still an outcome-based criterion, and it is one which enables us to include in our assessment thoughts about motives. In particular, we can now find relevant the question what other effects might flow from the motives which we would most probably have if we were to do that action.[13]

The point now is that if we were to decide that criterion 2 is preferable to criterion 1, we would have established that there couldn't be the sort of example of blameless wrongdoing that Parfit needs to show C to be undamagingly self-defeating. For the adoption of criterion 2 will have the effect that our assessment of act and of agent must coincide. For (2) allows us to include in our assessment of the act consideration of the other implications of the motives from which the act is or would be done. If the motive is one which is C-approved, it will be one whose presence leads to the best results overall; in which case the world in which the action is done must be one which is better in C's terms – in terms of outcomes.

So, is criterion 2 preferable to criterion 1? Parfit's use of the latter is perfectly standard, but that is no justification. We must, of course, consider this question in consequentialist terms. And in terms of outcomes, it seems undeniable that if all our acts satisfied criterion 2, things would go better in terms of outcomes than if we all restricted ourselves to criterion 1. So there is a direct consequentialist reason for preferring criterion 2.

My conclusion is therefore that C is damagingly self-defeating: that the way in which it defeats itself amounts to self-refutation, since there is a single sense of aim in which it both gives us an aim and tells us not to pursue it. The attempt to defuse this by judicious use of the act/agent distinction fails to work, since the best version of that distinction still leaves us with the same assessment of agent as of act.

IV

It might be thought that there is no point in arguing against Parfit's attempts to dissolve the apparent contradiction by appeal to the distinction between act and agent. After all, we are going to need such a distinction anyway, and however it comes, it is going to generate the sort of difference between rationality of act and that of agent, or between whether what we do is right and whether we are right to do it, which will give Parfit all he needs to keep going. But this would be a mistake. There are two sorts of ways in which the value of act and of agent can come apart. The first is that of blameless wrongdoing, and the second that of blameworthy rightdoing – that is, where we are wrong to do something which is in fact right.

The classic examples must be handled carefully, however. This is for two reasons. The first is that the act/agent distinction is in fact highly controversial, especially when we define the agent side of the distinction in terms of motive. This is because the distinction between act and motive is itself controversial.[14] This subject is worth a paper in itself; I only mention here the oddity of allowing that there is a good sense in which the pharisee is doing what he ought. The value of his motives seem to infect the value of what is done, not in the sense that the value of one can affect the value of the other (their being two independent objects), but in the sense that the motive is part of the action. With a different motive it would have been a different action.[15]

The second reason for caution is that it is not sufficient for Parfit's defence of S and C that there should be some distinction or other between act and agent. He needs the right one. Suppose we start by thinking of the *action* as a composite which we are attempting to decompose into, on the one hand, the qualities of the agent in doing that action and, on the other, the qualities of the doing which that agent did. There are four ways in which we could hope to do this, which correspond to four reasons for drawing *some* sort of act/agent distinction. Each reason creates its own distinction. The first reason is the need to say something about cases of error and/or ignorance. Where the error or ignorance is not culpable though the action goes wrong in some way, we feel that there is something here to approve of and something to disapprove of. One way to work this is to carve things up so that the approval goes to the agent and the disapproval to the action.[16] My own view about this is that Parfit is right to cope with this sort of problem by means of the objective/subjective distinction rather than the act/agent one.

Second, there is the need to distinguish long-term evaluations from short-term ones. We may feel that an agent is in general to be approved of because she is a person of goodwill and sensitivity, though here she allowed her prejudices to run away with her. There is no problem with this. Of course, we do need to make such a distinction to cope with the vagaries of moral experience. And we could announce that the long-term evaluations are of agents, while the short-term ones are of acts, and hope to focus the long-term ones on motives and the short-term ones on outcomes. We would then end up with Parfit's marriage of the act/agent distinction with the outcome/motive one. Sadly, however, this will not wash, for short-term evaluation may still be sensitive to motives – not of course to one's normal pattern of motivation, but to that operative in this unusual case.

The third reason is a sense that the action is effectively to be assessed as a change in the world, while the agent is to be thought of as a sort of intention in practice. Compared with the second reason, this pulls the agent back towards the particular case, but pushes the action out into the realm of mere events. But this cannot give us anything relevant to ethics. Events as such are not susceptible of moral assessment at all. We have only managed to separate act from agent here at the cost of removing the act from the moral realm altogether.

The fourth reason for drawing an act/agent distinction is the one Parfit has been concerned with: namely, the need to show that a theory which separates what it says about motives from what it says about aims is not contradictory. This is a much more specific need, designed to save a specific theory from a specific form of refutation, and I have been arguing that the attempt to run the act/agent and the outcome/motive distinction together does not work. My suggestion has been that we should focus our *moral* evaluation on what might be called the agent-in-acting, in a way that prevents either distinction from getting a grip. The qualities of the doer in the case must coincide with the qualities of the thing done, in a way that leaves no room for talk of blameless wrongdoing or blameworthy rightdoing. The relevant qualities of the action, conceived as an object of *moral* assessment, are the same as those of the agent in doing it (where there is no error or ignorance, of course).

I argued that in Parfit's four examples the relevant qualities of act and agent did in fact coincide, on the most plausible interpretations of S and of C. And once we have decided that for Parfit it will not do to identify the qualities of the agent with the subjective qualities of the act, have put aside thoughts about short-term and long-term evaluation, and have distinguished the sorts of qualities an act can have from those available to mere events, I see no further rationale for drawing the only sort of act/agent distinction which would save S and C from being worse than only indirectly self-defeating. The qualities of the doer in this case must coincide with those of the thing done. And this leaves no room for talk of rational irrationality or blameless wrongdoing in any way that will help to show it to be other than a contradiction to say with S that there is a single rational aim which it is not rational to pursue, or with C that there is a single moral aim which it is immoral to aim at.

V

In this final section I turn to consider whether, in arguing that S and C are worse than only indirectly self-defeating, I have not in fact cut the ground from under my own feet by undermining the argument that they are indirectly self-defeating in the first place.[17] If this were so, it would be very damaging to my main concerns. For the proof that S and C specify aims which they tell us not to pursue is based on the admission that they are indirectly self-defeating. Because they are indirectly self-defeating, there are circumstances in which they prescribe an aim for us and then tell us not to pursue that aim. And this is the root of the sort of incoherence that I have been trying to bring out. So it is important for me to agree that S and C are at least indirectly self-defeating. In what follows I argue that this is the case for S, leaving it open whether what can be proved for S can also be proved for C.[18]

Parfit gives two examples to show that S is indirectly self-defeating. These differ in style. The first is aimed at hedonists: that is, at those who hold that the life which goes as well as possible for oneself is the life in which one is as happy as possible. Parfit simply says that it is a well-established fact that happiness, when aimed at, is harder to achieve (p. 6). However, I am reluctant to rely on this 'well-established fact' alone. Parfit offers the case of Kate as a back-up. His conclusion is that 'on the hedonist theory, it would be worse for Kate if she was never self-denying' (p. 6).

This comes out in the following way. If one is never self-denying, one never does what (one believes) will be worse for oneself. The hedonist glosses this as 'one never does what (one believes) will make one less happy'. Kate is a hedonist, and is not never self-denying. She knows that if she worked only a little less hard on her books, they would be not much worse and she would be much happier overall. But she does not do this. She would only do it if she were never self-denying; but if she were to do it, she would in fact find her life boring. So it would be worse for her if she were never self-denying than if she had some other disposition.

Is there an alternative act which Kate could do and which would make her life go better for her in hedonist terms? Parfit assumes that there is: namely, that of working less hard on her books. But earlier we were led to question this. Since Kate would only do this act if she cared much less about her books, and since if she cared much less about her books she would find her life boring, the act of working less hard on her books is not one which would make Kate happier. Viewed in this way, Kate is already never self-denying. For she is already doing that act which of all the available alternatives makes her happiest. So her case hardly gives us an example in which S is indirectly self-defeating.

Of course, what is at issue is again whether to take a wider or a narrower conception of the comparison classes at issue in the relevant subjunctive conditionals (i.e. which notion of an available alternative to adopt), and this is a matter which I have already discussed. Its relevance here is that it offers us not one but two understandings of what it is to be never self-denying, in one of which Kate is never self-denying and in the other of which she is not. My point is that given my preference for the wider conception, I cannot use the example of Kate of show that S is indirectly self-defeating.

But Parfit has another example. The case of the driver stranded in the desert shows that it may be worse for me if I am never self-denying. For if I cannot lie convincingly, I will not be able to persuade you that when you have given me a lift out of the desert, I will repay you for your trouble. It would have been better for me if I were trustworthy – that is, sometimes self-denying.

One might reply to this as follows: 'Surely the best thing for me is that I should now decide to ask you for the lift and pay you for it later. If I fail to do this, I am failing to do what is required for my life to go, for me, as well as possible. And why should we accept that I cannot make that decision now?' Parfit's reply is that if I (know that I) am never self-denying, I cannot make that decision because I know that I will not keep to it when the time comes. It might be better for me to have a different set of motives, but as things are, the action of deciding to take the lift and pay for it later is not available to me. (Note that this argument adopts for the case of the driver the notion of an available alternative that I recommended in the case of Kate.)

This looks promising. We could allow that it shows that S is indirectly self-defeating. But there are two worries. First, in accepting Parfit's reply, we have removed from our driver the option of choosing, in accordance with the recommendations of S, the long-term action of asking for a lift for which he pays later. Here we are imposing on S a very short-term (atomistic) conception of an action. But haven't we already made critical remarks about such an imposition, with reference to the case of Kate? In fact, not. The sort of atomism we rejected there was one which considered actions in isolation from the motives, plans or projects from which they sprang or to which they contributed. The sort of atomism we are considering here is one which rejects the idea of a long-lasting or gappy action. We have not said anything yet against that sort of atomism.

But isn't this sort of atomism enormously implausible? It amounts to two assumptions: first, there cannot be extended or conjunctive actions such as getting a lift and paying for it at the end; second, I cannot now decide to do a 'delayed' action, one whose time has not yet come. Any 'decision' I make is only so much empty noise. If S is committed to these assumptions, it is *fantastically* implausible. For it entails that I cannot even now decide to go to the library, and that I cannot engage in any sort of long-term planning or project.

I am tempted to say, however, that S *is* committed to these implausible theses;[19] Parfit is right to hold that the driver cannot commit himself now to paying later. But I want to suggest that this constitutes a direct refutation of S. A self-interest theory of rationality which cannot capture the rationality of long-term planning is deeply flawed.

One might suspect that in convicting S of this gross implausibility, I have imposed on it a conception of an action to which it is not committed. But that would be exactly wrong. The point here is that the very short-term conception of an action which makes trouble for S is one generated by S itself. We might even go so far as to say that there is no question of somehow importing from outside the right conception of an action, to see how S fares with it. There is no independent source of such a conception, since each theory of practical rationality generates its own. S can hardly complain if we use against it a conception of an action which it itself provides.[20]

So I am still able to maintain that S is indirectly self-defeating. But I retain a distrust of the use of very complex examples such as those of the driver and of Kate. There is in both cases an oddity: the driver is weirdly transparent, and Kate would only work less hard if she worked much less hard. I prefer to use cases without such peculiarities; and anyway it would be comforting to have an example which would still work for a (probably incoherent) non-atomistic version of S. The classic hedonist paradox is still usable, and so is another example which I owe to David Boonin-Vail. If my strongest desire is to be likeable, and I make likeability my dominant aim, I will achieve this aim less well than if I had some other set of motives. Likeable people are not those who are centrally concerned about their own likeability, and who judge everything else by its conduciveness to their likeability. So a person whose dominant aim is to be likeable would do better not to be never self-denying. This example is not perfect; it still appeals to challengeable empirical claims about human psychology. But it is the sort of example that seems to me most persuasive. I believe that it is only one among many which, though simpler than Parfit's cases, do show that it is better in S's terms not to be never self-denying. This leaves me holding what I intended originally to hold: namely, that S is, but is not only, indirectly individually self-defeating.[21]

Notes

1 Parfit distinguishes between theories that are individually self-defeating (p. 5) and those that are collectively self-defeating (p. 27), but this distinction will not be relevant here.

2 I see no relevant difference here between having a set of motives and acting on that set, and some of the things I say later may depend on this. The only

relevant difference arises because of weakness of will. But Parfit has already argued (p. 5) that no real problems arise for S because of our failure to do what S commends or to act on motives of which S approves.

3   I add 'here' in order to show that we are here defining the notion of the agent's rationality in doing this particular action; the contrast between act and agent is to be drawn in the particular case; it is not the same as the contrast between long-term and short-term evaluation of the agent.

4   Two comments: first, notice again that this notion offers an evaluation of the agent in doing a particular act; it purports to be atomistic (cf. n. 2); second, in expressing C's criterion for agents using the notion of blamelessness I have remained faithful to Parfit's text, but lost the pleasing symmetry between S and C which would have remained had I expressed the agent criterion as a criterion of the conditions under which agents *act rightly* (they may act rightly in doing an action which is wrong). This would have left the notion of the right as the pivotal notion for C, as the notion of the rational is the pivotal notion for S. The crucial point for C, however, is not so much the pivotal term used as the general distinction between its commendation conditions or approval conditions for agents and for acts. We will return to this matter at the beginning of section 3.

5   Parfit's actual account says: 'if they never do what they *believe* would be worse for them in S's terms' (p. 6, my emphasis). But our previous discussion of the objective/subjective distinction shows that this addition makes no relevant difference.

6   Or, better, here is an outcome whose promotion should be your dominating concern, and you will best achieve it if it is not your dominating concern.

7   I owe this last point to Candace Vogler.

8   C is collectively, rather than individually, self-defeating (see n. 1).

9   Remember that C officially makes claims only about the worth of acts and agents. Of course, a full consequentialist theory will include claims about which features make one outcome more valuable than another (just as a full account of rationality will specify which features mean that one life is going better than another). But such a theory of value is technically distinct from any consequentialist criterion for acts and agents.

10 The only 'contradiction' I want to impute is the one involved in our being told both to have and not to have one and the same aim.

11 If my career is worth more than the minor wrongs I will commit to save it, then my subsequent actions will be right, and I will be right to do them.

12 Parfit argues otherwise, when he writes: 'it would be wrong of me to cause myself to lose this disposition [the disposition to help my enemy commit minor wrongs], since, if I do, my children will be killed' (p. 39). But this is a mistake; I can cause myself to lose this disposition and allow my career to be ruined, without my children being at risk. They are only at risk if I voluntarily abandon my career. Parfit recognizes this defect in a footnote added in the 1987 reprint, but I cannot see how the change in the example which he suggests there would improve matters, nor indeed that any change could.

13 In these terms we can rewrite the discussion of Kate. Is Kate's action of working as hard as she does rational? We might say that there is the same

distinction between a narrower approach to this question, which looks merely at the effects of Kate's act, and a broader approach, which asks more generally whether the world in which she does this is one in which things go better for her. Her act is not rational if we judge merely by its effects, but it is rational if we consider the effects of the pattern of motivation which would lead her to work less hard – namely that she would find her life boring. As things stand, life would go worse for her in the nearest world in which she worked less hard. But, unlike the case of Clare, the distinction between causal and broader approaches is not quite the point for Kate. For even if we looked merely at the effects of the individual action, we still have the choice between two answers. For what the effects of Kate's action are for Kate depend largely upon the pattern of motivation that generates the action.

14 For a good discussion of this point, see H. W. B. Joseph, *Some Problems in Ethics* (Clarendon Press, Oxford, 1931).

15 Mill says, in a long footnote to ch. 2 of his *Utilitarianism*, that 'he who saves another from drowning in order to kill him by torture afterwards does not differ only in motive from him who does the same thing from duty of benevolence; the act itself is different'. But he ascribes this difference entirely to a difference in intention. I want to say that a difference in motive has the same effect.

16 For more on this theme, see my 'Externalism for Internalists', in E. Villanueva (ed.), *Rationality in Epistemology, Philosophical Issues*, vol. 2 (Ridgeway, 1992), pp. 93–114.

17 David McNaughton brought this possibility to my attention.

18 Here is a possible defence for C: with criterion 1 C is undamagingly self-defeating, and with criterion 2 C is not self-defeating at all. I pursue this line of thought in the last chapter of my *Moral Reasons* (Blackwell, Oxford, 1993).

19 John McDowell persuaded me that I should say this.

20 This idea was suggested by John McDowell.

21 I am most grateful to John Broome, Richard Gale, David Gauthier, Brad Hooker, Dale Jamieson, John McDowell and David McNaughton for their comments on earlier drafts, and especially to Derek Parfit for forceful and really positive discussion and criticism.

2

Rationality and The Rational Aim

David Gauthier

I

'Many of us want to know what we have most reason to do. Several theories answer this question' (p. 3). Wanting to know what one has most reason to do might be understood simply as wanting to know what to do. But if I want to know what to do, a theory, whether about rationality or about morality, will not answer my question. Parfit's question must be understood another way. He supposes that S, the Self-interest Theory, gives this answer: 'What each of us has most reason to do is whatever would be best for himself' (p. 8).[1] One might then understand the question as asking what considerations give one sufficient reason for acting. The Self-interest Theory answers: considerations about what would be best for oneself.

Or so Parfit may claim. But let us consider what he tells us about S, as a theory about rationality:

> We can describe all theories by saying what they tell us to try to achieve. According to all moral theories, we ought to try to act morally. According to all theories about rationality, we ought to try to act rationally. Call these our *formal* aims. Different moral theories, and different theories about rationality, give us different *substantive* aims.
>
> By 'aim', I shall mean 'substantive aim'.... S gives to each person this aim: the outcomes that would be best for himself, and that would make his life go, for him, as well as possible. (p. 3)

A person who achieves the formal aim given him by S acts rationally and is rational. A person who achieves the substantive aim given him by S has his life go for himself as well as possible. How are these related? A natural supposition would surely be to treat the substantive aim given by a particular theory of rationality as its specification of the formal aim. Each theory of rationality provides an account of what it is to be rational; this account is formulated in the substantive aim that it gives each person. Thus, according to S, to be rational is to have one's life go for oneself as well as possible.

But this is not Parfit's view. He says: 'According to S, our formal aim is not a substantive aim' (p. 9). And he insists that S does not 'give to each person *another* substantive aim: to be rational, and to act rationally' (ibid.). Now of course, if the substantive aim were a specification of the formal aim, then it would be true that S did not give to each person *another* substantive aim, but in giving to each person the aim that her life go as well as possible, it would thereby give her the aim of acting and being rational. And Parfit denies this. Indeed, he says that 'In the case of some people, according to S, being rational would *not* be part of what makes their lives go better' (p. 10).

So what is Parfit's account of the relation between the formal aim, acting and being rational, and the substantive aim, having one's life go as well as possible? To answer this, we must know what, on Parfit's understanding of the Self-interest Theory, it is to be rational. But what can it be if not to act so that one's life goes as well for oneself as possible? And if this is what it is to be rational, then how can Parfit suppose that 'being rational would *not* be part of what makes their lives go better'? For if to be rational is to act so that one's life goes as well as possible (henceforth I shall take 'for oneself' as read), then surely if one is rational, one's life must go as well as possible. If one acts so that one's life goes as well as possible, then one's life goes as well as possible.

This last argument moves too quickly. But I shall defer discussing this; for the present we should note that Parfit does not give us a direct account of what it is to be rational. However, we might construct one for him, by taking what he says about rational actions, desires and dispositions, and supposing that, to be rational, one must always do what is rational, and have both 'the supremely rational desire' and 'the supremely rational disposition' (p. 8). And we may now apply this to S. Parfit says that according to S, 'What it would be rational for anyone to do is what will bring him the greatest *expected* benefit' (ibid.). He also says that according to S, 'The supremely rational desire is that one's life go as well as possible for oneself,' and 'The supremely rational disposition is that of someone who is never self-denying,' where to be never self-denying is never to do what one believes will be worse for one (ibid.).

On this reading, the formal aim given by S is that one always do what will bring one the greatest expected benefit, and desire that one's life go as well as possible, and be disposed never to do what one believes will be worse for one. And the substantive aim is that one's life go as well as possible. Parfit's examples show that the substantive aim is not a specification of the formal aim, and indeed that someone who adopts the formal aim may well fail to achieve his or her substantive aim. Suppose I am never self-denying. Then, if I promise to do what at the time of keeping or breaking my promise would be worse for me, I shall break the promise. Suppose I know that I am never self-denying. Then I cannot promise sincerely to do what would be worse for me. Suppose I am transparent. Then I cannot convincingly purport to promise to do what would be worse for me. But as in Parfit's example of my car breaking down in the desert (p. 7; I shall henceforth refer to this as 'the desert breakdown case'), it may be greatly to my advantage to make such a promise. Only a convincing promise to pay you a large reward will induce you to drive me out of the desert, and I have no other way out. So my life will go better if I make such a promise. If I am trustworthy, 'disposed to keep my promises even when doing so will be worse for me' (p. 7), I can make a convincing promise. If I am never self-denying, I cannot. So my life will go better if I am trustworthy, rather than never self-denying. But the rational disposition is to be never self-denying. If I follow my substantive aim, I shall, if I can, make myself trustworthy. But if I follow my formal aim, I shall be never self-denying. Thus the substantive aim is not a specification of the formal aim, and someone who adopts the formal aim may fail to achieve his substantive aim.

This argument may seem insufficient. In the desert breakdown case I do better to be trustworthy. But does this show that it is better for me to be trustworthy than to be never self-denying? Someone might object that even if being trustworthy is sometimes beneficial, at other times it is costly. Suppose you are gullible. You believe whatever you are told. Then, if I am never self-denying, I can falsely promise to reward you if you drive me out of the desert, knowing that I will not pay you. Whereas if I am trustworthy, I cannot avoid paying if I promise you a reward, and so do worse. The objector grants that if we restrict our attention to a particular case, we may think that the formal and substantive aims diverge, but he claims that from an overall standpoint the aims coincide.

A first response to this objection is that the overall benefits of being able to promise sincerely to do what will be worse for me may reasonably be expected to outweigh the overall costs of keeping promises when one could have got away with insincerity. A person need not make promises except when she expects to benefit thereby, and if she is rational (by the standard of S), she will not make promises except in such contexts. A person who frequently made foolish promises might of course suffer from his trustworthiness, but in making foolish promises, this person would already be acting in a way that was not best for him. Someone who could count on herself to make promises only when it would be best for her could expect to benefit from being trustworthy.

A further response rests on the fact that even generally trustworthy persons have been known to make false or insincere promises. There are occasions that call for trustworthiness; on other occasions one may do better not to be self-denying. Since our concern is with rationality and not morality, we need not hesitate here over the thought that selective trustworthiness may be a less than admirable characteristic. We need only note that a person must expect to do better overall if she is disposed to be selectively trustworthy rather than never self-denying, assuming of course that she is reasonably astute.

The objection fails. And so Parfit insists that although according to theory S never to be self-denying is the supremely rational disposition, yet being never self-denying is not part of the substantive aim that S gives to many, if not all, persons. Thus, according to Parfit, S may be indirectly individually self-defeating. 'It can be true that, if I try to do whatever will be best for me, this will be worse for me' (p. 5). And this is not because I will fail to do what is best for me. 'Even if I never do what, of the acts that are possible for me, will be worse for me, it may be worse for me if I am purely self-interested [i.e., never self-denying]. It may be better for me if I have some other disposition' (ibid.).

Parfit further claims that 'S implies that we cannot avoid acting irrationally' (p. 13). I shall not summarize his rather convoluted discussion, but reconstruct the argument in somewhat different terms. It is irrational for anyone to do what he believes will be worse for himself. It is therefore irrational for anyone to perform a self-denying act. But it is worse for one to be never self-denying. If one is never self-denying, then one has acted irrationally in not trying to acquire some other disposition, such as trustworthiness, that it would be better for one to have. If one has some other disposition, then one acts irrationally in performing the self-denying acts towards which one is sometimes disposed. Thus, whether or not one is never self-denying, sometimes one acts irrationally.

This argument is not conclusive. For it may be that one can do nothing about one's dispositions. If so, then one may be never self-denying without having acted irrationally. I shall therefore replace Parfit's claim by a weaker one: S implies that to the extent that the disposition to be never self-denying is in our control, we cannot avoid acting irrationally. According to the account of rationality that I have ascribed to Parfit, a rational person has the supremely rational disposition, and so the claim has this corollary: S implies that to the extent that the disposition to be never self-denying is in our control, it is rational to make oneself irrational, and irrational to remain rational. For the supremely rational disposition is to be never self-denying; but it is rational to acquire another disposition, thereby becoming irrational, and irrational to remain never self-denying and rational.

Earlier I questioned the view that if one acts so that one's life goes as well as possible, then one's life goes as well as possible. We may now see why. When I act so that my life goes as well as possible, I am not being self-denying. But if I am never self-denying, then I must expect my life to go worse than if I am disposed to perform acts some of which are self-denying. In so far as it is within my power to affect my dispositions, then, my life will go as well as possible only if I bring it about that I sometimes act so that my life does not go as well as possible.

II

Although S may be *indirectly* individually self-defeating, Parfit denies that it can be *directly* individually self-defeating. He says (p. 55) that if S were directly individually self-defeating, then it would be certain that if someone were successfully to follow it, he would thereby cause the substantive aim given him by S to be worse achieved than if he had not successfully followed it. But this is not so:

> S gives to me at different times one and the same *common* aim: that my life goes, for me, as well as possible. If my acts at different times cause my life to go as well as possible, I must in doing each act be successfully following S. I must be doing what, of the acts that are possible for me, will be best for me. So it cannot be certain that, if I always successfully follow S, I will thereby make the outcome worse for me. (p. 55)

Parfit's definition and argument may both seem puzzling. S may be indirectly individually self-defeating, yet it is not *certain* that if someone tries to achieve his S-given aim, that aim will be worse achieved than if he were disposed in some other way. Parfit shows that it is rational to expect this to occur, but nevertheless someone might never find himself in circumstances in which a self-denying disposition would benefit him. Why, then, does Parfit claim that for S to be directly individually self-defeating, it would have to be certain that a person who successfully follows it will cause his S-given aim to be worse achieved than if he failed in some particular way successfully to follow it? I agree with Parfit that success in following S does not guarantee that one will cause one's S-given aim to be worse achieved than it might otherwise be. But is it possible that someone might be successful in following S and yet thereby cause his S-given aim to be worse achieved than it might be? And if it is possible, then surely S could be directly individually self-defeating.

Recall Parfit's claim that S implies that we cannot avoid acting irrationally. If this is true, then it is not possible always successfully to follow S. If the disposition never to be self-denying is in my control, then if I remain never self-denying, I do what I expect to be worse for me, thus failing to follow S, or I cease to be never self-denying, and must expect sometimes to do what is worse for me, thus failing to follow S. If I begin by successfully following S, then I bring it about that I do not always follow S. So if the disposition never to be self-denying is in my control, then I must sometimes do what is worse for me, and the question whether S is directly individually self-defeating does not arise.

What if the disposition never to be self-denying is not in my control? Then if I have this disposition, it may be that I always act rationally, and so successfully follow S. It is worse for me that I am never self-denying, but nothing I do makes the outcome worse for me than something else I might do. And so Parfit's claim seems to be true, in that, in so far as it is possible always successfully to follow S, it is not directly individually self-defeating.

This last argument may seem mistaken. If I am never self-denying, then surely I do what is worse for me. For example, in the desert breakdown case I do not make the sincere promise that would elicit your assistance. What I do is worse for me than making that promise. But does this show that I do what is worse for me? I *cannot* make the promise. Knowing myself to be never self-denying, I cannot sincerely promise to reward you for driving me out of the desert. What I can do is limited by my disposition. I do what is best for me given that I am never self-denying. That it would be better for me were I differently disposed does not show that I fail successfully to follow S.

Is this right? Is what a person can do limited by his or her dispositions? If I am never self-denying, does it follow that I can perform only non-self-denying actions? Surely this is wrong; a person with a cowardly disposition may on occasion perform a courageous action. But this analogy misses the real point. Suppose that I am *firmly* disposed to be never self-denying. Then in deliberating about what to do, I consider the various alternatives, choosing an action that affords me an expected benefit at least as great as that of any action that I believe possible for me. The criterion of possibility here cannot include the condition that the action not be self-denying. An action can be shown not to be self-denying only by comparing its expected outcome with that of the alternative possible actions. Thus I select from the members of the set of possible actions one that, relative to that set, will involve no self-denial. Suppose that I am considering whether to pay you a reward for driving me out of the desert.

I take both paying you and not paying you to be my possible actions, and I consider which affords me the greater expected benefit and so involves no self-denial. If I choose not to pay you, believing it to afford me the greater expected benefit, I do not suppose that paying you would be impossible simply because it would be self-denying.

Now consider promising to pay you a reward. The claim is that it is not possible for me to *sincerely* promise to pay you a reward, if I believe that I am never self-denying and that paying you the reward would involve self-denial. But why? I believe that it is possible for me to pay you the reward. Indeed, I believe that I shall pay you the reward if paying you the reward will lead to my life going as well as possible. So why is it not possible for me to promise, even though I am disposed to be never self-denying? If my disposition does not make it impossible for me to pay you, why should it make it impossible for me to promise to pay you?

The answer, I think, is that promising requires that one suppose not only that it is possible to perform the promised act, but that one will perform it. It is not possible for me to promise – sincerely – to pay you, while holding the belief that I shall almost certainly not pay you. But if I am aware that I am disposed to be never self-denying, and that paying you would involve self-denial, then in all likelihood I hold the belief that I shall almost certainly not pay you. And then it is not possible for me to promise sincerely to pay you. Holding the belief that I shall not pay you excludes promising to pay you from the set of possible actions over which I deliberate. I do not decide against promising to pay you by assuming it to be possible and then finding that, relative to its alternatives, it would involve self-denial. Rather, I rule it out by realizing that given my beliefs about my dispositions and about what other actions would involve self-denial – beliefs that I hold prior to comparing promising to pay you with the alternatives – I cannot form the requisite intention. A person's possible actions are not directly limited by what she may be disposed to do, but they are indirectly limited by what, given her knowledge or beliefs about her dispositions, she can form the intention to do.

We may now return to the main point. Parfit claims that S is not directly individually self-defeating. As I have said, he seems to be right. A person who is able to affect whether she has the disposition never to be self-denying cannot always successfully follow S, so that the question of being worse off should she follow it does not arise. And a person who has the disposition but is unable to affect having it can successfully follow S without thereby causing herself to be worse off, but she is worse off in virtue of having the disposition. This latter person may be rational; according to S, as Parfit understands it, she does have the supremely rational disposition. But she is *cursed* by her rationality.

III

This conclusion should make us suspect Parfit's account of rationality. Even if we are willing to admit that rationality may not be an unmixed blessing, we should, I think, admit this with reluctance, and only when we are satisfied that our admission does not rest on misunderstanding rationality. I believe that there is a better understanding than Parfit offers, and one that avoids at least some of the unwelcome consequences of his account. I cannot fully develop such an understanding here, but taking comfort in the fact that Parfit's own discussion is sketchy, I shall offer an equally sketchy alternative.

My starting-point is the relation between the formal and the substantive aim given each agent by a theory of rationality. I have no objection to Parfit's idea that theories of rationality may be characterized primarily in terms of such aims; rather, I want to insist, as I suggested at the outset, that the substantive aim given by a theory of rationality is its particular way of giving content or substance to the formal aim that all such theories share. Thus I propose that we interpret S, the Self-interest Theory, as giving to each agent the aim that his life go as well for himself as possible, this being its way of specifying the formal aim of being rational that it must give him in so far as it is a theory of rationality.

I shall suppose that to be rational one must always do what is rational, and have both the supremely rational desire and rational dispositions. Although this is somewhat similar to the account of rationality that I ascribed to Parfit, I give a different content to what it is rational to do, and I do not speak of any disposition as supremely rational. Let us consider the question of rational dispositions first. Parfit supposes that for theory S it is possible to specify a disposition as rational without regard to the agent's circumstances, by relating it straightforwardly to the substantive aim given by the theory. Thus he supposes that, according to S, the supremely rational disposition is 'that of someone who is never self-denying' (p. 8). I propose, however, that a disposition is rational if and only if having it is most conducive to one's substantive aim. S gives one the aim that one's life go as well as possible; it therefore claims that a disposition is rational if, among those humanly possible, having it will lead to one's life going as well as having any other. Since, as Parfit has shown, to be never self-denying is self-defeating in terms of this aim, to be never self-denying is not always a rational disposition. If a selectively trustworthy person may expect to do better than someone who is never self-denying, and if there is no alternative better still, then selective trustworthiness is a rational disposition, and being selectively trustworthy is a necessary condition of being rational. But there need be no one disposition that, independently of an agent's circumstances, is sufficient to ensure that his life will go as well as possible, and thus I do not suppose that there need be a single supremely rational disposition.

The supremely rational desire, on Parfit's account of S, 'is that one's life go as well as possible for oneself' (p. 8). He says little about how this is to be interpreted. It would, I think, be clearly mistaken to suppose that a person is rational only in so far as she is directly motivated by the supremely rational desire. However, if we understand the supremely rational desire as that which in effect governs or regulates one's other desires, ensuring that a person's particular desires, at least in so far as they are motivationally effective, are compatible with her life going as well as possible, then I need not object to Parfit's account. If, as I have suggested, selective trustworthiness is a rational disposition, then on particular occasions a person should be moved by the desire to keep her promise, even though she may realize that she would do better to break it. But such a desire is fully compatible with her desiring that her life go as well as possible, in so far as she recognizes that did she not desire to keep her promises, she would expect to lose out overall; since she would be unable to make convincing promises in situations in which she could profit by doing so, or to receive benefits that depended on her fellows believing her to be trustworthy or reliable. Acting on those desires that make one trustworthy may be in itself a cost, but having those desires that make one trustworthy, at least in some relationships and with some persons, is a much greater benefit.

Let us turn to the claims of theory S about what it is rational to do. In taking the rational action to be what maximizes the agent's expected benefit (or utility, in the standard parlance), Parfit follows what in my view is the orthodox position advocated by the theory of rational choice. But, as we have seen, at least some agents – those who are capable of affecting their dispositions and who would do best to be selectively trustworthy, or at least not to be never self-denying – *cannot* always do what on this account is rational. On Parfit's view, not only are some persons cursed by rationality; others are condemned to irrationality.

Parfit's account connects rational action with rational motivation. A person who has the supremely rational disposition never to be self-denying and the supremely rational desire that his life go as well as possible will be moved to perform those actions that will bring him the greatest expected benefit. I propose to retain the connection between rational action and rational motivation, but of course in terms of what I have claimed to be rational dispositions, which are those that, given the agent's circumstances, will lead to his life going as well as possible. Thus I interpret theory S as claiming that what it would be rational for one to do is whatever one would be rationally motivated to do. In so far as selective trustworthiness is a rational disposition, it is rational to keep at least some of one's promises, even though doing so may be self-denying and not maximize one's expected benefit.

How does rational action relate to the substantive aim given by theory S? Parfit's account (p. 8) makes this relation simple and direct. One's aim is that one's life go as well as possible. Therefore, in any situation in which one has a choice among actions, an action is rational if and only if it may reasonably be expected to lead to one's life going as well as possible. But this simple relation is sacrificed by my alternative account. A particular action may be rational even though the agent does not expect it to lead to her life going as well as possible.

There is of course an indirect link between the rationality of an action and the agent's life going as well as possible. This link is provided by the connection between rational actions and rational dispositions. I have claimed that according to theory S, an action is rational if and only if it would be motivated by a rational disposition. This implies that if an action is rational, then it must be a member of a *set* of actions that are collectively performable, could be motivated by a particular disposition or set of compatible dispositions, and that would lead to the agent's life going as well as would the actions belonging to any set that would be motivated by some alternative possible disposition or set of compatible dispositions. Let us call such a set of actions an optimal dispositionally coherent set.

Consider once again the desert breakdown case. Suppose that I am disposed to prudent trustworthiness; I am prudent in making promises when I can expect to benefit from sincere promising, and I keep the promises I make. I promise to reward you if you drive me out of the desert; you drive me out, and I reward you. Rewarding you does not lead to my life going as well as would not rewarding you. However, the actions belonging to the set motivated by prudent trustworthiness – promising to reward you and rewarding you – lead to my life going at least as well as the actions belonging to any set that would be motivated by any alternative possible disposition, such as being never self-denying. There is, of course, a set of actions whose members would lead to my life going better than the set motivated by prudent trustworthiness – the set whose members are promising (sincerely) to reward you and not reward-ing you – but no single coherent disposition can motivate both members of this set.

Of course an action may belong to an optimal dispositionally coherent set and yet not be rational. Not rewarding you belongs to such a set – namely, the set of which it is the sole member. Being never self-denying provides adequate motivational basis for not rewarding you; thus dispositional coherence is readily satisfied. And optimality is evident: if

I do not reward you, my life will go better than if I perform any alternative action. But not rewarding you is not rational, since it is not motivated by a rational disposition. Furthermore, an action may be rational and yet belong to a sub-optimal dispositionally coherent set. Rewarding you belongs to such a set – namely, the set of which it is the sole member, since the alternative set of which not rewarding you is the sole member is an optimal dispositionally coherent set. But if an action is rational and belongs to a sub-optimal dispositionally coherent set, then this must be a subset of an optimal set given coherence by the same disposition. And if an action is not rational and belongs to an optimal dispositionally coherent set, then this must be a subset of a sub-optimal set given coherence by the same disposition. For a rational action is one motivated by a rational disposition, and a disposition is rational if and only if all of the actions it motivates collectively lead to the agent's life going at least as well as it would were she motivated by any other possible disposition. Thus an action is rational if and only if it belongs to a maximal set of actions that is given coherence by some disposition, and is optimal among dispositionally coherent sets.

At the end of section II I said that a person who was unable to affect her disposition never to be self-denying might be rational in having (according to Parfit's version of S) the supremely rational disposition, but that she would be cursed by her rationality. On the reformulation of S that I have been sketching, such a person is not fully rational, since *never* to be self-denying is not a rational disposition. To be fully rational, a person must be able to have those dispositions that lead to her life going as well as possible. And the lifetime optimal dispositionally coherent set of actions that are motivated by these dispositions may, and normally will, include some that do not in themselves lead to her life going as well as possible. Being disposed to perform such actions leads to her life going better than if she were disposed to perform only those actions each of which at the time of performance would lead to her life going as well as possible. The desert breakdown case illustrates this in terms of the effects of the agent's dispositions on what she is able to do; if she is, and knows herself to be, never self-denying, then advantageous acts of promising prove unavailable to her. But it may be helpful to conclude this part of my argument with a rather different example.

We are farmers; my crops are ready for harvesting now, and yours will be ready next week. If we harvest together, each of us will do better than if we harvest alone. You are therefore willing to help me with my harvesting now if you can count on me to reciprocate next week. But for whatever reason (perhaps I don't much care for you, and am selling my farm and moving away after the crops are in) we both know that next week I shall do better not to help you. If I am never self-denying, then next week I shall not help you; on the other hand, if I am disposed to reciprocity, then I shall. If I expect others to be fairly good judges of my dispositions, then I do better to be disposed to mutually beneficial reciprocity than to be never self-denying. The set of actions I am motivated to perform if I am disposed to mutually beneficial reciprocity makes my life go better, but not simply because this disposition enables me to perform advantageous acts, such as making sincere promises, that would not be possible for me were I never self-denying. Rather, my disposition gives rise to expectations by other persons that motivate them to act in ways that afford me opportunities that, even given my self-denying behaviour, make me better off than the opportunities I should have were I never self-denying.

This completes my sketchy reformulation of the Self-interest Theory of rationality. As I noted earlier, I do not want to endorse S as the correct theory of rationality, but only to offer an alternative and, I think, better account of what S claims than that given by Parfit. (It may not be the best account.) And in giving such an alternative I am of course intending to suggest how in general one should relate the formal and substantive aims of a theory of rationality, and determine what dispositions, desires and actions are rational according to that theory.

IV

Suppose that there is a very powerful demon whose rewards and punishments outweigh all other considerations in determining how well one's life goes. This demon issues rules to govern behaviour. But he does not reward obedience to his rules or punish disobedience. Rather, he rewards the disposition to obedience, and punishes all other dispositions. He does this by affecting one's opportunities, so that each person will enjoy more favourable opportunities if he or she is disposed to obey the demon's commands than if he or she is disposed in any other way. In this world the disposition to obey the demon's commands is rational – indeed, supremely rational. Since the demon does not reward actual obedience or punish disobedience, there may well be particular situations in which a person makes her life go less well by obeying than by disobeying. But on my interpretation of S this does not affect the rationality of the disposition to obedience, or of the particular obedient actions that it motivates.

Some persons think that there actually is a demon whose rewards and punishments are all-important in determining their fate; they regard this demon as god. Some of these persons may think that god directly rewards obedience and punishes disobedience, if not in this world then in the next one. They are rational if they are disposed to be never self-denying, for they are then led straightforwardly to obedience by considering how their lives, including their lives after earthly death, will go if they obey or if they disobey. Others, however, may think that god rewards those who are sincerely disposed to obedience without thought of the benefits and costs thereof. According to theory S as I have interpreted it, they are rational not if they are disposed to be never self-denying, but only if they are disposed to be obedient.

But other still may have a different belief about god's concerns. They may think that god rewards, not the disposition to obedience, but the belief that obedience is the supremely rational aim. They may think that those who consider that to be rational is to have one's life go as well as possible will experience opportunities inferior to those who consider that to be rational is to conform to the will of god. If they are right, what does theory S claim? Notwithstanding divine rewards, theory S claims that having one's life go as well as possible is the supremely rational aim. But it also claims that, in so far as it is within one's power, it is irrational to believe this, and rational to believe instead that obedience to god's will is the supremely rational aim. It claims that being disposed to obey god is rational. A disposition is rational if it makes one's life go as well as possible; the disposition that makes one's life go as well as possible is the disposition that would be most conducive to attaining the supremely rational aim, were that aim to be obedience to god's will. But it claims that one should believe that being disposed to obey god is rational simply because it is most conducive to the aim of being obedient, and not because it will make one's life go as well as possible. Indeed, if one believes that being disposed to obey god is rational because it will make one's life go as well as possible, then one's life will not go as well as possible. In effect, the belief that being disposed to obey god is rational is true only if it is held on false grounds. And theory S claims that an action is rational in so far as it conforms to god's will. But again, the real reason that this is true is not the reason why one should believe it. The real reason relates the action to a disposition that makes one's life go as well as possible, but one should believe it because the action is related to a disposition that is most conducive to obedience to god's will.

If there is a sufficiently powerful demon who rewards the belief that obedience to his will is the supremely rational aim, then it is rational to hold false beliefs about rationality. To hold such beliefs, one may need to be irrational; if so, then it is rational to be in this way irrational. Such rational irrationality is not ruled out by my formulation of theory S. And it could not be ruled out by any formulation that would leave it possible for a person's fate to depend on her beliefs about rationality. But its scope is significantly reduced. Rationality is a curse only if irrationality is directly rewarded. This is, I think, a significant improvement on Parfit's account.

V

Parfit supposes that it can be rational to cause oneself to act irrationally, and to do this in circumstances in which irrationality itself is not the direct object of reward, or rationality the direct object of punishment. To support this view he considers an example adapted from Schelling (pp. 12–13) , which I shall refer to simply as 'Schelling's answer'. An armed robber orders me to open the safe where I keep my gold, threatening to kill my children, one by one, so long as I refuse. I fear that even if I comply, he will kill us anyway, to prevent our identifying him later to the police. Fortunately I have a drug at hand that 'causes one to be, for a brief period, very irrational' (ibid.). I take the drug; the robber now 'can do nothing that will induce me to open the safe. Threats and torture cannot force concessions from someone who is so irrational' (p. 13). And since I am irrational, I am less likely to be able to identify him later. Thus 'making myself irrational is the best way to reduce the great risk that this man will kill us all' (ibid.).

Parfit describes my behaviour under the influence of the drug thus: 'Reeling about the room, I say to the man: "Go ahead. I love my children. So please kill them"' (ibid.). Observing someone behave in this way, we might well consider him irrational. But should we? Suppose you fully understand the situation. If someone said to you, 'Look at Gauthier! He's totally irrational,' you might well respond, 'Not at all. Crazy as he seems, and crazy as his behaviour would be in other circumstances, actually what he's doing is perfectly rational. He's best off acting in a way that bears no predictable relation to what the armed robber does or says. And that's exactly what he's doing.'

We might hesitate, though, to allow that my behaviour is rational. But I think this is because what I do is not under my control, and more especially not under my *reasoned* control. It is true that I do best to act in a way that escapes my reasoned control, but does this make my uncontrolled actions rational? Indeed, we might want to deny that my behaviour under the influence of the drug should be treated as a set of actions at all. But of course we could not then say that I am acting irrationally. The only action that we could judge rational or irrational would be my taking the drug, and that is a perfectly rational action according to theory S, whether we interpret it as Parfit does or as I propose.

But whatever we might intuitively be inclined to say, we must recognize that 'rationality' is a technical term in both Parfit's enquiry and my critique. In Schelling's answer the disposition that will make one's life go as well as possible is to act in a quite random and uncontrolled manner. On my account of theory S, it is therefore the rational disposition in such situations, and the actions to which it gives rise are rational actions. In most situations it would of course not make one's life go best to be disposed to act in a random and uncontrolled way. It is therefore not surprising that we should pre-theoretically characterize all random and uncontrolled behaviour as irrational. Someone who accepts theory S interpreted as I propose will think that in the unusual circumstances of Schelling's answer, our pre-theoretical characterization is mistaken. I find this unsurprising.

Parfit rejects the claim that he labels G1:

> If there is some motive that it would be both (a) rational for someone to cause himself to have, and (b) irrational for him to cause himself to lose, then (c) it cannot be irrational for this person to act upon this motive. (p. 13)

He thinks that Schelling's answer shows this claim to be false. I think it shows that our ordinary ideas about rationality and irrationality are sometimes mistaken.

Parfit also rejects the claim that he labels G2:

> If is rational for someone to make himself believe that it is rational for him to act in some way, it *is* rational for him to act in this way. (p. 23)

He supports this with an example that raises difficult issues for any theory of rationality, 'How I End My Slavery' (p. 22). He considers someone who rationally becomes a threat-ignorer – that is, someone who rationally comes to think it rational to ignore all threats. Faced with a threat-enforcer, who thinks it rational to execute all threats, and who has made an apocalyptic threat, he ignores it with the predictable apocalyptic result. He has rationally come to believe that it is rational for him to ignore the threat, but Parfit claims that his belief is false.

Given Parfit's interpretation of theory S, a person who comes to believe it rational to be a threat-ignorer no longer fully accepts the theory. But on my interpretation this is not so. If a person reasonably believes that his life will go best if he is a threat-ignorer, then according to theory S, threat-ignoring is for him a rational disposition, and ignoring a threat a rational action. It is compatible with theory S to believe it rational to ignore threats, and this belief may be true (although a person might have reason to believe it even if it were not). Should we conclude that on my interpretation of S, G2 is true? Specifically, should we agree that if it is rational to dispose oneself to be a threat-ignorer, and so to believe that it is rational to ignore all threats, then it is rational to ignore an apocalyptic threat despite what one expects to be the consequences? And should we welcome this conclusion?

Suppose that I may reasonably expect my life to go better if I am a threat-ignorer. I ignore various threats; on some occasions I find this costly, but this need give me no reason to reconsider or regret my disposition. Although I may be unaware of the specific situations in which being a known threat-ignorer has saved me from being the victim of a threat, I may reasonably believe that I have benefited more from such situations than I have lost from ignoring threats that have been subsequently carried out. But now suppose that you, a known threat-enforcer, issue an apocalyptic threat. You will blow us all up – you, me and our respective families – unless I give you the last piece in my box of chocolate fudge. I don't much want the fudge, but I am a threat-ignorer; I refuse you the fudge, and, as I expect, you blow us all up. This may be irrational on your part, but rational or irrational, given that I could and did expect it, do I not act irrationally in denying you the fudge? For now my disposition to threat-ignoring does not make my life go better – and not just in terms of my future expectations, but on balance. Although in the past I reasonably expected my life to go better overall if I were a threat-ignorer, I realize that if I now ignore your threat, that expectation will prove false, and my life will have gone worse overall. One might suppose that I should have qualified my disposition to be a threat-ignorer, so that I should not have extended it to apocalyptic threats. But I may reasonably have believed that any qualification would reduce its *ex ante* value, so that unqualified threat-ignoring offered me the best life prospects.

I have no easy resolution of the problem implicit in this example. There are self-denying dispositions that may reasonably be expected to make one's life go better overall. If one holds any of these dispositions, one is committed to perform particular actions that will not make one's life go as well as possible. But there are several different forms of commitment possible. The weakest is to be committed to particular costly actions only so long as one reasonably expects adherence to the disposition to be prospectively maximally beneficial. In defending the rationality of dispositions requiring this level of commitment, and of the actions they motivate, I accept the claim G1. Stronger is to be committed to particular costly actions so long as one reasonably expects

past and prospective adherence to the disposition to be maximally beneficial in comparison to what one would have expected from past and
prospective adherence to any other disposition. I also defend the rationality of dispositions requiring this level of commitment, and of the actions that they motivate. To this extent I accept the claim G2. Strongest
is to be committed to particular costly actions even if one recognizes that
past and prospective adherence to the disposition will not be maximally
beneficial in comparison with what one would have expected from past
and prospective adherence to some other disposition. This third level of
commitment requires that one adhere to a disposition in the face of its
known failure to make one's life go better. Can this be rational?

With this question my enquiry into rationality moves into an area not
charted by Parfit in *Reasons and Persons*. Such an area must be explored
elsewhere. I conclude by repeating what I have claimed. We should treat
the aim given us by a theory of rationality as explicating what it is to be
rational, and then consider the dispositions, desires and acts that it
recommends in the pursuit of the rational aim as themselves rational.
This is not Parfit's view. On his account dispositions, desires and acts are
rational if they are directed *at* the aim, not if they are directed *by* it. For
him the rational person is disposed to pursue the aim; for me the rational
person is disposed in whatever way will best lead her to achieve the aim.
Parfit supposes that theory S tells me that my reasons for acting are
considerations about what would be best for myself. I suppose that S tells
me that my reasons for acting are considerations determined by my being
disposed in the ways that are best for me. More generally, Parfit's view
implies that any theory of rationality tells me that my reasons for acting
are considerations about what would be conducive to the aim it gives me.
And I hold that any theory of rationality tells me that my reasons for
acting are considerations determined by my being disposed in the ways
that are most conducive to the aim it gives me. Were Parfit right, then
rationality would all too frequently be a curse from which, rationally, I
should seek to free myself, adopting irrational dispositions that would
motivate me to perform irrational acts so that I might better achieve the
rational aim. But perhaps it is only his view of rationality that proves a
curse, from which I have been seeking to free myself.

Note

1   Parfit does not accept S. Neither do I. But I believe that his account of S
    shows how he supposes the various parts of a theory of rationality – the
    specification of the formal aim and the substantive aim, the characterization
    of rational dispositions, desires and actions – are related. My concern in this

Rationality and The Rational Aim 41

essay is with these relations, and I use theory S to illustrate my differences with Parfit on these matters. I should note my gratitude to Parfit for reading an earlier draft of this paper and suggesting various clarifications and emendations, many – but as he will recognize, not all – of which I have accepted.

3
Which Effects?

Frank Jackson

Consequentialists judge actions by effects. But precisely which effects? This is one question with many strands. The strand I wish to pursue arises from Derek Parfit's discussion of some interesting examples in chapter 3 of *Reasons and Persons* – the chapter entitled 'Five Mistakes in Moral Mathematics'.

Consider the following example, which I will follow Parfit in referring to as the 'overdetermination case', taken from that chapter.

> X and Y [simultaneously] shoot and kill me. Either shot, by itself, would have killed me. Neither X nor Y acts in a way whose consequence is that an extra person is killed. Given what the other does, it is true of each that, if he had not shot me, this would have made no difference. (p. 70)[1]

There are a number of ways in which non-consequentialists could argue that X and Y act wrongly in this case. But what should consequentialists say about the case? (i) They might say that neither X nor Y act wrongly. Parfit declares this conclusion to be 'absurd' (p. 70). (ii) They might say that X's act *does* have a bad effect, on the ground that it causally contributes to a bad effect, and so it counts as wrong on straightforwardly consequentialist considerations: the same goes for Y's act. (iii) They might say that we cannot consider X's act in isolation from Y's. Although neither has a bad effect in itself, the pair of acts has a bad effect. Each act belongs to a collection of acts which has a bad effect, for had neither X nor Y shot, I would have lived. And it is by appealing to this fact that a consequentialist can show that what X did is wrong, and likewise that what Y did is wrong.

Parfit suggests that the third course is the way for consequentialists to go. I will be arguing that there are serious problems for this view, and that consequentialists should adopt the first line.

Preliminaries

The first preliminary concerns the usage of terms like 'effect', 'harm' and 'benefit'. Parfit and I are in agreement that the second line of response mentioned above would be a mistake. Although it is perfectly good English to say that an act has a bad effect when it plays a major role in bringing about something bad, still, in the sense which is central for consequentialism, such an act need not have a bad effect. For an act to have a bad effect or to harm in that sense is for it to *make things worse*: act A has a bad effect iff there is an available alternative to the act such that, had it been performed, things would have been better. Similarly, to have a good effect or to benefit is to make things better: act A has a good effect iff there is an available alternative to the act such that, had it been performed, things would have been worse. In what follows I follow Parfit's example and use these terms in this way.[2] In this sense, X's act in the overdetermination case does not have a bad effect, although it does play a major role in causing my death. This would be so even were the case one where X's act pre-empts Y's act – X's bullet kills me just before Y's arrives, say – so that Y's act plays *no* causal role in my death and X's act does all the causing.

How, then, can Parfit hold that what X does is wrong, and likewise, how can he hold that what Y does is wrong? He argues that effects *other* than the effects of the act in question should on occasion to be taken into account. Consequentialists who hold that only the effects of the act in question need to be taken into account make what he calls the 'Second Mistake in Moral Mathematics'. As he puts it, 'it is natural to assume

(The Second Mistake) If some act is right or wrong *because of its effects*, the only relevant effects are the effects of this particular act.' (p. 70)[3]

Parfit's view is that the overdetermination case shows that this dictum is false. For in his view it is evident that X does wrong; yet, as we have seen, X's act does not have a bad effect. It does not harm me. Ergo, we must look elsewhere to find the effect that makes X's act wrong. And the place to look, in Parfit's view, is at the effect of X's and Y's acts considered together. Although, had X not acted, things would have been just as bad for me; had X *and* Y both not acted, things would have been better for me. I would have lived. Thus, on his view, what makes X's act wrong is that it is a member of a collection of acts such that if each had been different in a certain way, things would have been better for me. It is the effect of X's and Y's acts taken together that we need to take into account to get what he holds to be the evidently correct answer that X acts wrongly. The same goes for Y. Accordingly, he concludes that the Second Mistake is rightly called a mistake.

Secondly, there is a reading of the Second Mistake on which it would be a simple blunder, and not a doctrine that could fairly be described as a natural one to assume. Suppose that I kill M, and that my act inspires someone else to kill N, and that N would not otherwise have died. Is it one of the effects of my act that N dies? The answer is clearly yes, and is yes on all seriously entertained versions of consequentialism. Hence, if we were to read the Second Mistake's dictum that the only effects relevant when evaluating a given act are the effects of that act, as meaning that we should *ignore the effects on other acts*, the Second Mistake would not be a natural one to make, and would not be one made by seriously entertained versions of consequentialism.

Moreover, so read, it would be beside the point in discussions of the overdetermination case. The problem in that case is not that *if we exclude from consideration effects on the acts of others*, X's act does not have a bad effect on me. It is that it does not have a bad effect on me, all effects included. For if X had not shot, Y would still have shot, and I would have died just the same. Parfit's concern is to explain how it is that X's act is wrong despite this fact, and he seeks to recover this answer not by observing that there is some effect of X's act that we failed to take into account, an effect involving someone else's actions, but by urging that we must take into account the effect of X's and Y's acts taken together, and in particular the fact that had both X and Y not acted, things would have been better for me.

I have laboured this point because although it is, I think, clear that Parfit intends to read the Second Mistake in a way that makes it a view which is attractive (and so worth arguing against), at one point he seems to read it in the less charitable way. At one point he suggests that certain co-ordination problems also show the error of the Second Mistake, and that they do this by showing that consequentialists should claim

> Suppose that someone has done the act, of those that are possible for him, whose consequence is best. It does not follow that this person has done what he ought to have done. He ought to have asked whether he is a member of some group who could have acted in a way whose consequence would have been better. If this is true, and *he could have persuaded this group to act in this way*, this is what he ought to have done. (p. 73, my emphasis)

He argues that this gives the 'second reason [in addition to that provided by the overdetermination case] why it is a mistake to consider only the effects of single acts' (p. 73). However, in the lesson that consequentialists are supposed to learn from co-ordination problems, we are asked to start by supposing 'that someone has done the act, of those that are possible for him, whose consequence is best', and then to grant that this is consistent with it not being the case that this person has done what he ought to have done, on the ground that it may be that he could have persuaded a certain group to act in a way which would have led to a better consequence. But in that case, he did *not* in the first place do the act of those that are available to him whose consequence is best; he only did what is best out of the acts available to him *minus* the option of persuading the others to act in a certain way. It seems here, therefore, to be being assumed that the Second Mistake involves ignoring options that involve effects on the acts of others.

In any case, from here on I am going to read the Second Mistake in the way which makes it a natural one for consequentialists to assume: namely, as the claim that the only effects which matter are the effects of the act in question but that (of course) we must include as possibly relevant all the effects of the act in question.[4]

I now turn to arguing that consequentialists should deny Parfit's intuition concerning the overdetermination case, and instead of embracing his view that the Second Mistake is a mistake, they should hold that neither X nor Y do anything wrong. I will start by presenting three considerations which I take to support this conclusion. I will conclude with some brief diagnostic remarks on possible sources of the (in my view) illusory appeal of the view that X and Y act wrongly in the overdetermination case and of the associated view that the Second Mistake is well named.

Three Reasons for Consequentialists to Deny the Intuition that X and Y Both Act Wrongly

(i) In the overdetermination case things would have been just as bad for me had X not shot, and likewise if Y had not shot. It is not just that I would have died had X not shot, but that though I might have died in a slightly different way, it would have been in an equally bad way; and likewise if Y had not shot. Also, there are no other relevant consequences for people other than myself. What happens if we remove these two special features of the example?

My first reason for saying that consequentialists should deny that X and Y act wrongly can be introduced by considering what seems to me a curious asymmetry in Parfit's attitude to what it is plausible to say about these two possible modifications of our example. Parfit describes a case where a relevant feature of the *manner* of my death is not overdetermined under the heading 'Case Two' (the original overdetermination case is 'Case One'), as follows: 'X tricks me into drinking poison, of a kind that causes a painful death within a few minutes. Before this poison has any effect, Y kills me painlessly' (p. 70). As in Case One, it is being supposed that had X not acted as he did, Y would still have acted as he did, and conversely. Hence, in both cases my death is overdetermined. The difference is that a morally relevant feature of the manner of my death – namely, how painful it is – is not overdetermined in Case Two. By contrast, in Case One, had X not acted as he did, my death would have been no better and no worse than it in fact was; and similarly if Y had not acted as he did, my death would have been no better and no worse than it in fact was.

Case Three is an example where there are effects on someone other than me. It runs as follows.

> X tricks me into drinking poison of a kind that causes a painful death within a few minutes. Y knows that he can save *your* life if he acts in a way whose inevitable side-effect is my immediate and painless death. Because Y also knows that I am about to die painfully, Y acts in this way. (p. 71)

Parfit observes rightly that in both Case Two and Case Three Y does not harm me – Y in fact benefits me, because things would have been worse for me had Y not acted as he did – but he takes a very different view as to whether Y's act is right in the two cases: 'Y acts wrongly in Case Two', but in Case Three 'Y is doing what he ought to do' (p. 71).

This is puzzling. We can see easily enough how a *non*-consequentialist might hold that Y acts wrongly in *both* cases. What is puzzling is how someone sympathetic to consequentialism could take *different* attitudes to Y's act in the two cases. Parfit's reason for holding that Y acts rightly in Case Three is that Y does not harm me and he benefits me and someone else. But in Case Two Y does not harm me, and he benefits me. How can the change from the benefit being to someone else and me to being to me alone *in itself* make the difference?

I think it is clear that consequentialists should hold that Y acts rightly in both cases. The crucial point is that Y makes things better, and this is what matters for consequentialists. Imagine that you are me in Case Two – the one in which Parfit holds that Y acts wrongly – and imagine that you know exactly how appalling the pain that X's poison is going to inflict on you will be unless Y steps in. The case will not be significantly different from those that dominate the literature on euthanasia. (Can it matter, particularly from a consequentialist viewpoint, whether the causal origin of my potential agony lies in a cancer, say, or in the action of X?) Would you not beg Y to step in with the painless lethal injection?

You may or may not be moved by this kind of consideration, and the host of associated ones in the literature relating to euthanasia in particular and consequentialism in general (not that it is only consequentialists who approve of euthanasia). I am not trying to make a contribution to that debate, but rather to highlight the fact that it is clear what consequentialists should say about Y in both Case Two and Case Three: namely, that he acts rightly.

I can now put the problem for holding that in the original overdetermination case, Case One, Y acts wrongly.[5] Y acts rightly in Case Three. Parfit and I are agreed on this, and on why it is true – it is true because Y benefits someone else and does not harm me. Now, as we have been arguing, there is no relevant difference between Case Three and Case Two; the fact that the benefit is to me and not another is not a relevant difference. Therefore, the right thing to say about Case Two is that Y acts rightly. But now we find ourselves in the following position if we insist that in Case One Y acts wrongly. If Y makes a difference for the better – in particular, benefits me – Y acts rightly. That is the lesson of Case Two. If Y makes a difference for the worse, Y acts wrongly (of course). And if Y acts in a way which makes no difference whatever, neither benefits nor harms, Y also acts wrongly. But we have three possibilities for an action: right, wrong and neither (neutral). Where did the neutral case go? If benefiting makes an act right and harming makes it wrong, then surely doing neither makes it neutral. To suppose otherwise is to make zero special in an essentially arbitrary way. Indeed, there is textual evidence that Parfit himself might be sympathetic to this line of thought. In the course of arguing that in Case Three Y acts rightly, he says that 'since Y's act is not worse for me it is morally *irrelevant* that Y kills me' (p. 71, my emphasis). It seems that it is making worse and making better that are the morally relevant considerations for being wrong and being right, respectively, in which case neither X nor Y acts wrongly (and neither acts rightly) in Case One.

(ii) The second consideration that makes trouble for holding that both X and Y act wrongly in the overdetermination case is that it runs counter to the whole thrust of consequentialist thinking about morality.

What other people will or would do is clearly in general relevant to deciding what I ought to do. If a 'friend' asks me for a loan of my revolver, saying that he plans to kill his parents, it is no use my defending my action of lending him the revolver by saying that *I* am not going to kill his parents. This is not controversial. What is controversial is whether the fact of who does or would do the killing is relevant in itself. Suppose he gives me the choice of killing one of his parents or of doing nothing, in which case he will kill both of them. Should I simply argue that I ought

to kill one of his parents, as the alternative is that both die, or should I
see as central the fact that if I kill one of his parents, it is *I* who does the
killing, whereas if I 'do nothing', *he* will do the killing?

This is a very familiar and hotly debated question, but I take it that
what is not in debate is where the consequentialist stands on it. If it really
is true that I am absolutely sure that my friend will carry out his threat to
kill both his parents unless I kill one of them, and if it really is true that
there are no other relevant consequences, then I ought to kill one of his
parents. In and of itself, who does the killing is irrelevant in the
consequentialist picture. But it is exactly this which a consequentialist
who thinks that both X and Y act wrongly in the overdetermination
case must deny. For such a consequentialist holds that X ought not to
shoot, but the difference between shooting and not shooting in the
overdetermination case is precisely a difference in who brings my death
about. That is the only relevant difference. If X shoots, he joins with Y in
killing me; if X refrains from shooting, it is all done by Y.

The response might be: so much the worse for the usual understanding of consequentialism. The overdetermination case shows that it is
wrong to think that the irrelevance *per se* of who performs an action is
central to consequentialism. But this would, I think, be too sanguine. To
hold that who does the action in question is in and of itself important is
to introduce agent-relative values, and to add them to one's account of
consequentialism threatens to denude consequentialism of any distinctive content. It is not for nothing that the denial of agent-relative values
is a standard feature of characterizations of consequentialism.[6]

(iii) The final difficulty I want to raise against holding that both X and Y
act wrongly turns on the difference between overdetermination proper
and causal pre-emption. Suppose that Y shoots at a rock and that the
bullet ricochets away harmlessly. Suppose that the noise of the shot has
no bad effects, that the news of his shooting does not encourage people
to be careless with firearms, and so on and so forth. Has Y acted
wrongly? Clearly not. Would it make any difference to this conclusion if
the rock were crushing me to death? Well, if he could have done something useful, he should not have been wasting time shooting at the rock;
but provided that Y could not in any way have prevented the rock from
crushing me, the fact that the rock was crushing me to death is neither
here nor there as far as the rightness or wrongness of Y's firing at the
rock goes. Moreover, consistently with all this, it could have been the
case both that the reason the rock was crushing me to death was that X
had rolled the rock on to me and that, had X not rolled the rock on to me,
the bullet from Y's gun would have struck and killed me instead of
ricocheting off the rock.

The original overdetermination case had then better be a case of overdetermination and not pre-emption. If X's shooting and killing me pre-empts Y's shot killing me, then it is not plausible that Y acts wrongly. It would be just like the rock case: not only would Y not harm me, but Y would not even be a partial cause of something bad which happens to me. But this conclusion means that Parfit must hold that the fine detail of what happens inside me is absolutely crucial in a way which is hard to believe. You see X and Y shoot at me, and see the bullets enter my body. I fall to the ground dead. You know that had X not shot, I would still have died. You know that had Y not shot, I would still have died. You know that had neither X nor Y shot, I would have lived. But is what you are witnessing a case of overdetermination or of pre-emption? That depends on the fine detail of what happens inside my body. If, for instance, X's and Y's bullets strike my heart at exactly the same time, then Parfit will say that both act wrongly; but if – as is more likely – one bullet does the deadly work a moment before the arrival of the other, then he must, as we have just seen, hold that only one of X and Y acts wrongly. Thus, the answer depends on what precisely happens inside me, in a way which could be accommodated within the deontologist's framework, but which is hard to make plausible from the consequentialist perspective.

Diagnostic Remarks[7]

Parfit is surely right that the immediately natural response to the overdetermination case is that both X and Y do wrong. For the immediately natural response is that wrong is done, and if not by X and Y, then by whom? But if our arguments above are right, this intuition must be explained away – or, at least, the consequentialist must explain it away. I have three suggestions as to the source of the intuition.

First, although consequentialists should not hold that both X and Y act wrongly, they can and should hold that there is something very wrong about X and Y. In the discussion of the overdetermination case we (following Parfit) neglected the distinction between objective and subjective rightness (and wrongness). From the consequentialist viewpoint (and at least some others), there is a fundamental distinction between the question of whether an act is subjectively right and whether it is objectively right. An act is objectively right if it *in fact* makes things better – that is, benefits – and subjectively right if (roughly) it is likely by the light of the agent's beliefs to make things better – that is, to benefit. Conversely, objective wrongness is a matter of actually harming, whereas subjective wrongness is a matter of being likely to harm according to the agent's beliefs. For example, if I know that there is a 90 per cent chance that throwing a brick out of the window of a high-rise apartment block in Manhattan will kill someone, and no chance that it will do any good, then in the subjective sense it is beyond question that I ought not to do it; whereas in the objective sense there is a 10 per cent probability that I am doing nothing wrong.

It is not controversial that there are these two senses. What is controversial is whether we should hold that (i) they are different but equal, or (ii) that the objective sense is primary in consequentialist ethical theory, or (iii) that the subjective sense is primary.[8] We were able to neglect the distinction thus far because the points we were making went through on either interpretation; but for what follows it is clearest if we suppose that X and Y know the facts that obtain in the overdetermination case, and think in terms of what is subjectively right and wrong for X and Y to do – though, of course, as they *know* the relevant facts, what is subjectively right (wrong) coincides with what is objectively right (wrong).

I can now say what is so wrong about X and about Y. It is essential for its being true in the overdetermination case that neither X nor Y harm me, both that X would still have shot had Y not shot, and that Y would still have shot had X not shot. But, that is to say, it is essential to the case that both X and Y would have shot *even in the situation where they would have harmed me.* The way things actually are in the overdetermination case, Y does not harm me; but this is true because X would have harmed me in a certain counterfactual situation. This very obviously does not reflect to X's credit. The same goes for Y. Y is such that had X not shot, he would still have shot, in which case he would have harmed me. This fact about Y does not reflect to Y's credit. The point is that although consequentialists should say that X and Y do nothing wrong, they can and should say that X and Y are people of bad character in that in a certain case they would have done wrong, and that this fact is revealed by the overdetermination case. In short, the case displays immorality, but immorality of character rather than immorality of action.

Secondly, a consequentialist can hold that it would be quite wrong of X and Y to get together beforehand, the night before, say, and reason as follows: 'We have always wanted Jackson dead. To date we have been restrained by the belief that it would be wrong to kill him. But now that we have been convinced that consequentialism should be framed in terms of the difference an action makes (that is, in terms of harm and benefit, as those terms are used above and by Parfit), we see that if we get together and overdetermine Jackson's death, we will achieve our goal and do so without doing anything wrong.'

They are wrong. They have overlooked the fact that what each does when they plan to get together and proceed with the overdetermined death makes things worse. It harms me. Hence, consequentialism does *not* let them off the hook. Although it implies that their acts at the time of shooting are not wrong, certain prior actions of each come out as wrong.

Thirdly, in practice, in many cases structurally like the overdetermination case something subjectively like the 'Share-of-the-Total View' is correct. Suppose that a group of people together ensure some desirable result. They each put in the same amount of time and effort, and the result is well worth the time and effort. How do we regard each individual's contribution to the overall good? Typically, we look on the matter in a share-of-the-total way. We share out the credit equally. But of course, often we overdetermine the good. Eighty of us agree never to walk on the grass, and this leads to the desirable result that there is not a track across the grass. But it might be that for each and every one of us it is true – and we can be pretty confident that it is true – that were he or she to walk on the grass, it would make no difference whatever to the appearance of the grass because (i) the others would still refrain from walking on the grass, and (ii) one person walking on the grass would make no relevant difference (I mean *no* relevant difference, not a tiny difference; we are not here concerned with what to say about tiny differences).

How, then, can we share out the credit equally? Indeed, it seems that on the approach I have been defending, nobody gets any credit at all. Because for each and every person it is true that they do not make a difference for the better; they bring about no benefit. But in practice it is very hard to be *certain* that the desired result is overdetermined. Typically, each person is in the situation of increasing slightly the probability of the desired result. True, most likely the desired result is overdetermined, so that each act brings about no benefit, and so, most likely, each act is not *objectively* right; but if the desired result is important enough, the increase in probability may be worth the effort, and the act may be *subjectively* right. And in such cases we can take a species of the share-of-the-total approach to each person's contribution to the *probability* of the desired result. Each of the eighty people who refrain from walking on the grass makes a roughly equal contribution to the probability of the desired result of trackless lawn. When each person says to themselves that they did their bit, this is very probably false if it means that they made things in fact slightly better; but it is true if it means that they made the probability of the desired result that bit higher. What they make a difference to is the probability. If the good secured by n agents acting in a certain way is G, what each can set against his or her name in such a case is not G/n, but $G (P' - P)$, where P' is the probability of G given that he or she acts, and P is the slightly lower probability given that he or she does not act.

A similar point applies to the original overdetermination case, of course. (I say 'of course', but I confess the point eluded me until a discussion at Otago.) In reasonably normal circumstances both X and Y will do the subjectively wrong thing in the overdetermination case. For X will not know for sure that Y would still shoot and kill me should he, X, not do so. Hence, by shooting, X raises the subjective probability according to him of my dying. Hence, it is only in the objective sense, or in the subjective sense in the special case where X *knows* that Y would still kill me, that X's act of shooting is not wrong. The same goes for Y's act of shooting, obviously.

I conclude that consequentialists should make the Second Mistake.[9]

Notes

1 It is being supposed that had X not shot, Y still would have, and conversely, that had Y not shot, X still would have.

2 See pp. 69, 70. I will not rehearse his arguments for the conclusion that it is the making a difference sense of 'harm' and 'benefit' which is central for consequentialists. They are collected under the heading of criticisms of the Share-of-the-Total View, the view that if n people get together to produce a good G, the good to be set against each person is G/n. As noted above, I agree with Parfit that this view is to be rejected. I will be offering at the end of the essay, however, an explanation of why in certain cases something like the Share-of-the-Total View feels right.

3 'But surely it is obvious that the possible effects of the alternatives to the act matter, so how can Parfit say that "it is natural to assume" that only the effects of this particular act are relevant?' But remember that Parfit is using 'the effects of this particular act' to stand for how things would be were this act performed by comparison with how things would be were this, that or the next alternative to it performed, and we are following this usage. On this usage, the Second Mistake is natural. Indeed, as indicated earlier, I will be arguing that it is not a mistake at all. Incidentally, I take the presence of the word 'its' in the statement of the Second Mistake to be a slip. I take it that the Second Mistake is that of supposing that if some act is right or wrong because of effects (no 'its'), the only relevant effects are the effects of this particular act. Parfit's idea is that there are acts which are wrong because of effects, not because of *their* effects, but because of the effects of collections of actions to which they belong.

4 Susan Hurley, *Natural Reasons* (Oxford University Press, Oxford, 1989), ch. 8, reads Parfit in this way. Indeed, I take it that she agrees with Parfit against me that the Second Mistake is a mistake.

5 From the consequentialist perspective. From now on I will sometimes drop this qualification, but of course my conclusions pertain throughout to what consequentialists ought to say, and my final target is Parfit's view that consequentialists should acknowledge the Second Mistake as a mistake.

6 See e.g. Samuel Scheffler, *The Rejection of Consequentialism* (Oxford University Press, Oxford, 1982). Parfit himself takes agent neutrality as a constitutive feature of consequentialism; see e.g. the discussion on p. 27.

7 I am much indebted to Parfit for convincing me that an earlier suggestion by way of diagnosis (made in 'Group Morality', in *Metaphysics and Morality*, ed. Philip Pettit et al. (Blackwell, Oxford, 1987), pp. 91–110) did not go to the heart of the problem (for why, see n. 8). At least some of what follows I owe to him (though I hesitate to be more specific).

8 Parfit appears to belong to the different-but-equal camp, going by how he introduces the distinction on p. 25. I happen to think that it is the subjective notion – spelt out in terms of expected value – which is fundamental; see my 'Decision-theoretic Consequentialism and the Nearest and Dearest Objection', *Ethics*, 101/3 (April 1991), pp. 461–82. I also think that this is the standard opinion; but for dissent see e.g. Peter Railton, 'Alienation, Consequentialism, and the Demands of Morality', *Philosophy and Public Affairs*, 13 (1984), pp. 134–71, and David Brink, 'Utilitarian Morality and the Personal Point of View', *Journal of Philosophy*, 83 (1986), pp. 417–38. I can now explain the remark in n. 7 that my diagnosis in 'Group Morality' did not go to the heart of the problem. In 'Group Morality' I argued that we must distinguish the moral status of individual actions and group actions. This is fine if it is objective rightness and wrongness that are in focus. But subjective rightness and wrongness make little sense for groups of persons as such, because it is individuals who have subjective probability functions.

9 I am much indebted to discussions with Philip Pettit, correspondence with Parfit, discussion arising from seminars at Otago, and especially to numerous discussions with the members of PH 533, Spring Semester, 1990, Princeton University.

4

Parfit and the Time of Value

Michael Stocker

1. Introduction

In Part 2 of *Reasons and Persons*, 'Rationality and Time', Derek Parfit discusses the rationality of basing preferences simply on time. He recognizes that many people would prefer to have suffered pain than have it still to be suffered – for example, to have undergone a painful operation rather than still have it to undergo. He suggests that pure time preferences may not be irrational; he also holds this about the contrary, temporally neutral preferences of Timeless, who cares as much about past as present or future pain (pp. 178–84 and 194–5). Parfit's favoured account of rationality, the Critical version of the Present-aim Theory, is silent on the rationality or irrationality of time preferences (see e.g. p. 135). But he seems, clearly enough, attracted to temporal neutrality, and indeed holds that we would be better off if we were like Timeless (p. 174).[1]

As indicated below, there are connections between this last claim and his ontological claims about personal identity, developed in later parts of the book. But I will examine time preference from an ethical and, more broadly, an evaluative standpoint. Sections 2–4 are concerned with some general ways in which time is relevant for ethics. Section 2 argues that time plays essential roles in the nature and value of what we are, do, experience and value. Sections 3–4 discuss the importance of the past for ethics and the difficulties that contemporary ethical theories have with this because of their practical-minded concern with guiding action. Section 5 concludes from these considerations that there are few ethically important pure time preferences. Sections 6–7 argue that past pain does not have the same evaluative importance as does present and future pain. This essay thus argues that some pure time preferences can be defended. But it is more concerned with helping us understand the complexity of the connections between time and value.

2. Our Temporalized Life and Values

Parfit suggests that the fact that something will occur on a future Tuesday is no reason for choosing or avoiding it (p. 124). Perhaps future-Tuesdayness is evaluatively irrelevant. But what about time in general?

If, quite generally, time were evaluatively irrelevant, pure time preferences could not be based on evaluative considerations, and to that extent could not be defended. But evaluatively, time is essential, not just relevant, to us and our lives. It helps determine both the sort and the amount of value of what we are, do, experience and value.

Let us start by noting that our most basic categories for moral understanding and evaluation – acts, experiences and lives – are temporalized.[2] Our acts are temporalized: they are in time, and, more important, they involve time. They take time, and they are concerned with getting things done at the right time and in the right temporal order; they involve plans, which themselves, and in the agency they involve, extend over time.[3]

So, too, our experiences are importantly temporalized. They take time, and they also have a temporal order. Without both, but especially without the latter, they might simply be the sensations that the *Philebus* (21C) suggests are available to sea creatures without reason – mere present sensations. To mention one point, some of our important experiences are about developments in our lives, such as past failure and presently growing success. If these and other important experiences are to have the undoubted importance they do have, they must reflect, and be part of, how things are in the world and for us. Otherwise, they would be false in many of the ways that, again, the *Philebus* (36Cff.) shows that experiences can be false.

These issues could be pursued through Kant and his discussions of time and experience. Or they could be pursued in more modern terms by showing how our important experiences are broadly psychological, rather than narrowly so – that is, they make essential reference to facts 'outside' the person who has the experiences, rather than only to internal ones. The value of experiences turns both on how they present themselves to us at a moment, or at a series of moments, and also on the fact that they are part of, and true to, our temporally extended lives. They are experiences of a self which is in time and for which temporality is of the essence.[4]

Other aspects of our lives are also temporalized. Consider, for example, the centrality of different periods of a life, such as childhood, adulthood and old age, for understanding ourselves and others. And of course, many sensibilities, abilities and virtues are importantly temporalized in relation to these periods of a life: for example, the courage and love of the young are, near enough necessarily, different from those of the mature or elderly.[5]

In addition, the elements of our lives, such as personal relations, projects and emotions, are also temporalized. So, for example, there are important differences between an intimate relationship that starts poorly and ends well and one that starts well and ends poorly. And lives can be importantly different sorts of lives because they have one rather than the other of these different sorts of relationships.

As with relationships, so with many activities and projects – for example, writing a book or building a house. Their temporal structure and direction are important, and at times essential, to their being what they are and having the value they do, as is their temporal location in a life. So, too, for such milestones in life as achieving success or coming to accept one's own mortality.

Many pleasures are temporalized. Aristotle and Mill argue that children's pleasures are not pleasures for adults. This is to say both that what pleases children does not please adults and also that the very pleasure is different. Even gustatory pleasures are temporalized. To take a small example, it can make a hedonic difference whether one has the last glass of wine with the main course or with dessert. Order of presentation is, after all, one of the important considerations of a gustatory aesthetic.

Here we should also remember Aristotle's arguments in books 7 and 10 of the *Nicomachean Ethics* that pleasures are, or are intimately tied to, activities. Just as those activities are temporalized, so are those pleasures. This, or course, also holds for the pains of not getting those pleasures, or the pains of failed Aristotelian activities.

I will conclude this list by noting that throughout our lives, proper timing is of great evaluative importance, and that it can involve the most difficult sort of evaluative judgement.[6] The difficulty and fineness of judgement to get the timing right shows, almost by itself, the evaluative importance of time and temporal order and structure.

Having good timing involves knowing not only what to choose, but when to choose it. As this makes clear, it is not merely objects of choice but also choices – acts of choosing – that are temporalized. This, of course, has already been seen. For many of the temporalized values mentioned above are not effects of choice and action, but constitutively part of choice and action. They are, or are parts of, Aristotelian activities, *praxeis* and *energeiai*.

Temporality, then, is absolutely central to our lives – both for living them and also for understanding and evaluating them. Differences in time are often not simply differences in time. They also make for differences in what occurs, and in the nature and amount of its value.

3. Ethics, Practical-mindedness and the Past

Let us now focus primarily on choice as choosing, and only secondarily on objects of choice. How, if at all, could time rationally bear on choice? The answer might seem simple. We can choose only what is, or is believed to be, in our power to get, effect and so on. But the past is not in our power; nor can we rationally believe that it is. Thus, past pain – as well as anything else that is past – cannot figure in rational choice.

Choice, then, is concerned with the present and the future, not also the past (see p. 168). This may explain why many contemporary ethical theories either simply ignore, or tell us to ignore, the past. For, on their view, ethics is, almost entirely, concerned with choice and with guiding action, with answering such questions as 'What should I do?'. It is thus difficult to see what ethical role they could find for the past.

Of course, practically-minded ethicists can recognize that the past has a causal bearing on present or future value. That half of a mile-long tunnel has already been dug is important. But it might seem that the past act, itself, now has no present or future evaluative relevance: what does have relevance is that now we have to dig only half a mile to complete the tunnel.

Practically-minded ethicists can also recognize that the past can bear conceptually on present or future value. Here are some examples. First, giving someone a book seems evaluatively different when it is the keeping of a promise rather than the giving of a gift.[7] But to keep a promise, a promise must have been made. Second, suppose that because of the way someone was abused as a child, she is now fearful of being alone with a man. I think that, because of the way it came about, such fear deserves special consideration. (See 'Success Theory', pp. 494 ff.) Third, justified punishment seems to require past misdeeds.

Many ethicists disagree, because they see as valuable only states of consciousness, only 'features of our lives that are introspectively discernible', as Parfit says of Preference-Hedonism (p. 494). So they hold, for example, that however the fear came about, even if it is entirely groundless, it deserves the same consideration. And they deny importance to the fact that a promise was made, and point instead to, for instance, the belief that one was made and the harm that will be occasioned by not doing what it is believed was promised. They handle punishment similarly.

We need not examine this argument. It is enough for us to have seen that ethics can be practically-minded, taking 'What should be done?' as its primary question, and still allow that the past can have evaluative relevance: by bearing causally or also conceptually on present or future value.

4. Another Ethical Role for the Past

As important as the practical is, it is not the whole of ethics. Nor is the past ethically important only in so far as its bears on the practical.

This is once again coming to be seen by ethicists. I say 'once again', since it is clearly the view of the great classical ethicists from Socrates at least through Mill. Despite their disagreements with each other on this and related issues, they rightly emphasize the ethical importance of character, motivation, moral psychology and much else that, if tempo-rally located at all, is located throughout our lives, and that concerns our past, not just our present and future. So, too, many of them rightly emphasize the ethical importance of a whole life: that one of the most important ethical enterprises is constructing, evaluating, understanding and living a good, whole life.

Rather than argue for this generally, I will apply it to our particular concern about the role of the past. Some agents and some ethical views are too practically-minded. They are too concerned with what they should do, and thus too concerned with the present and the future. If they are concerned with the past, it is only in so far as it bears on the present or the future. But the past, as past, has no essential importance for these overly practically-minded people. Put somewhat misleadingly, they are concerned only with doing, and not also with being.

These people need not be incoherent. At the least, it is possible not to be concerned with the past in ways that it is humanly impossible not to be concerned with the present or the future. Here we might compare the possibility of never turning attention to the past, thus never caring about what one should have done, with the human impossibility of never turning attention to the present or the future, thus never caring about what to do.[8]

With our classical ethicists, I fault these people on out-and-out moral grounds. Put summarily, they are not living well. They do not have good lives. A good life must, of course, be concerned with the present and the future – with the practicable. But it also requires self-understanding, including an appreciation of the past: for example, what one has done and been, how one has affected others, one's commitments and loyalties. We need, in short, to ask in an ethically charged and informed way, 'What sort of life have I had?'.[9]

We cannot simply walk away from our past, holding that what is past is past, and thus no longer of any concern. We must recognize and own that we now are the person we were. This in no way denies the possibility of change, conversion, forgiveness, redemption and the like. It is the basis for them.

Some might think that the ethical importance of such appreciations has to do simply with present and future action, and suggest that such evaluations as 'You should act with a proper appreciation of your past' give them their proper due. But that evaluation goes beyond telling us what we should do. It also tells us how we should be. And the reasons for being that way go beyond our acts. Even apart from its acts, the unexamined life is, in itself, a poor life, and self-understanding is, in itself, valuable.[10]

5. The Past, Temporalized Values and Pure Time Preference

Let us now turn to the bearing of my arguments about the evaluative importance of the past and the temporalization of values on the claim that pure time preference cannot be defended. I do not think that Parfit's ontology of persons can allow for these temporalized values, or that it can give proper importance to our concern with our whole life – either as already lived and now to be reflected upon, or as still to be constructed and given meaning to. These are so central to our evaluative concerns that I do not think we have any idea of how to evaluate those lives which Parfit's ontology allows, or, indeed, whether it will allow for what we can even recognize as lives.[11] This, if right, is harsh criticism of that ontology – if, that is, metaphysical views can be assessed by the evaluative and ethical losses and gains they entrain (see p. 177). But to take up the relation between Parfit's ontology and the view about time preferences to which he is attracted – namely, temporal neutrality – would change the standpoint from which we are examining that claim: from an ethical and evaluative one to a metaphysical one.

From our standpoint, that claim seems to allow evaluative importance to the past. Indeed, one natural way to take that claim is as holding, first, that the past, present and future are all ethically important, and perhaps also, second, that they should all be evaluated in the same ways. In later sections, we will find problems with the second of these.

And again from our standpoint, that claim seems to allow that values can be temporalized. It does this if it holds, as I think it does, that where instances of value differ only in time, and thus not also in value, preferences between them simply on the basis of the temporal differences could not be defended. But where values are temporalized, the instances differ in other, often evaluative ways, not just temporally. And thus the claim about pure time preferences is not about those values.

But then the temporalization of values raises questions about the importance of the claim that pure time preferences cannot be defended: the more values are temporalized, the smaller the ambit of that claim.

Now I have not argued that temporalization is so pervasive that every change in time makes for a difference in value. And it does seem that time differences do not always make for differences in value. Turning now to Aristotelian actions, which themselves are temporalized, for certain students there might be no evaluative difference between studying ancient history first and music second, or vice versa. What may be important is simply that, by the time they graduate, they have studied both.

But in many cases, the order of courses is evaluatively important. Thus, even if we know that there can be some cases within the ambit of the claim about pure time preferences, we may have no general way to know which they are.

Some may suggest that there is a way to know this. We could resort to time features such as future-Tuesdayness. And we could develop another range of cases by making the temporal difference large enough to be noticed, but small enough not to make any other difference – for example, drinking wine with the main course after four forkfuls versus after five, or three seconds versus four seconds after the fourth forkful. Here any preference, and especially insistence on either, might well seem at best childish, if not irrational.

In saying this, I might thus be agreeing that pure time preferences cannot be defended. But what I think is far more important is that to find a case where we may be able to be sure that no value differences are occasioned by temporal differences, we had to resort to trivial – and very silly – examples. And our thinking the forkful preferences irrational may well be a reflection of our seeing how unimportant it is to decide whether these options do differ in value.

It is unclear, then, how many important cases fall under the claim that pure time preferences cannot be defended. To this extent, it is unclear how important that claim is.

6.   Evaluations of Past Pain in Biographies

But it is also unclear whether it is right. As I will argue here, even if past pain has the same value as present or future pain, we still have good evaluative reasons to prefer that it occur at one of these times rather than another. Restricting attention to bodily pain, and to evaluations of such pain from mainly a first-person perspective, I will sketch two lines of support for my claim that past bodily pain is unimportant, or at least less important than present or future bodily pain. The first is through the examination of biographies: the second, taken up in section 7, is in terms of overarching evaluations, such as 'a good life'.

Earlier in this essay, I suggested that the past is important as the subject of reflection, understanding, criticism and the like. We must, of course, be concerned about the future – for example, about how we should live and what we should do. But we must also be concerned about the past: what sort of life we have lived, what sort of person we have been, how we have treated ourselves and others, what needs to be sustained, changed, rectified and the like, and so on. My claim about past pain is that precisely because it is past pain, it is often irrelevant to an appreciation of the life we have lived. And where it is relevant, its relevance is often less than when it was present or still to come.

It is obvious that all people have suffered and continue to suffer pain. They skin their knees, cut their fingers, suffer illnesses, undergo privations, and so on and on. Despite, or because, they are so commonplace and so trivial – at most mere distractions – such everyday pain does not get much of a serious mention, much less discussion in many biographies. Of course, if a person has endured serious and prolonged pain, then that may well be important. It may be important for the colour and tone – that is, the hedonic character – it gave the life: for example, the bitterness and difficulty, the painfulness, of the life. Its importance can also be, and often will be, not understandable in terms of painfulness, but in terms of how, if at all, the pain gave shape to the life: for instance, whether it disrupted the life, whether it left emotional or personal scars, whether the person developed strength and endurance or was weakened.

One way to explain these points is that the painfulness of bodily pain often seems a distraction or an interruption. It is a distraction from and an interruption to our active and, one might hope, interesting and pleasurable engagement with the world. Personifying bodily pain, we can say that it tries to seize and direct our attention, away from our activities and projects, toward our hurting, perhaps injured body. So understood, its importance lies not in itself – its own positive or negative features – but in what it prevents.

In assessing past pain, then, one question is whether it succeeded in reshaping or misshaping our life, in distracting us, in thwarting activity, in forcing our attention away from the world, to our hurting body. Often anyway, if we succeeded in doing what is important despite the past pain – if it did not distract or stop us – then it is now irrelevant or unimportant, or certainly less important than it was when it was in the present or the future.

My point here is that what is important about our past is, to some extent, the tone, but also the shape of our life: what and how we did with our life, what we did and what we became, what we made or failed to make of the world, our relations and ourselves. To the extent that past pain did not importantly affect that, it is evaluatively unimportant for appreciations of the life. As might be said, 'It has no importance now.' It has no meaning, in that it does not enter into our self-understanding. (I will return to this.)

The unimportance or lesser importance of past pain can also be seen by considering how we respond when we are told about pain. Suppose that we ask an eight-year-old how the day was and what happened, and as usual we are told about the pain of some minor hurt – today, of a skinned knee. I think we might well feel dismay, especially if we are the child's parent: not dismay at the child's having been hurt, but dismay at the fact that this is what sticks in the child's mind, that this is how the day was for the child. Our dismay is over the child's being, we fear, caught up in a life of passivity and being affected, rather than one of activity and doing; being someone caught up in self-pity, already living the life of a victim, who sees life and the world as defeating, if not positively hostile, who is undone by everyday trials and vicissitudes, who is weak and dependent.

These, of course, may be overblown, hyperbolic worries. There may well be other, far more benign characterological explanations of the focus on everyday pain. Or perhaps the explanation will be more external to the child: such a focus is just a passing phase – perhaps occasioned by a death in the family – that will soon be outgrown. But this is just my point: there is something strange, questionable and perhaps wrong with the focus on past pain.

My point about recounting pains was about 'ordinary' pains, not severe or prolonged pain. There is nothing untoward in a child's telling us about severe, recent pain: for example, the pain from breaking a collar-bone yesterday in a fall from a tree.

But even here, time plays some role. We may properly think little or nothing of it if middle-aged people include in the story of their lives that some time ago – for example, when they were children – they suffered chronic pain which cast a pall over their lives, or that they suffered a painful bone fracture. Yet we might still find it strange, in need of explanation, as raising serious questions, if they focus on the fracture, and even after all this time still get caught up in that pain.

We might suspect that they were, and still are, strongly affected by the injury and that they focus on the pain to stop themselves from examining those effects: for example, becoming a 'good child' who is afraid to defy authorities or take risks, becoming a person who sees the world as dangerous, unjust and hostile, and so on. Or we might suspect that they never received the care and sympathy they needed at the time, and that they still need it – to make it good even after all these years.

If this is right, we have another reason to think that the painfulness of even severe bodily pain is poorly suited to being part of an answer to 'What sort of life have I had?'. If it is important, at least much of its importance lies in what it showed about the tone of our life, as might chronic pain; and what it showed about our character and how it helped shape our character (for example, whether we then or now bear pain with courage, perhaps even grace, or with self-pity); whether we then or now engage with the world and with other people with trust or fear, as successful agents or victimized patients; our sort and level of self-confidence and our areas of optimism and pessimism. This, of course, is to give pain meaning for self-understanding.

On the other hand, the painfulness of present and future pain is an important consideration in determining what one should do. The painfulness of pain gives us a good reason, even if not a decisive reason, to avoid it.

Of course, if the present or future pain will impede action, this gives us a reason to avoid it: the same reason there is to do the action. And if the pain will help shape one's character in bad ways, or perhaps simply show its badness, this is a reason to avoid it. But even where one knows that the pain will not block or disrupt the action, and will not shape or show one's character in bad ways, one still has a reason to avoid the pain. And this is simply the painfulness of the pain.

If I am right, at least often, then pain is a temporalized evaluative consideration. It is usually relevant, and sometimes important or decisive, for present or future action, but irrelevant or less important for assessments of the past. This is also true for experiences: even if one can do nothing to avoid it, the painfulness is a reason to want not to experience it. But often, past painfulness is not a reason to want now not to have experienced it, or to mind that one did experience it.

Here it might be objected that my claim about the value of pain at different times is simply an artefact of my asking non-parallel questions about different times: about the present, 'What should I do?', and about the past, 'What sort of life have I had?'. But, the objection goes, I should have compared the 'What should I do?' with its grammatical parallel 'What should I have done?'. (Toward the end of section 7, I consider issues about the proper parallel in the present or the future to 'What sort of life have I had?'.)

Several points should be made in reply to this objection. First, I think we can show the rationality of pure time preference by showing that we have important concerns which differ in regard to time. And each of our non-parallel questions is important.

Second, in choosing which question about the past to compare with 'What should I do?', we have good reason to focus on the more important question. And 'What sort of life have I had?' seems more important than 'What should I have done?', in that the concerns informing the former seem more important than those informing the latter.

I have already discussed the importance of 'What sort of life have I had?'. One's past life informs all parts of one's life, and one's whole life, in a multitude of important ways. To be sure, 'What should I have done?' is hardly pointless. Answering it can provide lessons for present or future action. In addition, it can help show how well or poorly one understood and worked toward one's goals, the distractions one was prey to, and so on. It can also provide material for rethinking one's past and for imagining different pasts which one could, and perhaps should, have had instead. This, however, sustains my claim. For if these activities are pointful, not just empty regrets, fantasy and wishful thinking, they are less about what one should have done than they are about the sort of person one was and could have been. And thus, much of the importance of 'What should I have done?' has to do with how it helps in answering 'What sort of life have I had?'.

Third, just as past pain may be of no, or of diminished, importance to appreciations of a life, it can, in another way, be of no, or of diminished, importance for questions about what one should have done. This is shown to be true, I think, as the time of the pain recedes further and further into the past. I do not mean that as time changes, the answer to the question changes: that the day after one hurt oneself the answer to 'What should I have done?' is 'Keep out of trees with thin branches to avoid hurting yourself', but that sometime later that answer becomes false or less true. What I mean has, in effect, already been said: that as the time of the pain recedes, to focus on that past pain, and thus to concern oneself with that question, suggests something untoward, or at least in need of explanation.

This is important enough to put in a different but related way. Suppose I reflect on what I did some time ago, and come to see that I could have achieved the same goal by acting in a different way that would have occasioned less bodily pain – pain that only hurt, but did not help colour or shape my life. My conclusion might well be that, of course, I should have done that other act and avoided the pain. My conclusion could also, or instead, be that the pain makes no difference now; it is now unimportant. This is so even though, were I again faced with a choice between those ways of achieving that goal, I would think that the pain makes a difference and is important now – simply because it is or will be painful. (As the future case shows, 'It is not important now' does not follow from 'It is not hurting now'.) In this way, the time of the pain makes a difference to our concern with it.[12]

In this way, too, bodily pain differs importantly from such moral bads as an act of betraying a friend or abusing a child, and also from such combined moral-psychic-physical pains as that occasioned by being sexually or physically abused by a relative. Here the matter is somewhat complex.

At least in regard to doing, and perhaps also suffering, such moral bads, one may sensibly prefer that they be well in the past rather than still to come. There is, I think, a special horror to the realization that there is a real possibility that one will, or even could well, do such an act – a horror which may well be lacking in the realization that, in the past, one did such an act. Toward the past, sadness, regret, disgust, shame and repentance, rather than horror, can be more appropriate. But this, I think, has to do with temporalization – with why we prefer a life that matures to one that degenerates, a life that starts poorly and gets better to one that, traversing all the same points, goes downhill.

None the less, mere passage of time does not eliminate, or perhaps even lessen, the importance of these moral bads. (Of course, if it did – that is, if even apart from temporalization, these moral bads, by being past, were unimportant or less important – that would help show the rationality of pure time preference.) I do not mean that we should dwell on such issues, or that if we do dwell on them, that raises no questions. Rather, they are still important for us now, in that they should have been taken up in our appreciation of our past. In this way, they are part of our past that should inform how and what we are now.

7.   Past Pain and Overarching Evaluations

To put my point about past bodily pain and overarching evaluations, I will start with Aristotle. On his view, a good life, a life of *eudaimonia*, requires moral and intellectual development, success in important activities, especially political activities, good friends and family relations. To be sure, bodily pleasures are important. But even more important are the pleasures of doing those activities and doing them well. If these conditions are met, and if external circumstances are good enough, then one can have a life of *eudaimonia* – a happy or meaningful, fulfilling life.[13]

These conditions for *eudaimonia* can be met even if there is a significant amount of pain. To be sure, prolonged and severe pain can sufficiently impede a person from fulfilling those important conditions and thus preclude *eudaimonia*. But even though pain is bad (*NE* VII 13 and X 2), not every pain, nor even every serious pain, precludes *eudaimonia*. Otherwise, Aristotle would have to hold that human life can be free of significant pain – which he clearly does not. (See e.g. the opening chapters of *NE* II and the discussion of courage in books II and III.) Or he would have to hold that *eudaimonia* is beyond human reach – which he clearly does not. (See *NE* I 6. 1097a34.) Indeed, he writes that a person 'will not be dislodged from his *eudaimonia* easily, nor by ordinary misfortunes' (*NE* I 10. 1101a10ff., tr. Rackham). This suggests that pain need not even diminish *eudaimonia*.

Some may have trouble with accepting this as true of a happy life, thinking that if two lives differ simply in that one has somewhat less pain than another, then it must be at least somewhat happier. But there should be no trouble in accepting this about a meaningful or fulfilling life. Severe and prolonged pain can, of course, make it difficult or even impossible for a life to be meaningful or fulfilling – for example, by making it difficult or impossible to engage in significant activities and relationships. But smaller amounts of pain may have no effect here: two lives with only a moderate, usual amount of pain can be meaningful or fulfilling, and equally so even though one has somewhat more pain than the other.

Two objections should be considered here. First, against my claim that my own past pain is less important to me than my future or present pain, it could be argued that another's – for example, your – past pain had better be as important to me as that person's present or future pain. So, evaluating other people's pains differently, simply on the basis of when they occurred – as I might for my own pains – may well involve me in doing what is questionable, if not presumptuous and wrong: telling others the value or meaning of their lives. And, modifying a case of Parfit's, if I receive a letter stating that you will undergo a painful operation on 15 May, it does not seem that my sympathy should be affected by whether I get it on 5, 15 or 25 May.

I am moved by the content of this objection, but not as an objection to my claims. For, as stated at the outset of section 6, I am concerned mainly with the rationality of pure time preferences in regard to first-person evaluations. Thus, for the objection to be relevant, those evaluations would have to be sufficiently similar to second- or third-person ones. But I think they are importantly dissimilar. This, in fact, is suggested by what I take the objection to say: each of us is in a morally special position to understand, appreciate and judge our own lives.

And indeed, we do seem to have special authority and responsibility concerning ourselves. This encompasses such issues as who has primary care for each of us, who is in a position to determine the nature and value of the life, and also the different sorts of concerns we have in regard to ourselves and others. Here we should remember that many of our contemporary ethical theories devolve from concerns with legislation, especially welfare legislation; and we should also remember Kant's dictum that we should be concerned with our own perfection and the happiness of others.[14]

The second objection to my claim is, again, that I discuss non-parallel questions. It could be agreed that pain often makes little difference to a life – to a whole life – but that this does not have to do with the past as opposed to the present or the future. So it could be held that present or future pain figures equally little in questions about a whole life, such as 'What sort of life should I lead?' and 'At the end of my days, what kind of life should I hope to have had?'.

The claimed overestimation of the importance of present pain might be explained in terms of the moral psychology of attention. When thinking about one's present situation, one may naturally, if faultily, focus too much on what is present – especially if it tries to seize and direct our attention – rather than on how the present will or can be made to fit in with the rest of one's life.

Or perhaps the overestimation has to do with evaluative errors. The error might be, or stem from, not taking seriously the arguments of those ethicists who have claimed that bodily pain is far less important than other disvalues. One important train of argument here is that not even the greatest bodily pains could justify, even if they could excuse, serious moral wrongs: for example, the cowardly desertion of comrades in arms or of one's dependent children.

Or the error might be, or stem from, simply assuming that all pain is bad, and is better not had than had. Yet, as the following three points suggest, from the specific to the most general level, pain seems constitutive of a good life, and indeed of a human life. Thus, that general evaluation of pain is highly problematic, perhaps even mistaken.

First, many activities constitutively involve creating and dealing with pain. Sexual activities are obvious examples here. So are such sports as long-distance running, and many other feats of physical, emotional, or mental strength and endurance. And if fear involves pain, so are many amusements, such as fun-fair rides and horror tales and shows.[15] Here, of course, we control the difficulty and the pain, which may help explain why we like these pain-involving activities.

For, second, our world of life and action, unlike a magical or divine world, is, and seems constitutively to be, a world that quite generally confronts us with resistance, difficulty and pain. Just as we have trouble in understanding what ballet would be if there were no gravity to constrain but also enable the dancer, so we have trouble in understanding what action would be if it required only wishing, rather than effort, struggle and endurance. This, if right, helps explain why, third, many ethical virtues, such as courage and liberality, and many professional virtues, such as perseverance, have to do with the character we need to deal with resistance, difficulty and pain.[16]

I am sympathetic to these claims about the moral-psychological and evaluative status of pain, but I do not see how they bear on the rationality of pure time preference in regard to past pain. First, no matter how unimportant pain is for such present- or future-looking questions as 'What sort of life should I lead?', it is important for such other present- or future-looking questions as 'What should I do?'. And according to at least many contemporary ethicists, the last is the most important, or at least one of the most important, evaluative questions.

We thus see that there is a looseness, or some other sort of complexity, in the relations between those different present- and future-looking questions. The painfulness of present pain gives a present reason for action, even if, considered from the perspective of a whole life, it has no evaluative importance, or has evaluative importance only to the extent that, with other pains, it adds up to be too much. (Perhaps the special evaluative place of the present for pain plays some role in Parfit's giving the present quite generally a special evaluative place.) Thus, some considerations relevant to 'What should I do?' are not among those relevant for 'What sort of life should I lead?'. (This raises the question of whether one can always do what one should do and still not lead the sort of life one should lead.)

Second, if we are concerned with the question of pure time preference with regard to pain, we should be interested in the different roles pain plays in answers to various questions about the future. Once again, we see that as evaluative concerns differ, so do evaluations.

For the general topic of this essay – the time of value – it is important to see that what is in question is the importance of pain for a whole life, rather than its importance for appreciative judgements and evaluations. After all, my question about the future was 'What sort of life should I lead?'. And, if this is appreciative, it is also importantly concerned with choice and guiding action. As this suggests, taking stock of one's past is importantly different from thinking about and planning how one should, henceforth, live.[17]

So again, we see that asking what seems to be the same question – here, 'How should we evaluate this long period of a life?' – can, instead, be to ask importantly different questions if different times are involved. And we also see why among the important present or future comparisons to 'What sort of life have I had?', we find 'What should I do?' and 'What sort of life should I lead?'. We should not expect to find its future-tensed grammatical parallel, 'What sort of life will I have?', in so far as that concerns factual, predictive interests, not appreciative, evaluative ones.

Let us now turn to the value of pain itself. Third, some pains may well not be bad, and some may be worth enduring. But, so far as the above examples show, this is independent of the time of the pains – past, present or future.

Fourth, it would be dangerous for many contemporary ethicists – including, I think, Parfit – to argue that bodily pain, whether past, present or future, is not always bad or is less bad than is often thought. For they proffer such pain not only as typical of value, but also as one of the most important disvalues. Thus, to the extent that it is an unimportant or atypical disvalue, or is only sometimes bad, to see whether their ethical theories are important, we will have to see whether they are right about value in general or, at best, only about the evaluative peculiarities of bodily pain.

Finally, there is another danger – for the importance, not the truth, of the claim that pure time preference cannot be defended. As we have seen, that claim does not apply to those many temporalized values where time makes for an evaluative difference. To this extent, it is limited in scope. But suppose now that bodily pain is evaluatively unimportant. Then showing that such pain is within the ambit of the claim adds little to the importance of the claim.

But in any case, we have seen that the claim is mistaken. We have seen that pure time preference with regard to one's own bodily pain can be defended, even if it cannot be defended with regard to other people's pain or other bads (sections 5–7). Also, we have seen that the past is vitally important for ethics – contrary to practically-minded theories (sections 3–4). And we have seen that time plays essential roles in the nature and value of what we are, do, experience and value (section 2).[18]

Notes

1 I am very pleased to thank Derek Parfit for help here and elsewhere.
2 Material in this section is drawn from my *Plural and Conflicting Values* (Oxford University Press, Oxford, 1990), ch. 8, sect. 2.
3 On the importance of time for human life, especially human acts, see Christine Korsgaard, 'Personal Identity and the Unity of Agency: A Kantian Response to Parfit', *Philosophy and Public Affairs*, 18 (1989), pp. 101–32.
4 On the distinction between the broadly and the narrowly psychological, see e.g. Tyler Burge, 'Individualism and Psychology', *Philosophical Review*, 95 (1986), pp. 3–45; and Jerry A. Fodor, *Psychosemantics* (MIT Press, Cam-

bridge, Mass., 1987). For recent discussions of the importance of experiences being true or accurate, see e.g. Richard Kraut, 'Two Conceptions of Happiness', *Philosophical Review*, 88 (1979), pp. 167–97; Lynne McFall, *Happiness* (Peter Lang, New York, 1988); and John Bigelow, John Campbell and Robert Pargetter, 'Death and Well-Being', *Pacific Philosophical Quarterly*, 71 (1990), pp. 119–40.

5 See Aristotle, *Nicomachean Ethics* (*NE*), *passim* and *Rhetoric* II 12–14. See also Alasdair MacIntyre, *After Virtue* (University of Notre Dame Press, Notre Dame, Ind., 1981); Michael Slote, *Goods and Virtues* (Oxford University Press, Oxford, 1983); Annette Baier, 'Familiar Passions', unpublished paper read to the University of Cincinnati Philosophy Colloquium, 'The Concept of Emotion', March 1985; and Bigelow et al., 'Death and well-Being'.

6 My thanks are owed to Graeme Marshall here.

7 My thanks are owed to Frances Howard-Snyder here.

8 My thanks are owed to Jonathan Bennett here.

9 See Norman Care, *Living With One's Past* (Rowman & Littlefield, Lanham, Md., 1996), ch. 1.

10 My thanks are owed to Margaret Walker here. On that evaluation being of us and our acts, see my *Plural and Conflicting Values*, pp. 35–6 and 112–13; my 'Act and Agent Evaluations', *Review of Metaphysics*, 27 (1973), pp. 42–61; Norman Dahl, 'Obligation and Moral Worth: Reflections on Prichard and Kant', *Philosophical Studies*, 50 (1986), pp. 369–99; and Stephen Hudson, *Human Character and Morality* (Routledge and Kegan Paul, Boston, 1986).

11 See Korsgaard, 'Personal Identity and the Unity of Agency', and Mark Johnston, ch. 8 below. My thanks are owed to Johnston for help here and elsewhere.

12 My thanks are owed to Jonathan Bennett here.

13 On external circumstances, see John M. Cooper, 'Aristotle on the Goods of Fortune', *Philosophical Review*, 94 (1985), pp. 173–96. On whether *eudaimonia* is better understood in terms of happiness or meaningfulness and fulfillingness, see David Wiggins, 'Truth, Invention, and the Meaning of Life', *Proceedings of the British Academy*, 42 (1976), pp. 331–78; and Kraut, 'Two Conceptions of Happiness'.

14 My thanks are owed to Annette Baier here. See my 'Agent and Other: Against Ethical Universalism', *Australasian Journal of Philosophy*, 54 (1976), pp. 206–20.

15 On these last, see Michael Balint, *Thrills and Regressions* (International Universities Press, Madison, Conn., 1987).

16 On these issues, and their basis in Aristotle, see my *Plural and Conflicting Values*, pp. 63 ff.

17 My thanks are owed to Laurence Thomas here.

18 In addition to those mentioned above, my thanks are also owed to Jonathan Adler, Jeff Blustein, Chris Gowans, Elizabeth Hegeman, Lynne McFall, Liam Murphy, Ernest Wallwork and Terry Winant.

5

Parfit's P

Philip Pettit and Michael Smith

I Introduction

In *Reasons and Persons*, Derek Parfit describes two theories of rationality, the Self-interest Theory, S, and the Present-aim Theory, P. 'S and P are simply related: they are both theories about rationality' (p. 129). Parfit thinks that S represents an overwhelming orthodoxy. 'The Self-interest Theory has been believed by most people for more than two millennia' (p. 194). P is not a single theory, but rather a class of theories, and Parfit thinks that one of those versions of P which he describes as critical – CP – is the best theory. He rejects some versions of CP, but leaves a number of candidates in the field. 'We should reject the Self-interest Theory about rationality, and accept the Critical Present-aim Theory' (p. 450).

As theories of rationality, S and P say what we should do. Thus they may conflict, not just with one another and not just with other theories of rationality, but also with morality. S in particular is likely to conflict with morality. 'There are many cases where it would be better for someone if he acts wrongly. In such cases we must decide what to do. We must choose between morality and S' (p. 129).

One sort of moral theory with which S and P may conflict is the neutral sort of morality, N, which identifies a common aim that all are required to further. Parfit is concerned with the decision between theories – strictly, classes of theories – like S, P and N. We might describe these alternatives simply as theories about what we should do, specifying S and P more exactly as theories of rationality, N as a theory of morality. But it will be simpler to describe them all, in the spirit of Sidgwick (p. 129), as theories of rationality. In adopting this way of describing the alternatives, we do not beg any questions, least of all any questions against Parfit.[1]

Our primary aim in this essay is to provide a certain perspective on P

– in particular, on the group of CP-theories to which Parfit is sympathetic. We think that there are two kinds of theory that might be described as theories of rationality; one we cast as a background theory, the other as a foreground theory. This distinction will be congenial to Parfit, since he acknowledges a related contrast. Our main question is whether P-theories – particularly the preferred versions of CP – point us towards a background or a foreground theory of rationality.

The question proves to be worth pursuing, for answering it highlights various features of the theories Parfit has in mind. It turns out that all versions of P, including CP versions, can be seen as pointing us to a background theory of rationality, and that, seen in this role, they have affinities with decision theory and some variants of decision theory. It turns out on the other side that while uncritical versions of P cannot double as plausible foreground theories – in this they resemble decision theory – some critical versions can. A CP-theory can represent a plausible foreground theory, but only provided that the critical component – the component represented by C – bulks large.

Answering the question posed not only serves to highlight certain features of P-theories. It also provides a useful standpoint from which to examine Parfit's main argument against S: the argument that he describes as the 'Appeal to Full Relativity' (pp. 137–48). Looked at in the light of our discussion, that argument appears unnecessarily weak; it turns out that there is a stronger argument against S that is available to Parfit. If our primary aim is to provide a certain perspective on P, our subsidiary aim is to put Parfit under some pressure on this front.

In the next section we present the distinction between background and foreground theories of rationality. In the third section we consider P as a background theory of rationality, and then in the fourth section we look at it as a foreground theory. These sections serve to put P in perspective, in accordance with our primary goal. In the fifth and final section we pursue the subsidiary goal, using considerations raised by the earlier discussion to suggest a revision of the principal argument that Parfit presents against S.

II   Background and Foreground Theories

Parfit makes a distinction between 'explanatory' and 'good' reasons. Furthermore, he makes it clear that his concern is with reasons in this second sense. 'By "reason" I shall mean "good reason"' (p. 118). The theory of rationality bears on reasons in this sense, for it is a theory about what constitutes reasons as reasons – that is, as good reasons – and about what makes some reasons better than others.

But there is a distinction to be drawn among good reasons, a distinction between two different senses in which something may be described as a good reason. This distinction is important from our viewpoint, because it generates a distinction between two kinds of theory that may each be described as a theory of rationality. The one kind we cast as a background theory, the other as a foreground theory.

The first sense of reason is that of a rational spring. A set of beliefs and desires can be a spring for the formation of a new desire or the performance of an action: say, the desire for a particular option or the performance of the corresponding action. Equally, a set of beliefs can be a spring for the formation of a new belief: say, the belief in something that follows from the contents of the other beliefs. In each case the spring may be rational; it may be a type of intentional profile that makes it rational for an agent to form the relevant sort of output, the new desire or the new belief. Other things being equal, the beliefs and desires will make the new desire for the option rational if the desires involve a pro attitude towards options with a certain property and if the beliefs involve taking the option – perhaps uniquely – to have that property.[2] Other things being equal, the beliefs will make the new belief rational if their contents – the propositions that the agent believes – provide inductive or deductive support for the content of the new belief. Where the type of intentional profile in question makes the new type of desire or the new type of belief rational in this way, it constitutes a good reason for forming that desire or belief. It is a good reason in the sense of being a rational spring for the formation of that desire or belief.

The second sense of reason is that of a rational ground. When a set of beliefs is a rational spring for the formation of a new belief, then the common presumption among philosophers is that the contents of those beliefs are rational grounds for forming the new belief. Take the beliefs that if p, then q and that p. These beliefs are a rational spring for believing that q, at least if other things are equal (other things will not be equal, for example, if the belief that q is inconsistent with something the agent already believes). Where the beliefs are a rational spring for believing that q, the (alleged) facts that if p, then q and that p, will be a rational ground for forming that belief. They will constitute a good reason for the agent to form that belief in a different sense of good reason from that of a rational spring; indeed, the difference in sense is so great that it marks a difference in *category*, as we might say. Where the rational spring consists in an intentional profile, a belief-state type, the rational ground consists in an assumed state of the world 'intended'; it consists in the way things are believed to be.

We have illustrated the notion of a rational ground with reference to the theoretical case in which beliefs lead to belief. What about the practical case in which beliefs and desires lead to desire, and ultimately perhaps to action? In particular, what factor in a rational ground corresponds to a desire in a rational spring? Here, unlike the case with belief, there is no common presumption to provide guidance. Is the proposition that is to correspond to the desire that p the content proposition itself – the proposition that p? Is it the proposition that the agent desires that p? Is it the proposition that it is desirable to satisfy the agent's desire that p? Is it the proposition that it is desirable that p? Is it something else again? Or is there perhaps no right and wrong in the matter?

Our view, which we have defended elsewhere, is that the case of desire goes in fairly exact parallel to that of belief.[3] Just as beliefs in a rational spring correspond to certain potentially explaining and justifying propositions in a rational ground, so we think that desires in a rational spring also correspond to such propositions in a rational ground. The proposition that gives the content of a belief is what figures in the corresponding rational ground. Such a proposition is a potential explainer and justifier of having that belief in the sense that what is endorsed in assent to that proposition – the alleged fact that p – may explain, and will certainly justify, the belief that p. Our view, in parallel with this, is that the proposition that corresponds in a rational ground to a desire that figures in a rational spring is a potential explainer and justifier of having that desire. Corresponding to the desire that p will be, not the proposition that p, and not in general the proposition that one has the desire that p, but rather a proposition such that what is endorsed in assent to it makes the having of the desire suitably intelligible. With most desires the proposition will have to be that it is desirable in some way that p: it is only what is endorsed in assent to such a proposition that could suitably explain or justify the general run of desire.[4]

There are different accounts of what is endorsed in assent to a proposition like 'It is desirable that p'. They range from cognitivist accounts which take it to be a common-or-garden fact to non-cognitivist stories that represent it as a projected way of viewing the world: a soft fact, in some sense.[5] But such differences need not affect our story. The view we take is that for most desires it is such an alleged fact, whatever the ontological status the fact enjoys, which serves in a rational ground as the counterpart to the desire that p in a rational spring. Suppose then an agent acts on the desire that p together with a suitable instrumental belief: say, the belief that p can be made the case by taking a certain option O; suppose, in particular, that this desire and belief constitute a rational spring for the agent to desire, and choose, O. In that case our view suggests this: that the (alleged) fact that p is desirable – or whatever – combines with the (alleged) fact that p can be made the case by taking option O to constitute the corresponding rational ground: the ground in view of which the agent can rationally desire O and act accordingly.

We will not repeat our earlier argument for the view that rational springs and rational grounds relate on this pattern in the practical case. We do not need to, since Parfit obviously agrees. He is prepared to countenance a sense of good reason that corresponds to a rational ground rather than a rational spring. And he is prepared to recognize that what corresponds to a desire in the rational ground is not the ascription of the desire itself, and not the content of the desire, but rather a proposition that reveals why possession of the desire is suitably intelligible. 'In most cases, someone's reason for acting is one of the features of what he wants, or one of the facts that explains and justifies his desire. Suppose that I help someone in need. My reason for helping this person is not that I want to do so, but that he needs help, or that I promised help, or something of the kind' (p. 121).

One further comment on rational grounds. As we employ the notion, a consideration X may be a rational ground for an agent's desiring something even if it happens that the agent will promote the good in question better by avoiding thoughts about X in his day-to-day deliberations. Take the good of spontaneity. We are prepared to think that the desirability of spontaneity may be a rational ground for an agent's having the desires constitutive of spontaneous behaviour even though the best way for him to promote his own spontaneity will be by avoiding spontaneity-focused deliberations in the day-to-day. It may be a rational ground, because, on reflection, in giving a rational justification for his behaviour in general – in giving a rational self-justification – the good of spontaneity may be something that he needs to take into account. It is neither here nor there that the rational thing for him to do in his more concrete deliberations is to forswear thinking about his own spontaneity.

With the distinction between rational springs and rational grounds, we are in a position to distinguish between two kinds of theory of rationality. Think of the springs as occupying a background, machine-room role, while the grounds appear in the foreground, being the considerations to which the agent actually pays attention in giving a reflective justification for his actions. The background theory of rationality will focus on good reasons in the sense of rational springs, and the foreground theory will focus on good reasons in the sense of rational grounds. In each case the theory will try to identify conditions that are necessary, and perhaps even sufficient, for an agent to have good reasons in the appropriate sense and to be, to that extent, rational; we assume that, with creatures like us, rationality requires the having of good reasons in both senses. It will tell us what is necessary, and perhaps sufficient, in the appropriate forum, the background or the foreground, for rationality.

The theory in either sense may address both theoretical and practical rationality – it may address rationality in the formation of beliefs as well as rationality in the formation of desires and in the performance of actions – but we will restrict our attention, as Parfit does, to the practical case. Our only concern will be with the background and foreground theories of practical rationality, though we shall often omit explicit mention of the practical; it is to be taken as understood.

There are a number of constraints that a background or foreground theory can recognize as conditions of rationality, and, depending on how many are introduced, the theory can be more or less demanding. It may identify a coherence condition on springs or grounds: a condition to the effect that they are internally coherent, and coherent with other states of the agent, or other things the agent posits, in a suitable way. It may prescribe a condition of reflection that should be satisfied by an agent if certain springs or grounds are to be rational ones for him to act on: say, the condition that the agent is suitably thoughtful in forming or considering the springs or grounds in question. Or it may go for a laundering condition of some kind, requiring that the springs or grounds be only of certain preferred sorts: say, that they involve only evidentially well-supported beliefs or propositions, or only certain desires or goods.[6] Theories that are demanding will tend to impose severe laundering constraints, as in the utilitarian theory of practical rationality that the only rational desire to act on in the background, and the only rational ground to take into account in the foreground, involves the maximization of happiness.

Background and foreground constraints on rationality may interact in the sense that endorsing a particular constraint in either area may commit one to endorsing a corresponding constraint in the other. To endorse the background laundering constraint according to which it is rational to desire happiness is to commit oneself to the foreground laundering constraint according to which it is rational to take happiness into account as a ground of action, and vice versa. At the limit, as is probably already evident, a background or foreground theory may be so demanding – in particular, it may involve such severe laundering constraints – that it leaves no independent questions to be resolved in the other area. Thus the background and foreground forms of the utilitarian theory of practical rationality are mutually determining in this way: if it is uniquely rational to desire the maximization of happiness, then it is uniquely rational to act on the ground of maximizing happiness, and vice versa. But it is crucial to recognize that though there are these connections between background and foreground constraints, there are some constraints in each area without any corresponding constraint in the other.

This is why background and foreground theories can represent distinct areas of enquiry.

One might have expected that any foreground constraints would resolve all relevant background questions; for it is plausible to hold that an agent is rational to embrace certain beliefs and desires only if he has rational grounds for doing so: only if he has grounds laundered of certain unsuitable considerations, grounds reflectively endorsed, or grounds that cohere with one another in certain ways. But even if certain background constraints are determined by foreground constraints in this way, there may well be other background constraints to be identified. It may be, for example, that the rational agent should only form new desires – or, in the theoretical case, beliefs – that cohere in a certain way with the degrees of strength with which he holds his existing attitudes, where those degrees are determined independently of rational grounds; they are a subjective given. This, as we shall see, is the line that Bayesian decision theorists run.

What of the other possibility: that any background constraints of rationality will resolve all relevant foreground questions, rather than vice versa? Here a simple case serves to establish that this is not so. Suppose that we identify a set of constraints on the beliefs and desires that it is rational for an agent to act on. Suppose that, according to those constraints, if he has certain desires – desires that p, that q, or whatever – then it is rational for him to act on them; this is the sort of thing postulated, as we shall see, both by decision theory and by the uncritical versions of P. What does this say about what it is rational for him to do in the foreground, about what grounds it is rational for him to invoke in self-justification? It does not say enough to close all questions. For example, the rational thing for him to do in the foreground may be to look to the fact that he desires that p or that q; to look to the fact that it is desirable to satisfy such an experienced desire; or to look to the fact that it is desirable, as he sees things, that p or q or whatever.

The emerging picture is this. To commit oneself to a background theory of rationality, especially a comprehensive background theory, may be to commit oneself, at least partially, in the area of foreground theory; it may be implicitly to endorse certain foreground constraints. Equally, to commit oneself to a foreground theory of rationality, especially a comprehensive foreground theory, may be to commit oneself partially in the area of background theory. But even a fairly rich commitment in either area may not exhaust the commitments to be made in the other. There may be independent questions to be resolved on either side of the background–foreground divide.

In the next section we will focus on the background theory of practical rationality, the theory of what makes for rational springs of desire and therefore action. In the section after that we turn to the foreground theory, the theory of rational grounds for action. In each case we will be raising the question of where P fits, and in particular where the group of CP-theories to which Parfit is sympathetic fit. We want to see how P-theories relate to well-established rivals in each area.

III   P as a Background Theory

If we want to situate P among background theories of rationality, then the most useful thing to do will be first to look at the most standard theory in the area, and then try and relate other theories, P included, to that theory. So what is the most standard theory of background rationality, in particular background practical rationality? What is the orthodox account of the requirements that the potential springs of desire and action must fulfil if they are springs that it would be rational for an agent to satisfy?

The orthodox account is surely Bayesian decision theory. This theory holds that all that is required for an agent's springs of action to be rational – all that is required for an agent to be rational in serving them – is that they satisfy a certain coherence constraint. The springs of action which the decision theorist countenances are constituted by subjective probabilities and subjective utilities; these are degrees of belief and degrees of desire, where degrees are calibrated so that a rational agent will prefer something desired at a higher degree to something desired at a lower. The constraint which decision theory imposes on the subjective probabilities and subjective utilities of the rational agent is variously formulated, but in every version it comes out as a constraint of coherence.[7]

Roughly the idea is this. We focus on items of desire, items to which the agent attaches utilities, and in particular on items of desire that relate probabilistically to other desired items: thus we focus on an item like X which, as the agent sees things, will yield a desired item Y with probability $\frac{1}{4}$ and a desired item Z with probability $\frac{3}{4}$. The decision-theoretic constraint requires a rational agent to desire such an item with a degree that corresponds in a certain way to his degrees of desire for the different possible outcomes and to his associated degrees of probability. Specifically, to take the case given, it requires that the agent's utility for X be the sum of the utility he attaches to Y, multiplied by $\frac{1}{4}$, and of the utility he attaches to Z, multiplied by $\frac{3}{4}$. It requires the rational agent to conform to the rule of expected utility in the utility that he assigns to an item like X.

Let us describe an item like X as a complex object of desire: it is complex in so far as there are desired outcomes with which it is probabilistically associated. The constraint imposed by decision theory puts a requirement on the degrees of desire that a rational agent has or comes to have for such complex objects. The requirement is that the degree of desire should reflect the extent to which the object serves the agent's other desires according to his beliefs. This constraint is sometimes taken to suggest that there are simple objects of desire, and that rationality consists in instrumentally shaping one's desires for complex objects in the light of one's desires for simple ones. But the decision theorist may endorse the constraint without conceding that there are any simple objects of desire; he may work, as Richard Jeffrey does, with an atomless algebra of objects.[8] And even if he does believe that there are simple objects, he need not think that the rational agent's degrees of desire for those objects are any more primitive than his degrees of desire for more complex things.[9] This is why we describe the decision-theoretic constraint merely as a requirement of coherence among potential springs of action, a requirement of coherence among an agent's degrees of belief and desire.

Bayesian decision theory does nothing more in elucidation of rational springs than to require the coherence involved in the rule of expected utility. However, it is clearly possible to build more demanding theories of background rationality out of the theory.

Some theorists have required for rationality not only that a rational agent satisfy expected utility, but that he do so with regard to degrees of belief and desire that survive certain tests of reflection: they are considered probabilities and utilities. The basic idea here goes back at least to Sidgwick, and has been taken up by contemporary theorists like Rawls and Brandt and Gauthier.[10] Roughly, in order to be rational, we must satisfy the beliefs and desires that we would have if we were in possession of the relevant facts and could think clearly.

Other theorists have supplemented the coherence constraint of decision theory not with a constraint of reflection, but with a laundering constraint. Some of these have wanted to admit only subjective probabilities, only degrees of belief, that correspond to probabilities that are objective in some sense.[11] Others have required that an agent's degrees of desire should be ethically satisfactory, say through answering to some specified values: they have required this, if not for being rational, at least for being moral, and therefore for doing what one should. The agent must not only satisfy expected utility, he must satisfy it with regard to the utilities he ought to have, the utilities that reflect some particular values: in a phrase, he must desire according to expected value, not just according to expected utility.[12] There has not been much agreement on which desires or preferences are unethical, as Jon Elster notes. But there has been some. 'On most accounts these would include spiteful and sadistic preferences, and arguably also the desire for positional goods, i.e. goods such that it is logically impossible for more than a few to have them.'[13]

Although we have stressed that decision theory does not have to be understood as an instrumental theory of rationality, it should be clear that the theory – that is, the theory unmodified by reflective or laundering constraints – derives from the Humean, instrumental way of thinking of rationality. We take an agent's desires as given, and we treat the requirements of rationality as requirements for the satisfaction of those desires. This approach is distinctively Humean in spirit. Of course, the expected utility version of what it is to be rational, what it is to satisfy desires, is much more complex than anything which Hume envisaged, but that should not surprise us, given the use it makes of quasi-mathematical notions that do not figure in Hume. The greater complexity means that the theory places requirements on a rational agent's desires of a kind that Hume sometimes seems to rule out. Thus it requires that an agent's desires satisfy various subsidiary conditions of coherence; for example, it requires that an agent's preferences not be intransitive: if he prefers A to B and B to C, then he cannot prefer C to A. But this sort of requirement is not imposed wilfully. As things turn out, it makes no sense to require an agent to desire and act according to the rule of expected utility if he has an intransitive preference structure.

Not only is decision theory – that is, unconstrained decision theory – Humean in spirit, however. It also represents the most sophisticated attempt to give expression to the orthodox Humean notion of what practical rationality – background practical rationality – consists in. For that reason it stands out as the background theory of rationality which most contemporary philosophers, economists and social theorists would identify as orthodoxy. It explicates what John Rawls describes as the 'standard' and 'familiar' concept of rationality.[14] As we have seen, theorists of rationality – and especially morality – often constrain decision theory with different sets of reflective and laundering constraints. But the point to notice is that unmodified decision theory is for so many of them the natural place to start. It is the agreed rest position, the position from which other destinations are most easily reached.

With decision theory in place, we may now ask where P stands in relation to it. In its initial formulation – one amended in critical versions, as we shall see – P says that what an agent has most reason to do is whatever would best fulfil his present desires (p. 117). This statement brings out a striking contrast between P – in all versions – and decision theory. Decision theory says that what it is rational for an agent to do – what complex object it is rational to desire – is whatever best serves his desires *according to his beliefs*. P says that what he has most reason to do is whatever best serves his desires *in fact*. This might mean: whatever best serves his desires, given suitably objective probabilities as to how things will turn out. Parfit, however, takes it to mean: whatever actually best serves his desires, whatever will turn out to serve them best, however improbable its turning out that way is at the time of action. We can put this initial contrast between decision theory and P by saying that P objectifies decision theory.

This difference between decision theory and P-theories need not mark any disagreement. The question of what it is rational to do can be treated in either of two ways, as a question about what is subjectively rational or as a question about what is objectively so. The subjective question concerns what it is rational for an agent to do in the light of his beliefs, where the answer will vary with varying beliefs. The objective question bears on what it is rational for the agent to do in a sense – assuming there *is* a legitimate sense – in which the answer is not supposed to vary with a variation in the agent's beliefs; it is the question, as Parfit likes to phrase it, of what an agent has most reason to do. A complete theory of rationality, as Parfit agrees, will address both questions – though it may not treat them as of equal legitimacy or importance (pp. 25, 120, 153). This is unsurprising, since an answer to one will tend to suggest a line on the other. But though a complete theory will address both questions, it is common in discussions of rationality to focus on one or the other.

The difference between decision theory and P-theories is that decision theory is designed to answer the question about subjective rationality, whereas P-theories are generally formulated by Parfit to answer the question about objective rationality; they are presented as theories about what an agent has most reason to do. This is not to say that Parfit thinks that P-theories can only deal with the objective question. He opposes such theories to the Self-interest Theory, S, and just as he thinks that S has an answer to the subjective as well as the objective question, so he presumably thinks that P theories can be adapted to provide an answer to the subjective issue (p. 8). Indeed, the indications are that if they were adapted to cope with the subjective question, Parfit's P-theories would look very like decision theory; his discussion of S in this role suggests that they would make use of the decision-theoretic notion of expectation.

When we say that P objectifies decision theory, then, we do not say that it diverges from it. All we mean is that it represents a counterpart of decision theory – one that mentions desires but ignores beliefs – which is suited to dealing with the objective as distinct from the subjective question about rationality. Is P – strictly, the unqualified version of P – the only objective counterpart of decision theory? No, as already implicitly noted. A decision theorist of subjective rationality says that an agent should do whatever best serves his desires according to his beliefs. Asked to address the question about objective rationality – if he admits its legitimacy – he might say, not that an agent should do whatever actually best serves his desires, but that he should do whatever best serves his desires according to some appropriately objective probabilities at the time of action.[15] Such a theory might equally well claim to objectify decision theory.

Parfit introduces two amendments of the initially formulated doctrine, the doctrine that just objectifies decision theory. First, he assumes that the desires that a rational agent has most reason to satisfy – the desires which it is objectively rational for him to fulfil – are those that would survive a certain reflection on the agent's part: desires that he would have 'if he knew the relevant facts, was thinking clearly, and was free from distorting influences' (p. 118). The condition of reflection introduced here is the familiar sort discussed earlier in relation to decision theory. Notice in particular that it is reductively specifiable by reference to what are the facts, what are relevant unclarities, and what are typical distorting influences; reflection will have occurred whenever the agent operates in knowledge of the facts and in the absence of such unclarity or distortion. Parfit does not presuppose an independent notion of rational desire such that we could then characterize the condition where reflection has occurred, in a non-reductive way, as whatever condition is necessary for the formation of rational desire: whatever condition it takes to produce such desire. Parfit discusses only cases where the reflective condition is met, and we shall generally take the condition as given in what follows (p. 120).

So far the sort of P-theory envisaged comes to an objectified and reflective version of decision theory. Parfit also introduces a second qualification to the variants of P that he countenances, a qualification that amounts to a laundering constraint. He is prepared to countenance only critical versions of P: only CP-theories. P goes critical in virtue of two distinct sorts of constraint over and beyond the reflective condition (p. 119). One is a constraint already assumed, as we have seen, in decision theory: that the agent's desires overall satisfy coherence conditions like that of not involving intransitive preferences. This we may ignore. The other is a constraint on the content of individual desires and sets of desires.

Parfit requires that individual desires are not irrational in any intrinsic way, that they are not open to rational criticism. He cites as compelling examples of irrational desires those desires that would discriminate between pleasures and pains in some arbitrary way: desires like the desire to avoid pain except on Tuesdays (pp. 124–5). Parfit is also open to the possibility that some desires are rationally required, and that a set of desires may be irrational in content, through failing to contain such desires (pp. 119, 121–2). Thus the group of CP-theories that he is prepared to countenance covers a broad range, stretching from the weak sort that would just outlaw irrational desires like the ones mentioned to the strong sort that would represent some desires as rationally required.

Can we say more about the theories that belong to Parfit's preferred group? All theories that address the question of what it is objectively rational for an agent to do can be presented in CP terms; the CP structure is one of which *'every* possible theory about rationality is one version' (p. 194). But Parfit is hostile to some CP-theories. He rejects the CP version of S, CPS, according to which what a rational agent should do is whatever actually best serves the desire that is alleged to be supremely rational: namely, that things go as well as possible for an agent over the course of his life (p. 131). Equally, of course, Parfit rejects the null version of CP – null because the critical element vanishes – which would deny that any desires are rationally impermissible or mandatory (p. 194). Otherwise he is well disposed to CP-theories. Thus he is open to the idea that the desire that things go as well as possible for an agent over the whole of his life may be rationally required, even if not supremely rational (p. 135). And he is open also to the idea that the desire to further certain moral ends may be rationally required, and even indeed that it may be supremely rational (pp. 121–2, 133, 452). This theory, CPM, is the CP version of N, as CPS is the CP version of S.

We have situated Parfit's P-theories in the context of other background theories of rationality, presenting them in relation to decision theory and well-known variants of decision theory: those that would impose extra reflective and laundering constraints. All P-theories differ from decision theory in being formulated as objectified theories, as theories that are addressed to the question about objective rather than subjective rationality. And CP-theories differ from unmodified decision theory – though not, of course, from the constrained variants – in being subjected also to reflective and laundering constraints.

This presentation of P-theories should be useful in providing a perspective on them. It does not jar with anything that Parfit himself says, except in one minor respect. It suggests that Parfit overstates the novelty of his own theory and the standing of S. 'It has been assumed, for more than two millennia', Parfit says, 'that it is irrational for anyone to do what he knows will be worse for himself' (p. 130). S is, he tells us, 'the verdict of recorded history', and he therefore worries that we will find 'absurdly rash' his rejection of S in favour of P, and in particular CP (p. 194). But these claims about S are overstated, and this anxiety is groundless.

While there have certainly been adherents of S for more than two millennia, over the last 200 years it has been even more widely assumed that it is not irrational for an agent to do what he knows will be worse for himself. ' 'Tis not contrary to reason', as Hume put it, 'for me to chuse my total ruin, to prevent the least uneasiness of an Indian or person wholly unknown to me.'[16] Hume transformed our way of thinking about practical rationality, and that transformation has culminated, over the past half-century, in the development and widespread acceptance of decision theory as a formal model of practical rationality. It is decision theory, unconstrained by the requirement that the rational agent's desires answer to the specific value of furthering his own interests, that now enjoys the status Parfit claims for S over the last two millennia.

P-theories are closely related to decision theory, as we have seen. Unqualified versions of P objectify decision theory, while the critical versions, in particular those that Parfit himself favours, also impose certain reflective and laundering constraints. Thus the endorsement of a CP-theory in preference to S – or even in preference to unconstrained decision theory – does not represent an 'absurdly rash' move. On the contrary, it is likely to seem a natural and reasonable initiative.

IV   P as a Foreground Theory

Our discussion in the last section shows that it is perfectly natural to take P-theories as background theories of rationality. There is more difficulty, however, in taking them as foreground theories, as we shall now see. It turns out that the unqualified version of P, and some of the critical versions too, cannot plausibly be taken in a foreground role. This is not a criticism of those theories, but an interesting fact about them. It indicates that they should be seen as theories which address only background questions of rationality. In this limitation, as we shall see, these theories resemble decision theory.

The background theory of practical rationality is concerned with what makes for rational springs of action. The foreground theory addresses the parallel question of what makes for rational grounds of action. We saw that a background theory may look to constraints of coherence, reflection or laundering in formulating the requirements of rationality. Equally, a foreground theory might look to constraints of such kinds. It might say that what is required for certain grounds to be rational is that they cohere with one another in a certain way; that they are grounds that the agent would endorse on reflection; that they exclude certain unsuitable sorts of considerations; or a mixture of such things.

The two sorts of constraints that are actually most invoked in the foreground theory of rationality are coherence and laundering constraints. The best-known constraint of coherence has it that if a consideration gives an agent a good foreground reason – a rational ground – for doing something, and if it mentions a particular individual, time or place, then considerations that differ at most in the particular mentioned must give rational grounds to any individual in the position of the agent. It would be incoherent to acknowledge the one consideration as a good reason without acknowledging the others as good reasons. This is the constraint of universalizability. It means that if I am given a good reason for doing something by the fact that a particular individual is in need, then anyone in my situation would be given a good reason for doing that sort of action by the fact that any relevantly similar individual was in need. And it also means, to take a slightly more complex example, that if I am given a good reason for doing something by the fact that it will help my child, then anyone in my situation would be given a good reason for that sort of action by the fact that it would help his or her child.

Theories of foreground rationality often also introduce laundering constraints on the considerations that may rationally justify an action from an agent's point of view. Thus a theory might prescribe that the fact that an action will cause one pain constitutes a good reason *pro tanto* for not doing it, or that the fact that an action will cause one pleasure always constitutes a good *pro tanto* reason for doing it. Again, a theory might prescribe that the only consideration that can rationally justify an action to an agent is the fact that so acting will maximize happiness generally. And so on through other salient examples.

It should be clear that a satisfactory theory of background rationality will not necessarily double as a satisfactory theory of foreground rationality. That is to say, a formula as to what one has good or most reason to do may constitute a satisfactory theory as it applies to rational springs without constituting a satisfactory theory, or even a half-sensible theory, as it applies to rational grounds. Suppose we endorse decision theory: we think that any set of subjective probabilities and utilities will constitute rational springs for an agent to act on, provided they satisfy the coherence constraint associated with the agent's maximizing expected utility; moreover, we think that these are the only rational springs there are. This does not mean that we will take decision theory to provide also a satisfactory theory of foreground rationality: a theory that closes the foreground questions which, as a background theory, it leaves open. These will include questions to do with whether the rational agent should focus on considerations about which desires he has, considerations about the desirability of satisfying those desires, or considerations about the desirability of the things he desires.

Our own view is that decision theory sticks entirely to background matters, and has nothing to say on such foreground questions. Someone who thinks that decision theory serves also in a foreground role – the business school enthusiast perhaps – will take a very different view. He will hold that the decision-theoretic formula offers advice on how to deliberate, suggesting that the agent should consult his own degrees of belief and desire in deciding how to act; he should consult these, rather than the alleged facts that support them, the facts about what is so and about what is desirable. We think that what is proposed here has little merit or sense.

As a foreground theory, decision theory would say that any suitable set of subjective probabilities and utilities will constitute rational grounds for an agent to take into account in self-justification, and indeed that there are no other sorts of rational grounds available. It would counsel the agent to consider the state of his beliefs and desires with a view to determining in every choice the option which best serves those beliefs according to those desires, the option which maximizes expected utility. But it would be crazy to prescribe that an agent should deliberate only from considerations as to what he believes and desires, as distinct from considerations as to what is the case or what is desirable. We cannot seriously entertain the possibility that the rational agent should not consider the things he believes – that p, that if p then q, and so on – in deriving and justifying new beliefs, but should rather consider the fact that he believes that p, believes that if p then q, and the like. Neither can we countenance the possibility that he should not consider the factors that serve to justify and explain his desires – that an option will help a friend, that it will make him famous, or whatever – but should rather focus on the desires themselves.[17] We need not argue the point, since Parfit would obviously agree with us. He is explicit, as we have seen, on the case of desire: 'my reason is not my desire but the respect in which what I am doing is worth doing, or the respect in which my aim is *desirable* – worth desiring' (p. 121).

We have seen that Parfit's P-theories represent fairly reasonable proposals on matters of background rationality, being objectified and, in the case of CP-theories, reflective and laundered versions of decision theory. The question now is what a P-theory would amount to as a theory of foreground rationality, a theory as to the grounds which a rational agent will take into account for choice. The question in particular is whether it would make for a foreground theory of a more plausible kind than decision theory or whether, like decision theory, it is best seen as a purely background theory.

The unqualified version of P, a version rejected by Parfit himself, says that the rational thing for an agent to do in any situation is what best serves his desires in fact. It will be clear that this version of P cannot serve as a foreground theory any more successfully than decision theory. Apply the P-formula to resolving foreground rather than just background

questions, and it would have the rational agent restricted to a consideration of the state of his desires. The unqualified version of P is subject to
the complaints just made about decision theory as a foreground theory,
complaints which we assume that Parfit would support. Thus this version
of P should be seen only as a background theory of rationality.

At the other extreme from the unqualified version of P are the critical
versions which qualify P to the extent of taking a particular sort of desire
to be supremely rational. We are thinking here of CPS, which confers
this privilege on the desire that one's life go as well as possible, and CPM,
which gives a similar status to certain moral concerns: say, the utilitarian
concern with overall happiness. Such theories can serve as reasonable
theories of foreground rationality – certainly as theories less mad than
decision theory – because they can be taken to prescribe as grounds for
the rational agent to consider, not matters to do with the satisfaction of
a desire that the agent happens to have, but rather matters concerning
what would be desired if the agent were fully rational: the rational
agent's own well-being or the happiness of sentient creatures overall. It
is not crazy to claim that the only rational ground for choosing something
is that it is supremely rational to desire it.

What now of Parfit's preferred group of CP-theories? These, as we
have seen, will include theories as strong as CPM, theories that represent
the desire for some moral end as rationally required and supremely
rational. There will be no difficulty, as we have just seen, in taking such
theories in a foreground as well as a background role; there will be no
problem in seeing them, not just as telling us the desires it is rational to
satisfy – only those that serve the supremely rational desire – but also as
offering counsel on the grounds it is rational to invoke in deliberative
self-justification.

But Parfit's preferred theories also include theories that are very weak
in the critical dimension: theories that rule out only desires that are
irrational in certain conspicuous ways – say because they distinguish
arbitrarily between different instances of a certain sort of pleasure or
pain. What is the position going to be with such theories? Will they be
capable of doubling in a foreground role? Or will they be better taken,
like decision theory and the unqualified version of P, as theories of a
purely background kind: theories that do not address, or that address
only in part, questions about the grounds that it is rational to invoke in
deliberation?

What sorts of grounds would such a weakly critical CP-theory prescribe that the rational agent should consult in deliberation? Because it
insists that certain desires and patterns of desire are intrinsically irrational, it will certainly rule out certain considerations from being taken
into account by a rational agent. The rational agent will not be moved, at

bottom, by the thought that pains are undesirable except on a Tuesday; he will not be moved by judgements of desirability that fit a pattern whereby X is more desirable than Y, Y than Z, and Z than X; and so on. But for the rest, it seems, such a minimally critical version of CP, interpreted as a formula for resolving foreground questions, would simply tell the rational agent to look to the state of his own present desires, provided they meet certain minimal conditions of reflection, in determining what to do. And in that case it follows that the theory would run into the same troubles as decision theory if it were taken as a theory of foreground rationality. It would prescribe as grounds that are uniquely appropriate for rational choice considerations that Parfit himself tells us do not in general constitute such grounds. For these grounds do not concern the worth or desirability of actions.[18] We should take a theory of this kind to be a theory that addresses background, not foreground, questions about rationality.

As against this line of argument someone may say that every foreground theory of rationality must acknowledge that there are some desires which an agent will have without reasons – hankerings, hungers and the like – which will provide *pro tanto* foreground reasons, of themselves, for action: that is, for acting so as to satisfy them. So what is supposed to be so counter-intuitive about the foreground proposals that a weakly critical CP-theory would put forward?

There are two points to make. First, the sorts of desires quoted in analogy are unusual, having a dual aspect as producers of action and as phenomenological yearnings, and it is going to be strange if a theory – a weakly critical CP-theory – treats other kinds of desires as of the same sort: say, if it treats in this way my desire to write a novel, be kind to friends, or become famous. Second, even it were fair to treat other kinds of desire like these phenomenological inclinations, this would not support the conclusion that such desires offer, of themselves, foreground reasons to act. If I act on a phenomenological desire, my foreground reason must be that it is desirable in some way to satisfy it, not just that I have the desire; the latter reason could be as much a reason to get rid of the desire, say by therapy or by resort to a cold shower, as it would be a reason to satisfy it.[19] The first of our two points shows that the objection is based on a strained analogy, the second that it is based on an analogy which fails to deliver the required result.

We saw in the last section that any P-theory – in particular, any of the CP-theories countenanced by Parfit – can pass muster as a background theory of rationality. In this section we have seen that some strongly critical CP-theories, including CPS and the sort of CPM which Parfit keeps in his preferred group, can reasonably double as foreground theories too. But we have also seen that the unqualified version of P, and less strongly critical CP-theories, cannot reasonably be taken in this role; they cannot reasonably be taken as offering advice on rational grounds for deliberation. Like decision theory, such theories are better taken as doctrines addressed solely to questions of background rationality.

V Parfit's Case against S

Our argument so far serves to put P-theories – in particular, the CP-theories preferred by Parfit – in some perspective. We hope that it throws light on their relations with other theories of rationality and on their capacity to answer the different sorts of questions that come up in the background and foreground areas. The argument does not support any criticism of Parfit, except in the suggestion that he overstates the standing of S and the novelty of his own proposal.

In this final section, however, we do mean to offer a challenge to Parfit. We consider one of his main arguments against S – the Appeal to Full Relativity (pp. 137–48) – and find that his failure to be explicit about the distinction between background and foreground theories of rationality leads him astray. In that argument the unqualified version of P is evidently treated as a foreground theory, and as a foreground theory that is plausible in its own right. For reasons rehearsed in the last section, such an argument should convince no one, least of all Parfit himself. But though the argument as presented does not succeed, our discussion reveals that a closely related, and indeed stronger, argument remains available. The criticism we offer, therefore, is constructive in effect, and Parfit may find it congenial.

Parfit introduces his argument[20] with these remarks:

> Sidgwick's moral theory requires what he calls Rational Benevolence. On this theory, an agent may not give a special status either to himself or to the present. In requiring both personal and temporal neutrality, this theory is *pure*. Another pure theory is the Present-aim Theory, which rejects the requirements both of personal and of temporal neutrality. The Self-interest Theory is not pure. It is a *hybrid* theory. S rejects the requirement of personal neutrality, but requires temporal neutrality. S allows the agent to single out himself, but insists that he may not single out the time of acting. He must not give special weight to what he *now* wants or values. He must give equal weight to all the parts of his life, or to what he wants or values at all times.
>
> Sidgwick may have seen that, as a hybrid, S can be charged with a kind of inconsistency. If the agent has a special status, why deny this status to the time of acting? We can object to S that it is *incompletely relative*. (p. 140)

Parfit's argument against S is a pincer argument that S is incoherent in recommending a partiality to self over others but an impartiality as between present and future times. Parfit endorses a principle of full relativity or partiality: this is the Appeal mentioned. According to this principle, reasons – in particular, the allegedly compelling reasons countenanced by S – should be fully relative if they can be relative at all: they should be fully relativized to persons and times if they can be relativized to either (pp. 140–1). His defence of the principle is that any grounds for going relative in one way will be grounds for going relative in the other. If we go agent-relative in the theory of what it is rational to do, arguing that the question before me as an agent is what there is most reason for *me* to do, we should go time-relative also, on the grounds that equally the question that I face is what it is rational for me to do *now*: I should say that what it is rational for me to do is whatever will promote the good for me now (pp. 142–3). Thus, the pincer argument says, the defender of S should give up his theory in favour of either a fully relative theory or a fully neutral one; he should say that what it is rational for an agent to do is to promote the good generally over all people and times or to promote the good for himself now. He should not treat 'I' and 'now' in less than an even-handed way (p. 148).

This argument is directed principally against S as a foreground theory, arguing that S offends against a certain coherence constraint. The argument is that we cannot rationally justify our conduct to ourselves by appeal to considerations that are only incompletely relative, such as the consideration that this option will be beneficial for me over a range of times. The rational agent who considers conforming to S – the agent who thinks that there are rationally compelling considerations of the kind cited by S – is enjoined by the pincer argument to prefer to countenance considerations that are fully neutral or fully relative. Thus, on Parfit's account, the argument produces an instability result for the Self-interest Theory. It means that the theory is a half-way house between foreground theories recommending that we act on fully relative and fully neutral considerations. We should cease to look for a theory of compelling reasons altogether, or we should reject S in favour of one of the extreme positions.

But though the argument is directed principally against S in a foreground role, it tells against S in a background role as well. If we are required rationally to abjure any foreground theory of compelling considerations, such as S, or to reject S as a foreground theory in favour of a theory that recognizes fully relative or fully neutral considerations, then in the theory of background rationality we must forswear any demanding theory like S – any theory requiring a certain desire – or we must reject S in favour of theories that launder desires uniformly: theories which require rational desires to have either fully relative or fully neutral contents. We cannot endorse a theory like S which casts as supremely rational a desire that is intertemporally neutral but interpersonally relative.

The account of Parfit's argument offered so far is silent on the question of what constitutes the good which S says the agent should promote for himself over his life as a whole. S says that an agent should act so that his life goes as well as possible, but in our account of this argument against S we have said nothing about what it is for a life to go as well as possible. S may be interpreted in any of a number of different ways, depending on what the good for a person is taken to be. Thus S will vary in its concrete significance, Parfit says, as the good is equated with pleasure or the fulfilment of the agent's desires or the realization of an objective benefit like knowledge (p. 4).

When Parfit develops his pincer argument against S, he does so under a particular interpretation of the good: namely, an interpretation which equates the good for an agent with the fulfilment of his desires (p. 137). On this construal, S says that the only considerations that can rationally justify his conduct to an agent are those that concern the satisfaction of his desires over his lifetime. The pincer argument alleges that he should, rather, act on fully relative or fully neutral considerations: considerations to do with what will satisfy his desires now or considerations to do with what will satisfy people's desires generally.

What doctrine prescribes that the rational agent should act on considerations about what will satisfy people's desires generally? Rational Benevolence, in something like Sidgwick's sense: specifically, utilitarianism in a desire-centred form. And what doctrine prescribes that the rational agent should act on considerations to do with what will satisfy his own desires now? The Present-aim Theory, Parfit tells us (p. 140; see also p. 135). And here we see the promised dénouement. In pressing his pincer strategy against S, Parfit commits himself to the view that, of the two foreground theories of rationality that are to be preferred to the desire-fulfilment version of S, the fully relativized alternative is P in the unqualified form that says that the rational agent should do whatever would best satisfy his present desires.

But this has to be a mistake on Parfit's part, since we know he thinks that considerations regarding their desires do not in general give people good foreground reasons to act: that they should act instead on considerations that serve to explain and justify their desires, considerations as to the worth of what they desire (p. 121). We think that he could never have made this mistake if he had applied the background–foreground distinction to his discussion of good reasons and of theories like S and P. It is a pity that though he appears to be committed to such a divide, he did not give more explicit attention to it in his treatment of these topics.

What is the effect of admitting, as we think Parfit should admit, that one of the pure alternatives with which he seeks to destabilize the desire-fulfilment version of S is an alternative that has to be rejected out of hand? Surprisingly, the effect is to strengthen the case against this form of S. Parfit's destabilizing argument is that anyone who adopts a theory of compelling reasons like S has a reason to prefer a fully relative theory or a fully neutral one. But if the fully relative theory is not a real option, then the argument would seem to establish that anyone who adopts S has a reason to prefer a fully neutral theory. We might cast the argument as follows, in the form of a *reductio*. The relativization countenanced in adopting the desire-fulfilment version of S leads in consistency to full relativization; but full relativization is in this case quite objectionable, involving the adoption of the unqualified version of P as a foreground theory; so relativization of the sort involved in this form of S should not be tolerated. So stated, the argument resembles the case made by Thomas Nagel in *The Possibility of Altruism* against the relativization of foreground reasons.[21] If we are to countenance compelling reasons of the kind alleged by the desire-fulfilment version of S, then, we should countenance only neutral reasons as compelling.

Someone may say that while we have shown that Parfit has a *reductio* strategy available against S, with the good interpreted as desire-fulfilment, we have not shown that he has such a strategy available under other interpretations of the good. It is true that we have not shown this, but it turns out that something close to the more general result can be established. This is surprising, since it makes it even less explicable why Parfit should have thought that he had only a destabilizing argument available against S.

The other interpretations of the good for a person that Parfit cites equate it with pleasure or with a more objective good like knowledge (p. 4). Suppose, then, that the good is taken as pleasure or knowledge. The Self-interest Theory will prescribe that the rational agent should take considerations about the promotion of his own pleasure or knowledge over his lifetime as supremely compelling: as considerations that trump everything else. The pincer argument says that, on the contrary, if such trumping considerations are countenanced, then the only coherent recommendations are either that the agent should act on considerations about the promotion of pleasure or knowledge generally – the fully neutral position – or that he should act on considerations about the promotion of his pleasure or knowledge now – the fully relative position. Thus it appears that the mid-way position S is unstable.

But in this case, as in the argument with the good taken as desire-fulfilment, it appears that Parfit has the resources available to do more than just destabilize S. He himself points out that if we apply relativization to the hedonistic version of S, so that the happiness of me now is what counts, we are led to an 'absurd' view (p. 142; see also p. 135). And in that same context he does not even mention knowledge – or any other such good – as the sort of thing that might plausibly be held to be in the interest of me-now; he would therefore presumably regard the theory that would focus on present knowledge rather than present pleasure as equally, if not more, absurd. But if the pincer argument shows that a neutral theorist who goes to S ought in consistency to go to a position that is rated absurd, then the argument does more than destabilize S; it reduces S to absurdity and, among theories that countenance compelling considerations, establishes the unique superiority of the neutral position.

The lesson of these reflections is that not only does the introduction of the background–foreground distinction help in situating P-theories relative to decision theory and other theories of rationality. It also helps us to see that Parfit goes astray in the course of one of his main arguments against S: specifically, in thinking that he has only a destabilizing strategy available against S, when a *reductio* strategy is accessible from the very considerations he musters. This charge may not be uncongenial to him. Not only is S unstable, as he alleges. It involves a sort of relativization that leads to near-absurdity.[22]

Notes

1　True, we abstract away from the distinction between what is subjectively and what is objectively rational, which is important in Parfit's work, but we shall lift that abstraction later.

2　Donald Davidson, 'Actions, Reasons and Causes', in *Essays on Actions and Events* (Clarendon Press, Oxford, 1980), pp. 3–19.

3　Philip Pettit and Michael Smith, 'Backgrounding Desire', *Philosophical Review*, 99 (1990), pp. 565–92. See too a paper written five years after 'Parfit's P': viz. 'Freedom in Belief and Desire', *Journal of Philosophy*, 93 (1996).

4　Michael Smith, 'Valuing: Desiring or Believing?', in *Reductionism, Explanation and Realism*, ed. David Charles and Kathleen Lennon (Oxford University Press, Oxford, 1992), pp. 323–60. For a later, fuller treatment, see *The Moral Problem* (Blackwell, Oxford, 1994), esp. ch. 5. Why do we say 'with most desires'? Because with some desires – visitations like hungers and hankerings – the rational ground for acting, if there is one, will be that it is desirable to satisfy such urges. See the discussion at the end of section IV.

5　See e.g. Simon Blackburn, 'How to Be an Ethical Anti-realist', in his *Essays in Quasi-Realism* (Oxford University Press, Oxford, 1993), pp. 166–81.

6 Robert Goodin, 'Laundering Preferences', in *Foundations of Social Choice Theory*, ed. J. Elster and A. Hylland (Cambridge University Press, Cambridge, 1986).

7 Ellery Eells, *Rational Decision and Causality* (Cambridge University Press, Cambridge, 1982).

8 Richard C. Jeffrey, *The Logic of Decision*, 2nd edn (University of Chicago Press, Chicago, 1983).

9 Philip Pettit, 'Decision Theory and Folk Psychology', in *Essays in the Foundations of Decision Theory*, ed. M. Bacharach and S. Hurley (Blackwell, Oxford, 1991), pp. 147–75. For a later, fuller treatment, see Pettit, *The Common Mind: An Essay on Psychology, Society and Politics* (Oxford University Press, New York, 1993), esp. ch. 5.

10 See Henry Sidgwick, *The Methods of Ethics* (Dover, New York, 1966), bk 1, ch. 9; John Rawls, *A Theory of Justice* (Oxford University Press, Oxford, 1971), sect. 64; Richard Brandt, *A Theory of the Good and the Right* (Oxford University Press, Oxford, 1979), ch. 6; and David Gauthier, *Morals by Agreement* (Oxford University Press, Oxford, 1986), ch. 2.

11 See e.g. D. H. Mellor, 'Objective Decision-Making', *Social Theory and Practice*, 9 (1983), pp. 289–310.

12 See e.g. Frank Jackson, 'A Probabilistic Approach to Moral Responsibility', in *Proceedings of the 7th International Congress of Logic, Methodology and Philosophy of Science* (1983), ed. R. Barcan Marcus et al. (North-Holland, Amsterdam, 1986), pp. 351–66; Mellor, 'Objective Decision-Making'; Susan Hurley, *Natural Reasons* (Oxford University Press, Oxford, 1989).

13 Jon Elster, *Sour Grapes* (Cambridge, Cambridge University Press, 1983), p. 22.

14 Rawls, *Theory of Justice*, p. 143.

15 See Mellor, 'Objective Decision-Making'.

16 David Hume, *A Treatise of Human Nature*, ed. P. Nidditch (Clarendon Press, Oxford, 1968), p. 416.

17 Pettit, 'Decision Theory and Folk Psychology'.

18 Notice that this argument turns on the assumption that Parfit's condition of reflection, as mentioned in section III, is reductively specifiable.

19 See Gary Watson, 'Free Agency', *Journal of Philosophy*, 72 (1975), pp. 205–20.

20 Parfit introduces this second of two arguments in the course of providing the S-theorist with a reply to the first. The first argument is an implausibility charge of a kind that is familiar and, by his own admission, unprovable (pp. 130–6). It counters the S-theorist's claim that it is supremely rational to desire that things go as well as possible for oneself over one's life with cases where it seems rational for an agent to satisfy desires – say, moral concerns – that require the frustration of self-interest. This would tell against S in either background or foreground role. The S-theorist replies to this argument that he does not have to assume all three of the elements involved in S: viz. that the agent should promote (1) the good, (2) for himself, (3) over his life. He assumes the first two elements – that the good for the agent provides a reason – and he offers an argument for the third – that if the good

for the agent provides a reason, then it does so in a time-neutral way. Parfit uses against this reply a principle that is later strengthened into the Appeal to Full Relativity. That appeal is meant to undermine the reply as well as to provide a second argument against S.

21 Thomas Nagel, *The Possibility of Altruism* (Oxford University Press, Oxford, 1970). Parfit distinguishes his own destabilizing argument from Nagel's (p. 144).

22 We are grateful for the useful discussion this paper received when it was presented at the annual conference of the Australasian Association of Philosophy, Sydney, 1990. We are also grateful for comments received from Frank Jackson, Lloyd Humberstone and Graham Oddie. We are greatly indebted to Jonathan Dancy and Derek Parfit for detailed comments on an earlier draft, and are also in Dancy's debt for helpful exchanges on the interpretation of *Reasons and Persons*.

6

Rational Egoism and the Separateness of Persons

David O. Brink

Derek Parfit's wide-ranging and important book *Reasons and Persons* defends interesting and often revisionary claims about morality, rationality and personal identity in imaginative and resourceful ways. Two of the book's central themes are the nature of individual rationality and the way in which our views about it interact with our views about the nature of persons. In his discussion of these issues, Parfit examines the way in which different views of rationality treat matters of intertemporal and interpersonal distribution. He exploits parallels between these two distributional dimensions in order, among other things, to challenge rational egoism, or the 'Self-interest Theory' as he calls it. Whereas Sidgwick acknowledged a similar challenge to egoism but did not think it sound,[1] Parfit thinks that it constitutes a decisive objection to egoism. This is an important challenge. But, like Sidgwick, I believe that egoism's commitment to the separateness of persons provides a rationale for its asymmetrical treatment of intertemporal and interpersonal distribution. And because Parfit's reductionist claims about personal identity appear to challenge the separateness of persons, I shall consider his claims and argue that the egoist rationale is compatible with reductionism about personal identity.

This is an adaptation, with significant revisions, of material from my 'Sidgwick and the Rationale for Rational Egoism', in *Essays on Henry Sidgwick*, ed. B. Schultz (Cambridge University Press, New York, 1991). Some of the revisions were made during a Fellowship that I held at the Center for Advanced Study in the Behavioral Sciences, funded by an Old Dominion Fellowship from the Massachusetts Institute of Technology and by grants from the National Endowment for the Humanities (#RA-20037-88) and the Andrew W. Mellon Foundation. I would like to thank these institutions for their support. I would also like to thank audiences at Stanford University, University of California at Irvine, Massachusetts Institute of Technology, Middlebury College, and the Sidgwick conference at the University of Chicago for helpful discussion of these issues. Special thanks go to Jonathan Dancy, Stephen Darwall, Terry Irwin, Diane Jeske, Derek Parfit, Sydney Shoemaker, Alan Sidelle and Jennifer Whiting.

1 Practical Rationality: Interpersonal and Intertemporal Distribution

Practical reasoning involves assessing alternative courses of action and deciding what to do. Alternative actions will typically have different implications for the amount of benefits and harms produced and their distribution among persons and across time. If we assume that, other things being equal, the rationality of an action is proportional to the amount of value it would produce, then we can understand theories of rationality as concerned with the way in which benefits and harms rationally ought to be allocated *among persons* and *across time*.

Theories might be classified by what they say about *whose* welfare matters. On one view, only the agent's own welfare should have non-derivative rational significance for her; actions must benefit the agent in some way to give her reason for action. Although no labels seem entirely satisfactory, we might call such a view *agent-biased*. On alternative views, an agent has reason to benefit others independently of any contribution (causal or constitutive) that this makes, directly or indirectly, to her own welfare. Again, no labels seem entirely satisfactory, but let us call any view that demands concern for others that is rationally non-derivative *impartial* or *altruistic*. There are many different interpretations of impartiality. I will assume that all versions are universal in the scope of their other-regarding concern, so that the agent has some non-derivative reason to be concerned about anyone's welfare. But impartiality or altruism, as I am understanding it here, does not, as such, attach equal weight to everyone's interests. It is only a *person-neutral*, or *impersonal*, conception of impartiality that does this. On this view, an agent has equal non-derivative reason to be concerned about anyone's welfare; in deciding what to do, she should consider only the magnitude of the benefits she can produce.

Theories of rationality might also be classified by their attitudes towards the *temporal location* of benefits and harms. On one view, only present benefits should have non-derivative rational significance for the agent. We might call such a view *present-biased*. On alternative views, an agent should be *temporally impartial* in the sense that she has non-derivative reason to be concerned about benefits at any time. One form of temporal impartiality is *temporal neutrality*. On this view, an agent has equal non-derivative reason to be concerned about benefits and harms at any time; the temporal location of a benefit or harm should itself be of no rational significance to her.

Rational egoism claims that an agent has reason to do something just in so far as doing so contributes to her own overall happiness or welfare.

As such, rational egoism is agent-biased. This aspect of egoism is one way of articulating the common thought that I have special reason to be concerned about my own life and welfare. But rational egoism is not present-biased, because it assigns equal importance to benefits and harms of equal magnitude at different times in the agent's life. Indeed, egoism is not just temporally impartial; it is temporally neutral. Its temporal neutrality represents a natural articulation of the common belief that I rationally ought to be just as concerned about future goods and harms as about present ones (of equal magnitude), and that preference for a smaller present good at the cost of a greater future good is a sign of irrationality. Rational egoism is, therefore, a *hybrid* theory of rationality: it is temporally neutral but agent-biased.

Egoism can be contrasted with two *pure-bred* theories of rationality: a fully neutral theory and a fully biased theory. We might call the fully neutral theory *neutralism* or, following Sidgwick, *rational benevolence*; we might call the fully biased theory *presentism*. Neutralism is both temporally neutral and person-neutral; it holds that an agent has reason to do something just in so far as it is valuable, regardless of whom the value accrues to or when it occurs. Presentism, on the other hand, is both temporally biased and person-biased; it holds that an agent has reason to do something just in so far as it is in his own present interest.

Rational egoism and its rivals are defined *structurally*, by their attitudes to the distribution of benefits and harms across time and among persons. These theories do not themselves say what constitutes a benefit or a harm. *Subjective* theories of welfare claim that an individual's good consists in, or depends importantly upon, certain of her psychological states. For instance, *hedonism* identifies a person's good with her having pleasurable mental states or sensations. *Desire-satisfaction* theories claim that something is in an individual's interest just in case it would satisfy her actual desires or the desires that she would have in some preferred epistemic state. By contrast, *objective* theories of welfare identify a person's welfare or happiness with certain character traits, the exercise of certain capacities, and the possession of certain relationships to others and the world, and claim that these things are good for the agent independently of their producing pleasure for her or being the object of her desire. Like Parfit, I want to focus on a structural worry about egoism's hybrid character. For this reason, wherever possible, I shall abstract from the different versions of egoism and its rivals that result from incorporating different evaluative assumptions.

Because rational egoism has a hybrid structure, it may seem arbitrary. It may seem that we should distribute goods and harms by the same principles within lives and across lives. In *The Methods of Ethics* Sidgwick raises, but ultimately rejects, this parity argument as a possible difficulty for egoism (*ME*, pp. 418–19). In *The Possibility of Altruism* Thomas Nagel makes a similar parity argument on behalf of altruism.[2] In chapter 7 of *Reasons and Persons* Parfit argues that Sidgwick underestimated the power of the parity argument. Like Nagel, he accepts parity and rejects egoism, but he draws different conclusions. Though Parfit is sometimes content with the parity claim that is agnostic between the fully neutral and fully biased pure-breds, he seems to think that the natural conclusion of the parity argument is fully biased presentism. For his own 'Present-aim Theory' is fully biased, or, as he says, fully 'relative'; he takes it to be the main challenge to egoism (p. 117), and he treats the parity argument as part of the 'Appeal to Full Relativity'.

2 Parfit's Assumptions

Parfit describes his own rival theories in somewhat different terms than those I use for mine. His three rivals are the fully relative Present-aim Theory, P, the hybrid Self-interest Theory, S, and the fully neutral morality, or Neutralism, N. P tells each agent to aim at what will best achieve his present aims (p. 92). S tells each agent to aim at what will make his life as a whole go as well as possible (p. 3). And N seems to tell each to aim at the best outcome overall (pp. 94–5, 126, 138–44). Parfit also distinguishes between hedonistic, desire-fulfilment and objective list theories of value (p. 4).[3] Because I shall formulate and assess Parfit's arguments in terms of my distinctions, I should comment briefly on ways in which our assumptions differ.

First, we are both concerned with the way in which theories of practical rationality distribute benefits and harms across persons and across time. But whereas Parfit contrasts relative and neutral distribution, I contrast biased and neutral distribution, and see neutral distribution as a special case of impartial distribution. Though I shall focus on neutral forms of impartiality, I think that it is important to recognize, as Sidgwick and Nagel do, that perhaps the most significant fact about the egoist view of interpersonal distribution is that it rejects impartiality; it recognizes only derivative reason to benefit others. This fact also explains why I speak of temporal or personal bias, rather than relativity. As agent relativity is generally understood, a reason is agent-relative if its general form involves essential reference to the person who has it.[4] But many theories besides S and P are agent-relative, including many that recognize non-derivative reason to benefit others. For example, C. D. Broad sketched a theory that he called 'self-referential altruism', according to which one has non-derivative reason to benefit others, but the weight or strength of one's other-regarding reasons is a function of the nature of the relationship in which one stands to the beneficiary.[5] Self-referential altruism is agent-relative, but it is impartial or altruistic because it recognizes non-derivative reason to benefit others. If the most significant aspect of the egoist's account of interpersonal distribution is that it does not recognize non-derivative reason to benefit others, then it is misleading to focus on agent relativity here, as Parfit does, because this puts some impartial or altruistic theories, such as self-referential altruism, in the same camp as egoism, rather than in the same camp as neutralism. If so, the focus here should be on what I call agent bias – the denial of non-derivative concern for others – rather than agent relativity.

Second, I construe all three structural rivals as theories of rationality. Unlike Parfit, who sometimes construes the fully neutral theory as morality, I want to treat it as a theory of rationality, just like the other two theories; this makes their rivalry clearer, and allows us to assess the parity claim in a more straightforward manner. This will be clearest if we think of the fully neutral theory, as Sidgwick did, as rational benevolence; it stands to rationality as utilitarianism or consequentialism stands to morality.

Third, Parfit's P is in some ways different from presentism. P claims that one has reason to do something just in so far as it would satisfy one's present desires or aims; whereas presentism claims that one has reason to do something just in so far as it would promote one's present interests or happiness. I think there are two different ways to understand P and its relation to presentism.

On one reading, P's focus on present aims, rather than present interests, of the agent is very significant. On this view, P is not primarily a view about how to decide among beneficial and harmful alternatives; rather, it reflects assumptions about the purely instrumental character of practical rationality, according to which action is rationally assessable only in so far as it is instrumental to the satisfaction of the agent's desires or aims. But this Humean, or instrumental, conception of P is not a conception of the intertemporal and interpersonal distribution of benefits and harms.[6] Interesting as this conception of P is, it is not a good structural rival to egoism.[7]

Alternatively, we might not regard P's focus on present aims, rather than present interests, of the agent as very significant. For we can understand P as a special case of presentism: namely, presentism with a desire-satisfaction theory of value. But in the present context we should focus on presentism, rather than its special case P. This is because the parity argument aims to compare three theories that abstract from different possible claims about value and make competing claims about intertemporal and interpersonal distribution. This is how egoism and neutralism are formulated; the third member of the triad should also abstract from claims about value and make claims about intertemporal and interpersonal distribution. If so, the fully biased theory should be presentism, not P.[8]

These are my main reasons for formulating the structural parity issue as I do. The differences between Parfit's formulation and my own should cause neither confusion nor distortion.

3   The Parity of Intertemporal and Interpersonal Distribution?

Unlike neutralism or presentism, rational egoism is a hybrid theory of rationality; it is temporally neutral and agent-biased. Can this hybrid character be justified? Is it reasonable to treat time and person differently, as egoism does? Or is egoism an unhappy compromise between the two pure-breds? Egoism is committed to saying that it makes all the difference *on whom* a benefit or burden falls, and none whatsoever *when* it falls. On reflection, this may seem arbitrary. As Sidgwick notes, in discussing the 'proof of utilitarianism',

> I do not see why the axiom of Prudence [rational egoism] should not be questioned, when it conflicts with present inclination, on a ground similar to that on which Egoists refuse to admit the axiom of Rational Benevolence. If the Utilitarian [neutralist] has to answer the question, 'Why should I sacrifice my own happiness for the greater happiness of another?' it must surely be admissible to ask the Egoist, 'Why should I sacrifice a present pleasure for a greater one in the future? Why should I concern myself about my own future feelings any more than about the feelings of other persons'. (*ME*, p. 418)

The egoist asks the neutralist, 'Why should I sacrifice my own good for the good of another?'. The egoist doubts that concern for others is non-derivatively rational. But the presentist can ask the egoist, 'Why should I sacrifice a present good for myself for the sake of a future good for myself?'. The presentist doubts that concern for one's future is non-derivatively rational. These doubts may seem parallel. We must decide where among lives and when within lives to locate goods and harms. Because both are matters of position or location, we may think that they should be treated in the same way. Parfit does (p. 140). He writes:

> As a hybrid, S can be attacked from both directions. And what S claims against one rival may be turned against it by the other. In rejecting Neutralism, a Self-interest Theorist must claim that a reason may have force only for the agent. But the grounds for this claim support a further claim.

> If a reason can have force only for the agent, it can have force for the agent
> only at the time of acting. The Self-interest Theorist must reject this claim.
> He must attack the notion of a time-relative reason. But arguments to
> show that reasons must be temporally neutral, thus refuting the Present-
> aim Theory, may also show that reasons must be neutral between different
> people, thus refuting the Self-interest Theory. (p. 144)

If present sacrifice for future benefit is rational, why isn't sacrifice of one
person's good for the sake of another's? In this way, the appeal to parity
may support neutralism. This is roughly Nagel's view.[9] His primary aim
is to argue against egoism's agent bias and in favour of impartiality, or
altruism, and he relies on the parity of intertemporal and interpersonal
distribution to do so. Just as the interests of an agent's future self provide
him with reasons for action now, so too, Nagel argues, the interests of
others can provide him with reasons for action. Failure to recognize
temporal neutrality involves temporal dissociation – failure to see the
present as just one time among others – and failure to recognize impartiality, or altruism, involves personal dissociation – failure to recognize
oneself as just one person among others.[10]

Nagel's remarks about the 'combinatorial problem' show that he is
sceptical of an impersonal interpretation of impartiality.[11] None the less,
his appeal to parity seems to require neutralism and not just impartiality.
For he appeals to parity to argue from egoism's temporal neutrality to
non-derivative concern for others. But if intertemporal and interpersonal distribution must be isomorphic, and we accept a temporally neutral interpretation of intertemporal impartiality, then we seem forced to
accept a person-neutral interpretation of interpersonal impartiality.

Alternatively, we might treat time and person as parallel and argue
from the agent bias that egoism concedes to temporal bias, in particular,
present-bias. If my sacrifice for another is not rationally required, it may
seem that we cannot demand a sacrifice of my current interests for the
sake of distant future ones. If so, we will think that it is only the present
interests of the agent that provide her with non-derivative reason for
action. Though Parfit mentions Nagel's fully neutral response to parity,
it is the fully biased response that he develops and thinks Sidgwick
anticipated (pp. 137–44).

4   Egoism and the Separateness of Persons

Whereas Parfit thinks that egoism cannot meet this challenge, Sidgwick
thinks this challenge is unanswerable only on a very extreme kind of
scepticism about personal identity. The passage in which Sidgwick raises
the parity theme continues this way:

It undoubtedly seems to Common Sense paradoxical to ask for a reason why one should seek one's own happiness on the whole; but I do not see how the demand can be repudiated as absurd by those who adopt the views of the extreme empirical school of psychologists. . . . Grant that the Ego is merely a system of coherent phenomena, that the permanent identical 'I' is not a fact but a fiction, as Hume and his followers maintain; why, then, should one part of the series of feelings into which the Ego is resolved be concerned with another part of the same series, any more than with any other series? (*ME*, pp. 418–19)

Sidgwick sees the presentist's challenge to egoism, but thinks we can meet this challenge, because it depends upon denying that persons persist. Later, he suggests that the *separateness of persons* is what underlies rational egoism.

It would be contrary to Common Sense to deny that the distinction between any one individual and any other is real and fundamental, and that consequently 'I' am concerned with the quality of my existence as an individual in a sense, fundamentally important, in which I am not concerned with the quality of the existence of other individuals: and this being so, I do not see how it can be proved that this distinction is not to be taken as fundamental in determining the ultimate end of rational action for an individual. (*ME*, p. 498)

In these two passages Sidgwick appeals to the separateness of persons to justify egoism. I think he must suppose that the separateness of persons has both *metaphysical* and *normative* aspects. On the one hand, the separateness of persons involves recognition of ourselves as numerically distinct and temporally extended entities. But Sidgwick seems to think that this metaphysical claim commits us to normative claims as well. The second passage suggests that to recognize myself as distinct from others and temporally extended requires me to adopt patterns of concern that exhibit a bias towards myself. On one reading, the bias is supposed to be legitimated by prior recognition of the separateness of persons. But this seems to leave the process of legitimation unexplained. Alternatively, we might understand Sidgwick to be suggesting that the bias is part of what constitutes the separateness of persons. Though Sidgwick does not develop this suggestion, it seems not unreasonable.

It might be claimed that part of what it is for me to be a distinct person who persists through time is for me to form and act from a particular perspective on the world. Part of having and acting from a particular perspective involves forming and acting on intentions and goals in ways that display self-concern. Some of this self-concern involves backward-looking displays of trust. I form my intentions and goals as the result of

my own previous deliberations. Though I can take account of other
people's opinions in my own deliberations, forming my own intentions
involves accepting and endorsing my own previous deliberations, even
when I have reason to suspect that they have been imperfect and that the
deliberations of others are likely to have been better. Other parts of this
self-concern are forward-looking. Whereas some of my desires are impersonal in nature, many of them are personal. For instance, if I am
trying to prove a certain theorem, not only do I want the theorem to be
proved, but also I want to be the one to prove it, and this personal desire
structures my plans and activities. We can see that my personal desire is
not purely instrumental to the satisfaction of my impersonal desire by
noting that my aims would not be fully accomplished if someone else
were to prove the theorem, even if her proof were superior to the one I
would have offered.[12] It seems an important part of what makes people
distinct that they form and act on such personal desires.[13] Indeed, if
people's activities were not governed for the most part by personal
desires, it is hard to see how there could be impersonal desires that
valuable lives be led. What does a valuable life consist in if not, in large
measure, the satisfaction of suitable personal desires?[14] Intentions are
like personal desires, because one always figures in one's own intentions.
I always intend to bring something about through my own actions. For
instance, I may want my children to be raised well, but I intend to do
things to bring this about, typically by raising them myself. And this
intention is not satisfied if others take my children, without my consent,
and raise them well, even if they raise them better than I would have.
And, of course, having such self-involved intentions gives rise to a generalized concern for one's own future (e.g. anticipation, fantasy and anxiety) and further self-involved intentions as a way of ensuring that one
will be able to fulfil these original intentions. Moreover, in adopting intentions, I treat the object of my intentions and subsidiary objectives as
more or less fixed in ways that constrain my future deliberations.[15] For
example, if I intend to finish my article this coming summer, this con-
strains deliberation about the scheduling of the family vacation and
about whether to accept other professional commitments. But then,
when I adopt self-involved intentions, the associated self-concern must
also constrain my deliberations in ways that preclude seeing myself
merely as a resource for the production of impersonal value.

Another part of what it is for me to be a person with a particular
perspective on the world is that I am located at a particular point in a
network of interpersonal relationships and commitments, even if the
place I occupy in this interpersonal network changes over time. I form
friendships, marry and raise children, and these relationships help define
my life. Part of standing in such relationships to intimates is for me to

make them the object of my personal projects. I want to do certain things with them and for them, and I value these activities out of proportion to their impersonal value. In fact, my concern for those to whom I stand in special relationships shapes my conception of my own interests and the standards by which I judge my life to be a success.

If so, part of what it is for me to be a distinct, temporally extended person is for me to have a particular perspective on the world that displays a concern for my past and future self that is not proportional to the impersonal value of my activities. But then part of what it is for me to be a separate person is for me to be unwilling to sacrifice my interests without appropriate compensation. This would be one way of explaining the links Sidgwick seems to see between the separateness of persons and demands that sacrifices be compensated (*ME*, pp. 171, 174, 404, 498, 499, 501, 502).[16]

This appeal to the separateness of persons provides a rationale for egoism's hybrid character. The metaphysical separateness of persons plays two roles in this rationale. First, it is supposed to explain the appropriateness of the normative claim that it is unreasonable to make uncompensated sacrifices. Second, this compensation principle and the metaphysical separateness of persons explain the asymmetry between intrapersonal and interpersonal distribution. For there is automatic *intra*personal compensation, but no automatic *inter*personal compensation. Compensation requires that benefactors also be beneficiaries, and for compensation to be automatic, benefactor and beneficiary must be one and the same. In the diachronic, intrapersonal case, one's sacrifice of a present good for a (greater) future good is rational, because there is compensation later for the earlier sacrifice; benefactor and beneficiary are the same. This explains temporal neutrality. But in the interpersonal case, benefactor and beneficiary are different people; unless the beneficiary reciprocates in some way, the agent's sacrifice will be uncompensated. This explains agent bias.

Before we discuss the adequacy of this rationale, we should perhaps explain some implications of temporal neutrality and agent bias.

5 Temporal Neutrality

Because diachronic, intrapersonal compensation is automatic, it is the importance of the agent's interests, and not their temporal location, that determines what an agent has most reason to do. As Sidgwick claims:

Hereafter *as such* is to be regarded neither less nor more than Now. It is not, of course, meant, that the good of the present may not reasonably be preferred to that of the future on account of its greater certainty: or again, that a week ten years hence may not be more important to us than a week now, through an increase in our means or capacities of happiness. All that the principle affirms is that mere difference of priority and posteriority in time is not a reasonable ground for having more regard to the consciousness of one moment than to that of another. (*ME*, p. 381; cf. pp. 111–12, 124n.)

As Sidgwick notes, this kind of temporal neutrality is perfectly compatible with the claim that rational *planning* should take into account the uncertainty of my continued existence. We can explain this point by drawing a useful distinction between *subjective* and *objective* rationality (cf. p. 153; *ME*, pp. 207–8, 394–5). Claims of objective rationality are claims about what an agent has reason to do given the facts of a situation, whether he is aware of these facts or in a position to recognize the reasons that they support. Claims of subjective rationality are claims about what the agent has reason to do given his beliefs about his situation or what it would be reasonable for him to believe about his situation. The egoist can admit that the existence of my near future is more certain than the existence of my distant future, and that this epistemic fact should affect what it is subjectively rational for me to do; he claims only that in so far as I have both present and future interests, they provide me with equally strong objective reasons for action.

Temporal neutrality claims that what I now have most reason to do is what will most advance my overall good. This may require present sacrifices for my future benefit (now-for-then sacrifice). In one sense, this requires acting on interests that I do not now have, but this does not require me to act as if I now had those interests. For instance, it does not require me to eat or buy foodstuffs now in order to satisfy my future hunger. Where temporal neutrality requires now-for-then sacrifice, it requires only that I act now so as to be able to secure my later good at that time. For instance, it requires only that I set aside or employ my resources now so that I will then have the means available to satisfy the hunger that I will have later.[17]

6   Agent Bias

Because I am a separate entity, I am not automatically compensated by benefits to another, and this makes interpersonal sacrifice problematic. But compensation does not imply that others cannot be beneficiaries of the agent's actions; it requires only that the agent be an appropriate beneficiary. For instance, agents will often receive benefits in return for those they confer, as in most systems of co-operation for mutual advantage. In this way, the egoist can often justify being a reliable benefactor (cf. *ME*, pp. 164–70, 499–503).

The egoist may also be able to justify other-regarding action and concern as a kind of 'false target' for promoting the agent's own good. Sidgwick insists on the so-called paradox of egoism, according to which an agent may best promote her own interest not by doing things with the aim of maximizing her own welfare, but by developing concerns for people and activities for their own sakes (cf. *ME*, pp. 48, 136, 403). The paradox of egoism is supposed to explain why even hedonistic egoists should care for others for their own sakes.

Finally, versions of rational egoism that employ an objective conception of welfare have additional resources for justifying other-regarding conduct and concern. Many objective conceptions of welfare recognize a variety of social or other-regarding components in a person's good. They claim that family relationships, friendships and social relationships involving mutual concern and respect make our lives more valuable than they would otherwise be. By having friends and co-operating with others on a footing of mutual concern and commitment, we are able to exercise new capacities, secure ourselves against a variety of misfortunes, and generally extend our interests in new ways. On such views, the good of others is *part of* my own good; if so, benefits to them are benefits to me. On such a view, my reason to benefit others is derivative from my reason to benefit myself, but my concern for others is not purely instrumental. If such a view can be defended, it will allow for the possibility of interpersonal compensation, and so provide the basis for a robust defence of other-regarding conduct and concern on egoist grounds.

Of course, it is an open question exactly how far such strategies can be used to provide agent-biased justification of other-regarding conduct and concern. My immediate purpose is only to forestall possible misunderstandings of the commitments of agent bias and to insist that the success of such strategies *is* a genuinely open question.[18]

7 The Egoist Rationale

According to Sidgwick, the separateness of persons explains why the egoist holds a hybrid theory of rationality consisting of agent bias and temporal neutrality. The egoist will see no reason to follow the neutralist, who infers person neutrality from temporal neutrality. Stages of other people are not stages of me, present or future, and as a result, I may not be compensated for my sacrifices to others. The egoist will see no reason to follow the presentist, who infers temporal bias from agent bias. Unlike the stages of other people, my future self is a stage of me, and therefore

I do receive compensation when I make present sacrifices for my own future benefit. Diachronic, intrapersonal compensation is automatic; interpersonal compensation is not.

Because the egoist offers a rationale for rejecting parity, egoism's hybrid character cannot be represented as arbitrary or unmotivated. Indeed, on this rationale, whereas there is a kind of asymmetry in the egoist's treatment of intrapersonal and interpersonal distribution, this asymmetry reflects a deeper, symmetrical treatment of these two distributional dimensions. Though egoism is intertemporally neutral but interpersonally biased, both commitments follow from the separateness of persons and, in particular, the compensation principle. Egoism applies the compensation principle to both intrapersonal and interpersonal contexts: because there is automatic intrapersonal compensation, egoism is temporally neutral; because there is no automatic interpersonal compensation, it is personally biased.

The compensation principle is not uncontroversial. Its most controversial aspect, I believe, is its claim that uncompensated interpersonal sacrifice is unreasonable. But neither is this claim absurd.

Sidgwick motivates the compensation by appeal to the separateness of persons. We can explain the link, I have suggested, if the compensation principle expresses a form of self-concern that is itself constitutive of the separateness of persons. Even if we do not suppose that special concern is itself constitutive of the separateness of persons, it is commonly believed that we do have special reason to be concerned about our own lives that we don't have with regard to the lives of others. The rationality of an agent's actions seems not in general to be proportional to the good that she does. The compensation principle provides one explanation of why such special concern is appropriate.

Moreover, the compensation principle provides a natural explanation of traditional worries about the rational authority of morality. The basis of this worry is the claim that morality requires agents to benefit or respect others in ways that seem to constrain the pursuit of their own interest or happiness. But in supposing that there is a difficulty in defending the rational authority of other-regarding moral demands, we seem to assume that the rationality of sacrifice requires compensation, as the compensation principle claims.

It might be said that these claims do not require anything as strong as the compensation principle or egoism's agent bias. For the compensation principle implies that I have no reason to make an uncompensated sacrifice for another, no matter how small my sacrifice and how large the benefit it would confer on another, and agent bias implies that I have no non-derivative reason to benefit others. By contrast, it might be claimed, special concern and traditional worries about the authority of morality could be explained by weaker assumptions. We might not require full compensation for all sacrifices; we might not require compensation for small sacrifices, and we might apportion compensation, where we give it, in light of the seriousness of the sacrifice and the amount of benefit conferred by it. This might result in a more subtle kind of personal bias. On one such view, agents have non-derivative reason to benefit others, but, all else being equal, their self-regarding reasons are weightier than their other-regarding ones. By our definitions, such a theory would be impartial or altruistic, but it would assign weight to reasons according to an *agent multiplier*. In fact, the resulting theory might resemble Broad's self-referential altruism, construed here as a theory of rationality. These weaker assumptions would still allow us to make sense of special concern and raise worries about the authority of morality, provided morality contains more neutralist elements. Moreover, something like self-referential altruism might seem like an intuitively attractive compromise between agent bias and person neutrality.

But this apparent appeal is a source of trouble in the present context. For the structural objection to egoism assumes the parity of intra-personal and interpersonal distribution; parity, it is assumed, requires a pure-bred conception of rationality. But self-referential altruism is nei-ther agent-biased nor person-neutral (it is altruistic with an agent multi-plier), much less fully biased or fully neutral. It is itself hybrid, with a vengeance, and so can provide no comfort to the friends of parity and pure-breds.

Indeed, if parity is a virtue, then the egoist can exploit parity to argue against self-referential altruism. As I have indicated, egoism respects parity at a deep level, because it justifies agent bias and temporal neutral-ity by applying the compensation principle to both intrapersonal and interpersonal contexts. Paradigmatic forms of rational deliberation in-volve deciding to take some course of action that one would otherwise view as indifferent or harmful as a means or necessary condition to doing something else that is best overall. This familiar sort of now-for-then sacrifice is rational precisely because the agent is suitably compensated later for her present sacrifice. Indeed, intrapersonal sacrifice seems justi-fied if and only if it is adequately compensated. This is what explains temporal neutrality. But the very compensation principle that justifies temporal neutrality in intrapersonal contexts justifies agent bias in inter-personal contexts. If we believe that intrapersonal and interpersonal distribution must be regulated by the same principles, then this very familiar and attractive explanation of temporal neutrality requires us to reject self-referential altruism.

Moreover, some versions of rational egoism can help themselves to whatever appeal self-referential altruism might have. As I will explain below (in section 16), rational egoism can justify concern for others, on the agent's part, proportional to the strength of the psychological relations in which they stand to him, by representing such relations as extending the agent's own interests.[19] If so, we may be able to represent the central claims of self-referential altruism as theorems of rational egoism.

Finally, it is important to notice that the egoist's opponent in the parity argument relies on a compensation principle. The parity argument treats the egoist's demand, 'Why should I sacrifice my interests for another?', and the presentist's demand, 'Why should I sacrifice my present interest for my future interests?', as parallel. So Parfit's attempt to argue from egoism's agent bias to presentism's full bias appeals to the need for compensation, because egoism challenges neutralism by appealing to the need for compensation. Moreover, Nagel seems to assume something like the compensation principle when, in discussing the combinatorial problem, he rejects the interpersonal balancing that a person-neutral theory allows by appeal to 'the extremely strict position that there can be no *inter*personal compensation of sacrifice'.[20] Compensation is a controversial demand, but it is not the issue in this structural debate.

The egoist rationale also rests on the metaphysical separateness of persons. Sidgwick thinks that these metaphysical assumptions about personal identity are seriously challenged only by Humean views about personal identity. And Parfit claims that his own reductionist view of personal identity subverts egoism. Later (sections 9–16), I will discuss whether this egoist rationale is compromised by reductionist views of personal identity. But Parfit explicitly claims that the parity argument does not depend upon any special assumptions about personal identity (p. 139). This I deny. As long as agents are metaphysically distinct, interpersonal compensation is problematic; as long as agents are temporally extended, diachronic, intrapersonal compensation is automatic.

My purpose here is not to provide a full-blown defence of rational egoism or to argue that its pure-bred rivals are untenable. In particular, I have not claimed that the compensation principle is unproblematic or that the implications of agent bias and temporal neutrality are fully acceptable.[21] What I have argued is that there is a principled rationale for the hybrid character of egoism; indeed, egoism respects parity in so far as it regulates intrapersonal and interpersonal distribution by the same compensation principle.

8   Temporal Neutrality and the Bearers of Reasons

The presentist might claim that we have not appreciated the force of his appeal to full bias or relativity. The egoist insists that intrapersonal compensation is automatic, because benefactor and beneficiary are the same. This assumes that it is the temporally extended being – the person – that is the agent and the bearer of reasons for action. But the presentist might aim to challenge this natural assumption. The egoist is being asked to explain why the interests of my present self should be sacrificed for the benefit of my future self. This may make it look as if it is a person-stage, *me-now*, rather than me, who is the bearer of reasons. If so, the egoist's rationale would seem to fail. Me-now can fairly complain that it is being asked to make an uncompensated sacrifice. After all, the benefits of its sacrifice accrue not to me-now but to me-later. Me-now seems no more compensated for its sacrifice to me-later than I am by my sacrifice to you. Perhaps the compensation principle forces us to reject egoism in favour of presentism.

The issue seems to depend on whether we think of the agent and the bearer of reasons as the temporally extended person or as a person-stage. There is automatic intrapersonal compensation, but interstage compensation is problematic. We may ask the egoist whether *my present self* (me-now) has reason to sacrifice its interests for those of my future self (me-later). Or we may ask instead, as Sidgwick and Parfit both do, whether *I* have reason to sacrifice my current interests for the sake of my future interests.[22] The egoist can answer the second question; I am compensated for a present sacrifice by a (greater) future gain, because that future self is a part of me. Temporal neutrality seems threatened if and only if we formulate the challenge this first way. Though Parfit makes the appeal to full relativity or bias, this appeal to person-stages is not part of his view (pp. 95, 135, 139–45). None the less, it provides a defence of presentism that is worth considering.

We normally suppose that persons are agents and the bearers of reasons. Talk about person-stages may seem to be merely a convenient way of talking about persons at particular times. If so, egoism's temporal neutrality is secure, for there is automatic intrapersonal compensation. But even if we agree that person-stages are entities in their own right, perhaps four-dimensional entities,[23] is there any reason to think that they are agents?

It might be said that practical reasoning is necessarily temporally indexed. My deliberations are always about what I should do, plan, omit or postpone *now*, and I must deliberate on the basis of my *current* beliefs, aims and values.[24] But this does not show that agency must be understood in terms of person-stages, rather than persons. For as I have described this aspect of practical reasoning, it connects deliberation and action with what is true of agents at particular times; it does not involve commitment to person-stages.

Indeed, the suggestion that agents are person-stages is problematic, not just unmotivated. Its plausibility depends upon the 'life-span' of a person-stage. If the appeal to temporal bias is to be part of an appeal to full bias, and if this appeal is supposed to show that person-stages, rather than persons, are agents, then person-stages must be understood as time-slices or temporally minimal cross-sections of a person's life. Otherwise, the appeal to bias would not be full or complete. Call such a temporally minimal person-stage a *person-slice*.

It is difficult to regard person-slices as agents. For one thing, this conception of agency requires that person-slices have interests. If me-now is to be an agent concerned to advance its own interests, me-now must have interests. But it is not clear that person-slices do have interests (cf. p. 135). Whether the entity me-now can have interests depends upon which theory of welfare is correct.

If pleasure is a simple, qualitative sensation or mental state and a hedonistic theory of welfare is correct, then perhaps me-now has interests. Person-slices may contain qualitative mental states, such as pleasure. However, this is not the only version of hedonism. On a more plausible version, pleasure and pain are functional states: pleasure is a mental state or sensation such that the person having it wants it to continue and will, *ceteris paribus*, undertake actions so as to prolong it, whereas pain is a mental state or sensation such that the person having it wants it to cease and will, *ceteris paribus*, take action to make it stop (cf. p. 493; *ME*, pp. 42–3, 46, 127, 131, 402). But according to this version of hedonism, pleasure is already a state that is essentially the state of a temporally extended entity. If so, the bearer of pleasures cannot be a person-slice.

Moreover, hedonism seems an implausible theory of welfare, because a large part of a person's good seems to consist in his *being a certain sort of person* – that is, a person with a certain sort of character who exercises certain capacities and develops certain kinds of personal and social relationships. This is true not only on objective theories of value, which take welfare to consist in being a certain sort of person, but also on desire-satisfaction theories of welfare. Our desires are the desires of temporally extended beings, and the content of most of our desires is conditioned by this fact. If so, our conception of interests and welfare (i.e. of what makes a life go well) is fundamentally *diachronic*. And this implies that it is temporally extended beings, as the egoist assumes, rather than person-slices, who are the bearers of interests.

Not only is it doubtful whether person-slices have interests, it is also questionable whether having interests is sufficient for having reasons for action. A person-slice will not persist long enough to perform actions or receive the benefits of actions. If so, then person-slices cannot have reasons for action even if it is possible for them to have interests. Indeed,

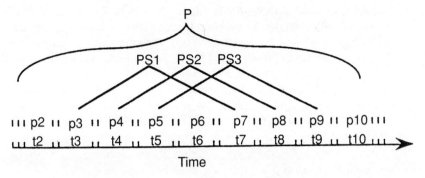

Figure 6.1 Overlapping temporal parts

more generally, as we have noted, a paradigmatic form of intrapersonal practical reasoning involves deciding to make short-term sacrifices as a means or necessary condition of achieving valuable goals. The rationale for such now-for-then sacrifice is that it is compensated; sacrificer and beneficiary are the same. The presentist also appeals to the compensation principle. But if agents are conceived of as person-slices, then we must reject one of our clearest paradigms of practical reason as irrational. Indeed, it is unclear what scope this view leaves for practical reasoning.

What if we construe person-stages, not as person-slices, but as temporally extended, cross-sections of a person's life? Call such a person-stage a *person-segment*. Person-segments, unlike person-slices, can have some interests and can live long enough to perform and receive some of the benefits of actions. The appeal to full bias, so construed, would also seem to challenge rational egoism's temporal neutrality, because me-now, conceived as a person-segment, may not be compensated for its sacrifice to me-later, conceived of as a later segment of the same person.

However, appeal to person-segments leads to a proliferation of agents and consequent indeterminacies in questions about practical deliberation that are troubling and unnecessary. Person-segments are made up of temporally related series of shorter person-stages (e.g. slices) and so contain parts that also belong to other person-segments; that is, person segments overlap. Consider a person consisting of person-stages, including stages p2 through p10 (figure 6.1). The person segment PS1 consisting of person-stages p3 through p7 contains within it, for example, part of the person-segment PS2, consisting of p4 through p8, and part of the person segment PS3, consisting of p5 through p9. Suppose the time is t6. If, as we normally assume, it is the person P that is the subject of practical deliberation, the egoist rationale allows us to identify her reasons for action. If person-segments are agents, whose reasons for action should we be concerned about now: those of PS1, those of PS2, or those of PS3? (This names only three of infinitely many possibilities.) Of couse, we can identify the reasons for action of each of these entities. But reasons for action are supposed to be related in some way to practical deliberation. Whose practical deliberation is in question?

The friend of person-segments might reply by arguing that some person-segments are more *salient* than others. Person-segments are individuated temporally, but some display more internal psychological coherence and integrity than others. Some segments of a person's life cut that life at its psychological joints, whereas others do not. So, it might be argued, at any point in time, the subject of practical deliberation should be identified with the salient person-segment existing at that time.

This suggestion reduces, but does not eliminate, indeterminacy. This is because salient segments will themselves overlap. Psychological change is generally fairly continuous, but proceeds at different rates along different dimensions of someone's personality. Even if there were mutual interaction among all aspects of a person's psychological make-up, there would still be distinguishable cognitive and affective aspects of a person's mental life whose development and careers would be staggered (cf. linguistic skills, mathematical skills, athletic skills, political beliefs, tastes in food, friendships, and career goals and expectations). This is just to say there are a great many different psychological joints at which to cut for salience. If so, there will be overlapping salient segments, producing significant, even if less extreme, proliferation and indeterminacy. Indeed, so long as the person is herself a salient segment, at any time there must be at least two possible agents on the person-segment view.

Moreover, these person-segments, salient or otherwise, do and must interact and co-operate. They do interact and co-operate, much as distinct individuals interact and co-operate in groups, in order to plan and execute long-term projects and goals. They must interact and co-operate if only because they have to share a body and its capacities in order to execute their individual and collective goals, much in the way that individuals must sometimes interact and co-operate if they are to use scarce resources to mutual advantage.[25] Indeed, both the ease and the necessity of interaction among person-segments will be greater than that among persons, because the physical constraints and the reliability of fellow co-operators are greater in the intrapersonal case. But this means that person-segments will overlap with each other; they will stand to each other and the person much as strands of a rope stand to each other and the rope. Though we can recognize the overlapping strands as entities, the most salient entity is the rope itself. So, too, the most salient entity is the person, even if we can recognize the overlapping person-segments that make up the person.

In this way, person-segments represent a rather arbitrary stopping place. If the appeal to full bias argues for agents with shorter life-spans than persons, then an appeal to *full* bias ought to argue for person-slices as agents. But if, as I have argued, that conception cannot be maintained, then it seems arbitrary to settle on person-segments. Once we extend the life-span of the agent beyond that of a person-slice, it seems that we should keep going until we reach the entity with the most natural borders: namely, the person.

These appear to be reasons for preserving the normal assumption that it is persons that are agents. But is this assumption itself incoherent? I have identified the person with a temporally extended entity, some of whose parts lie in the future. But then the person is in one sense 'not all there' at the time of deliberation and action. How then could the person be the agent who deliberates and acts and possesses reasons for action?

This raises difficult issues, but I doubt that they threaten the assumption that it is persons that are agents.[26] Notice, first, that person-slices seem to be the only candidates for agency that avoid some form of this objection. For person-segments extend from the instant of deliberation or action into either the future or the past (or both); so person-segments are also entities with parts that are 'not all there' at the time of deliberation or action. Only one person-slice is 'all there' at this time. But we have already seen that such a conception of agency is indefensible. We might, therefore, wonder whether the agent or entity whose interests determine what rationally ought to be done need be 'all there' at the time of action.

Consider an analogy with nations. We speak of nations as actors that enact legislation, start wars, and so on. We also think of nations as having interests and acting in their interests. But a nation is composed, at least in part, by its entire current population. And there is certainly some sense in which the entire population does not enact legislation or start wars. Instead, certain individuals or groups act as representatives of a larger, spatially dispersed group of which they are members. We do not conclude that nations cannot be actors or the bearers of interests. Instead, we conclude that a nation can act when its deputies act on behalf of the national interest – that is, the interest of the spatially dispersed group. Similarly, the present self can act as representative of the temporally dispersed entity, the person, by acting in the interest of this being. If so, then the fact that the temporally extended person is 'not all there' at the time of action is not a reason to deny that it is the actor or the entity whose interests determine what agents have reason to do. On this assumption, there is automatic diachronic, intrapersonal compensation, and so compensation does justify temporal neutrality.

9 Rational Egoism and Reductionism about Personal Identity

As we have seen, Sidgwick thinks that rational egoism appeals to the separateness of persons, and that it would be seriously challenged by a Humean account of personal identity (*ME*, pp. 418–19). Nor is such linkage between personal identity and our attitudes towards self-concern and future concern uncommon. Butler claims that special concern for oneself and moral responsibility would be undermined by Locke's account of personal identity in terms of memory connectedness.[27] In part 3 of *Reasons and Persons* Parfit likens his own reductionist account of personal identity to the views of Locke and Hume, and argues, among other things, that reductionism undermines egoism's temporal neutrality (pp. 139, 307–20). Because my concern is whether reductionist accounts of personal identity undermine egoism's hybrid rationale, I shall assume that Parfit's main arguments for reductionism are successful, and ask whether his conclusions about egoism follow.

Reductionism and non-reductionism begin as accounts of when two person-stages are stages of the same person; that is, both offer accounts of the relation of co-personality. Though Parfit characterizes the dispute between reductionism and non-reductionism in different ways, an important difference, for our purposes, is that whereas reductionists think that co-personality just consists in the holding of certain other familiar physical or psychological relations among these person-stages, non-reductionists claim that co-personality does not just consist in other, more basic relations but must remain a 'simple and unanalysable', 'further' fact (pp. 210, 240). Parfit defends a version of *psychological* reductionism, according to which personal identity just consists in psychological continuity and/or connectedness, with the right kind of cause, or 'relation R', as he calls it (p. 215). Of these two relations, psychological connectedness is explanatorily prior (cf. pp. 204–9). Person-stages p1 and p2 at times t1 and t2 are psychologically *connected* just in case the psychological states of the later stage are causally dependent, in the right way, upon the psychological states of the earlier stage. For example, different stages in a life will be connected in so far as actions at one time fulfil prior intentions, goals held at one time reflect prior deliberations, memories at one time depend upon past experiences, and other beliefs and desires are maintained from one stage to the other. Well-connected selves are likely to be similar psychologically. But psychological similarity and connectedness can diminish over time. Thus, p1 can be psychologically connected to p2, and p2 can be psychologically connected to p3, but p3 need not be, and is unlikely to be, as closely connected with p1 as p2 is. A series of person-stages p1 through p*n* is psychologically *continuous* just in case the members of every pair of temporally contiguous stages in this series are psychologically connected. It follows that p1 and p*n* can be psychologically continuous even if they are not psychologically well connected or connected at all.

Parfit argues that what matters in our continued existence is not personal identity itself, but relation R (this is supposed to be demonstrated by fission cases, of the sort I discuss in sections 14–16 below). Because R includes psychological connectedness as well as continuity, and the different parts of a life can be more or less closely connected, Parfit thinks that psychological reductionism undermines the temporal neutrality of rational egoism and makes it rational for us to be less concerned about our distant future than about our near future.[28]

10 Metaphysical Depth

Parfit claims that co-personality is metaphysically 'less deep' according to reductionism than it is according to non-reductionism. As a result, he thinks, once we accept reductionism, we should reject egoism's temporal neutrality. The idea seems to be that if identity over time is less deep, intrapersonal compensation is compromised (pp. 309–12).

We can concede that co-personality is less metaphysically deep according to reductionism, in so far as reductionism claims that co-personality can be analysed in familiar and unproblematic terms. But there is no general reason to suppose that this kind of metaphysical depth affects the justification of concern. This is because our concern about some entity or property may attach to its *functional role*, rather than to its metaphysical or compositional *analysans*. For instance, it seems that a materialist should be no less concerned to prevent pain (her own or that of another) than a dualist,[29] and, *ceteris paribus*, I should care just as much for mint chocolate-chip ice-cream upon learning its chemical composition. Similarly, it is not clear why becoming convinced that a future self's being me consists in its being part of a (non-branching) R-related series of selves or stages should make me any less concerned about that self. The relevant claim in the egoist rationale is that persons are metaphysically distinct and temporally extended; the rationale does not seem to require any particular metaphysical account of this fact.

Sometimes our beliefs about the metaphysical *analysans* of some entity or property will, or should, affect its role in our conceptual network in certain ways. For instance, we may learn that some gustatory properties of mint chocolate-chip ice-cream supervene on its saturated-fat content, and this may affect its desirability. But then we need an account of how the particular *analysans* to which the psychological reductionist appeals justify a change in our attitudes. Metaphysical *depth* does not establish this.

There are other ways in which Parfit does, or might, think that reductionism undermines egoism. Let us look at these.

11 A Discount Rate for Concern

Parfit's principal argument that reductionism undermines egoism's temporal neutrality applies to the normal, non-branching cases where relation R and personal identity both obtain. Relation R is what matters. According to Parfit, relation R consists of psychological continuity and/or connectedness. But psychological connectedness is a matter of degree, and, in particular, can and does diminish over time. Because relation R is what matters and it consists of psychological connectedness as well as continuity, Parfit claims, it is not irrational for me, all else being equal, to care more about my near future than about my more distant future. In fact, he thinks that a kind of discount rate that proportions concern to psychological connectedness is rationally acceptable.

> My concern for my future may correspond to the degree of connectedness between me now and myself in the future. Connectedness is one of the two relations that give me reasons to be specially concerned about my own future. It can be rational to care less, when one of the grounds for caring will hold to a lesser degree. Since connectedness is nearly always weaker over long periods, I can rationally care less about my further future. (p. 313)

As Parfit notes, this is a discount rate with respect to connectedness, but not with respect to time itself (p. 314). His discount rate should, therefore, be distinguished from the discount rate with respect to time that C. I. Lewis calls 'fractional prudence'.[30] Egoism is neutral with respect to time itself, and so must deny fractional prudence. But egoism's temporal neutrality is also inconsistent with Parfit's discount rate, because temporal neutrality requires a kind of equal concern for different parts of one's life. The magnitude of a good or a harm should affect its rational significance. But temporal neutrality implies that the temporal location of a good or a harm within a life should be of no rational significance. If so, then, all else being equal, an agent should be equally concerned about goods and harms at any point in his life. In particular, if near and more distant future selves are both stages in his life, then, other things being equal, an agent should have equal concern for each, even if the nearer future self is more closely connected with his present self.

Indeed, Parfit's claim about the discount rate seems too modest. He insists only that this discount rate of concern for one's future is not irrational; he does not claim that it is rationally required. Though the friend of temporal neutrality must deny the more modest claim as well, the reductionist argument, if successful, surely supports the stronger claim that a discount rate of concern is rationally appropriate where the relations that matter hold to a reduced degree. This is because concern should track and be proportional to the relations that matter.

Such a discount rate is incompatible with egoism's temporal neutrality. But reductionism does not imply a discount rate, and we should not accept one. There are two main grounds for rejecting a discount rate.

12   Two Forms of Psychological Reductionism

Parfit's argument requires that what matters is psychological connectedness as well as continuity (C&C), for it is only connectedness that will normally diminish over time; my distant and near future selves are both continuous with my present self. Now one form of reductionism would claim that relation R consists *only* in psychological continuity (C). If it is only C that matters, then I have no less reason to be concerned about my distant future than about my near future, because each is equally continuous with my present and past selves, even if each is not equally well connected with my present self.[31] Hence, it is not reductionism *per se*, but only Parfit's version of reductionism in terms of C&C, that threatens egoism's temporal neutrality.

Throughout much of Parfit's discussion, he is agnostic about whether the relation that matters is C or C&C (pp. 207, 262, 271, 279, 283). His only explicit argument for C&C, as against C, is that we are averse to many possible losses in psychological connectedness; thus, connectedness 'matters to us' (pp. 301–2). But our aversion to losses in connectedness does not require understanding reductionism in terms of C&C.

The clearest cases of aversion to substantial psychological change involve cases that I regard as *corruption*, where I become a less attractive person. But a natural explanation of this aversion is that it is to the *disvalue* of the psychological profile I would be acquiring, and not to loss of connectedness *per se*. This alternative explanation of my aversion is reinforced by the fact that I presumably would not be averse to loss of psychological connectedness involved in a psychological change that I have reason to regard as an *improvement*, provided that I am responsible for the change in ways that establish psychological continuity.

Indeed, because Parfit believes that what matters is C&C, he faces a problem explaining why we have reason to improve ourselves in ways that involve significant psychological changes. If what matters is C&C, then it becomes more difficult to explain how a person has prudential or agent-biased reason, as he surely seems to, to undergo a process of 'improvement' – even though it is agreed that the person emerging from the process is better off than the person beginning the process.[32] Indeed, if C&C is what matters, the more significant the improvement, the less prudential reason there is to undertake it.

At one point, Parfit suggests that my reasons to be concerned about the person who emerges when I undergo a psychological change depend upon both (1) the degree of connectedness between that person and myself prior to the change and (2) the value of the new psychological profile (p. 299). But (2) is something the egoist can happily admit – in so far as an agent is concerned to promote her own interests, she must be concerned with changes that are better for her – and requires no special claims about personal identity. And (1), I suggested, seems implausible, even when conjoined with (2), and may gain specious plausibility from its association with (2).

Failure to improve oneself is a form of imprudence. So Parfit must think that this phenomenon that we misleadingly describe as a form of imprudence is properly criticized as immoral, rather than irrational (pp. 318–20). Though the terms of criticism change, Parfit may think that the assumption that it is C&C that matters involves no net change in our evaluations. But moral criticism and rational criticism may play different roles in our overall evaluation of behaviour. Moreover, Parfit's view seems likely to affect our moral attitudes towards this phenomenon. For he must think that his version of reductionism makes interference with what we misleadingly call failure to improve oneself justifiable in terms of the harm principle, rather than as paternalism. But if, as Mill claims, interference under the harm principle is more easily justified than paternalistic interference, then Parfit must conclude that his version of reductionism makes interference with such conduct easier to justify.

These changes seem inadequately motivated. Self-improvement seems to be a paradigmatic form of agent-biased rationality. In so far as Parfit's view implies that failure to undertake such changes is not subject to such criticism, this is grounds for scepticism that C&C is what matters.

To undermine egoism's temporal neutrality, therefore, Parfit must not only defend psychological reductionism, but must provide a better argument for believing that it is C&C, rather than C, that matters.

13 Equal Concern

Moreover, Parfit's own form of reductionism fails to support a discount rate. The possibility that is supposed to undermine rational egoism is the case in which my distant future self, though continuous with my present self, is less well connected with my present self than is my near future self. This possibility does not threaten temporal neutrality even if, as Parfit assumes, connectedness as well as continuity matters. This possibility demonstrates only a fact about the relation *among the parts of my life*, not a fact about the relation *between these parts and me*.

Parfit claims to be discussing what people have reason to do, but his argument is plausible only if it is person-slices or segments, rather than persons, who are agents. Suppose I consist of a series of R-related person-stages p1 through pn at times t1 through tn (figure 6.2). The time is t1. Though p5 and p30 are equally continuous with my present self, p5 is better connected with my present self than p30 is. We can see how there is less of what matters between p1 and p30 than there is between p1 and, say, p5. This explains why *p1* or *some person-segment ending in p1* should be less concerned about the welfare of p30 than *it* should be about the welfare of p5. But P is not identical with p1 or any person-segment ending in p1, and the welfare of p30 is every bit as much part of P's welfare as is the welfare of p5. So this fact about the degree of connectedness between p1 and p30 does not affect p's reasons for action. And, as I have argued (section 8), it is persons, and not person-slices or segments, who are agents. Because all parts of a person's life are equally parts of her life, even if they are R-related to each other in varying degrees, benefits and harms are equally benefits and harms to her, regardless of their temporal location in the R-related series that is her life.

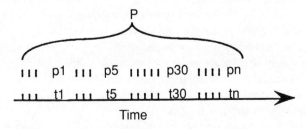

Figure 6.2 A person and her parts

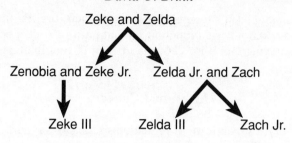

Figure 6.3   Relatives

But then diminished connectedness over time does not threaten temporal neutrality.

At one point, Parfit considers and rejects the sufficiency of an egoist appeal to this claim that all parts of a person's life are equally parts of that life (pp. 315–16). He appeals to an analogy with relatives. He claims that although all members of an extended family are equally relatives, this does not justify equal concern among them; for instance, it would not give my cousin as strong a claim to my estate as my children (p. 316). Is this a good analogy? Consider the following case (figure 6.3). Grandpa Zeke and Grandma Zelda have two children, Zeke Jr. and Zelda Jr. With his wife, Zenobia, Zeke Jr. has one child, named Zeke III; with her husband, Zach, Zelda Jr. has two children, named Zach Jr. and Zelda III. Parfit wants to say that whereas it is true that these people are all equally relatives, it does not follow that, say, Zeke Jr. should be as concerned about Zelda III (his niece) as he should be about Zeke III (his son); for instance, Zelda III does not have the same sort of claim on Zeke Jr.'s estate as Zeke III does. But to focus on the concerns of Zeke Jr. or the disposition of his estate is precisely the interpersonal (intrafamily) analogue of taking a person-stage, rather than the person, as the agent in the intrapersonal case, and I have argued against doing this. The intrafamily analogue of the person (in the intrapersonal case) is the family itself. Thus, the correct intrafamily analogue would focus on the distribution of some asset that belongs to the entire family. Here neutrality seems appropriate in light of the fact that all are equally parts of the family, even if some are more closely related than others. Thus, if Zelda Jr. is acting as the trustee of the family corporation, then, other things being equal, she ought to allocate as large a share of dividends to Zeke III (her nephew) as she does to Zach Jr. and Zelda III (her own children), even though Zach Jr. and Zelda III are more closely related to each other and to her than any of them is to Zeke III.

As long as we focus on the attitude appropriate for a whole to take towards any one of its parts, the relations that its parts bear to each other are, *ceteris paribus*, irrelevant.[33] And as long as persons are the relevant whole, this vindicates egoism's temporal neutrality.

14 Egoism and Fission

Parfit focuses on how reductionism might undermine egoism's temporal neutrality. But one might think that reductionism undermines egoism's agent bias. Fission cases provide an independent, even if less general, argument against rational egoism. As I have explained it, egoism relies on the compensation principle. Automatic compensation seems to require that the *very same person* who is benefactor be beneficiary. This condition may not seem to be satisfied in fission cases, even though the products of fission are R-related to the subject of fission. And, as Parfit effectively argues, it seems rational for the subject of fission to be concerned about all fission products that are R-related to her (ch. 12). If so, fission may seem to undermine egoism's agent bias.

Consider the following case. Tom, Zeke and Zach are identical triplets and become involved in a serious car accident. Zeke and Zach are brain-dead; Tom is not, but his body is hopelessly mangled. Assume that it is possible to transplant Tom's brain into Zeke's body and that this preserves Tom's psychological continuity. If we do this (case 1), we regard Tom as the surviving recipient and Zeke as the dead donor (Zach is simply dead). Assume that half the brain is sufficient to sustain psychological continuity. If half of Tom's brain is seriously damaged and we transplant the healthy half into Zeke's body (case 2), Tom again survives. If, however, Tom's entire brain is healthy and we transplant half of it into Zeke's body and half into Zach's (case 3), then we have a case of fission. Call the recuperating patient in Zeke's body Dick and the one in Zach's body Harry. There is just as much psychological continuity between Tom and Dick and between Tom and Harry as there was between Tom and the recuperating patient (i.e. Tom) in cases 1 and 2. Sam and Fred are series of R-related person-stages, each of which begins with Tom's stages. The important features of fission can be represented as in figure 6.4.

As Parfit notes (p. 256), there seem to be four ways to describe what happens to Tom and his relationship to Dick and Harry.

1 Tom does not survive fission; in particular, he does not survive as Dick or as Harry.
2 Tom survives as Dick, rather than Harry.
3 Tom survives as Harry, rather than Dick.
4 Tom survives as Dick and as Harry.

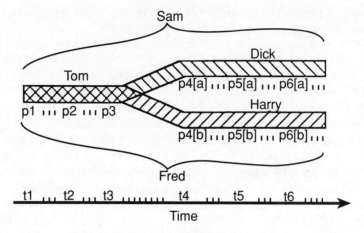

Figure 6.4 Fission

Each answer is initially hard to believe.

Against (1), we might note that there is just as much psychological continuity between Tom and Dick and between Tom and Harry as there was between Tom and the recuperating patient (i.e. Tom) in cases 1 and 2. If Tom survives in cases 1 and 2, how can he fail to survive fission? Surely, he has the same reasons to be concerned about Dick and Harry in case 3 as he did to be concerned about himself in cases 1 and 2. As Parfit says (p. 256), how can a double success be counted a failure?

But neither (2) nor (3) seems plausible. Dick and Harry have exactly equal claims to being Tom. It is true that one, but not the other, could none the less be Tom. But in virtue of what facts would one of them, rather than the other, be Tom? Dick and Harry are precisely symmetrically placed in their physical and psychological relations to Tom. If we have rejected non-reductionism, their claims to be identical to Tom must stand or fall together.

But they cannot both be Tom; (4) must be false. Identity is a transitive relation. And it seems clear that Dick is not the same person as Harry; they wake up in different hospital beds, have distinct streams of consciousness, and go on to lead different lives. But if Dick is not identical to Harry, then Tom cannot be identical with Dick and with Harry.

The best response is to accept (1) and claim that Tom does not survive fission. The transitivity of identity requires that any analysand of the relation of identity must be one–one, rather than one–many. But psychological continuity is a one–many relation. So whereas fission preserves psychological continuity, it cannot preserve identity. But because fission seems to preserve what justifies concern, we should conclude that what principally matters as far as the rationality of concern goes is psychological continuity, rather than personal identity *per se*.[34]

However, this response raises a problem for egoism. Because Tom survives transplants 1 and 2, he has good egoist reason to be concerned for the recuperating patient in both cases. Because Tom does not survive transplant 3, it looks as if he can have no egoist reason to be concerned about Dick or Harry; it seems he could not be compensated for any sacrifice he might make on behalf of Dick or Harry. But he bears the same (intrinsic) relationships to Dick and Harry in case 3 as he does to his recuperating self in cases 1 and 2. Fission involves *interpersonal psychological continuity*. It seems that Tom should be just (or nearly) as concerned for his fission products as for himself. If what principally matters is psychological continuity, not personal identity *per se*, then fission seems to demonstrate that an agent can have non-derivative reason to benefit others. In this way, fission might seem to undermine agent bias.

15 Egoism with Intracontinuant Compensation

If the egoist accepts reductionism, she may want to claim that maximal series of R-related person-stages – call them *continuants* – are the bearers of reasons for action. Indeed, reductionism would seem to imply that continuants are the entities with the most natural borders and, hence, are the most suitable agents (cf. section 8). The egoist could then reformulate the compensation principle in terms of continuants, rather than persons (though psychological continuants will normally be single persons).[35] According to this proposal, it is the two continuants Sam and Fred, rather than Tom, who have reasons for action. Because they each survive fission, each can be compensated for sacrifices that Tom might make; intracontinuant compensation will be automatic. Sam and Fred will have some common reasons and some competing reasons corresponding to their common and competing interests. We could even construct a notion of Tom's reasons out of the reasons common to Sam and Fred and an equitable accommodation between their competing reasons. For instance, we might claim that Tom has reason to take care of his health and to divide his estate equitably between Dick and Harry.

This strategy does introduce a kind of ambiguity about the subject of practical deliberation at t3, somewhat akin to the sort of ambiguities generated by the proposal that it is person-segments, rather than persons, that are the bearers of reasons for action (see section 8). But that proposal generated infinitely many possible subjects of practical deliberation in every case; the present strategy generates ambiguities only in fission cases and, even here, only as many alternatives as there are fission products.

Some of these claims may initially sound a little strange. But in many ways fission *is* strange, and I cannot see anything obviously implausible in this egoist proposal.

16 Egoism with Interpersonal Compensation

Alternatively, we might retain the original formulation of the compensation principle in terms of persons, rather than continuants, and reconcile the rationality of Tom's concern with Dick and Harry and the compensation principle by claiming that Dick's good and Harry's good are *part of* Tom's good.

I think it makes sense to claim that there can be people A and B who are related such that B's good is a part or component of A's good and that, in such cases, A benefits directly from B's benefit. This sort of relationship is most commonly thought to obtain where A and B are intimates – for instance, spouses or very close friends. Where A and B are intimates, the ground for regarding B's good as part of A's good (and vice versa) seems to be that A and B interact with each other on a regular basis and help shape each other's mental life. To a large extent, the experiences, beliefs, desires, ideals and actions of each depend upon those of the other. Of course, these are the sorts of conditions of psychological continuity and connectedness that are maximally realized in the *intra*personal case. Here they are realized to a very large extent in the *inter*personal case, and this is what grounds our claim that B's interests extend A's and that B's good is part of A's good (and vice versa). We might say that B stands to A as 'another-self'.[36] Now fission represents the limiting interpersonal case; Dick and Harry share Tom's goals and other psychological traits to the maximal extent possible, and they acquired these traits by a direct causal process from Tom. Indeed, fission cases seem to present the clearest case for claiming that one person's good is part of another's.

Unlike intimates who have ongoing interactions, Tom does not have an ongoing relationship with either Dick or Harry; indeed, he does not temporally overlap with either of them. Tom passes on his traits to Dick and Harry, and ceases to exist in the process. In this way, the relationship between Tom and Dick and Harry is highly *asymmetrical*; Dick and Harry owe their existence and nature to Tom, but not vice versa. For this reason, the parent–child relationship may present a better interpersonal model for the fission case than the relationship between spouses or friends. In many parent–child relationships the child's physical and psychological nature are to a significant degree a causal product of the parent's physical and psychological nature and activities, but not vice versa. This is how we can explain the common views that the parent's interests are extended to the child's welfare, that the child's welfare is part of the parent's good, and that the parent's interests can extend beyond her own existence. The continuity between Tom and both Dick and Harry is even greater than that between parent and child; this is our ground for claiming that Dick and Harry extend Tom's interests and for claiming that Dick's good and Harry's good are part of Tom's.

Of course, the asymmetrical character of the psychological relationship is clearest in the normal, intrapersonal case. In the normal, nonbranching case, relation R both extends the agent's interests and extends the agent. Tom is a person who consists of a non-branching series of psychologically continuous person stages p1 through p3. This psychological continuity from p2 to p3 extends Tom's interests in the sense that p3 inherits, carries on, and carries out p2's projects and plans. In this nonbranching case, it also extends Tom's life. In the fission case, however, relation R does not literally extend Tom's life, because neither Dick nor Harry is Tom. But, by virtue of being fully psychologically continuous with Tom, Dick and Harry will each inherit, carry on, and carry out Tom's projects and plans (though presumably in somewhat different directions over time). This seems to be a good ground for claiming that Dick and Harry extend Tom's interests, in the very same way that his own future self would normally extend his interests, even if they do not literally extend his life.

If so, interpersonal psychological continuity extends the agent's interests in much the way that intrapersonal psychological continuity does. An agent's future welfare is a constituent of her overall good. As such, she has reason to be concerned about her future for its own sake, as part of her overall good. In a similar way, if another's good is a constituent of the agent's overall good, then she has reason to be concerned about the other for his own sake, as part of her overall good. If so, the egoist can recognize derivative but non-instrumental reason to be concerned about others.

Nor is the scope of this egoist justification of other-regarding concern limited to one's fission products or intimates. Dick and Harry are, by hypothesis, maximally continuous with Tom. What makes fission a case of interpersonal psychological continuity is that continuity takes a one–many form. But we have seen that there is interpersonal psychological continuity in other cases – for instance, between intimates. If so, what distinguishes between future stages of myself and future stages of my intimates? The answer, according to psychological reductionism, must be that there is more continuity between myself now and myself in the future than between myself now and my intimate in the future. According to psychological reductionism, what distinguishes intrapersonal continuity and interpersonal continuity (in non-branching contexts) is the *degree* of continuity. There are more numerous and more direct psychological connections – between actions and intentions and among beliefs, desires and values – in the intrapersonal case. And where the connections between links in a chain are all weaker, continuity between any points in the chain will also be weaker. If so, we can see that I am more weakly continuous with my intimates than I am with myself. We can also see how I might be continuous with others, besides my intimates, even if more weakly so. I interact directly with others, such as colleagues and neighbours, and this interaction shapes my mental life in certain ways, even if the interaction in such cases is less regular than is my interaction with intimates, and even if the effect of such interactions on my mental life is less profound than is the effect produced by interaction with my intimates. Moreover, I interact with a much larger network of people indirectly, when the psychological influence between me and them is mediated by other people and complex social institutions, though the continuity thus established is, as a result, weaker. Indeed, the nature of my relationships to others and of the bonds between us are a function of the degree of interpersonal psychological continuity between us. If an agent's interests are extended in so far she is psychologically continuous with others, then the egoist can justify derivative but non-instrumental concern for others that is proportional to the amount of psychological continuity that exists between the agent and others.[37] If so, the egoist can justify a familiar kind of interpersonal discount rate. The central claims of self-referential altruism about other-regarding conduct can stand, not as axioms of practical rationality, but as theorems derived from an agent-biased theory.[38]

17 Conclusion

Rational egoism has a rationale for its asymmetrical treatment of intertemporal and interpersonal distribution that relies on the separateness of persons. The separateness of persons suggests the principle that it is unreasonable for agents to make uncompensated sacrifices. If we apply the compensation principle in both intrapersonal and interpersonal contexts, we explain temporal neutrality and agent bias; intrapersonal compensation is automatic, whereas interpersonal compensation is not. But then there is nothing arbitrary about egoism's hybrid structure; at a deeper level, it treats intertemporal and interpersonal distribution the same. I have tried to defend this rationale against two main challenges that Parfit's discussion naturally suggests. One might defend the fully biased presentism by arguing that it is person-slices or segments, rather than persons, that are agents and subjects of compensation. But it is persons that engage in practical deliberation and possess reasons for action; if so, temporal neutrality assures intra-personal compensation. Though the egoist rationale does appeal to the separateness of persons, it is not undermined by reductionist accounts of personal identity. The reductionist should accept temporal neutrality; all else being equal, agents should care equally about different parts of their lives, even if these parts are not equally related to each other. Nor does the reductionist account of fission undermine agent bias. If we continue to think of agents as persons, concern for those to whom one is R-related can be reconciled with agent bias by recognizing how interpersonal psychological continuity makes interpersonal compensation possible. Alternatively, if we think of agents as continuants, rather than persons, then concern for others to whom one is R-related can be reconciled with agent bias by recognizing how interpersonal psychological continuity makes intracontinuant compensation possible. If so, rational egoism's commitment to the separateness of persons explains its asymmetrical treatment of interpersonal and intertemporal distribution in a way that is metaphysically robust.[39]

Notes

1   Henry Sidgwick, *The Methods of Ethics*, 7th edn. University of Chicago Press, Chicago, 1907); hereafter *ME*.
2   Thomas Nagel, *The Possibility of Altruism* (Princeton University Press, Princeton, 1970), esp. pp. 16, 19, 99–100.
3   Parfit is attracted to what he calls a *Critical* version of P, CP, which tells each agent to aim at what will best achieve his present rational aims (pp. 94, 118–19). Rational aims exclude any intrinsically irrational desires, and include any desires that are rationally required. Because any aims might, in principle, turn out to be intrinsically irrational or rationally required, Parfit concludes that any possible theory of rationality can be represented as a version of CP (pp. 193–4). But these claims about CP are misleading. First, CP is not best represented as a version of P. Aims that are rationally required may concern things that are not the object of my actual or counterfactual desires; though I should desire them, I may not, not even under ideal epistemic conditions. But in so far as 'my rational aims' concern things that may satisfy none of my desires, CP should simply define rational action in terms of achieving those things now, not in terms of my present aims or desires. In this way, CP is more akin to presentism than to P. Nor is it helpful to think of CP in terms so broad that any theory counts as a possible version of CP

as long as CP is a rival to other theories and is fully relative (biased). For these purposes, CP is best understood as a version of presentism with an objective theory of value.

4 See Thomas Nagel, *The View from Nowhere* (Oxford University Press, New York, 1986), pp. 152–3.

5 See C. D. Broad, 'Self and Others', repr. in *Broad's Critical Essays in Moral Philosophy*, ed. D. Cheney (George Allen & Unwin, London, 1971), pp. 262–82.

6 On an instrumental view, as Hume famously observes, ''Tis not contrary to reason to prefer the destruction of the whole world to the scratching of my finger. 'Tis not contrary to reason for me to chuse my total ruin, to prevent the least uneasiness of an *Indian* or person wholly unknown to me. 'Tis as little contrary to reason to prefer even my own acknowledg'd lesser good to my greater, and to have a more ardent affection for the former than the latter' (David Hume, *A Treatise of Human Nature*, ed. P. Nidditch (Clarendon Press, Oxford, 1978), II.iii.3, p. 416).

7 An instrumental conception of P might also be thought to forge a link between normative or justifying reasons and explanatory reasons. We explain an agent's behaviour when we 'rationalize' it as an attempt to satisfy certain desires she had, given her beliefs. This may suggest that behaviour that is rationally justified is behaviour that would fulfil the agent's desires, or at least those desires she would have if she met certain epistemic conditions.

8 The fact that Parfit's preferred version of P is CP, in which the agent's aims sometimes play no essential explanatory role, makes it clearer that his fully relative P can, and should, be understood as presentism (cf. n. 3 above).

9 Nagel has revised his views in *View from Nowhere*, chs 8–9. Whereas *Possibility of Altruism* denied that there are agent-relative reasons, *View from Nowhere* recognizes some agent-relative reasons.

10 Nagel, *Possibility of Altruism*, pp. 16, 19, 99–100.

11 *Ibid.*, ch. 13, esp. pp. 134–42.

12 Contrast John Perry, 'The Importance of Being Identical', in *The Identities of Persons*, ed. A. Rorty (University of California Press, Los Angeles, 1976), pp. 67–90.

13 If personal desires essentially refer to the person who has them, then they appear to presuppose personal identity. If so, it may seem that personal desires cannot help constitute personal identity. The apparent circularity of treating personal desires as an ingredient of personal identity is like the circularity of treating memory as an ingredient of personal identity, and the solution is the same. We can appeal to 'quasi-memory', which is like memory except that it presupposes continuity, rather than identity, in our account of personal identity (p. 220). So, too, we can appeal to 'quasi-personal desire', which is like personal desire except that it presupposes continuity, rather than identity, in our account of personal identity.

14 Cf. Jennifer Whiting, 'Friends and Future Selves', *Philosophical Review*, 95 (1986), p. 579.

15 See Michael Bratman, *Intention, Plans, and Practical Reason* (Harvard University Press, Cambridge, Mass., 1987).

16 A similar claim linking the separateness of persons with a claim that the *morality* of sacrifice requires compensation is a familiar theme from recent moral philosophy. In charging that utilitarianism fails to recognize the separateness of persons, critics often complain that it allows interpersonal balancing, and so permits uncompensated sacrifices. (Cf. Nagel, *Possibility of Altruism*, pp. 138, 142; John Rawls, *A Theory of Justice* (Harvard University Press, Cambridge, Mass., 1971), pp. 23–4, 26–7, 29, 187–8, 191; and Robert Nozick, *Anarchy, State, and Utopia* (Basic Books, New York, 1974), pp. 31–4.) However, we should find the compensation principle more plausible as applied to rationality than as applied to the morality of sacrifice, to the extent that we regard the moral point of view as an impartial one and the rational point of view as the agent's personal point of view. For discussion of the compensation principle as applied to morality, see my 'The Separateness of Persons, Distributive Norms, and Moral Theory', in *Value, Welfare, and Morality*, ed. R. Frey and C. Morris (Cambridge University Press, New York, 1993), pp. 252–89.

17 Recognition of this fact may tend to undermine the force of some of Parfit's other criticisms of egoism, on the ground that its temporal neutrality requires us to act now on past desires that we no longer have and on future desires that we do not yet possess (cf. ch. 8, esp. sects 59–61). But to pursue these issues would require a fuller discussion of the commitments of temporal neutrality than I have space for here (I hope to pursue these issues elsewhere).

18 I explore egoist strategies for justifying other-regarding conduct and concern more fully in my 'Rational Egoism, Self, and Others', in *Identity, Character, and Morality*, ed. O. Flanagan and A. Rorty (MIT Press, Cambridge, Mass., 1990), pp. 339–78, and 'Self-love and Altruism', *Social Philosophy and Policy*, 14 (1997), 122–57.

19 See my 'Rational Egoism, Self, and Others' and 'Self-love and Altruism'.

20 Nagel, *Possibility of Altruism*, p. 142.

21 For example, Parfit raises some interesting questions about temporal neutrality (Pt 2, ch. 8), which I cannot pursue here.

22 Sidgwick says: 'it must surely be admissible to ask the Egoist, "Why should I sacrifice a present pleasure for a greater one in the future? Why should I concern myself about my own future feelings any more than about the feelings of other persons?"' (*ME*, p. 418). Parfit says: 'A Present-aim Theorist can ask, "Why should I give weight *now* to aims which are not mine *now*?"' (p. 95).

23 Cf. Mark Heller, 'Temporal Parts of Four-dimensional Objects', *Philosophical Studies*, 46 (1984), pp. 323–34.

24 For example, Williams bases his reservations about temporal neutrality on the thought that 'The correct perspective on one's life is *from now*' (Bernard Williams, 'Persons, Character, and Morality', repr. in his *Moral Luck* (Cambridge University Press, New York, 1981), p. 13).

25 Cf. Christine Korsgaard, 'Personal Identity and the Unity of Agency: A Kantian Response to Parfit', *Philosophy and Public Affairs*, 18 (1989), pp. 101–32.

26 Perhaps the difficulty arises only if we are realists about temporal parts, and perhaps the proper moral of the difficulty is that we should reject realism about temporal parts. The defence of presentism that I am considering in this section presupposes a realism about temporal parts. If we reject realism about temporal parts, this hurts presentism, not egoism.

27 Joseph Butler, *The Analogy of Religion*, appendix 1, repr. in *Personal Identity*, ed. J. Perry (University of California Press, Los Angeles, 1975), p. 102.

28 I will not discuss the 'Extreme Claim', which Butler accepts and Parfit discusses (pp. 307–12), according to which reductionism completely undermines any special concern for oneself and one's future. Because I think that egoism survives even Parfit's more moderate claim, there's not much reason to discuss the extreme claim directly.

29 Cf. Sydney Shoemaker, Critical Notice of Derek Parfit, *Reasons and Persons*, *Mind*, 94 (1985), p. 451 (repr. as ch. 7 below).

30 See C. I. Lewis, *An Analysis of Knowledge and Valuation* (Open Court, La Salle, Ill., 1946), p. 493.

31 I do think that continuity, like connectedness, can be a matter of degree. If, of two chains A and B, the links in A are better connected than the links in B, then the end-points in A will be more continuous than the end-points in B. However, this does not affect my present point, which assumes only that there is continuity within a chain despite a constant rate of diminished connectedness.

32 Compare Aristotle's discussion of the puzzle about whether to wish one's friend the good of divinity in *Nicomachean Ethics*, tr. T. Irwin (Hackett, Indianapolis, 1985), VIII 7, 1159a5–11. Aristotle claims that one who cares about the friend for the friend's own sake would not wish this good on him, because the friend would not survive the transformation. While Aristotle's claim seems plausible, C&C's corresponding claims about the (ir)rationality of self-improvement seem implausible. Aristotle's claim is plausible, because it is plausible to think that the species or genus to which an individual belongs is an essential property of that individual; whereas it seems implausible to think that an individual's current psychological profile is essential to that individual's persistence in the way that C&C seems to require.

33 Of course, all else is not equal if the relations among the parts of a whole are such that a given part is a less important part of the whole than others (e.g. as my fingernail is a less important part of my body than my heart). In such a case, treatment of the parts as equals may not support equal treatment of the parts. But notice that this will be a result of the relation between that part and the whole, and not simply between that part and other parts. Notice too that this is compatible with temporal neutrality.

34 If so, Parfit is wrong to claim, as he does (pp. 259–60, 278–9), that it is an 'empty question' which of the four answers is right, because they all describe the same outcome. I am unsure myself whether psychological continuity, rather than identity, is all that matters; if it can matter that psychological continuity takes a unique or non-branching form, then identity will have some independent value. However, it is enough to get this challenge to

egoism off the ground that psychological continuity has significant independent value.

35 This suggestion is similar to Lewis's view; see David Lewis, 'Survival and Identity', in *Identities of Persons*, ed. Rorty, esp. pp. 24–9. Lewis seems to want to identify persons and continuants; however, I do not. I think that brains or brain parts and the psychological continuants they support make up one person if and only if they are *functionally integrated*.

36 This phrase comes from Aristotle's justification of friendship in *Nicomachean Ethics*, bk IX, 1166a30–2, 1170b6–8. For further discussion of Aristotle's justification of friendship and its relevance to egoist justifications of other-regarding concern, see T. H. Irwin, *Aristotle's First Principles* (Clarendon Press, Oxford, 1988), ch. 18.

37 I discuss various issues about the scope and weight of the reasons that emerge from this sort of justification of other-regarding conduct and concern in 'Self-love and Altruism'.

38 In fact, this egoist justification of concern for others to whom one is R-related allows an egoist justification of temporal neutrality even on the assumption (rejected in sect. 8) that person-segments, rather than persons, are agents. Person-segments have reason to care about future segments to whom they are R-related. Assume, contrary to fact, that person-segments are agents. Temporally contiguous person-segments will be strongly R-related, and so the earlier segment will have egoist reason to benefit the later segment, even if C&C matters, despite the non-identity of the person-segments. In the case of temporally distant person-segments that are psychologically continuous but not well connected, the earlier segment will have egoist reason to benefit the later segment just in case C alone matters.

39 *Postscript* (added August 1995). Whereas my commitment to temporal neutrality requires me to reject an intrapersonal discount rate (sects 11–13), I think I would like to accept an interpersonal discount rate, not unlike the one recognized by self-referential altruism, as at least part of the correct view about rationality and morality (sect. 16). This asymmetry need not be problematic, as I hope to explain. But it may be hard to justify a familiar interpersonal discount rate if we believe that it is continuity (C), rather than continuity and connectedness (C&C), that matters. Continuity can admit of degrees; if of two chains A and B the links in A are better connected than the links in B, then any points in A will be more continuous than any points in B. So, for example, I am better connected and more continuous with myself in the future than I am with others, even intimates. But I may be equally continuous with many others, even if I am not equally well connected with all of them. This can be illustrated in terms of friendship. Let us say that friends are friendship-connected. Suppose that X is friends only with Y, whereas Y is friends also with Z. All else being equal, X is as friendship-continuous with Z as she is with Y, though she is friendship-connected to Y but not to Z. A familiar interpersonal discount rate, of the sort recognized by self-referential altruism, would claim that, all else being equal, X has more reason to be concerned about her friend Y than about her

friend's friend Z. We can endorse this claim if both C&C matter. Apparently, we cannot endorse it if only C matters, for X's friend Y and her friend's friend Z are equally continuous with X. So whereas if C alone matters, we could justify a self–other asymmetry, we could apparently not justify a familiar interpersonal discount rate. For this, connectedness, as well as continuity, must matter. Defending an interpersonal discount rate this way may seem inconsistent with my rejection of an intrapersonal discount rate (sects 11–13). In one way, it is; in another way, not. In this essay I offered two reasons for rejecting an intrapersonal discount rate. First, I pointed out that Parfit's argument for an intrapersonal discount rate requires that it be C&C, rather than C alone, that matters, as only connectedness normally diminishes over the course of a life. But, I argued, we might well suppose that it is C, rather than C&C, that matters, in part because this seemed necessary to justify prudential reasons for self-improvement (sect. 12). Second, I argued that Parfit's argument for an intrapersonal discount rate does not work even if C&C both matter, because it confuses parts and wholes (sect. 13). But it seems that I cannot appeal to the first argument against Parfit's discount rate and appeal to the significance of C&C to defend an interpersonal discount rate. I am now inclined to think that it was mistaken and unnecessary to suppose that the first argument should stand on its own. I still think that Parfit offers no good reasons for thinking that it is C&C, rather than C, that matters, and that his argument for a discount rate has a problem justifying prudential reasons for self-improvement. But we can avoid a discount rate and problems about the prudential justification of self-improvement and defend temporal neutrality, without denying that connectedness as well as continuity matters, provided we avoid what I think is Parfit's confusion of parts and wholes. For we can give prudential reasons for undertaking psychological improvements that diminish connectedness among one's parts by appeal to the need for a person to have equal concern for all her parts, regardless of the relations among them (sect. 13). This requires me to rest my case against the intrapersonal discount rate on the second argument. It would also allow me to accept an interpersonal discount rate while rejecting an intrapersonal one.

7

Parfit on Identity

Sydney Shoemaker

Each of the four parts of Derek Parfit's impressive and important book deserves detailed examination, and nothing short of another book could give detailed examinations of them all. Here I will focus exclusively on the discussion of personal identity that constitutes Part 3 of the book. The broad outlines of this account will be familiar to those who have read Parfit's well-known 1971 paper 'Personal Identity'.[1] The two targets of that paper – the view that personal identity is perfectly determinate (that questions of personal identity always admit of a yes or no answer) and the view that 'what matters' in survival is personal identity itself – are also among the main targets here. Parfit believes that we are naturally disposed to accept a 'non-reductionist' account of personal identity. According to this account, persons are 'separately existing entities', whose existence is all-or-nothing and does not consist in the holding of certain relations between mental events and bodies, and whose identity is perfectly determinate. Unity of consciousness is explained in terms of 'ownership' of different experiences by such a separately existing entity. And it is the continued identity of the entity of this sort one is that 'matters' – this is the focus of the special concern one has for one's future existence and well-being. But while this is what we tend to believe, according to Parfit, it is not what we should believe. Parfit champions a 'reductionist' account according to which we are not such separately existing entities, and according to which personal identity consists in facts that can be described 'impersonally', more specifically in 'non-branching psychological continuity and connectedness' (I shall sometimes abbreviate this 'psychological C&C'). We have psychological continuity when a person remembers his earlier deeds or experiences, or when an intention formed at one time is fulfilled at a later time, or when

First published as a Critical Notice of *Reasons and Persons* in *Mind*, 94 (1985), pp. 443–53. The present version is slightly abridged.

there is persistence of psychological traits over time – and psychological continuity consists in there being a chain of overlapping psychological connections. It is partly because psychological connectedness varies in degree that there can be cases in which personal identity is indeterminate. And it is psychological C&C, rather than personal identity *per se*, that 'matters'. What makes it rational (to the extent it is) for me to have a special concern for my well-being at a future time is the fact that my present states stand to my future states in the relations of psychological C&C that are constitutive of personal identity. But in so far as the holding of these relations justifies future concern, it would do so even when, because of 'branching', the relations do not constitute identity. Thus, if I split into two people (as in David Wiggins's example in which the hemispheres of someone's brain are separated and transplanted into different bodies), and my present stage is equally connected with the future stages of both, I should have the same concern for their future well-being as I should have for my own in ordinary cases, even though, strictly speaking, I can be identical with neither. And even in cases in which the future person is myself, I can be justified in having less concern in some cases (for example, when the future person-stage is temporally remote) because the degree of connectedness is less. This can justify treating different parts of a person's life as if they were different persons; thus, Parfit thinks, 'boundaries between persons' have less moral significance than they are given by common-sense morality and non-utilitarian moral theory. On this view, the notions of desert and entitlement have either less application than they are usually supposed to have (and, Parfit thinks, than they would have if the non-reductionist view were true), or, on an extreme version of the view, none at all.

Such a brief summary cannot do justice to the richness of Parfit's development of these ideas. The striking examples in his earlier treatments of this topic are supplemented here with many others that are equally striking, and Parfit shows great skill in marshalling hypothetical cases to enhance the plausibility of his position and undermine intuitions that conflict with it.

An important addition to Parfit's defence of his reductionist account of personal identity is the 'Combined Spectrum' argument he gives in reply to an argument of Bernard Williams directed against psychological C&C accounts. Parfit reconstructs Williams's argument so that it is based on what he calls the 'Psychological Spectrum' – a spectrum of possible cases in which it is held fixed that a future person will have one's present body, and in which one's degree of psychological C&C with that person ranges from a high degree at the 'near' end of the spectrum (the case of normal persistence) to none at all at the 'far' end (where the future person has a set of mental states totally unrelated to one's present ones).

Relying on the assumption that personal identity is always determinate and on the plausible claim that there is no point along the spectrum of which it is true that in all cases on the near side of it the future person is oneself while in all cases on the far side of it the future person is not oneself, Williams argues that even in the case at the far end the future person is oneself, and therefore that psychological C&C is not necessary for personal identity.

Parfit first counters this with the 'Physical Spectrum', a range of possible cases in which the amount of psychological C&C is held constant while the degree of bodily continuity is varied. At the near end is the case in which one continues to exist in the normal way, and as we move along the spectrum from this case, more and more of one's brain is replaced (by exactly similar bits), the case at the far end being the case in which all of it is replaced. Reasoning parallel to that used in the first case leads to the conclusion that bodily continuity is not necessary for personal identity. (Although Parfit does not point this out, if we use as the case at the far end of both spectra Williams's example in which one's body switches mental states with the body of someone else, the two 'Spectrum' arguments lead to incompatible conclusions as to which of the future persons is oneself.)

Parfit's Combined Spectrum argument undermines the common assumption of these two arguments, namely, that personal identity must be determinate. This time both physical continuity and psychological C&C are gradually reduced as we move along the spectrum from the normal cases – more and more of my brain is replaced, *and* more and more of my memories and other psychological traits are replaced by ones not connected or continuous with my present states. At the far end of the spectrum is a case in which the future person is someone whose body and psychological make-up are exactly like those of Greta Garbo at age 30, and in which there is neither psychological nor physical continuity between my present state and the state of that future person. Here no one will say that the future person is me. But, as before, there will be no point along the spectrum of which it will be plausible to say that in all cases on one side of it the future person is me, while in all cases on the other side he or she is not. Here we have no choice but to abandon the requirement that personal identity must always be determinate; and this not only undermines Williams's argument based on the Psychological Spectrum, but refutes one of the central theses of the non-reductionist view.

Another effective new argument is also a reply to an argument of Williams. To avoid violating the transitivity of identity (for example, to block the conclusion that the two offshoots in a 'fission' case are identical to one another in virtue of both being psychologically C&C with the original person), a psychological C&C account must incorporate

a 'no-branching' provision or 'no-competitors' clause; and once it does
so, it cannot satisfy the conditions that (1) whether a future person will
be me must depend only on the intrinsic features of the relation between
us, and cannot depend on what happens to other people, and that (2)
whether personal identity holds cannot depend on a 'trivial fact'.
Williams regards this as refuting such accounts. Parfit argues convincingly that *no* plausible criterion of personal identity (including the physical continuity criterion favoured by Williams) can satisfy both of these
requirements. And he suggests that the plausibility of the requirements
derives from a pair of analogous requirements which *are* met by his
reductionist view – (1') that the answer to the question of whether I
stand to the future person in the relation that matters must depend only
on the intrinsic features of my relation to the future person, and (2') that
the relation that matters in personal identity cannot hold or fail to hold
because of a trivial difference in the facts. If identity itself were what
mattered, these would be equivalent to Williams's (1) and (2). But Parfit
plausibly maintains that identity is not what matters – that if I split into
two people, both will be related to me in the way that matters.

The foregoing, and much else in this part of the book, seems to me
admirable. But despite my considerable agreement with Parfit's views, I
am left with some substantial misgivings. I begin with a worry about his
characterization of reductionism.

Parfit is fond of comparing persons with such entities as clubs and
nations, and apparently what are supposed to correspond to the members of clubs and the citizens of nations are the 'experiences' of persons.
If this comparison is taken seriously, the resulting view seems rather
like Hume's (except that Parfit never suggests that there is anything
'fictional' about personal identity). He characterizes the reductionist
view as saying that the facts in which personal identity consists can be
given an 'impersonal' description. Sometimes this seems to mean something fairly weak: namely, a description in which there is no actual
reference to any specific person. But sometimes he suggests something
stronger, as when he says, citing Lichtenberg, that 'because we are not
separately existing entities, we could fully describe our thoughts without
claiming that they have thinkers' (p. 225). This suggests that the only
entities referred to or quantified over in impersonal descriptions are
entities that could exist without there being persons – just as the people
who are in fact members of clubs could exist without there being clubs.
Yet the descriptions do refer to such mental entities as thoughts and
experiences. At one point (p. 211) Parfit proposes to use the word 'event'
rather than 'state' in referring to such entities, precisely because a state
must be a state *of* some entity, whereas this is not true of events. Apparently, then, he does not think of experiences and the like as entities that

of their very nature require subjects. This goes with an ambivalence Parfit seems to have towards the characterization of persons as subjects of experience and other mental items. While he allows that a person is something distinct from its brain, body and experiences, and something correctly said to be the subject of experiences, he repeatedly says that it is *because of the way we talk* that it is true that persons are subjects (see pp. 223, 225, 226, 251, 341). This suggests that he thinks that persons are logical constructions out of entities whose existence does not require that they be states of persons or other 'subjects' – entities whose existence is not 'adjectival' on mental subjects, in the way seeings are adjectival on seers, deeds are adjectival on doers, or (for a non-mental example) dents are adjectival on dentable surfaces.

This is certainly the way Hume thought of his 'perceptions'. But it seems questionable that there are any entities that fill the bill. Examples given of experiences are typically examples of experienc*ings* – and experiencings are patently adjectival. Moreover, it is not only the grammatical structure of our talk about experiences (and other mental events) that makes questionable the view that they have the status of Humean perceptions – that is, that their existence is independent of, and in some sense more fundamental than, that of the subjects that have them. If any sort of causal or functional account of the mental is correct, what constitutes a given mental state or event as being of a particular mental kind (e.g. an experience or belief having a certain content) is its being so related to a larger system to which it belongs as to be apt to play a certain 'causal role' in the workings of that system – and the existence of such a system will be just what Parfit regards as constituting the existence of a person. On any such view there will be a necessary ontological dependence of experiences (etc.) on the existence of persons or other mental subjects.[2] I suspect that if reduction requires an 'impersonal description' of the sort Parfit sometimes seems to have in mind, it will be impossible to have a reduction of personhood and personal identity without having a reduction of mentality as well – the impersonal description will have to be in physical or functional terms.

A weaker characterization of reductionism which would suit many of Parfit's purposes would be as follows. Take the issue between the reductionist and the non-reductionist to be over the status of the relation Russell called 'co-personality' – that is, the relation that holds between different experiences, person-stages, etc., just in case they belong to one and the same person. (In John Perry's terminology, co-personality is the 'unity relation' for persons.) The non-reductionist can be presumed to hold that this relation can be characterized *only* in the way I just characterized it – that is, in a way that makes essential use of the notion of personal identity. The reductionist holds that this relation can be given an independent characterization which allows it to be used in giving a non-trivial and non-circular account of the identity conditions for persons. This would permit a non-branching psychological C&C account of personal identity to be reductionist (as Parfit takes it to be), even if what it takes to be the co-personality relation (non-branching psychological C&C) cannot be characterized without quantification over entities – for example, experiencings – whose existence is adjectival on subjects. I shall henceforth assume that reductionism can be understood in this weaker way.

My most serious misgivings concern what Parfit says about non-reductionism. This is supposed to be the position we all naturally believe. And while Parfit thinks that it is false, he thinks it might have been true. His arguments for reductionism are in large part arguments against non-reductionism. And he apparently thinks of these arguments as empirical. What makes it unreasonable to believe in non-reductionism is the fact that there is no empirical evidence (although there might have been) for the existence of Cartesian egos or other 'separately existing entities', that there is good empirical reason to believe that the carrier of psychological C&C is the brain, and that the 'division of consciousness' observed in actual cases of surgical separation of the hemispheres of the brain shows that unity of consciousness is not explained by ownership by a subject. From all this it appears that the falsity of non-reductionism is empirical rather than a priori. And Parfit not only thinks that non-reductionism might have been true and that it is the view we naturally believe; he thinks that many of the attitudes we have would (or might) be reasonable if it were true, but can be argued to be unreasonable given that it is false. These include attitudes towards death, concern for our own self-interest, and non-utilitarian moral attitudes.

If the dispute between the reductionist and the non-reductionist is an empirical one, then when the former says (as Parfit does) that personal identity 'necessarily' involves or consists in certain things, he must have in mind nomological or metaphysical necessity rather than conceptual or logical necessity. This is not always how Parfit appears to view the matter. He relies heavily on imagined cases – for example, those involving 'teleportation', splitting of persons, and the like; and imaginability seems more relevant to claims of conceptual possibility and necessity than to claims of nomological or (Kripkean) metaphysical possibility and necessity. And when he argues for the psychological C&C version of reductionism over the physical continuity version (for example, when he argues in an appendix against Nagel's view that we are essentially our brains), the argument seems most naturally read as an a priori one based on our intuitions about possible cases, and ultimately on our concepts. Still, much of the time Parfit does seem to view the issues as empirical.

When he discusses imaginary cases, he is often at pains to say that the impossibility of these cases is only 'technical'; this suggests that he regards them as nomologically, or at least metaphysically, possible, and therefore that the sort of modality at issue, in his claims about what personal identity 'necessarily' involves, is metaphysical or nomological rather than conceptual, and a posteriori rather than a priori. And this of course goes with his claim that non-reductionism could have been true. Let us look, then, at his argument for that claim.

The argument rests on the imaginary case of a Japanese woman who has memories of living the life of a Celtic warrior in the Bronze Age. Some of these memories are confirmed by archaeological investigation in such a way as to leave no doubt that they are veridical; and since there is found to be no physical continuity between the Celtic warrior and the Japanese woman, the conclusion is forced on us that 'there is some purely mental entity which was in some way involved in the life of the Japanese woman, and which has continued to exist during the thousands of years that separate the lives of these two people' (p. 227). And, says Parfit, 'A Cartesian ego is just such an entity.' We are to imagine that further evidence shows that the existence of this ego is all-or-nothing.

I will not dispute the logical possibility of our discovering all this. But does this give us a case in which non-reductionism is true? If it does, it ought to give us a case in which the psychological C&C account of personal identity is false, since Parfit classifies this as one version (the one he favours) of the reductionist view. Yet it appears that in making these imagined discoveries we would be using psychological C&C as our epistemological criterion of personal identity – it is, after all, the memory connectedness of the Japanese woman and the Celtic warrior that would lead us to identify them. But given Parfit's intuitions about other cases, it is rather a mystery how he thinks the use of psychological C&C as our criterion of personal identity could lead us to the empirical discovery that personal identity does *not* consist in psychological C&C.

Parfit himself allows, later in the same chapter, that a dualist could be a reductionist about personal identity (see p. 241). So why in this case should the discovery of Cartesian egos be taken to establish, or support, non-reductionism? Perhaps the answer is that the dualist version of reductionism that Parfit has in mind is either a Humean bundle theory or a theory according to which the immaterial carrier of psychological C&C is an entity whose existence (like that of the brain) is not 'all-or-nothing'. If so, what is crucial about the Japanese woman case is that the existence of the carrier is discovered to be all-or-nothing.

Supposing for the moment that we could discover this, there are two possibilities: either the identity of this all-or-nothing immaterial entity necessarily goes with psychological C&C, or it does not. Parfit allows that one version of the latter supposition may be 'unintelligible'; this is the 'featureless Cartesian view', according to which the Cartesian ego that I am might cease to exist and be replaced by another which inherits all of my psychological characteristics. And Parfit seems committed to rejecting the possibility of persons being such entities by what he says about brains. He thinks that if all of someone's mental states are transferred to a different brain, the person goes with the states and acquires a new brain – or at any rate, that we make no mistake if we choose to describe the case in that way. It seems arbitrary to hold this and not to hold, as John Locke did, that it is likewise true that if all of someone's mental states are transferred from one immaterial substance to another, the person goes with the states. Presumably Parfit would also hold that if a brain is wiped clean of all of its mental states (or mental-state realizations) and all traces of its past, and then becomes the carrier of a new stream of psychological C&C, it becomes the brain of a new person (or at least that this description of the case is permissible). In the absence of reasons for treating brains and immaterial entities differently, he ought likewise to say that a new person comes into existence if an immaterial entity is wiped clean of its states and a new stream of consciousness begins in it. Here again he should follow the lead of John Locke, the original C&C theorist. So it would seem that Parfit should say that persons should not be identified with such immaterial entities unless it is discovered that the identity of such entities necessarily goes with psychological C&C.

But if this is to support non-reductionism, we will have to establish further that while the identity of these entities necessarily *goes with* psychological C&C (the necessity being, I suppose, Kripkean metaphysical necessity), it does not *consist in* it. Indeed, we will have to establish that it does not consist in anything at all (for establishing that it consists in something else would merely establish a different version of reductionism, not the truth of non-reductionism). It can be doubted whether this is even coherent. But even if it is, it seems obvious that nothing we could imagine discovering in the Japanese woman case could support such a view about the immaterial entities there discovered. If it is to be an empirical discovery that the identity of these entities goes with psychological C&C, how on earth do we trace their histories when we are in the process of discovering this? And how do we discover *empirically* that their identity consists in nothing, despite necessarily going with psychological C&C?

In response to the latter question it might be said that what would show that the identity of these entities consists in nothing (and so cannot consist in psychological C&C) is the fact that it is all-or-nothing. But this raises the further question of how we could discover in the first place that the identity of these entities is all-or-nothing, if we do not yet know what their identity involves. Moreover, as I shall now try to show, there is no incompatibility between the existence of so-and-so's being all-or-nothing and the identity of so-and-so's consisting in something – for example, in psychological C&C. This, if correct, undermines one of Parfit's main ways of distinguishing between reductionism and non-reductionism.

The existence of brains, Parfit says, is not all-or-nothing. But it seems imaginable that this should have been otherwise. It might have been the case that mental states are realized in the brain 'holistically', and that none of the brain can be removed without instantaneously destroying all consciousness and all life. Borderline cases between the existence of a functioning brain and the non-existence of one, and also borderline cases between the continued existence of a brain and its replacement by a different one, might be nomologically ruled out. Suppose also that a brain cannot remain biologically alive without retaining some appreciable degree of psychological C&C with its past states. And suppose (what may, for all I know, be the case) that teleportation, brain-state transfers, half-brain transplants, etc. are all metaphysically impossible (although conceptually possible). If all this were so, then (for us, anyhow) personal identity would necessarily go with brain identity, the latter would necessarily go with psychological C&C, and both sorts of identity would be perfectly determinate. Our existence would be all-or-nothing. Such difficulties as there may be in imagining the discovery of this are, I think, minor compared with those involved in imagining the discovery that we are all-or-nothing Cartesian egos.

But would such a discovery show that personal identity does not consist in psychological C&C? Surely not. In the envisaged situation, our reason for saying that the identity of a person necessarily goes with the identity of a brain would be precisely the discovery that the identity of a brain necessarily goes with psychological C&C. It is perfectly conceivable that there should be two sorts of creatures, both of which qualify as persons (given the sorts of psychological states they have), one of which is such that the identity of creatures of that sort necessarily goes with the identity of all-or-nothing brains (in the way just imagined), and the other of which is such that this is not so (they are the way Parfit thinks we are). We have a single notion of a person, and of personal identity, which we could use in talking about creatures of both sorts, and of both we could say that their identity consists in psychological C&C. Using psychological C&C as our criterion, we could discover that it is true of the first sort of creatures, and false of the second, that their identity necessarily goes with the identity of their brains, and that their existence is all-or-nothing. We might even put this by saying that the existence of persons of the first sort is found to 'consist in' the identity of their brains; but this would clearly be a different sense of 'consist in' from that in which the identity

of both sorts of creatures consists in psychological C&C. To avoid confusing these senses, we might do better to say instead that the identity of
the first sort of creatures is *realized in* the identity of all-or-nothing brains
– it is realized in this because their psychological C&C is realized in this.

I have been allowing that there is a sense in which it can be a matter
for empirical discovery whether entities of a certain sort have all-or-
nothing existence and whether their identity is always determinate. But
this is compatible with its being the case, and may even require, that the
identity of such entities over time consists in the holding of some sort of
'unity relation' (to use John Perry's term) between successive stages or
events, and therefore that a reductionist theory is true of them. For the
empirical question will be whether the way in which the unity relation
(e.g. psychological C&C) is realized allows there to be 'borderline cases'
of identity – that is, cases such that it is conceptually indeterminate
whether the degree to which the unity relation holds is sufficient to
constitute the continued existence of an entity of that sort. Imaginable,
and so conceptually possible, borderline cases may, or may not, be ruled
out as nomologically or metaphysically impossible by laws of nature and
modes of realization.

There are good reasons for thinking that indeterminacy of identity is
a semantic phenomenon rather than a metaphysical one. No ordered pair
of entities in the world can be such that it is indeterminate whether its
first member is identical to its second.[3] But the truth of a statement of
identity can be indeterminate owing to indeterminacy in the reference of
its terms.[4] It is this sort of indeterminacy that is ruled out by the discoveries imagined above; roughly, we discover that the existence of persons
is all-or-nothing by discovering that such vagueness as there is in the
concept of a person is neutralized by facts about the world which rule out
imaginable borderline cases of personhood and personal identity, and so
render the reference of 'person' in this world (although not in other
possible worlds) perfectly determinate. Plainly this is not establishing
that persons have a certain metaphysical status, and *a fortiori* it is not
establishing that they have a metaphysical status incompatible with
reductionism. What we cannot coherently suppose, I think, is that there
are two sorts of entities in the world: those whose identity is determinate
and those whose identity is not, and that it is an empirical question which
sort we are. The issue between reductionism and non-reductionism is
misconceived if it rests on that supposition.

If, as Parfit thinks, non-reductionism is false, and if, as I am inclined to
think, no empirical discoveries could show (or could have shown) it to be
true, it seems reasonable to conclude that it could not have been true –
that it is not, on examination, a coherent doctrine. This may or may not
call into question the claim that non-reductionism is what we are all

naturally disposed to believe. But I think it does call into question Parfit's view that many of our attitudes, about our own future well-being and about morality, would (or might) be justified if non-reductionism were true but are not justified (or are more questionably justified) given that reductionism is true. And I think this latter claim is questionable even if we allow, for the sake of discussion, that non-reductionism might have been true.

What Parfit frequently says is that on the non-reductionist view personal identity is, or involves, a 'deep further fact', and that it is this deep further fact that would, or might, justify attitudes that cannot be justified if reductionism is true – certain sorts of special concern about one's future well-being, or the assignment of importance to 'boundaries between lives' that goes with claims about moral desert. But suppose that, as I suggested earlier, the issue between reductionism and non-reductionism is over the status of the relation of co-personality – roughly, the reductionist affirms while the non-reductionist denies that this relation is identical with some relation (such as non-branching psychological C&C) that can be characterized other than as the relation that holds between different experiences, stages, etc. just in case they belong to the same person. Does co-personality come out as something 'deeper' on the non-reductionist view than on the reductionist view? The non-reductionist does say that co-personality is something 'over and above' psychological continuity and any other such relation you care to mention. But what is it beyond these? The only answer is: co-personality. And this is a relation which the reductionist also recognizes. In a sense the reductionist and the non-reductionist recognize the same relations and agree about which ones hold; the difference is only that the reductionist identifies relations the non-reductionist holds to be distinct. It is hard to see how a relation's being non-identical with any relation of a certain sort makes it especially 'deep', or especially important. To use an analogy, dualists affirm, while materialists deny, that mental states like being in pain are irreducible to physical states; but it would be odd to give this as a reason for saying that suffering is a 'deeper fact', and therefore matters more, on the dualist view than on the materialist view.

It is of course Parfit's view (which I agree is made plausible by a consideration of 'splitting' cases) that 'what matters' is not personal identity as such but the psychological C&C that normally constitute it. But he appears to think that *qua* constituted by these, as it is on the reductionist view, personal identity matters less than it would if non-reductionism were true. He regards as 'defensible' both the 'Extreme Claim', which says that attitudes of special concern for one's own future are justifiable only if non-reductionism is true, and the 'Moderate Claim', which says that even if reductionism is true, we can be

justified in having some special concern for our own futures. And the
version of the moderate claim that he quotes from an earlier article of his
compares the importance of personal identity on the non-reductionist
view and its importance on the reductionist view to, respectively, the
brightness of the Sun and that of the Moon at night (p. 309). But while
Parfit seems to saddle reductionists with the burden of either justifying
their special concern or admitting that it is irrational, we are told nothing
about why personal identity would matter *at all*, or about why special
concern would be justified *at all*, if non-reductionism were true – nothing,
that is, except the unsatisfactory claim that on the non-reductionist
view personal identity involves a 'deep further fact'. Similarly, we are
given nothing except this unsatisfactory claim in explanation of Parfit's
view that (non-consequentialist) notions of moral desert and commitment have a more unproblematic application if non-reductionism is true
than if reductionism is true (here again Parfit finds 'defensible' both an
'extreme' claim which holds that these notions apply only if non-
reductionism is true and a 'moderate' claim that allows them application
if reductionism is true), and his view that distributive principles of justice
have less weight if reductionism is true than if non-reductionism is true.

Parfit does argue persuasively that his reductionist position provides
an argument against the Self-interest Theory of rationality, the view that
what it is rational for one to do, on any occasion, is whatever makes one's
life as a whole go best. What 'matters' according to the reductionist view
is not identity as such (which is all-or-nothing), but the holding of certain
relations. Since these relations include psychological connectedness, and
since connectedness varies in degree, it is reasonable to reject the 'requirement of equal concern' that is built into the Self-interest Theory –
the requirement that 'A rational person should be equally concerned
about all parts of his future'. One can rationally care less about one's
further future, because connectedness is nearly always weaker over
longer periods.

It seems clear from the discussion of the Self-interest Theory in Part
2 of the book, where a number of other arguments against it are given,
that Parfit's concern to refute it is in part a concern to defend the
rationality of morality – for the Self-interest Theory holds that it is
always irrational to sacrifice one's own interests to those of others, or to
the demands of duty. It does not seem that the argument against the Self-
interest Theory based on the reductionist view of personal identity helps
in this defence of morality. The Self-interest Theorist who is persuaded
by the argument could stick to his view that what is rational is always
what is in one's own interest, but move to a different account of what is
in one's own interest–one according to which an action is in one's own
interest to the extent that it promotes well-being in the 'future selves'

psychologically C&C with one, where the weight given to the well-being of a 'future self' is greater or lesser depending on the extent to which it is psychologically connected with one's 'present self'. This seems to me the theory a proponent of the Self-interest Theory should move to if he becomes persuaded of reductionism and of the claim that what matters is psychological C&C, and if he wants to retain the spirit of his original view. And this theory poses as great a threat to the rationality of morality as does the original Self-interest Theory.[5] Parfit does mention such a revised version of the Self-interest Theory, but what he says about it does not seem to meet the point just made. One thing he says is that the revision 'breaks the link between the Self-interest Theory and what is in one's own interest' (p. 317). But this is true only on the *old* conception of what is in one's interest; and, in any case, he says nothing to show that it breaks this link in a way that helps morality. He also says that the revised theory is not a version of the Self-interest Theory but is instead a version of what he calls the 'Critical Present-aim Theory' – a theory which says that what it is rational for one to do is whatever best achieves what, at the time, one (not irrationally) wants or is rationally required to want. But elsewhere he tells us that any theory, even including the original Self-interest Theory, can be construed as a version of the Critical Present-aim Theory – so the fact that the revised theory is a version of it is no reason for saying that it is not also a version of the Self-interest Theory. I am not of course recommending the revised theory; my point is only that if the original Self-interest Theory needs to be refuted if we are to defend the rationality of morality, then so does this one, and that it is not refuted by considerations about what matters in personal identity. (It may be that a sufficient argument against both theories is that they do imply the irrationality of desires to help others or do one's duty; this seems to be what Parfit's first argument against the Self-interest Theory in Part 2 amounts to.)

Parfit's discussion of personal identity is full of rich and fascinating detail – much more than I have been able to cover here. Like all of the book, it amply repays careful study.[6]

Notes

1 *Philosophical Review*, 80 (1971), pp. 3–27.
2 For a related point, see my 'Personal Identity, A Materialist's Account', in Sydney Shoemaker and Richard Swinburne, *Personal Identity* (Blackwell, Oxford, 1984), esp. pp. 98–101.
3 See N. Salmon, *Reference and Essence* (Princeton University Press, Princeton, and Blackwell, Oxford, 1981), pp. 244–5. See also Gareth Evans, 'Can There Be Vague Objects?', *Analysis*, 38 (1978), p. 208.

4 See H. W. Noonan, 'Vague Objects', *Analysis*, 42 (1982), pp. 3–6, and 'Indefinite Identity: A Reply to Broome', *Analysis*, 44 (1984), pp. 117–21. See also 'Sydney Shoemaker's Reply', in Shoemaker and Swinburne, *Personal Identity*, pp. 145–6, n. 5.

5 Here I am indebted to Richard Moran.

6 I am grateful to D. Brink, R. Farr, H. Hodes, P. Gasper, A. Sidelle, J. D. Trout, M. Wachsburg and J. Whiting for helpful comments on an earlier draft of this review.

8

Human Concerns without Superlative Selves

Mark Johnston

In Part 3 of *Reasons and Persons* Derek Parfit argues that since a so-called reductionist view of personal identity, and hence of continued existence, is correct, survival, or continued existence, is not important in the way we naturally think. What matters, or what is of rational significance in survival, can be secured in cases in which people do not continue to exist, but are replaced. There is no reason to turn down a painless and practically undetectable replacement by the right sort of replica, even if one is convinced that this involves one's own death! Survival is not everything it has seemed to us to be. In more recent work Parfit seems attracted by the idea that since reductionism is true, no one *deserves* to be punished for even the great wrongs they committed in the past. He goes on to suggest that the very idea of just compensation is based on a mistake about the nature of personal identity.[1] Reductionism thus appears to show that, contrary to our primordial and habitual practice, the facts of personal identity and difference are not 'deep enough' facts around which to organize our practical concerns and patterns of reason-giving.

The issues raised by Parfit's arguments force consideration of fundamental questions about the relations between metaphysics and our practical concerns. Do we, as Parfit maintains, have a false metaphysical view of our nature as persons? How far does such a false metaphysical view guide us in our ordinary activities of reidentifying and caring about people? How much should the discovery that we have a false metaphysical view of our nature impact upon our practical concern with survival?

Because these questions loom, the topic of personal identity is an excellent test case for what I have elsewhere labelled 'Minimalism' – the view that metaphysical pictures of the justificatory undergirdings of our practices do not represent the real conditions of justification of those practices.[2] The minimalist has it that such metaphysical pictures are mostly theoretical epiphenomena; that is, although ordinary practitioners may naturally be led to adopt such pictures as a result of their practices and perhaps a little philosophical prompting, the pictures have relatively little impact on the practices themselves. For there are typically other bases of the practices. To this the minimalist adds the claim that we can do better in holding out against various sorts of scepticism and unwarranted revision when we correctly represent ordinary practice as having given few hostages to metaphysical fortune.

In the particular case of personal identity, minimalism implies that any metaphysical view of persons which we might have is either epiphenomenal or a redundant basis for our practice of making judgements about personal identity and organizing our practical concerns around this relation. About personal identity Parfit's claim is that although we are habitual non-reductionists, taking ourselves to be 'separately existing entities distinct from our brains and bodies', reductionism is true. So we must focus on the senses in which reductionism is true, and on how these might be relevant to Parfit's revisionary proposals.

How to be a Reductionist

Under the general heading of reductionism about personal identity, Parfit maintains:

1   The fact of a person's identity over time just consists in the holding of more particular facts about psychological and physical continuity (p. 210).
2   These 'more particular' facts can be described without presupposing the identity of the person in question (ibid.).
3   Because the more particular facts can hold to various degrees, the facts of personal identity can sometimes be factually indeterminate (pp. 216, 236–44).
4   As (1) implies and (3) illustrates, the facts of personal identity do not involve the existence of separately existing entities distinct from brains and bodies whose survival would always be a determinate matter (p. 216).

Parfit often uses 'reductionism' to denote a combination of (1)–(4) with what he believes inevitably follows: that is, that personal identity is not what fundamentally matters (e.g. p. 275). Since I am interested precisely in whether this claim does follow, I shall use 'reductionism' only as a name for (1)–(4).[3]

The crucial idiom of some facts consisting in the holding of other facts is not pellucid. Parfit himself disarmingly expresses doubt about the adequacy of his characterization of reductionism: 'It is likely that, in describing a Reductionist view about identity, I have made mistakes. Such mistakes may not wholly undermine my arguments' (p. 274). Some further clarification of reductionism is thus in order.

Let us first distinguish between analytical and ontological reductionism. Both are theses about some given fact-stating discourse. Analytical reductionism is the thesis that each statement cast in the discourse in question has an analytically equivalent statement in some other discourse which shares with the first no vocabulary other than topic-neutral expressions. Two statements are analytically equivalent just in case it is a priori and necessary that they have the same truth-value. While the notion of a fact is not well constrained in philosophical discussions, the following idea has at least some appeal: if two empirical statements are analytically equivalent, then they do not have different fact-stating potential.[4] So an analytic reductionism about the discourse in which claims of personal identity over time are cast would then have it that this discourse has no fact-stating power peculiar to it. This gives a very strong sense to the thesis that there are no 'further facts' of personal identity. However, the thesis in that sense is not plausible in itself, and even if it were, Parfit is in no position to endorse it. For he argues that we could have had good empirical evidence against reductionism. For example, if we had checkably accurate apparent memories about past lives, this might support the view that we had separable souls, and could be reincarnated. So no reductionist equivalence holds as an a priori matter.[5]

Ontological reductionism is not a thesis about the analytic redundancy of the vocabulary of a given discourse. It is a thesis to the effect that making statements in the discourse in question carries no commitment to entities other than those spoken of in some other, philosophically favoured discourse. Constructions out of the entities described in the favoured discourse may be allowed.

Thus, for example, many believe that while propositional attitude predicates cannot be analysed away in favour of purely physical predicates, there is none the less no special ontology peculiar to mentalistic discourse: every mental event or state is a physical event or state.[6] So also, those who believe that discourse about value cannot be analysed away in favour of discourse which does not employ evaluational predicates may nevertheless deny that there are extra evaluational properties, like G. E. Moore's non-natural goodness, superadded to the physical properties of things.[7]

While many ontological reductionists in fact express themselves in the idiom of identity, as with the claim that every mental event is a physical event, an ontological reductionist may also express herself in the idiom of constitution. Many of us are ontological reductionists when it comes to talk of clay statues. Clay statues are nothing over and above, are wholly constituted by, the quantities that make them up. But they are not identical with such quantities, as is shown by the fact that the quantities could survive under conditions in which no clay statues survive.[8]

Now although the notion of a fact is not well constrained in philosophical discourse, the following seems very plausible: facts involve things having properties at times, so the fact that a is F at t is the fact that b is G at t' only if $a = b$ and the property of being F is the property of being G and $t = t'$. So even when quantity Q is the quantity which wholly constitutes the statue of Goliath before and after some fire, the fact that the statue of Goliath survived the fire is not the same fact as the fact that Q survived the fire. For Q is not identical with the statue of Goliath. Here, then, is a clear and unworrying sense in which the fact that the statue of Goliath survived is a different, and in that sense further, fact than the fact that Q survived. This is not because the statue of Goliath is a superlative entity existing separately from the matter that makes it up, but for a reason that is in one way 'less deep' and in another way more deep (if one wants to follow Parfit and speak in those terms). It is because material objects and *a fortiori* art-objects are in a different ontological category from the quantities of matter that make them up.

Is ontological reductionism with such ordinary further facts a live option in the case of personal identity? On many plausible views it is. Here is one such view. People, at least the ones with which we deal, are essentially human beings. That is to say, a human person survives only if enough of an important part of the organism which constitutes him survives. What makes the important part – the brain – important is that it is the organ of mental life. On a less demanding, and perhaps more plausible, version of the view, it is enough that a physically continuous descendant of one's brain survives, so that one might survive if one's neurons were slowly replaced by bionic units. On this view there is never anything more to us than bodies and brains (and in certain science-fiction cases bionic parts which might have gradually taken over from our brains). Talk of human minds is just overly substantival talk of the mental functioning of particular human beings. It is not talk of the mental substances which inhabit human organisms. There are no such things.[9]

However, on this view human beings still cannot be identical to their bodies, to their brains, or to mereological sums of their bodies and brains. The idea that I am identical to my body, or to my body and brain taken together, is refuted by the fact that I might survive even if my body were destroyed. So long as my brain were kept alive and functioning – for example, by transplanting it into another receptive and de-brained body – I would go where my functioning brain goes, and would continue to exist even though the only part of my original body left was my brain.[10] Nor am I identical to my brain. When I report my weight as 160 pounds, I am not like the driver of a heavy truck who calls out to the bridge-master 'I weigh 3 tons.'

This means that although personal identity does not involve the persistence through time of Cartesian egos or mental substances, there are further facts of personal identity. Although Reagan does, and always did consist of, nothing more than a living body, the fact that he survived Hinckley's shots is not the fact that his body (including his brain) survived. Nor is it the fact that Reagan's brain survived. Nor is it the fact that part of Reagan's body that is other than his brain survived. Although these are all facts, the fact that Reagan survived is a further fact, thanks to the difference in category between persons and their bodily parts. Of course, we have yet to see how this difference in category could be important to rationality and morality.

So far, all of this is compatible with reductionism as Parfit himself characterizes it. Over a striking couple of pages Parfit adverts to a position which claims that (a) a person's existence just consists in the existence of his brain and body and the occurrence of a series of interrelated physical and mental events; and (b) a person is an entity that is distinct from a brain and body and such a series of events. Parfit writes:

> if this version [of Reductionism] is consistent, as I believe, it is the better version. It uses our actual concept of a person. In most of what follows we can ignore the difference between [this version emphasizing constitution and the version emphasizing identity]. But at one point this difference may have great importance. (p. 212)

The point cited by Parfit turns out to be several points, including the whole of chapter 14 of Part 3.[11] Unfortunately, Parfit does not make explicit how the better version of reductionism would make a difference at these points. It may therefore be worth seeing just how the better version bears on *most* of the argument of Part 3 of *Reasons and Persons*.

Let us call the better reductionism, the reductionism I have illustrated by the view that we are essentially human beings, reductionism with ordinary further facts. This differs from non-reductionism, which has it that personal identity involves what we might call superlative further facts – further facts involving the persistence of mental substances or Cartesian egos. Reductionism with ordinary further facts passes Parfit's crucial test for a reductionism: it allows that the facts of personal identity may sometimes be indeterminate. For example, the view that we are essentially human beings is formulated in terms of a vague necessary condition on continued existence of persons: enough of a person's brain (or brain-surrogate) must be kept functioning if that person is to survive.[12] No good explication of our ordinary concept of personal identity over time will find already implicit in our use of the concept an exact specification of how much is enough. As wielders of the concept of persons as human beings, we are not committed to the view that there is a precise point at which the victim of gradual but terminal brain damage ceases to be. By contrast, Parfit's construal of the idea of persons as Cartesian egos requires that there is such a point. The existence of Cartesian egos is supposed never to be an indeterminate matter.

Another important contrast with non-reductionism is this: of the ordinary further facts about the identity and difference of persons recognized by the better reductionism, Parfit holds that they are *fixed* by the facts about mental and physical continuity and connectedness. To put it in the now standard philosophical jargon: unlike the superlative further facts, the ordinary further facts of human personal identity *supervene* upon the facts of mental and physical continuity and connectedness. That is to say that no two possible situations alike with respect to the latter facts differ with respect to the former facts. The idiom of constitution of facts is best understood in these terms.[13]

Given widespread scepticism about the availability of analyses of significant parts of our discourse and a well-founded disbelief in superlative entities – Cartesian egos, superadded values, the moving NOW, human agency as uncaused initiation of action, etc. – the plausible general position is an ontological reductionism which allows that facts about microphysics may make up the, or a, fundamental supervenience base. On this view, the whole of the manifest world of lived experience is made up of ordinary further, although supervening, facts. There will then be a general philosophical temptation to disparage such facts and the concerns organized around them because they do not involve the superlative entities of speculative metaphysics. When in the grip of this temptation, the superlative entities can seem to be the only things which would give the required privilege to the discourses in which we state further facts. Had the superlative entities existed, and stood in the right relation to the discourses in question, then those discourses would have had an external point, and the interests which we reproduce, nurture and guide by means of those discourses would have had an external and independent justification.

The best defence against this tempting line of thought is a minimalist account of the justification of our practices. To acquire a feel for minimalism, consider what is in many ways its hardest case, the case of free will. According to the minimalist, when, for example, we hold someone responsible for an act, there are a variety of possible factual discoveries which would defeat the particular claim of responsibility – discoveries about coercion, automatism, the agent's radical ignorance of what was involved, and so on. And if it could be shown that, in such particular ways, no one is ever free, then this would radically undermine the whole practice of attributing responsibility. But in the absence of such discoveries, the mere observation that freedom does not consist in uncaused initiation of action is not itself a criticism of the practice. We should want to know exactly what role was played in the practice by the picture of agency as uncaused initiation of action, and not just that ordinary practitioners have a natural tendency upon philosophical prompting to spin out the picture of uncaused initiation. That the practice of attributing responsibility depends for its justification on facts about free agency, and that ordinary practitioners given the right sort of philosophical urging picture those facts as involving uncaused causings, does not settle it that the practice of attributing responsibility depends for its justification on facts about uncaused causings. The picture of uncaused causings may have only a minimal role. It may be epiphenomenal to the practice, or it may be only a redundant basis for the practice. The existence of this minimalist position shows that nothing can be made of the mere absence of superlative further facts. Hence the practical irrelevance of the *sheer* claim that the ordinary further facts are 'less deep' than the superlative further facts, where this just amounts to the observation that they do not involve superlative entities. If such an observation were by itself sufficient to discredit our practices, then all the concerns which have a purchase in the manifest world and cannot be captured as concerns about collections of microphysical facts would be discredited. Philosophy would have won an all too automatic, and probably Pyrrhic, victory over human life. It would have to begin again by scaling its standards of justification down to human size.

It may help to have another example of the rather abstract point about the practical dispensability of belief in superlative entities, states or processes. Arthur Prior argued that one cannot rationalize or show the point of rejoicing in the recent cessation of pain without making sense of present-tensed facts like the fact that one's pain is now over. Such facts are further facts. They are not identical to facts concerning what comes tenselessly after what. Moreover, mere knowledge of what comes tenselessly after what – for example, that 9 p.m. on 8 April 1990 is a time after the end of one's pain – is not sufficient to rationalize such rejoicing. Someone could suffer every evening with a bad digestive pain

which lasts for two hours. At 8 p.m. on 8 April 1990, after being in pain
for an hour, he recognizes that the pain he is undergoing will end by 9
p.m. But he is not then in a position to rejoice in the recent cessation of
pain, only in the fact that it will cease. There is a simple reason for this;
it is the reason he would express by saying at 8 p.m., 'My pain is not yet
over.'

One ought to be able to defend such tense-ridden attitudes and concerns without relying on the metaphysical picture which naïve thought
about time sometimes generates – the picture of the moving NOW which
noodles along at the well-regulated rate of one second per second, as
reality grows at one temporal end and diminishes at the other. After all,
how exactly does the extra process involving the moving NOW help to
make sense of my rejoicing that my pain is over? I could anticipate the
way the moving NOW moves toward and past the time at which my pain
ends just as I could anticipate some other event pre-dating and post-
dating the end of my pain. The picture of the moving NOW is just something we fall back on in imagination when we think about the nature of
tensed facts. But so far as our tense-ridden concerns go, all the temporal
becoming we need is the temporal becoming that McTaggart famously
and unpersuasively denied: that is, the existence of facts about what is
happening, what has happened, and what will happen.[14] These ordinary
further facts – *further* facts because not equivalent to facts about what
tenselessly follows what – quite reasonably shape and support our tense-
ridden concerns. It would be grotesque to abandon all such concerns
simply because one does not believe in the moving NOW. The picture of
the moving NOW is at most epiphenomenal to our tense-ridden concerns:
it may naturally emerge out of reflection on the nature of the facts
underlying such concerns, but it is not what we rely upon to justify these
concerns.

Self-concern and Self-referential Concern

Of course, these illustrative claims about free will and the moving NOW
require much more argumentative detail. My purpose here is to provide
the detail in favour of this minimalist claim: self-concern does not require
a Cartesian ego or a superlative further fact. To appreciate the independent reasonableness of self-concern, it helps to appreciate its place in a
wider pattern of self-referential concern, directed outwards from one's
present self to one's future self, one's friends, family, acquaintances,
neighbourhood, and so on. Typically, each of us finds him or her self
within a network of personal and institutional relationships, as a member
of a given family, a friend of particular friends, an acquaintance of

various acquaintances, a colleague of certain colleagues, an officer of several institutions. In the best case, one more or less identifies with each of these – that is, cares for their good in a non-derivative way. To be non-derivatively concerned for one's family, for example, is to care about the weal and woe of its members, perhaps also to care for the family's collective weal and woe, *and* to care about these things for the sake of the family and its members, not simply because their weal and woe contributes to other things one cares about, such as one's own good, or the flourishing of one's community, or the world's becoming a better place. Not only is it reasonable to have such a non-derivative concern for one's family, but a family member who had only a derivative concern would be regarded as lacking a kind of attachment which is often a central part of living a significant life. So too with one's identification with, or non-derivative concern for, one's future self. One can fail to identify with one's future self. But this will seem reasonable only if there is some considerable reason to inhibit the natural tendency to so identify, the natural tendency around which is built one's concern that one's own life continue, go well, and be worthwhile.

So there is a pattern of concern which is self-referential – it is *my* life, *my* friends, *my* acquaintances, *my* community, about which I especially care. However, this self-referential pattern of concern is not thereby egoistic. In valuing non-derivatively the well-being of others, I am motivated to act on reasons other than the promotion of my own well-being. Thus, many of us are prepared to sacrifice a considerable amount of our own well-being in order that the lives of our parents, children or friends go better. As the bonds of attachment and loyalty weaken, we are much less naturally and easily moved to sacrifice. For most of us, the claim of our common human family is felt to be comparatively weak alongside more parochial claims.

However, such a parochial bias is not necessarily at odds with generalized benevolence, the non-self-referential desire that the world should go better, that suffering should be lessened, and that all should be provided with reasonable opportunity to flourish. For although our strongest and most vivid concerns are self-referential, we are not evaluational solipsists. We do not, and need not, believe that our lives, our family, our friends, are especially distinguished from an impersonal point of view. We naturally have the thought that others equally legitimately have their own distinct self-referential patterns of concern, and are thereby responding to values as real as those to which we are responding. We recognize that the things worth valuing go far beyond our vivid parochial concerns.

Because what counts as a reasonable set of concerns is a holistic matter, and because we are prepared to find reasonable various trade-offs between the extremes of a thoroughly parochial and a thoroughly impersonal concern, it is difficult to say anything specific and plausible about what is rationally required – that is, what it would be irrational not to care about. None the less, since giving some non-derivative weight to self-referential concerns is probably part of many, if not all, such acceptable trade-offs, we can at least say that it is *reasonable, or defensible*, to have a non-derivative, though not inevitably overriding, concern for oneself, one's family, one's friends, one's acquaintances and one's nation. On the face of it, such limited self-referential concern is among the easiest of things to justify. Much is justified only in terms of such concern. Indeed, in order to get into the frame of mind in which limited self-concern and loyalism need justifying at all, one has to take the view that to justify a concern is to show how having it would make the world go better. But we may as well ask: what justifies the concern that the world should go better? Nothing does, or at least, nothing else does. The concern that the world go better, like self-referential concern, is a basic pattern of concern. That is not to say that these basic concerns cannot be defended against the claim that they are unreasonable. In barest outline, the defence of self-referential concern would be that we find it utterly natural, and that, at least so far, critical and informed reflection on such concern has not made it out to be unreasonable.

Parfit is rightly leery of one sort of argument from the naturalness of our concerns to their being reasonable. Against the argument that special concern for one's future would be selected by evolution, and so would remain as a natural fact, however the theoretical arguments come out, Parfit writes: 'since there is this [evolutionary] explanation, we would all have this attitude even if it was not justified. The fact that we have this attitude cannot therefore be a reason for thinking it justified' (p. 308).

The present argument from naturalness takes a different form. It appeals to a broadly coherentist view of justification. The concerns that are justified are those which will continue to stand the test of informed criticism.[15] Concerns that are natural and fundamental have a certain kind of defeasible presumption in favour of their reasonableness; they cannot all be thrown into doubt at once, for then criticism would have no place from which to start. In my view, just as it would be a mistake to attempt a direct and conclusive justification of our basic beliefs about the external world, so it would be a mistake to attempt a direct and conclusive justification of our basic self-referential concerns. What can be said by way of justifying such self-referential concerns is that they are utterly natural concerns, and that, so far at least, informed criticism has failed to discredit them. The defeasible presumption in their favour is so far undefeated. And here the main issue may be joined. Parfit maintains that a crucial piece of information, liable to rationally displace our self-concern, is the fact that the Cartesian picture of our nature is mistaken: we are not separately existing entities distinct from our brains and bodies. There are not the superlative further facts of personal identity which Cartesianism describes.

However, locating self-concern within the broader framework of self-referential concern raises doubts about the exact relevance of Parfit's anti-Cartesian observations. Who would suppose that non-derivative concern for our friends and acquaintances depends for its justification upon substantive metaphysical views about the relation of friendship and the relation of familiarity? Just as these concerns require only the ordinary fact that one has friends and acquaintances, so self-concern seems only to require the ordinary fact that one exists and will exist. What Parfit sees as a lack of 'metaphysical depth' in such a fact – for example, that one's continued existence does not involve the persistence of a Cartesian ego or anything else that would mark a metaphysical joint in the world – seems not to disqualify it from playing an organizing role in one's thought about one's future and past. Even if our thought about ourselves has Cartesian elements, the reasonableness of our self-concern does not crucially depend on the truth of the Cartesian picture.

Parfit aims to show otherwise by means of detailed investigations of the cases of fission and the Combined Spectrum, cases in which, he claims, the facts of personal identity come apart from what it is rational to care about in caring about survival. But as we shall see, the most that follows is that self-concern might be sensibly extended in certain bizarre cases, were these cases ever in fact to arise.

What Happens if we ever Divide?

Future-directed self-concern is both the concern that one will have a future and a non-derivative concern for one's well-being in any such future. The vivid sense that one will *oneself undergo* certain experiences in the future gives one's future-directed self-concern its special and urgent quality. One can imaginatively extend one's consciousness forward in time, anticipating what the future course of one's experience and action will be like from the inside. This is a particular application of a general imaginative capacity to grasp what it is like to undergo experiences. One can imagine what it might be like to be Dan Quayle running for President: one looks out at the by then more pacified press corps, one struggles to remember the script, one vaguely senses one's syntax jumbling in one's mouth, and so on. While imagining Quayle undergoing all this might make one embarrassed for Quayle, it will not arouse one's *self*-concern (unless one is badly deluded about who's who). Of all the actual future candidates whose consciousness can be imagined from the inside, at most one, as a matter of fact, will be physically and psychologically continuous with one's present self in rich and important ways. It is this matter of fact which allows one to give a uniquely directed future focus to self-concern – there is in fact at most one future person whose mental and bodily life is a continuation of one's own.

Given this, philosophers' preoccupation with the case of fission need not be seen as a penchant for amateurish science fiction, but as an attempt to explore the consequences of suspending this matter of fact around which our uniquely focused self-concern is formed. If the fission case is playing this role, then it cannot be a deep objection that fission is neither medically nor physically possible.[16] Such *per impossibile* thought-experiments might none the less teach us something about the relative importance of things that invariably go together. Something we value non-derivatively may be shown to be a mere concomitant of what is really important.

Enough by way of excuse for the fission case. In that case we are to imagine a doubling up of processes either one of which, had it occurred without the other, would have secured the continued existence of a given person. For example, consider a patient Luckless, whose body is badly degenerated and whose right hemisphere is utterly dysfunctional. Luckless has one chance of continuing to exist: his left hemisphere can be transplanted into a receptive and de-brained body. If we let 'Lefty' abbreviate the description 'the person who after the operation is made up of Luckless's original left hemisphere and the new body', then on many accounts of personal identity, Luckless would be Lefty.[17] Given the right sort of specifications of the brain of Luckless (having to do with not too much lateralization of mental functioning), many accounts would also allow that Luckless survives in the variant case in which only his right hemisphere is viable and is transplanted into a receptive and de-brained body – in that case Luckless is Righty. But since we have no problem imaginatively providing receptive and de-brained bodies, we should consider the case in which the transplanting of both Luckless's hemispheres takes place. In this case, is Luckless Lefty, Righty, neither Lefty nor Righty, Lefty and Righty considered as parts of a sum, or both Lefty and Righty in a way that requires Lefty to be Righty despite their spatial separation?

No answer is wholly satisfactory. Each answer violates one or other of a set of principles each of which holds up without exception in our ordinary practice of reidentifying persons. The relevant principles are:

1 Whether some process secures the survival of a given person logically depends only upon intrinsic features of the process; that is, it does not also depend on what is happening elsewhere and at some other time.
2 No person is at one time constituted by two or more separately living human bodies.
3 No person is spatially separated from himself in the manner of an instantiated property.

These principles produce a contradiction when taken in conjunction with the assumption built into the fission case: namely, that persons lack one of the prerogatives traditionally ascribed to substances – that is, essential unity. Thus, entertaining fission involves entertaining the idea that each person has two (or more) subparts such that the survival of either one of these subparts in the right environment can secure the survival of the person. Part of the importance of the fission case is that by imaginatively violating essential unity it illustrates how we might not be mental or physical substances. Such a violation is very surprising from the point of view of our ordinary practice of reidentifying persons, a practice which takes it for granted that a person has at most one future continuer of his physical and mental life.

There are determinate facts about personal identity in specific cases only if our concepts of a person and of being the same person determinately apply in those cases. When a case necessarily violates some principle relatively central to our conception of persons and their identity over time, the concepts of a person and of being the same person over time may not determinately apply in that case, so that there may be no simple fact about personal identity in that case. This is how it is in the fission case. Hence the various philosophical accounts of who is who in the fission case are best seen as proposals about how to extend our practice to a case where it presently gives no answer. Parfit takes essentially this line about the facts in the fission case. He writes that the question of who is who is 'empty', and then goes on to say that the best way to view the case (extend our practice to the case?) is to take it that no one is identical with either of his fission products. One might balk at the argument Parfit offers against the contending resolutions.[18] However, the important points are that, relative to our practice as it stands, the fission case (i) violates the ordinary presupposition of essential unity; (ii) is, as a result, an indeterminate case; and (iii) also violates a presupposition of our future-directed self-concern by providing more than one future person to continue an earlier person's mental and bodily life. These last two points are crucial for a proper assessment of the practical upshot of arguments from the fission case.

What Matters when we Divide?

Parfit claims that the practical upshot of the fission case is quite general: that personal identity does not matter. This, he claims (p. 262), is something that a reductionist must accept. As an ontological reductionist who believes in ordinary further facts, I deny it, and deny it on reductionist grounds.

The question of whether personal identity matters may be clarified as follows. Consider self-referential concern, and in particular self-concern. As they stand, these concerns, or at least those of them not directed at institutions and plural subjects, are *structured* in terms of the relation of personal identity. It is the person with whom I am identical that I am especially concerned about, along with the persons identical with my family members, friends and acquaintances. We can imagine an alternative pattern of special concern structured around R – psychological continuity and connectedness – rather than around identity. Let us call this alternative pattern of concern 'R-variant concern'. Since R involves the relation of psychological connectedness, a relation that holds to varying degrees, R-variant concern will most plausibly be scalar, dropping off as psychological connectedness weakens across lives.[19]

In so far as Parfit is advocating what he calls the Moderate Claim – that it is R, and not identity, which fundamentally matters – he is maintaining that reason is on the side of adopting R-variant concern in the place of what I have called self-referential concern. Since R-variant concern is also in a certain way self-referential, being a concern for the R-descendants of people with whom *I* now have certain relations, we can distinguish when we need to by referring to ordinary self-referential concern, or ordinary concern for short. (Parfit also considers an Extreme Claim which has it that not even R matters fundamentally. This would imply that not even R-variant concern is rationally defensible. More on extreme claims below.)

The fictional device of teletransportation can be used to make vivid the details of R-variant concern, and hence the import of the Moderate Claim. In standard teletransportation, a person's body is scanned and destroyed by the scanning, while at another, possibly distant point a cell-by-cell replica is created in an instant with available matter and the information obtained from the original body by the scanner. Teletransportation thereby secures that R holds between the person with the original body and the person with the newly made body. However, R holds because of an abnormal cause – the operation of the scanner and the reproducer – as opposed to the normal cause – the persistence of a functioning brain.

I am among those who regard the teletransporting scanner and repro-ducer as a xerox machine for persons with the unfortunate property of destroying not only the original body but the original person. That this is the case seems vividly illustrated when we consider standard teletransportation alongside branch-line teletransportation, in which the scanner collects information without destroying the original body. In this case it is obvious that a xerox or replica of the original person is produced at some distance from the original body.[20]

Suppose branch-line xeroxing were used to provide personnel for a deep space probe whose mission would never return it to earth. Suppose that those about to be xeroxed believe that it is just xeroxing – that is, they believe that they will be scanned, will survive the scanning, and that R-related replicas will be produced. Given this belief and beliefs about the horror of the mission, each person facing xeroxing strongly prefers that his 'replica' rather than he is sent on the mission. This is a manifes-tation of ordinary self-concern. Each has a bias in favour of himself and his own welfare as against that of strangers who happen to be R-related to him.

The Moderate Claim implies that this is a mistake. Even given the horrors of the space mission, there is no good reason for them to prefer that their replicas be sent off in the space probe. For the Moderate Claim is that it is R, and not personal identity, that matters. R will hold between any person before branch-line teletransportation and his replica. Indeed, we can easily imagine cases in which replication results in the original person being more strongly connected psychologically to his replica than to his later self: the scanning may produce as an after-effect mild psycho-logical disorientation in the original person. In these cases in which a person can anticipate that his replica will be more psychologically con-nected to him than his future self will be, the Moderate Claim implies that he should be more concerned for his replica, and so should prefer that his replica be left to live out the better life on earth. Such are the consequences of R-variant concern.

Related points apply to the other special relations which provide the bases for the rest of our ordinary self-referential concerns. If I believed the Moderate Claim, I would believe that everything which it is rational for my friend to care about in caring about survival would be secured if in the near future he were replaced by his replica. Indeed, in the case of a more psychologically connected replica, I would believe that he should prefer the survival of the replica to his own survival. Suppose it is settled that either my friend or his about-to-be-generated replica will be sent into deep space. When my friend is asleep, his replica will be produced. My friend will wake with some memory loss, and will be uncharacteris-tically irritable for a week. At the end of the week he will be whizzing past Neptune, while his calm, clear-headed replica has taken over his life on earth. If I believed in the Moderate Claim, I would believe that my friend has good reason *antecedently* to prefer this outcome to the alternative one. But how, then, can I be more discriminating on his behalf than I believe he ought to be on his own behalf? I ought antecedently to prefer that his replica be left behind with me and his other close friends. Identity itself is to be given no non-derivative weight within R-variant concern. Friendship, with its bias against substitution *salvis amicitiis*, a bias that is stronger as the friendship is more intimate, has come to an end.

To bring out the inhuman element in all this, imagine my friend discovering that I held this view about his upcoming space trip – that I preferred the clearer-headed replica to be left on earth. My friend might reasonably object that I did not care for him for his own sake, that he was for me simply a stage in a potential parade of persons appropriately tied together psychologically. Indeed, my readiness to be more attached to a more psychologically connected replica shows that *he* is not really the object of my friendly concern. I seem to care about psychological relations more fundamentally than I care about particular people.

There would be something right about these rebukes. Friendship does constitutively involve valuing the friend for his own sake and not being disposed to weaken the bonds of friendship just because of some psychological change in the friend. If I believe that I should transfer my affections to a person I am just about to meet, and so have not shared my life with, then the claim of friendship, as opposed to the claim that I find my so-called friend admirable, agreeable, genial, *simpatico*, is thrown into doubt. And as friendships become more intimate, all this is more pronounced. We can understand a husband who cares little when he discovers that his wife recently replaced her lost wedding-ring with a replica produced by the branch-line method, but what are we to think of a husband who would remain just as calm in the face of his wife's imminent replacement in his life by her replica. He is not exactly like the man who can easily transfer a long-standing love to a newly met identical twin of his lover. He may not simply love a type which his wife exemplifies. On the other hand, he does not simply love his wife as a person, but rather as a stage in a potential parade of persons. Perhaps there is something very sad about this, even if his wife would not object to being loved in this way, having been won over to the ways of R-variant concern. People have become secondary to the R-interrelated parades they head.[21]

That is to say, if the Moderate Claim were true, ordinary self-referential concern with its special place for people would be an indefensibly limited pattern of concern. On the required variant pattern, we would care as much for the R-related descendants of our friends, lovers, family and acquaintances. This is what the claim that it is not identity but R (psychological continuity and connectedness) that fundamentally matters comes to. As a defender of this claim, Parfit is not simply committed to saying that it would be acceptable to adopt R-variant concern. Rather, this is rationally required – ordinary concern is irrationally limited as it stands.[22]

This seems on the face of it a very strong result to extract from reductionism about personal identity, a thesis to the effect that the holding of personal identity over time consists merely in the holding of patterns of psychological continuity and connectedness, and therefore not in the persistence of a Cartesian ego. Parfit's argument for the claim that R, and not identity, is what matters comes in two distinguishable parts. First, he takes the case of fission to provide an argument that one should not be specially concerned that R holds uniquely between oneself and some future person. Then, by claiming that for a reductionist teletransportation is not significantly worse than ordinary survival, he argues that we should not be specially concerned that the holding of R be secured in the normal way – as a result of the activity of a unified physical basis of mental life.

About the case of teletransportation Parfit writes:

> My attitude to [the] outcome should not be affected by our decision whether to call my Replica me. I know the full facts even if we have not yet made this decision. If we do not decide to call my Replica me, the fact
> (a) that my Replica will not be me
> would just consist in the fact
> (b) that there will not be physical continuity,
> and
> (c) that, because this is so, R will not have its normal cause. (pp. 285–6)

Parfit continues:

> Since (a) would just consist in (b) and (c), I should ignore (a). My attitude should depend upon the importance of facts (b) and (c). These facts are all there is to my Replica's not being me. When we see that this last claim is true, we cannot rationally, I believe, claim that (c) matters much. It cannot matter much that the cause is abnormal. It is the *effect* which matters. And this effect, the holding of Relation R, is in itself the same. (p. 286)

Parfit talks about deciding to call my replica by standard teletransportation me because he believes that the case of teletransportation is a case in which the facts of personal identity are indeterminate. As in the case of fission, he believes that there is a best extension of our practice of making judgements of identity to that case – one is not identical with one's replica.

Since the argument for indeterminacy we gave in the case of fission has no strict analogue in the case of teletransportation (see n. 20), I do not agree that teletransportation is an indeterminate case. Even standardly imagined teletransportation is a case of xeroxing,[23] so (a) is just a fact. But when it comes to settling what matters, we should consider both hypotheses.

Take first the hypothesis that teletransportation is an indeterminate case. We saw that one presupposition of our future-directed concern was that at most one future person will continue our mental and bodily life. Another presupposition of future-directed concern is that given any future person there is a simple matter of fact as to whether this person is oneself or not. The idea that there may be no answer to this question initially boggles future-directed concern. When we discover that the determinacy of personal identity is not guaranteed in every case, we should look to see if there is a plausible way of extending ordinary concern to those cases in which its presuppositions are violated. One promising idea is this: look to see if in the indeterminate case a significant core of the relations which ordinarily constitute identity is none the less to be found. Since we have an indeterminate case, so not a case of non-identity, some such significant core will be there. As a way of coping with the failure of the presupposition of determinacy, one could reasonably take the holding of that significant core as a good surrogate for determinate identity. On the hypothesis that teletransportation is an indeterminate case, the significant core – the core which accounts for it not being a simple case of non-identity – is the holding of R. *So in teletransportation understood as an indeterminate case we have good reason to care about R much as we would care about identity*. The good reason comes from a sensible way of extending our self-concern to a case it is not as yet made for. But the crucial point is that we have here simply grounds for a *local* extension of our self-concern in those cases in which a crucial presupposition of that concern is violated. In the cases which make up ordinary life, in which the presupposition of determinacy is satisfied, there is no effect upon the reasonableness of organizing our concerns in terms of identity. No movement to R-variant concern is warranted. Even in the case of branch-line replication one still should not care for one's replica as one cares for oneself. For one is determinately not identical with one's branch-line replica.

Within Parfit's own framework this way of admitting but quarantining his claims about what concerns are reasonable in indeterminate cases will seem surprising. Parfit's central motivating idea is that what is important about the indeterminate cases he discusses is that those cases show that something crucial to our concerns – the superlative further fact of identity – is not only missing in those cases, but is always missing. But in discussing these cases it would be begging the question to assume that the superlative fact is crucially important to us. These very cases are themselves supposed to show that in the absence of the superlative further fact, we have no reason to care fundamentally about identity. But they do not show this. They are indeed cases in which something crucial to self-concern's getting a purchase is missing – namely, an ordinary, determinate, further fact of personal identity or difference. But in almost all ordinary cases this is not missing; there is an ordinary, determinate, further fact of personal identity or difference. Hence the very limited relevance of indeterminate cases.

Given the alternative hypothesis that one simply does not survive teletransportation, it patently does not follow that since the fact (a) that my replica will not be me just consists in the two facts (b) that there will be no physical continuity, and (c) that R will not have its normal cause, therefore 'my attitude should just depend upon the importance of facts (b) and (c)'. Rather, the defender of ordinary concern will argue *from above*: it is not that one should have a bizarre non-derivative preference in favour of R being secured by the functioning of human tissue instead of a machine. Instead, the first way of securing R is just a necessary condition for one's continued existence. Since, under mildly optimistic assumptions about one's future, concern for one's continued existence is eminently sensible, it is eminently sensible to have a derivative concern that R be secured by the persistence of one's brain. One needs no brute partiality for processes involving organic molecules in order to defend ordinary concern.

Some might think that this argument from above just produces a stand-off because it is merely equipoised with Parfit's argument 'from below' – namely, that since personal identity consists in brain-based R, and since a strong non-derivative preference for brain-based realization of R is hardly defensible, it follows that R is about as worth caring about as identity is. But as against the idea of equipoise, the argument from below is no counter-consideration at all. It is disastrously flawed. First, as we shall see, it depends on a fallacious additive picture of values. Second, it cannot be consistently applied unless one is prepared to embrace nihilism.

This second point readily emerges from the general plausibility of a denial of superlative further facts. It may well be that all the facts in the manifest world of lived experience supervene upon micro-physical facts – that is, facts about how the basic properties are distributed over some fundamental field or plenum. Particular ontological reductions for every object, event, state and process in the manifest world will locate for each its own particular patterns of constituting facts in the fundamental realm. Now take any valued object, event, state or process and the fact that it exists, obtains or occurs. That fact will be constituted by facts about micro-physical properties, facts about which one will have no particular non-derivative concern. If one took the argument from below seriously, one would conclude that the previously valued object is not worthy of concern. Generalizing the argument, we derive nihilism: nothing is worthy of concern. But this is not a proof of nihilism. It is a *reductio ad absurdum* of the argument from below. We should not expect to find the value of the things we value divided out among their constituents. That is to say, the argument from below depends upon a fallacious addition of values.

The Argument from Intrinsic Features

Parfit's main argument from the fission case is that although one's forth-coming fission could not promise (determinate) identity or continued existence, nothing worth caring about in caring about one's continued existence is missing. For, Parfit claims, whether one has reason to be especially and directly concerned for some future person can depend only on the intrinsic features of the relation between oneself and that future person (p. 263). In fission one stands in a relation to Lefty which is in all intrinsic respects like the relation one stands in to Lefty when only Lefty proves viable. But when Lefty alone proves viable, one is identical to Lefty. So, by Parfit's principle that only intrinsics matter here, it follows that in fission one gets something that is as much worth caring about as identity or continued existence. Indeed, a corresponding application of Parfit's principle to one's relation to Righty implies that one gets what matters twice over. Although it is a necessary condition of identity, uniqueness does not in fact matter; that is, it is not a reasonable object of concern. So identity is not what matters. What matters are the more particular relations which hold twice over in the fission case.

Whence the plausibility of the crucial principle that whether one has reason to be specially and directly concerned about some future person depends only on the intrinsic aspects of the relation between oneself and that future person? Certainly not from the plausibility of the general claim that extrinsic features do not matter. We often take extrinsic features to be highly relevant to how we evaluate some fact or relation.[24] Rather, whatever plausibility Parfit's principle has seems to derive from what we earlier saw to be a presupposition of future-directed concern: namely, that at most one future person will continue one's mental and bodily life. In taking ourselves to be unified substances, we suppose that we will have at most one such future continuer, hence that whether some process represents our continuation depends only upon intrinsic features of that process, *and hence that* whether some process is rightfully taken to ground direct future concern can depend only upon intrinsic features of that process.

If this is the basis of the appeal of the crucial principle that only intrinsic features matter, then to use that principle to show something about what matters in the fission case is to try to walk out on a branch one has just taken some trouble to lop off. The very case of fission itself undermines essential unity, violates the presupposition that one will have at most one continuer, threatens the ordinary idea that only intrinsic features matter to identity, and so undermines the basis for the principle that only intrinsic features can matter. Thus no one is in a position to appeal to this last principle in the fission case. The plausible basis of the principle is undermined in the very description of the fission case.

None the less, I do think that it is reasonable *although not rationally required* to extend one's future-directed concern in the fission case, so to care about each of one's future fission products as if each were oneself. Although I could understand someone doing otherwise, I would not make a significant sacrifice to have someone intervene in my upcoming fission to ensure that only the transplanting of my left hemisphere proved viable. And this is my reaction even though I believe that only then would I determinately survive the procedure. Sydney Shoemaker adopts the same attitude in his discussion of fission, and concludes with Parfit that identity cannot be what matters fundamentally.[25] Have we at last hit upon a successful argument for Parfit's desired conclusion, or at least a weakened version of it: namely, that it is at least reasonable to take the view that identity never matters fundamentally, so that moving to R-variant concern is at least reasonable?

No, we have not. It is one thing to conclude that in the fission case (neurally based) R, and not identity, is the relation in terms of which one should extend one's special concern. But as we saw with the quarantining manoeuvre above, it is quite another to conclude that quite generally it is (neurally based) R that matters. Fission is a case in which at least two presuppositions of our special concern are violated. The first is that it is always a determinate matter whether one is identical with some given future person. The second is that at most one future person will continue one's mental (and physical) life. When such presuppositions are violated, future-directed concern neither determinately applies nor determinately fails to apply. It is reasonable to try to find a natural extension of such concern for such cases. In that regard, an appealing idea is to look for a significant core of the relations which constitute identity in the determinate cases. If we are reductionists who emphasize the importance of a continuous physical basis for mental life, then we will find in the fission case a reasonable basis for a local extension. In such an indeterminate case it will then seem reasonable to extend our concerns in accord with the holding of neurally based R. This relation holds twice over, and to the same degree as in some cases of determinate identity: for example, when only Lefty survives. If we instead take ourselves to be essentially human beings, then the important core of what constitutes identity is still discernible in the fission case: that is, the persistence of enough of the brain to be capable of continuing the mental life of the original subject. This important core also holds twice over in the fission case. So were we ever to face fission, it would be reasonable to care about our fission products as we would care about a future self. *But this is not because identity is never what matters; rather, this is because caring in this way represents a reasonable extension of self-concern in a bizarre case.* Of course this does not mean that we might not have further practical reasons to avoid fission – for example, in order to avoid intractable squabbling over spouses, houses and jobs. It is just to say that there is no inevitable and universal objection to it from the point of view of appropriately extended self-concern. The resultant impact on ordinary self-referential concern would be much more local and conservative than the move to R-variant concern. With one possible class of exceptions, locally modified concern would differ from ordinary concern only in certain bizarre cases which may never in fact arise. Identity would always in fact be what matters. The exceptions involve gradually coming into being and passing away. On a reductionist view of personal identity, there may be no fact of the matter as to just exactly when a person begins to exist and when he ceases to exist. In such cases what is indeterminate is whether we have a person at all. As a result, there will be no determinate fact of personal identity. This is slightly less surprising than the situation in Parfit's indeterminate cases, for in those cases there was a determinate fact about a person existing at one time and a person existing at another. What was indeterminate was whether these were the same person.

However, since the presupposition of determinacy is violated in cases involving coming into being and passing away, an extension of self-referential concern may again be reasonable. We should look in such cases for an important core of the relations which make up identity in the determinate cases – for example, overlapping links of strong mental and physical connections across time. And we should extend our concern to the extent that such strong links hold. Such an adjustment represents only a possible deviation from ordinary concern. Ordinary concern may implicitly have made just such an accommodation already.

In any case, neither R nor brain-based R nor the persistence of enough neural capacity to continue mental life would be the relation around which our self-referential concerns are almost always organized. Identity would keep this privileged role. Within locally modified concern the importance of R or the other relations in a few cases would be parasitic on the importance of identity.

A telling case from Susan Wolf nicely highlights the differences between R-variant concern and locally modified concern. Suppose with Wolf that small children are not very strongly connected psychologically to the adults they will become. R-variant concern would have us care considerably more for our present children than for the adults they will eventually become. But then, as Wolf asks, why should a parent reduce the happiness of the child she loves so much in order to benefit a remote adult she loves so little? R-variant concern will give no special weight to the obvious answer: that one loves the person the child is, and the remote adult is that person. As a result, R-variant concern would find little place for disciplining children for the sake of the adults they will become. If parents acted accordingly, the results would probably be pretty bad.

Wolf argued from these and other bad effects of R-variant concern to it not being reasonable to adopt such a pattern of concern.[26] Parfit jibs at the whole strategy of argument, suggesting that reasonable adjustment to the discovery of error may none the less have some bad effects. Parfit also hopes that the good will outweigh the bad.[27] (He might also have added that on his view a consequentialist morality will take up some of the slack in direct parental concern.) The present point is not Wolf's point that because R-variant concern would be nasty, brutish and pretty short-lived it is therefore not a reasonable adjustment. The point is rather that the move to R-variant concern is not a reasonable adjustment because it is much more radical than the indeterminate cases require. Reasonable adjustments are those in accord with what Quine called the 'maxim of minimum mutilation'. A much less radical adjustment is the move to locally modified concern.[28] Given a merely local extension of ordinary concern for the indeterminate cases, the ordinary practice of child-rearing will remain unchanged. For personal identity holds determinately between the child whom one now loves and the adult he will become. The extension of concern for cases of indeterminacy does not apply. Nor will it apply in a massive core of ordinary cases.

All this suggests that there is a false apparatus of generalization at the heart of Parfit's arguments against identity-based concern. If the fission case showed that a presupposition of such concern was *always* violated, then there would be general consequences for our concerns. So, if the existence of a superlative further fact were such a presupposition, the general consequences would threaten. What is evidently not there in the fission case, the superlative further fact, is never there. However, since the relevant presupposition of self-concern is the holding of the determinate, ordinary fact of personal identity or difference, the case has no effect beyond the imaginative fringe.[29] What is not there in the fission case is almost always there. Identity is still almost always what matters.

The Combined Spectrum

Similar remarks apply to the third of Parfit's main examples, the Combined Spectrum. In the Combined Spectrum there is a series of possible cases. In the first case in the series I undergo as little psychological and physical change as possible. In the next case I undergo a slight amount of psychological and physical change, in the next case slightly more, and so on, increasing gradually case by case until in the last case the psychological and physical changes are so extreme that it is clear that I cannot survive them, or indeed any of the radical changes near this end of the spectrum. Parfit writes: 'it is hard to believe that there must be . . . a sharp borderline somewhere in the Spectrum [which separates the cases in which I survive from those in which I do not survive]' (p. 239). That is to say, we have a region of indeterminacy within the spectrum; cases in that region are such that there is no sharp yes or no answer to the question whether or not I survive in those cases. How is one to proportion one's degree of concern for the people around after the various changes that occur across the spectrum? The psychological and physical connections decline uniformly across the spectrum. Parfit's account of what matters might therefore suggest that the plausible pattern of concern declines uniformly with the decline in psychological, and perhaps physical, connections. Parfit tells us that physical continuity and physical similarity will only have some slight importance, except in the case of 'a few people who are very beautiful [where] physical similarity may have great importance' (p. 217). Putting this complication about the physical relations aside for a moment, it does seem plausible in the Combined Spectrum to adopt a pattern of concern which, at least within the zone of indeterminacy, declines uniformly with the decline in psychological connectedness. But is this not to admit that what fundamentally matters is not identity, but the holding of psychological connectedness?

No, it is not. The plausibility of proportioning future concern in accord with psychological connectedness arises from two factors. One is the now familiar idea that by way of a local extension of ordinary concern it is reasonable to organize future concern in an indeterminate case around some significant core of the relations that constitute identity. Here one's version of reductionism will be relevant. Those who believe that human persons are essentially human beings, and who, as a result, think that the persistence of enough of the physical basis for one's mental life is crucial for identity, will reasonably proportion future concern within the zone of indeterminacy in accord with the degree to which the same neural capacity to subserve a relatively rich mental life persists. Depending on the details of the operative intrusions, this may grossly correlate with the holding of significant psychological connections. Psychological reductionists, who think that the facts of personal identity consist in the holding of psychological connections, will directly proportion concern to the degree to which the psychological connections hold. As we move into the zone of indeterminacy, these physical and mental relations weaken to a degree not found between successive stages of a single life. Future-directed concern should be weakened accordingly, progressively so as we move through the indeterminate zone.

The second source of the plausibility of the idea that future-directed concern should drop off gradually as psychological connectedness drops off comes from the reasonable concern that one have, in one's future self or in another, an excellent future executor for one's ongoing projects. This needs some explanation.

Imagine someone who is dying of an incurable illness. A central project of his last years has been the completion of a certain book. No doubt this project has an essentially *self-involving* aspect – that is, it is the project that *he himself* complete the book in question – so that the demand inherent in the project cannot be satisfied unless he carries out the project himself. As the end approaches, it becomes clear to the dying man that he will not complete the book. His self-involving project is doomed. However, unless he is completely self-involved, he will think that considerable value attaches to the non-self-involving counterpart of his self-involving project – that is, the project that *someone* complete his book in much the way he would have completed it. (Notice that this project is still self-referential.) Furthermore, completion of the book in this way would give significance to the dying man's efforts in his last years. So he seeks an executor of his project – someone well equipped to carry out the non-self-involving counterpart of this project. The more a given person has access to the dying man's intentions, notes and drafts, the better executor he will be. The more a given person has relevantly similar psychological dispositions, the better executor he will be.

The moral is quite general. Consider the cluster of relatively long-term projects which give momentum and significance to one's life. So long as one is not utterly self-involved, it is reasonable to hope for a good future executor of those projects, *whether or not that executor is identical with oneself.* In fact, always or for the most part, the only way to have even a pretty good executor is to determinately survive, and not change too much psychologically. But the Combined Spectrum is precisely a case in which in the zone of indeterminacy one may get a pretty good executor without determinately surviving. Hence, reasonable concern for an executor is not essentially tied to one's own future existence. We need only add that so long as the social environment remains relatively stable, some future person will probably be a good executor of one's present projects to the extent that he is psychologically connected to oneself. Since in general we want good future executors of our projects, it seems quite reasonable to proportion one aspect of one's future-directed concern in accord with psychological connectedness. So in the Combined Spectrum this implies some proportioning of future-directed concern in accord with the degree of psychological connectedness found in the case in question. And while the local modification prompted by indeterminacy applies only within the zone of indeterminacy, *this* proportioning will apply not just within the zone of indeterminacy but across the whole spectrum.

Part of the importance of this talk about executors and proportioning is that it brings out that, in caring about our futures, we reasonably want a package deal: as well as our future existence, we want the means to make that future existence a worthwhile continuation of our present life. Too often, even in the best work on the topic of personal identity, we are presented with an exclusive choice of the form: 'What matters, personal identity or the psychological continuations?' As against what the question presupposes, the natural view is that both matter, and that either part of the package is less attractive on its own.[30]

So in the Combined Spectrum there are two grounds for allowing one's concern to drop off across the zone of indeterminacy as psychological connectedness drops off. One is that one's chance of having a good executor is thereby dropping off. The other is that as psychological connectedness drops off, one of the central core of identity-constituting relations is dropping off.

Just to anticipate an objection, consider two close cases in the spectrum, one at the remote end of the zone of indeterminacy and the other just beyond. In the first case, someone survives who is not determinately not me but who is very disconnected from me psychologically and physically. In the second case, someone only slightly more disconnected but who is determinately not me survives. I would not be inclined to make a significant sacrifice to secure the first outcome rather than the second. But rather than being an objection to our proposed scheme of discounting, this seems to me to be what the scheme implies. By the time we have reached the remote end of the zone of indeterminacy, physical and psychological connections have worn out to a great extent. So neither the

concern organized around the constituting core of identity nor the concern for an executor has much purchase.

A point of proper emphasis should be added. I may not have thought
of the best way of extending identity-based concern across the zone of
indeterminacy in the Combined Spectrum. The main point is that, like
the case of fission, the Combined Spectrum requires only a local modification of future-directed concern. Given the local modification, identity
is still almost always what matters. So much for the immoderate position
expressed by the so-called Moderate Claim.

Metaphysics and Criticism

Revisionism has so far fared pretty badly. Parfit's arguments for the
Moderate Claim are met by quarantining our reactions to the indeterminate cases and by recognizing the fallacy in the additive argument from
below. The ordinary supervening facts of personal identity and difference are a real and sufficient basis for self-referential concern. It is not a
probative argument against our identity-based practices that they are not
superimposed upon superlative metaphysical joints. It is enough that
those practices respect the differences among the lives of human beings.
So far in the case of personal identity, the doctrine that I have elsewhere
called 'Minimalism' seems vindicated: metaphysical pictures of the underpinnings of our practices do not represent what crucially has to be in
place if those practices are to be justified.

That is not to say that conservatism must inevitably win the day
against an ambitious practical revisionism. The philosophy of personal
identity need not leave everything as it is. The criticism of metaphysics
can have a practical role. That criticism, at least when it is criticism of the
idea that one or some or all of our practices can be justified in terms of
a demand for them built into the things themselves, is often an important
prelude to a successful revisionary criticism of the specific practices in
question. A metaphysical picture – in effect a concrete instance of the
idea of an independent demand in the things themselves[31] – can help
cement a false sense of the necessity of our practices, depriving the
imagination of alternatives, thereby reducing practical criticism to the
condition of a device in the service of banal meliorism. But pointing out
that the rightness or legitimacy of our practices can never be the solitary
work of nature or supernature is not itself to criticize those practices.
Rooting out false necessity is better understood as a prolegomenon to
criticism. The critical meat is the defence of a concrete alternative.

None the less, in the case of personal identity, it may seem that the relevant prolegomenon must also be the end of the matter. The idea of a radical practical criticism of our identity-based practices, the idea of defending a concrete alternative to these practices as an alternative which better serves our legitimate interests, can seem incoherent. For, as our defence of the centrality of self-referential concern implies, many of our legitimate interests require the language of personal identity for their very formulation. We seem of necessity deprived of an independent practical lever against our identity-based scheme of concern. Any envisaged benefit within the proposed alternative could not literally be a benefit for us as opposed to the differently conformed entities recognized within the alternative scheme.

As against this defeatism, I simply want to mention the possibility that we might be more protean than we appear to ourselves to be. Our turning out to be human beings may be more a matter of what turns out to be personal identity for us as we now are, than a matter of what it always must be, however we might refigure our concerns and expectations. That is to say, what instantiates the relation of personal identity for us may in a certain sense be up to us, a matter more dependent upon our identity-based concerns than it might initially seem. Because human being is just *one* way of instantiating personhood, we might be able to remain the same persons, and so the same subjects of benefit and loss, even if we ceased to be always and only human beings. *If* this were so, and if we could articulate a radical defect in the condition of being always and only a human being, we might find a real critical basis for radically refiguring our concerns and expectations. But that, as they say, is another story.[32]

Notes

1 Derek Parfit, 'Comments', *Ethics*, 96 (1986), pp. 832–72.
2 See Mark Johnston 'Is There a Problem About Persistence?' *Proceedings of the Aristotelian Society*, supp. vol. 61 (1987), pp. 107–35; *idem*, 'The End of the Theory of Meaning', *Mind and Language*, 3 (1988), pp. 59–83; *idem*, 'Constitution is not Identity', *Mind*, 101 (1992), pp. 89–105; *idem*, 'Objectivity Refigured', in *Realism and Reason*, ed. J. Haldane and C. Wright (Oxford University Press, Oxford, 1992), pp. 85–130.
3 I shall not discuss (2). In the most recent reprinting of *Reasons and Persons* Parfit seems to weaken his claim about impersonal descriptions.
4 This has only some appeal as an account of the identity of facts, because some will want to add a further structural condition of the sort discussed below. But adding this condition here would simply reinforce the argument in the text.
5 For an argument to the same effect, see my review of Sydney Shoemaker

and Richard Swinburne, *Personal Identity* (Blackwell, Oxford, 1984) in *Philosophical Review*, 96 (1987), pp. 123–8, esp. p. 128.

6 See Donald Davidson, 'Mental Events', in *Essays on Actions and Events* (Oxford University Press, Oxford, 1980), pp. 207–25. What are mental properties on this view? Perhaps they are rather gerrymandered sets of physical events. I discuss this issue in 'Why Having a Mind Matters', in *Actions and Events*, ed. E. LePore and B. McLaughlin (Blackwell, Oxford, 1985), pp. 408–26.

7 Evaluational properties may be no more than dispositions with physical properties as their categorical bases – i.e. wholly constituted by such physical properties. For such an ontological reductionism without analysis see my 'Dispositional Theories of Value', *Proceedings of the Aristotelian Society*, *supp. vol.* 68 (1989), pp. 139–74.

8 Some sophisticated philosophical objections to this view are addressed in my 'Constitution is not Identity'.

9 Such a view, while at odds with substance dualism, is compatible with a property dualism which finds mental properties to be radically unlike physical properties, and not reducible to them.

10 All this is discussed in more detail in my 'Human Beings', *Journal of Philosophy*, 84 (1987), pp. 59–83.

11 *Reasons and Persons*, p. 212, n. 10.

12 This is typical of conditions on identity over time. See my 'Is there a Problem about Persistence?'.

13 On supervenience see J. Kim, 'Concepts of Supervenience', *Philosophy and Phenomenological Research*, 45 (1984), pp. 153–76.

14 Perhaps the ordinary further facts of tense are categorial facts having to do with our way of constructing our experience of the world. The ordinary further facts of personal identity may be similarly categorial, having to do with our way of constructing our activity in the practical world. For such a suggestion see Christine Korsgaard's fascinating paper 'Personal Identity and the Unity of Agency: A Kantian Response to Parfit', *Philosophy and Public Affairs*, 18 (1989), pp. 101–32. For an attempt to deal with the initial logical problems with the idea that we constitute ourselves by way of our practical concerns and activity, see my 'Relativism and the Self', in *Relativism: Interpretation and Confrontation*, ed. M. Krausz (University of Notre Dame Press, Notre Dame, Ind., 1989), pp. 441–72.

Parfit writes (pp. 165–86) that 'it cannot be irrational' to abandon our tense-ridden concerns if there is no temporal becoming. Perhaps this is plausible if one means by temporal becoming what McTaggart meant – the existence of tensed facts. On McTaggart's argument against temporal becoming, see M. A. E. Dummett, *Truth and Other Enigmas* (Duckworth, London, 1983), pp. 351–7.

15 For a development of this idea and its relation to the concept of value, see my 'Dispositional Theories of Value'.

16 As against John Robinson, 'Personal Identity and Survival', *Journal of Philosophy*, 85 (1988), pp. 319–28.

17 Why the explicit mention of the description? So that the terms 'Lefty' and

'Righty' are not mistaken for rigid designators – i.e. designators which designate the same thing in every possible situation in which they designate anything. If they were rigid designators, then it would be incoherent to say that Lefty would have been Luckless but for the existence of Righty. Nothing is contingently identical with itself.

18 It is too extreme to say, as Parfit does, that other views of fission grotesquely distort the concept of person. For more on fission as an indeterminate case, the view that we could be repeatable across space, and a reply to Parfit's specific attempt to rule out David Lewis's proposal, see my 'Fission and the Facts', *Philosophical Perspectives*, 3 (1989), pp. 85–102.

19 On pp. 313–15 Parfit claims that it is defensible and rational for someone persuaded that R is what matters to have a scalar concern which involves caring less for one's future self as psychological connectedness weakens. However, in the context of Parfit's total discussion, a stronger claim seems warranted. Given that such a scalar concern is very plausible in the Combined Spectrum, one of the two cases central to Parfit's defence of the view that it is R that matters, the form of R-variant concern best motivated by Parfit's discussion is scalar, dropping off as psychological connectedness weakens.

20 Robert Nozick's Closest Continuer Theory, the theory that one is identical with the closest of one's close enough psychological and perhaps physical continuers, would invalidate the argument from the obvious xerox claim about branch-line teletransportation to the xerox claim about standard teletransportation. By indicating that the intrinsicness principle ((1) above) is plausible for ordinary practitioners, I mean to imply that Nozick is wrong about the status of his theory. The Closest Continuer Theory, because it is at odds with (1), is an extension of our practice. This extension is not forced upon us. Principles (1)–(3) are not inconsistent with the description of teletransportation and the branch-line case unless we add what is on any view not utterly obvious – i.e. that we survive teletransportation. So if we are describing how our practice as it stands applies to teletransportation, we should apply principle (1). Hence, when we take the obvious view that branch-line teletransportation is a case of xeroxing persons, it follows that standard teletransportation is xeroxing persons too.

21 Contrast the easily confused case of series-persons. In 'Relativism and the Self' I argue that there could be persons who naturally and spontaneously take themselves to survive teletransportation and who might not be wrong about this, at least if certain further conditions were satisfied. They would be, in Thomas Nagel's useful term, series-persons. Love among series-persons would be strongly individuated love for particular series-persons, not love for parades of series-persons. No series-person should rebuke his friend for caring for his teletransportation product. But he could rebuke his friend for preferring his clearer-headed back-up produced by branch-line teletransportation.

22 Cf. p. 262: 'If we are Reductionists, we *cannot* plausibly claim that of these two relations it is identity that matters.'

23 For us and our kind, at least.

24 In his fine 'Surviving Matters', *Nous*, 24 (1990), pp. 297–322, Ernest Sosa provides the obvious examples of exclusive ownership, winning, unique achievement and intimacy.

25 Shoemaker and Swinburne, *Personal Identity*, p. 121.

26 Susan Wolf, 'Self-Interest and Interest in Selves', *Ethics*, 96 (1986), pp. 704–20.

27 Parfit, 'Comments', p. 833.

28 An obvious but unsustainable objection is that the move to locally modified concern, unlike the move to R-variant concern, leaves us without a uniform basis for our self-referential concerns. There is a uniform basis. We are to organize our concerns around personal identity, and in those cases in which it is only sort of true or partly true that personal identity holds, we are to extend identity-based concern.

29 Suppose that fission took place all the time. Then our concepts would come under such strain that we might resolve indeterminacy by altering our concept of personal identity. Since we take personal identity to be what matters, a nice way of doing this would be to ignore those ontological conservatives who believe in a sharp distinction between particulars and properties and allow that under special circumstances splittable particulars can share some of the traditional prerogatives of instantiated properties – i.e. they can be multiply located at a time. For an argument that this is not incoherent see my 'Fission and the Facts'.

30 David Lewis's paper 'Identity and Survival', in his *Philosophical Papers*, vol. 1 (Oxford University Press, Oxford, 1985), pp. 55–77, is built around the assumption that one needs some complex apparatus of temporal parts to make the answer 'identity and the psychological connections' acceptable.

31 For this idea of metaphysics see my 'Objectivity Refigured'.

32 For part of the story, and in particular for a detailed account of how we might be protean in just the way suggested in the text, see my 'Relativism and the Self'. For help with this essay I would especially like to thank Derek Parfit and Jamie Tappenden. Peter Unger offers a somewhat similar deflationary treatment of Parfit's central cases in his *Identity, Consciousness and Value* (Oxford University Press, Oxford, 1990).

9

Has Kant Refuted Parfit?

Simon Blackburn

From the Opinion that Spirits are to be known after the manner of an idea or sensation, have risen many absurd and heterodox tenets, and much scepticism about the nature of the soul.

Berkeley, *Principles*, § 137

1 The Unity Reaction

It is not obvious that there is a specific problem of personal identity, beyond any problem that might exist about the identity of rather large mammals over time. How could there be? We are rather large mammals, albeit ones with complex psychologies, as well as the other properties mammals share. Complex psychologies give a set of properties that can persist, or fade, or change altogether, along with the other properties we share with animals. They give us a psychological form that is in important respects universal, so that it could be duplicated, and shared with others of our kind who have had the same experiences or have the same mental traits. But it is not clear how that introduces any special problem of identity. If we can count chimpanzees well enough over time, we can equally count persons. And if we are not unduly troubled by concocted stories of fission or fusion, or Sorites-generating changes of chimpanzees, nor should we be with equivalent stories about persons.

While we adopt a third-person perspective, thinking of the identity of friends and relations over time, there is no specific problem. The ordinary changes of life leave us knowing whom to love or punish; if extraordinary stories leave us any more baffled than do those told about splitting and coalescing animals, plants or ships, then it is only because we find it harder to shrug our shoulders. We find it more important to know who is who than what is what. But it is hard to see that this attachment is of much significance; nor would it be likely to survive constant occurrences of fission and the rest. In the case of a friend who undergoes some kind of fission, we can easily become reconciled to having two friends with some pleasing characteristics where before we had only one; or, if we adopt a Lewis arithmetic, where before we thought we had only one. If we knew this was going to happen, we would avoid future-tense ascriptions implying uniqueness, just as we would avoid talking about the scenery further along the road if we knew that the road branches into two forks.

If there is a specific problem, it must come from within the first-person perspective, and indeed this is how it seems. My past is not such a problem: told that I am one of two twins who emerged from a 'splitting' operation, or that I am the result of a commingling of two or many different previous persons, I may be surprised, but I am not knocked off imaginative balance. It is the future that is baffling. A prospect of fission is suddenly urgent, because I do not know what to expect. Take the pure case in which two descendent selves emerge from some operation, and one wakes painfully in noise in a uniformly red room, and the other wakes painlessly in silence in a uniformly green room. However symmetrical the split or however we juggle the properties that fall to one character and the properties that fall to another, there seem in prospect to be only three possibilities: at that time either I will experience pain, noise and red, or lack of pain, noise and green, or I will not awake at all. There seems, in advance, to be no other relevant possibility. Nor is there any solution to be found in blurring the boundaries, by saying in effect that it will be somewhat like waking in green painless silence, and somewhat like the other. Because at the later time there is nobody who has an experience a bit like one and a bit like the other, whatever that might mean: there are two people with their crisply different experiences, and that is all. I may be the one, or I may be the other, or I may be with my forefathers.

Equally with split-brain cases. However these are described from the outside (and the *actual* description is by no means as straightforward as 'two streams of consciousness' accounts make it), we cannot well imagine what it would be for me to both have the experience of concentrating hard upon a physics problem at a time and be concentrating hard upon the words of my friend at the same time. Concentrating hard upon physics means being immune to the chatter of my friend, and vice versa. Rather, such imagining degenerates into imagining me doing one thing while some recalcitrant part of my body does another or perhaps some result pops out of my mouth, perhaps to my surprise.[1]

I shall call this reaction to such cases the 'Unity Reaction'. I suggest that the only specific problem in the area is that of understanding and giving due weight to the unity reaction.

Its due weight may indeed be very little. One suggestion is that the unity reaction is simply a hangover from a Cartesian or pure ego theory of the self. But this is surely the wrong way round. It is not as if a Cartesian theory of the self has any independent appeal: it is surely more probable that the unity reaction is taken to be a buttress to that theory, rather than appearing as a consequence of it. It is not, for example, as Parfit suggests, that people think there is empirical evidence for Cartesianism (in telepathy, apparent reincarnation and so on) and then become led to the unity reaction via that theory, or pretence of a theory. It is rather that the same imaginings that are present in the unity reaction lead people to think they see how stories of reincarnation and the rest could be true. I think I can imagine how it would be for me to have to serve a future life, and hence see how it might be happening for someone else.

In fact, belief in reincarnation and the rest simply could not underpin the unity reaction, because so far as that belief goes, the self could be quite generally fissiparous, with a long, multi-incarnation history one possibility among others: simply by revealing one case of extended unity, the stories put no empirical or conceptual difficulty in front of frequent disunity. Yet that is what our imaginings do. They are therefore not to be explained by prior fantasies of having been Napoleon or Cleopatra, or prior gullibility when others claim so to have been.

Of course, the unity reaction is only wrongly taken to be a buttress to a Cartesian theory. Such a theory explains the reaction by supposing that there is a definite something whose unity is unaffected by whatever is happening to the animal and its psychology, and that either ends up in the red noisy room or the green quiet room or quits the scene altogether. Kant showed that such a hypothesis is quite useless. Yet we should notice that it is only if we believe in such a thing that the problem raised by the unity reaction remains a specific problem of *identity*. Otherwise it is instead the problem of understanding a certain kind of thought, and of seeing how it connects with other thoughts about the self.

Another suggestion is that whatever the original motivations towards the unity reaction, we can train ourselves out of it, and that it would be better, both metaphysically and even ethically, if we did. This is the claim I want to query here. I shall do so by taking another Kantian standpoint, that of the active subject of thought and action. Kant thought of the unity of the self as forced by the need to acknowledge this standpoint, and it is this line of his thought that I want to explore. If it is right, we have to deny a central theme of Parfit's book, which is that a non-practical, 'constitutive' metaphysics of the self can play any part in diminishing the distinctive force of a practical stance such as egoism. What happens when we think what to do is sufficiently different from anything that happens when we think of links between empirical constituents of the world to leave egoism, or other ethical stances, unscathed by this kind of metaphysics.

What I want to propose is that a certain kind of activity, with a consequent purely formal unity of the self, is involved in any kind of practical reasoning. The question 'How will it be for *me*?' maintains an absolute, but formal, grip on this activity. If this is right, it goes some way to explaining the compulsive grip of the unity reaction, or the sense that we must give an answer in the familiar thought-experiments – a compulsion that entirely survives the awareness that the empirical self will have dissolved or merged or split in the cases set up. Similarly, I may want to set about seeing Venice, and this is a project that is successful, of course, only if I do. It is not a project that succeeds if someone related by a chain of continuous and connected states, as a child might be, goes there. Of course, ethically, if I am nice, it may 'matter' to me as much or more whether the child gets there, but it is not the same, and it is a subterfuge to substitute the ethical issue of what matters for the personal question of what to expect.

We might put the conclusion by saying that even if Parfit's metaphysics survives, its ethical consequences are less than he imagines. But a farther-reaching way of putting it is to doubt whether in this region metaphysics is exhausted by the one range of considerations, or, in other words, to wonder whether the standpoint of practical reason is not itself a constraint on anything we can regard as the entire truth about persons (hence my epigraph from Berkeley). But before entering these deep waters, I shall say a little about the more orthodox, 'Strawsonian' objection to Humean, and Parfitian, reductionism.

2 Reductionism

It is often said that Parfit's theory of persons is an update of Hume. It is a sophisticated version of a 'bundle' theory. Then it is said that, like Hume's theory, it is vulnerable to a Kantian refutation. The usual idea is that Kant's refutation undercuts the 'atomistic' basis in the particular self-standing perceptions that make up the primitive ontology of Hume. Equally, an update would undercut the basis of psychological states such as quasi-remembering, that, with relations of continuity and connectedness, and together with physical states of body at a time, make up that of Parfit. Undercutting the basis means showing that Hume or Parfit get the priorities wrong. The individual person or self precedes the individual experience or mental state or perception that it possesses. The individual psychological state might be thought of as adjectival or adverbial compared to its subject, dependent upon it like a dent is dependent upon a dented surface, or a state of travelling at a certain velocity is dependent upon an object travelling. Similarly, the 'quasi-memory' or mental state abstracted from the question of its truth as an intentional state presenting a state of affairs may be quite parasitic upon the ordinary memory, in the way that Kant thought illusion was 'merely the reproduction of previous outer perceptions, which, as has been shown, are possible only through the reality of outer objects'.[3]

The argument here is bound to be complex, because Parfit's position is supposed to be consistent with admitting the existence of persons as owners of experience. So perhaps Parfit can give the Kantian whatever ingredients he thinks he needs. For example, if 'first-person thinking', or 'I-thoughts', are found to be essential to any kind of thinking, or even to the possibility of experience itself, Parfit can apparently reply that he offers no objection to any such thinking, provided, of course, that it is conducted in the light of the reductionist truth about ourselves. It is not obvious that the Kantian wants to hold out for more than this. Parfit tells us that the 'best-known version' of a non-reductionist view is the claim that we are Cartesian egos (p. 228). And whatever Kant's need for a subject of experience is, it is emphatically not the need for Cartesian egos. These are things whose nature and identity conditions form a subject of their own, explorable by the rational psychologist and bringing a separate source of determinacy to questions about identity. Kant does more than share Parfit's hostility to any such notion. Whereas for Parfit it is a contingent fact that nature does not give us sequences of events that make it reasonable to think in Cartesian terms, for Kant any such thinking, in the face of any course of experience whatsoever, would be illusory.[4] So the distance, if there is one, between them is constrained at each end: Parfit being not quite so Humean, and Kant not nearly so Cartesian, as they might initially sound.

Parfit believes that although persons exist, we could give a complete description of reality without claiming that they exist. These claims have an air of tension, and have led some to suppose that Parfit is really little better than an error theorist about owners of experience, doing no more than playing along with what is really on his view an unfortunate way of talking.[5] The Humean analogy with communities illustrates the difficulty. We might want to claim that a community is an entity distinct from its citizens just because communities have different criteria of identity – they survive changes of citizenry, changes of territory – and can be theorized about in ways that reflect this. But then how can someone not describing reality in terms of communities still be giving a complete description of reality? He might have all the *facts*, it has to be said, without grouping them in those terms. But what about, for example, the

fact that some territory contains two different communities? Either missing out the grouping is missing out a fact, or the original description
contains enough to 'include' such a fact. But descriptions include facts
only because of their logical implications, so this is really the option that
the description gives a base set of facts from which any truth put in terms
of communities can be deduced a priori (for any contingent premises
must be in the description already, if it is to be complete). But in this
case we are not really giving the base description without claiming that
communities exist. The claim that they do at least follows from what
we do describe. It seems better, then, to say only that though persons
exist, we could give a complete description of reality without claiming
that persons exist in so many terms. The fact that they do would only
be implied in whatever else is given in the complete impersonal
description.

Turning the issue into one of whether an impersonal description
counts as complete seems, then, to turn it into an issue about deducibility. But it is not clear that this is the appropriate idiom for ontological
questions. Deducibility is in some respects too weak a notion for ontology, since as well as any question about what follows from what, the
question of the independent standing of the entities mentioned in the
premises is bound to be difficult. But in other ways deducibility threatens to be too strong a requirement: a statue consists in the particles in
their relations, but to whom is a deduction of propositions about the
statue from propositions about the particles open? The metaphysical or
ontological truth about the statue is fairly evident, but it is not at all
evident that there exists some complete description of some selected
particles yielding deductions of truths put in terms of statues. So far as
ontology is concerned, we might do better without any mention of descriptions, by substituting the thesis that we, or perhaps God, could give
not a complete description, but a complete reality without making (separate) provision for the existence of persons. Once the bodies are given,
and relations of 'non-branching continuity and connectedness' amongst
self-standing psychological states, persons follow. This is the idea behind
the supervenience of the person on the basic ontology and relations
between its elements.

Once we have got here, unease about priorities looms. It can take two
forms. The first is that the atoms and their relations, the psychological
states and the relations of continuity and connectedness, could not be
what they are were they not parts of the life of a person. But it is worth
noticing that there may be nothing necessarily vicious even if this is true.
For we might be able to see how the 'particles' come to be what they end
up being by their relations to others, when still it is the fact of their
standing in these relations that in its turn makes up the whole. A tune can

be a sequence of sounds, even if a sound 'being what it is' in some place in the tune is in turn partly dependent upon that place. There is only a problem if the elements are irreducibly dependent on the whole, as if the tune depends for its very existence on the sounds, and they depend for *their* very existence on the tune. This is not true of the tune and the sounds, because we can see how even if the sounds are altered by being surrounded by others, we can properly think of the altered sequence arising from the original atomistic elements. But even this is quite complex. If we thought of sounds as essentially dependent on context, so that a sound in a melody or chord literally could not occur outside it, then it would be truer to say that sounds are abstractions from melodies or chords, rather than that these are constructions out of sounds. I do not suppose we consistently think like this about sounds. But it is easy to doubt whether we have any conception of the individual 'perception' or psychological state in abstraction from its ownership by a subject. If this form of the objection stands, then we, the theorists, are mistaken in allowing the Hume–Parfit priority to individual states.

The more subtle version of this problem goes via the content of peoples' thoughts. Suppose that among the states making up a normal life are self-conscious thoughts, activities and imaginings that depend upon a conception of the self and its future and past existence. Suppose these thoughts include those indicated by the unity reaction. Then it would be as if the Parfitian self (small s) depended for its existence on people thinking, wrongly, in terms of an irreducible Self (capital S). The threat is that enough basic thoughts involve a self-conception that cannot itself be built on Humean or Parfitian atoms. We might try taking what Bernard Williams called in ethics a 'Government House line' about that, simply acknowledging that the vulgar proceed under an illusion about themselves. But this line is not open to Parfit. First, it is central to Parfit's programme of ethical reform that the reductionist view is wholly believable: 'We can believe the truth about ourselves' (p. 280). But second, in so far as the threat concerns basic and essential thoughts, we have no way of contemplating a change: giving up whatever conception of the Self they involve would be giving up thinking altogether. So the two forms of threat may turn out to be equally strong. But they each depend on finding some Kantian line of thought that undermines the reductionist's starting-point.

3   The Self in Space

So the focus is on the psychological atoms from which the Parfitian construction starts, and the question is whether these are essentially and constitutively involved with a strong notion of a Self: a Self that cannot, to fulfil its role, be replaced by a reductionist's substitute.

There is one approach to this issue that I shall not pursue. If we take a resolutely third-person approach to selves, their psychological states and their identities, then it will seem very perverse to start with psychological states and relations of continuity and connectedness between them. This is because it is so plausible to think of any such states only as states of persons, no more a good starting-point for ontology than dents and bruises: dangerous abstractions from sentences describing the dispositions and functioning of people. The reason why I shall not pursue this is already apparent in my emphasis on the unity reaction. Banning the Hume–Parfit priorities in favour of a third-person world will seem like sweeping the unity reaction under the carpet in favour of a problem-free third-person solution, and this, I am arguing, fails to engage with what troubles us.

The Kantian lesson, well-taught by Strawson, can be outlined, at the risk of simplification, like this. We concentrate on the fundamental capacity of conceiving of experience as experience of a world of independently spatially arrayed objects. This is not possible without organization or synthesis, and Kant distinguishes three stages: the synthesis of apprehension, which is just the emergence of appearance in consciousness; synthesis in imagination, or memory, which is the building up of the enduring three-dimensional object from the successive perceptions of its parts; and finally synthesis of recognition in a concept, which is the recognition of numerical identity of perceived object in the succession of experiences.[6] The aim is to show that such synthesis is at the same time the synthesis of self-consciousness: the feat of seeing experience as experience of a spatially arranged, objective world is at the same time the feat of seeing myself as one entity within that world, with a distinctive spatial position and history in time. Without that self-consciousness the succession of experience would remain unconceptualized: it is this synthesis that alone prevents experience from being a 'rhapsody of perceptions'.[7] The difficulty is to connect this line of thought with the unity of apperception, or indeed with the unity of anything at all, except, of course, the external objects whose individuation is the subject of synthesis. Even an out-and-out bundle theorist, and certainly Parfit, can surely reply that all Kant here shows is that for a sequence of experiences to be what it is (experience of an objective, spatially extended world) it must possess, first, an order, and second, the material for certain kinds of imagination or disciplined used of memory and organization, enabling it to represent one perception as related to a previous one in a way that allows them to be synthesized as views of the same object. Without that much we have 'less even than a dream'. The problem is to say why each of the experiences needs to be ascribed to an enduring subject, the same on each occasion.[8] We can pose the problem in programming terms. For a system accurately to represent when a sequence of images is to be classified as one object or several will require considerable order in the sequence and an ability of the programme to 'recognize' that order and synthesize a solution in the light of it.[9] But it would not, on the face of it, require that the programme 'represents' itself to itself, adding an 'I' to accompany its representations. After all, it does not appear to itself (the camera does not typically appear in the photograph), and it need have no ability to make anything of a scene in which it does.

The argument now proceeds to another stage. If this is all a programme can do, it is incapable of making discriminations that we can make. Furthermore, it is essential to our mastery of the concepts of space and time that we can make them. The ability is to distinguish between similar scenes at different places, and to use the fact of our own location to determine whether a memory was of one or another thing at a time. If we did not do this, we could not give a determinate content to memory as memory of a particular thing, since there would be no anchorage of the original experience to one object or another. This anchorage is given by a unified self subject to a speed limit in space, whose position at different times determines possible objects of memory.[10]

We can see the justice of this line of thought. Suppose I am the recipient of information from a source or sources of totally unknown and unguessable position. Then any attempt to build up a picture of the world relying upon them is blocked. If one report has it that a noisy red object is approaching and another that there is a green patch on a red object that is approaching, there is no reason for me to interpret the second report as picking up reference to the first, and if all sources of information had this disembodied quality, I could not know or guess at the occupancy of the world or worlds on which they report. This familiar line of argument shows that without the thought of an anchored spatial location for a source of information, no conception of the objective world can emerge.

But it is very doubtful indeed whether this line of thought delivers any result inimical to Parfit. The general drift is not towards giving myself a foundational unity through time, but towards seeing awareness of my point of view as one position in space, identified, like all positions, by the stable spatial relations of objects. My experience is indeed experience as from a point of view; this point of view is itself located, as are the objects it presents, and like them – in fact, exactly like the one I think of as my body – it moves only in restricted regions at restricted speeds. But no special unity of the subject emerges from these thoughts, because nothing is needed by way of unity or identity or speed limit of the subject beyond what is also needed by way of stability in the other objects in space. And for this nothing is required beyond the stability of my body. But we are familiar with the thought that the identity through time of my body is not an all-or-nothing matter, that it will permit of borderlines and slippery slope arguments, and in some actual or imagined circumstances there will be no unique right answer as to whether it has survived or not. We cannot justify the hard-edged quality of the unity reaction this way.

To avoid misunderstanding, I should say that when I compare the stability needed from something that can be thought of as 'my past point of view' with the stability of my body, I am by no means implying a 'bodily criterion' of personal identity, or closing off the possibility of teletransportation and the like. I am simply making the point that in order to accommodate the Strawsonian argument, nothing more stringent or irreducible about personal identity is required, than is required of moderately stable items of the ordinary world. As far as this point goes, the speed limit requirement and the possibility of building a picture of an objective space with me having one point of view upon it could be met by other means: law-like teletransportations of moderate frequency, or leisurely flotations away from the body of the kind C. D. Broad used to like.

We can now suggest that there is inevitably something self-defeating about trying to undermine Parfitian reductionism from this direction. The aim is to show that an impersonal, or Humean, description of a course of experience, or sequence of perceptions, or experiential route, is not a satisfactory basis for reduction, because the basis is contaminated by an indissoluble reliance on the self, destroying its credentials as a genuinely impersonal ontology. But in the execution of the aim, the post-Strawsonian plays along with the initial ontology. His strategy is to build up the richness necessary in a sequence of experiences for them to contain the material for their putative bearer to think in terms of a self and a world. Far from undermining the initial starting-point, this strategy, if successful, might seem more like a vindication of it. It could be described as showing how any appearance of a need for irreducible reference to a self in our thought is in fact superficial, explicable through the need for nothing more than a stable location, or point of view, conceived of as that from which the information about the world is gathered. I think this gap between the aim and the strategy is inevitable: once we have the 'objective perspective' on the self and the world, we are bound to be thinking in terms of a sequence of experiences and a sequence of physical states. What else is there to think of? And once we do this, a Parfitian or Humean metaphysics is equally predictable, for nowhere in this flux is there material for an all-or-nothing unity of the self. Once finding myself is thought of as finding a stable place amongst the other stable constituents of space, from which information is conceived as being processed, then reductionism is on home ground.

This is far from a knock-down argument. Indeed, I am strongly tempted to suppose that something more than I have found can be extracted from the priority of empirical synthesis over 'Humean', atomistic experience. Nevertheless, the difficulty encourages me to try another, not incompatible, line that can be extracted from Kant.

4 Activity

Some post-Strawsonian commentators on Kant admit that there is little in the Transcendental Deduction to suggest that Kant is primarily concerned with the location of an empirical self in an external world.[11] In fact, the Strawsonian construction covers the ground that Kant introduces in connection with empirical consciousness, which 'depends on circumstances or empirical conditions'.[12] But Kant explicitly distinguishes pure apperception from empirical apperception.

> Consciousness of self according to the determinations of our state in inner perception is merely empirical, and always changing. No fixed and abiding self can present itself in this flux of inner appearances. Such consciousness is usually named inner sense, or empirical apperception. What has necessarily to be represented as numerically identical cannot be thought as such through empirical data. To render such a transcendental presupposition valid, there must be a condition which precedes all experience, and which makes experience itself possible.[13]

In giving us the 'I think' that can accompany all my representations, pure apperception gives us something prior to empirical consciousness; it gives us something necessary to any power of combination or thought, prior to sensible intuition, and capable of exercise in empirical consciousness or elsewhere.

Kant's concern is to emphasize the place of agency in thought: the unity of consciousness with which he is concerned is the unity of an act, bringing into being any determinate combination of a manifold. But action here is not contrasted with cognition. Without action, no understanding, and hence no judgement or experience, is possible.

> This we can always perceive in ourselves. We cannot think a line without drawing it in thought, or a circle without describing it. We cannot represent the three dimensions of space save by setting three lines at right angles to one another from the same point. Even time itself we cannot represent, save in so far as we attend, in the drawing of a straight line (which has to serve as the outer figurative representation of time) merely to the act of the

synthesis of the manifold whereby we successively determine inner sense, and in so doing attend to the succession of this determination of inner sense.[14]

Action is lost in the sideways perspective described at the end of the last section. Even on the surface the loss produces a strain when we try to think of an element in a course of experience 'doing' something, as we surreptitiously do when we think of an element of a series of experiences making use of information, or as Strawson does when he talks of a series of experiences building up a picture of a world.[15] The strain is not merely superficial, or due to the relative unfamiliarity of the idea of an experience doing something. It arises from the attempt to combine two fundamentally opposed perspectives: the practical perspective of judgement and agency and the passive, 'sideways' perspective of an objective ontology.

So far I think many commentators would agree. But they would not agree that anything promising lies down this road. It seems to lead, in Kant's thought, to a hopelessly transcendental self: a thing whose judging operations are responsible for time itself, and whose noumenal freedom is compatible with the sway of determinism over the entire world that we know. If this is the end-product, then it naturally seems better to avoid such strands in Kant, and retreat to the safer ground of connecting empirical self-consciousness with the exercise of other spatial capacities.

If Kant is right that the two perspectives of agency and judgement, on the one hand, and of anything found in an objective, Humean or Parfitian ontology, on the other, simply do not mix, then it will be tempting to give complete metaphysical sovereignty to the latter, and to downgrade the former as at best a question of a necessary illusion somehow required for thinking of oneself as other than passive. Other writers have taken up the practical challenge to Parfit that seems implicit in Kant. But I believe that the tendency (and it is extremely natural) is to allow the reductionist metaphysics, but to try to sever it from its ethical consequences, as if the glass wall separating myself from others can come down metaphysically, but be allowed to remain at least moderately important in practical reasoning. Korsgaard, for example, shares Parfit's view that persons are not 'deeply or metaphysically separated', although she wants to give greater place to an agent-centred, personal concern for my future, analogous to my personal concern for the future of larger organizations of which I am a part: my family or state.[16] And it is indeed easy to worry whether any reminder that we conduct our judgement 'as if' there were a transcendental unity involved, rather than indicating a reservation about the Humean or Parfitian approach, represents a prejudice that with their help we should overcome.

But I want to suggest that we should beware of separating objective, constitutive questions from 'merely' forensic or regulative questions so easily. It may be that it is no good shrugging off the latter and pretending to conduct all our reasoning as if the former alone mattered. It will be a pretence, because reasoning – and that includes thinking of any kind at all – cannot be understood in that way. When I deliberate, I wonder what to think or do: I do not try to predict, passively and from the outside, what I shall do. When I judge, I wonder what to say about something: I do not try to predict, passively and from the outside, what I shall end up saying about it. These activities proceed under the discipline of reason, and hence are subject to norms, and they involve myself as an agent, not as the latest stage of a bundle of separately individuated psychological states. When I think, I as it were take charge of the bundle, and it is only from the outside perspective that this is to be thought of as the passive arrival of more states for it. Parfit is concerned that we can believe the (reductionist) truth about ourselves; Kant is more concerned that we can think the truth, and that includes above all the truth that we can think.

Unfortunately, the metaphor of two perspectives, one active and one empirical and objective, is misleading. Although it is better than thinking in terms of two ontologies – the transcendental versus the empirical self – it is not as if the metaphor is happy either. We understand perspective first in connection with objective spatial order, where we have some sense of one order coexistent with different points of view. It is not so clear what one world, coexistent with, first, an empirical objective point of view, and second, an active one, could be. Any attempt to describe it would, surely, be to describe it from the point of view of description – namely, the empirical, objective standpoint. I suspect that Kant never entirely overcame this difficulty.[17] With this caveat I shall continue to talk of the two perspectives, for our concern will not be with anything 'seen' within the perspective of agency, but with the nature of that perspective and our obligations towards it in our theory of the self.

If Kant is right to separate the two perspectives as he does, the later use he makes of the separation need not be quite as objectionable as it sounds.[18] The central idea has to be that

> When we consider actions in their relation to reason – I do not mean speculative reason, by which we endeavour to explain their coming into being, but reason in so far as it is itself the cause producing them – if, that is to say, we compare them with [the standards of] reason in its practical bearing, we find a rule and order altogether different from the order of nature. For it may be that all that has happened in the course of nature, and in accordance with its empirical grounds must inevitably have happened, ought not to have happened.[19]

Reason in its practical bearing gives us a 'rule and order' different from the order of nature in the following sense. Suppose I am wondering what to do when, say, my guests arrive. In wondering whether to show my holiday slides or offer a drink, I am not wondering how events, under their empirical determinations, will unfold. I am wondering how to unfold them. And if later I wonder whether I should have offered a drink instead of showing the slides, again, I am not speculating about causes, but reliving the moments of deliberation and either endorsing or regretting the practical reasoning they represented. I can look back at myself as an empirical part of the causal patterns, of course, as we do when we distance ourselves from some of our motivations; but this is necessarily different, and necessarily not the only relation the thinking, active mind has to its world.

Kant connects the active perspective with freedom and with independence of time. To take the former first: saying that as I contemplate the future in this frame of mind, I conceive of myself as free is ambiguous. It is true that as I do so, I necessarily think of possibilities as open, for just as I abstract from the empirical order, so I abstract from the causation that its particular evolution may impose. It is not true that I therefore have a determinate conception of myself as both agent and cause but at the same time exempt from empirical causation. Saying any such thing is attempting to assimilate the active perspective to the passive, or the self as agent to the objective ontology of unfolding states, and this is exactly what we must not do. Keeping both points in mind is not easy, but it is easier if we remember the reservations about the metaphor of twin perspectives on the one reality.

It is harder to make sense of the independence of the active self from the temporal order of events. But a preliminary remark might be this. When I present myself imaginatively as in a situation where I might decide to do something, just as I am not concerned with predicting the empirical sequence of events within which my action will take place, so I need not be concerned with its temporal location. Nor need I be concerned with my relation, as future agent, to my present empirical self – I need not be speculating about the train of causal relations my future self bears to me now, nor about the members of my present bundle of memories, character traits, and so on, that I shall take with me in its execution. We will see more of this in the next section. But it has to be said that although we can deliberate without specific reference to particular times, this is hardly defending the doctrine that we here engage a mode of thought somehow logically prior to, or distinct from, our awareness of time.

If Kant is right to insist on separating the reasoning perspective from the ordinarily empirical or substantive one, we might expect that some misrepresentation of reasoning arises from a purely empirical approach. A good example of the kind of misrepresentation possible seems to me to be given by Parfit's treatment of 'Present-aim Theory' versus 'Self-interest Theory' versus 'Morality' in chapter 6 of *Reasons and Persons*. As he sets it up, Self-interest Theory, which counsels that it is uniquely rational to do what is best for ourselves, occupies an unstable middle ground between Morality, which counsels us that it is rational to take into account other peoples' interests, and Present-aim Theory, which counsels us that it is uniquely rational to do what would best fulfil our present aims and desires. The idea is that just as self-interest over time introduces a wider perspective than the present, so morality introduces a wider perspective than self-interest; any advantage self-interest has over present aim is equally an advantage that morality has over self-interest. The detail need not concern us, for what is interesting is the perspective from which 'my present aims' are in principle one factor in a practical reasoning process – a factor which one theorist is making paramount and that other theorists want to make subsidiary. The 'objectification' of the self is evident. For what actually happens in practical reasoning is that my present aims are not one factor in a calculation; rather, my desires and other conative states form the medium through which I take in the different factors. I do not say 'What are my aims?', and then decide from some vantage-point independent of those aims how much to take those aims into account. Rather, I look at the factors that do matter to me – anything from how much it costs or hurts me, to how much it will cost or hurt me tomorrow, to how much it costs or hurts everybody – and make a decision. My present aims are visible only in a sideways look at my reasoning that makes some of these matter and others not. But they do not come in twice, first as determining the way the factors are selected and weighed, and second as factors themselves, amongst others. In this respect my present aims are like the eye through which the visual scene is presented, but which forms no part of the scene itself.

Of course, one can attempt a more detached perspective from which one tries to see some of one's present aims as less important or more absurd than they seem from the inside. But one does not thereby float free of using other present desires and aims, or reasoning in the light of them, any more than when one looks at one's eye one escapes the need to use one's eyes to do so. Any theory of practical reasoning that sees one's present conative state as one factor amongst others in some process of reasoning conducted in a different sphere altogether is guilty of the objectification of the self that Kant is fighting.[20]

In her sympathetic discussion of these matters, Carol Rovane points out the kind of 'sideways' point of view involved:

Parfit tempts us not with the chance of a lifetime, but the chance of two (or more) lifetimes in which we can divide labor so as to make more of our dreams come true . . . If I were to branch, he would say, I (I*, we?) could both write my book and become an accomplished musician whereas in this life I must choose between them.[21]

And she proposes an ethical way out of the discomfort we face when considering such possibilities: 'Persons who branch must know this about themselves sufficiently in advance so that they have, in consequence of their foreknowledge, an attachment to the consequences of branching' (p. 376). This attachment is to overcome the sense of alienation or simple indifference that a person might otherwise have on being told that a branch in some quite different part of the world was equally a descendant of the same original self. But again, we should notice that the perspective is resolutely objective, or third-personal. The attachment to writing my book or becoming a musician is exactly like an attachment to my children doing so. It comes not from any sense of *my* living through it, but simply from a benevolent desire that someone else, albeit someone to whom I am closely connected, does so. It fails to engage the unity reaction, precisely because the question of what it will be like for *me* (evenings in front of the word processor are not like evenings at the piano, so which will it be?) is ignored.

If we thank Kant for stressing the primacy of agency and the traps of trying to conceive of it from within an impersonal perspective, what difference does it make to the theory of personal identity? None, I believe, if our subject is the issue of whether a 'fixed and abiding self' can present itself in the flux of inner and outer appearances. In other words, none if the subject is approached as it always is when we try to describe the conditions for personal identity through time and relate them to the causal and spatial ordering of temporally successive states.

5 Imagination and Unity

The reductionist ontology is held to determine ethical consequences. Parfit talks of its liberating effects, enabling him to be concerned less about the rest of his own life, and more about the lives of others. He finds that it breaks down the 'glass wall' separating himself from others (p. 281). The drift is towards less concern with self and more with general utility. It is perhaps worth pointing out that with a little imagination the impact may be quite the other way: since it is good for *anyone* to visit Venice, and since my 1992 self has, as it were, not been there much more than you have, it might appear equally proper to buy it (as others would have it, buy myself) a ticket as buy you one. But this is not the heart of the matter.

It is difficult to connect the active perspective with the 'unity of apperception', or indeed with the unity of anything at all. But this is not so much a problem as a guide. Kant himself thinks of the unity as a purely formal unity: it is not a unity connected in any way with empirical conditions or 'criteria of identity' of anything whatsoever.[22] When we deliberate, or reason through situations in which, as we put it, we imagine or remember ourselves, it is obvious that we do not find presented as part of the content a single entity – oneself – meaning that in the story we monitor some kind of unifying relation that it supposedly bears to a present self.[23] On the contrary, a typical imaginative narration simply specifies that it is oneself: 'Don't just think of Napoleon surveying the battlefield, imagine that you are in his shoes.' And we obey by adopting a first-person perspective, not by laboriously adding to the stories some fancied connections to the present.

As Williams points out, the right thing to say about such imaginings is that the self, as an object of reference somehow sustained throughout their content, simply drops out. Instead of the dangerous formula 'imagining myself being Napoleon' or 'imagining that I am Napoleon', we have a pretending, or 'fantasy enactment of the role of Napoleon' – a fantasy involving only me, here, now, and Napoleon, or perhaps Napoleon's history as I conceive it to have been.[24] I am not here presented empirically, as part of the narration. If we say that the self is fantasized as present in this kind of case, that is simply through the fact that a first-person perspective is adopted. Treating it as part of the scene because of this would be exactly like Parfit's treating first-person aims as merely part of the field of considerations present in deliberation, or (arguably) like Berkeley's mistake in treating the perceiving self as part of the content of a piece of impersonal imagining.

Once this is understood, then it is easy to see how the Cartesian 'I' gets a foothold. It arrives because, as Williams puts it, we have a kind of speculation which can 'perhaps rather compulsively' make sense – namely, one in which the self is happily imagined to be there just the same, whatever the proposed changes of empirical facts and continuities.[25] But if this is a misinterpretation of the content of such speculations, all is saved: there is in them no pure ego that only accidentally has my history and set of characteristics and locus.

Williams comes upon these kinds of case by contrast with what he thinks of as less problematic cases of 'participation' imagery – that is, roughly, imaginings in which a first-person perspective is adopted, as it would be if the narration of the imaginings is presented as 'I am sitting in a racing car/watching a battle/waking in a green room'. The less problematic cases, he believes, preserve enough of the empirical self for the 'myself' to retain its ordinary reference to the empirical me as person, body or bundle. 'It is, for instance, relative to my real wants, ambitions, and character that the imagined happenings are, to me in them, satisfying or upsetting.'[26] And of course one can take into a fantasy one's own skills or memories, as if one imagined oneself at Austerlitz, with one's knowledge of twentieth-century artillery.

Nevertheless, it seems wrong to infer that in these kinds of case there is a transfer of reference into the content of the narrative. To use Williams's own analogy, the mistake would be like supposing that because I am acting a character who in fact has quite a lot of my characteristics, I am therefore acting myself. Whereas the truth is that it is irrelevant to what I am doing whether the character maintains any of my characteristics or not: in either event I am putting on a persona, and although it may be more or less difficult, depending on how much the persona resembles me, this does not change the logic of the activity. In my Walter Mitty moments I imagine myself winning the Grand Prix and being garlanded by adoring fans, but whether or not I add to the fantasy 'and while it happens, I shall be the same old me with a house, a wife and two children, thinking of Kant' or whether I add 'and while it happens I shall be planning how to collect my Nobel Prize for mathematics' is, as it were, a matter of taste.

We are familiar with the idea that 'I' cannot be substituted by any battery of descriptions, for that leaves open the question whether it is I who satisfies the descriptions. My parallel point is that when I reason about the future, the 'I' cannot be substituted by something with some favourite battery of links to my present self, for that leaves open the question whether it is I who experiences one thing or another at the end of the links.

We can connect this with Miss Anscombe's tantalizing suggestion that 'I' has no referring role like this. In the uses I am interested in, we do not transfer a reference when we imagine ourselves winning races, watching Austerlitz and so on. Miss Anscombe is right that in 'I imagined myself at Austerlitz' the 'myself' is not referential (but you imagined it, for all that). And when we conduct practical reasoning, the question 'What will it be to me?' takes me into my first-person perspective, rather than introducing another object into the imagined scene. And this is quite unlike the 'What will the Eiffel Tower/Mrs Thatcher/the whales be like?' when we carry a straightforward reference into the future, noting as well as we can what changes and links need preserving for the thought-experiment to be well conducted. Of course, still less do we need to place ourselves as we are now empirically into an imagined scene, as when, with the tastes and activities of a twenty-year-old, we imagine a projected retirement, unintelligently mourning being unable to do things that we will not then want to do. The whole point is that the empirical self, just as much as links of connectedness with it, is unrepresented in the narrative. The same is true in the hard case of imagining my own funeral. Here I can take up one perspective (that of a witness) and imagine watching the body (how wrinkled I became, I might think) and my friends. But while I am doing this, I am not in the narrative, even if my body is. Or I can imagine from the inside being stiff and experiencing nothing; I can flicker between the two, in order to try to convince myself that it is really *my own* funeral. But I cannot simultaneously place myself inside and outside the coffin. The unity reaction holds absolute sway.[27]

6   The Glass Wall

This sketch of a Kantian opposition to Parfit leaves many questions unresolved. We would want to say more about relating the active and the passive, and more about ordinary, referential uses of 'I' (these two topics might turn into one). I should mention too that although the unity reaction has here been connected with the active self, it is not only when we consider what to do, but even when we consider what we shall be experiencing, that it maintains a grip, and the connection here is obscure. More could be said, too, to disentangle what is legitimate and inevitable in our capacity for this kind of thought from its flavour of illusion, as if it were presenting us with a unity that actually has no foundation, for the sake of practical affairs and morality. Instead, I shall close by making a few less theoretical remarks about the bearing of all this on Parfit's ethical intentions. Certainly, I believe that a proper view of the active versus the objective perspective requires that the former not be relegated to a 'merely' practical, non-metaphysical source of thoughts that do not aspire to constitutive truth. Nevertheless, its proper place yields some consequences for Parfit's ethical standpoint.

If practical reasoning is essentially conducted from within a first-person perspective, imagining *my* doing something is a very different matter from imagining *someone else* doing something. The imagining is quite different, and if what I have said is right, this difference is absolute, and will not succumb to indeterminacies in constitutive questions of identity of anything through time. Now it does not follow that we should respect this difference in ethics. We might offer the advice: 'Try to think of your taking the compromised job, shooting the innocent sacrifice, etc., just as a case of *someone* doing it', and we might commend people for succeeding in doing this ('Someone had to do it'). But it is fairly clear that we should not always do this. Even from a virtue-ethics or a motive-utilitarian standpoint, we can see why we could want to encourage in me a greater propensity to recoil from the prospect of my doing something than from the prospect of someone doing it. It is our own actions, after all, whereby we do anything at all, including remonstrating with other people who do things. The situation that I am in as a practical reasoner is always first a situation in which I have to decide what I should do. If, inside that perspective, particular boundaries between myself and others become salient, it is impossible to believe that this is to be regretted.

Of course, there will be cases and cases. My recoil may be not an exercise of virtue, but an exercise of squeamishness, or of other failings like fear or false pride. We all know the discomfort of benefitting from the fact that some people will do things that we would not bring ourselves to do. But these cases by no means undermine the distinctive priority of the first-person viewpoint. They merely show that there is a task of deciding what ought to be unacceptable from within that viewpoint, and of then deciding what boundaries one would wish generally observed from within it, and what benefits one might be willing to forgo if such a change in peoples' characters came about. The metaphor of a glass wall is in fact a very good one: my future as an agent lies in a single tunnel, but not one that prevents endless awareness of the decisions and the scrutiny of those in other tunnels. What constraints on action I should find as I look towards my own future doings is a matter of ethical argument, but the constitutive question of what separates the tunnels has no independent effect on it.

Notes

1 The difficulty of describing split-brain patients in other terms is made plain in Grant Gillett, 'Split Brains and Personal Identity', *Mind*, 95 (Apr. 1986), pp. 224–9.

2 Immanuel Kant, *The Critique of Pure Reason*, ed. N. Kemp-Smith, 'The Paralogisms of Pure Reason', A342–405; B407–32. Credit should also go to Locke, *Essay*, bk II, ch. 27, §§ 10, 12, 19.

3 Kant, *Critique of Pure Reason*, B277.

4 Parfit is rightly criticized for generally treating this issue as contingent, in Sydney Shoemaker's Critical Notice, *Mind*, 94 (1985), pp. 447–9; repr. here as ch. 7, pp. 140–2.

5 Quassim Cassam, 'Kant and Reductionism', *Review of Metaphysics*, 43 (Sept. 1989), pp. 75–7. Shoemaker (ch. 7) points out that Parfit repeatedly says that it is because of the way we talk that persons are subjects of experience: he cites *Reasons and Persons*, pp. 223, 225, 226, 251, 341.

6 Kant, *Critique of Pure Reason*, A99–106.

7 Ibid., A157, B196.

8   This problem is forcefully and lucidly presented in Cassam, 'Kant and Reductionism', pp. 87–91. See also Thomas Powell, *Kant's Theory of Self-Consciousness* (Oxford, Oxford University Press, 1990), ch. 1.

9   'Images' here just stands for information of any kind: the problem need not be a specifically visual one, although (not surprisingly) that makes it easier to visualize.

10 Cassam, 'Kant and Reductionism', pp. 91–2. Cassam rightly quotes Shoemaker, 'Persons and their Pasts', in *Identity, Cause, and Mind* (Cambridge, Cambridge University Press, 1984), pp. 19–48.

11 Cassam, 'Kant and Reductionism', p. 93.

12 Kant, *Critique of Pure Reason*, B140, p. 157. The importance of this was impressed upon me by John Kenyon.

13 Ibid., A107, p. 136; see also B132, p. 153.

14 Ibid., B155, p. 167.

15 P. F. Strawson, *The Bounds of Sense* (Methuen, London, 1966), pp. 105–6.

16 Christine Korsgaard, 'Personal Identity and the Unity of Agency: A Kantian Response to Parfit', *Philosophy and Public Affairs*, 18 (1989), esp. pp. 124–7.

17 I inveigh against supposing that there is any easy use of the 'two perspectives' metaphor to resolve conflict in 'Enchanting Views', given to the Gifford International Conference on the work of Hilary Putnam, and published in *Reading Putnam*, ed. Peter Clark and Bob Hale (Blackwell, Oxford, 1994).

18 I am talking only of the First Critique. The attempt to connect noumenal freedom with pure susceptibility to the moral law is another matter, as everyone knows.

19 Kant, *Critique of Pure Reason*, A550, B578, p. 474.

20 I first put this as an objection to Parfit in a seminar conducted by Professor Hare in, I believe, the summer of 1983. It may be that the ethical squeeze on Self-interest Theories that Parfit wants can still be created, by separating aims with a current self-centred content (me-now) from aims with a future self-interested content (me-later) and from altrustic aims (you-now or you-later). The point would be that it is not the fact that an aim is a present aim that matters, but that its object is a state of me-now. Parfit's ethical point would be that if me-later is allowed as a proper aim, why not you-now, or you-later?

21 Carol Rovane, 'Branching Self-Consciousness', *Philosophical Review*, 99 (1990), p. 374.

22 Kant, *Critique of Pure Reason*, A105, p. 135; A363, p. 342.

23 See also Powell, *Kant's Theory of Self-Consciousness*, p. 165.

24 B. Williams, 'Imagination and the Self', in *Problems of the Self* (Cambridge University Press, Cambridge, 1973), pp. 42–4.

25 Ibid., p. 43.

26 Ibid., p. 39.

27 Williams strikes me as ambivalent on the relevance of these matters to personal identity. Although in the magnificent 'The Self and the Future', in his *Problems of The Self* (Cambridge University Press, Cambridge, 1973),

pp. 46–63, he rightly seems to highlight what I have called the unity reaction, in 'Imagination and the Self' the general drift is to downplay the significance of imaginings for the topic. I would like this essay to act as some kind of link between the two, preserving the core of each. I am indebted to Jay Rosenberg and Geoff Sayre-McCord for the request to say something about the funeral case.

10

People and their Bodies

Judith Jarvis Thomson

I

The simplest view of what people are is that they are their bodies.
That view has other attractions besides its simplicity. I feel inclined
to think that this fleshy object (my body is what I refer to) isn't something
I merely currently inhabit: I feel inclined to think that it *is* me.
This bony object (my left hand is what I refer to) – isn't it literally
part of me? Certainly we all, at least at times, feel inclined to think
that we are not merely embodied, but that we just, all simply, *are* our
bodies.

What stands in the way of adopting this simple and attractive
view?

Some people would say that the manner in which death ordinarily
comes on us stands in the way of adopting it. Some people's deaths issue
from total destruction of the body, as in an explosion, but that is not the
ordinary case. Suppose Alfred and Bert are people who died of a disease,
in their beds. Their bodies did not go out of existence at that time. So if
Alfred and Bert went out of existence at that time, then they are not their
bodies.

But did Alfred and Bert go out of existence at that time? Don't people
who die in bed just become dead people at the time of their deaths? Cats
who die in bed become dead cats at the time of their deaths; why should
it be thought otherwise in the case of people? Can't there be some dead
people as well as some dead cats in a house after the roof falls in? The
answer surely is that there can be.

You might have wondered why I have been talking in the plural, of
people. I did so because the only available candidate in the singular for
the plural 'people' is 'person', and philosophers do not use 'person' as a
mere innocuous singular for 'people': 'person' in the hands of a philosopher trails clouds of philosophy. 'Dead people', like 'dead cats', causes

no one any discomfort; but 'dead person', unlike 'dead cat', causes a philosopher (though not, I think, a non-philosopher) to feel at best anxious.

Locke said that a person is 'a thinking intelligent being', and I think he meant that a thing is a person at a time *t* only if it is a thinking intelligent being at *t*, so if we agree with him, we must of course conclude that nothing is, at *t*, both dead and a person. I think he meant us to conclude also that a thing is a thinking intelligent being at *t* only if it is thinking at *t*; and since he said that consciousness is essential to thinking, I think he meant us to conclude also that a thing is a thinking intelligent being at *t* only if it is conscious at *t*. So if we agree with him here too, we must of course also conclude that nothing is, at *t*, both unconscious and a person. Thus nothing is at any time both a person and dreamlessly asleep. But then what on earth could persons *be*? Consciousnesses? Are there such entities as consciousnesses?

Did Locke believe that persons are people? That persons are ordinary men or women, children or infants? Locke said: 'if it be possible for the same Man to have distinct incommunicable consciousnesses at different times' – and he plainly did believe this possible – 'it is past doubt the same Man would at different times make different Persons.' Now one way of interpreting this passage is to take Locke to be relativizing identity – that is, to take him to be saying that the following can be the case: *x* and *y* are the same man, and each is a person, but *x* and *y* are not the same person. Interpreted in this way, Locke does believe that some persons are men. But I think it best to take him to believe that no person is a man, though a man may 'make' a person, and indeed a different person at different times.[1]

Whatever is to be said about how we should interpret Locke, it will in any case be just plain people – ordinary men, women, children and infants – that I will be concerned with throughout. And a thing can certainly be, at *t*, both a man and unconscious. Even a man in a coma. (Isn't it perfectly clear that that is Nancy Cruzan, the very woman herself, lying in that hospital bed?) A thing can even be, at *t*, both a man and dead. ('Dead men tell no tales' is true, but that is not because nothing is both dead and a man.)

Some philosophers may say 'Okay, I give you people. They're just their bodies. What interests me is instead persons, persons not being people.' But I suspect that most philosophers who write on these matters would not give me people in this easy-going way; I think it *is* people whom they mean to be writing about. Most of them do take seriously some theories about the entities they are writing about that are incompatible with the view that those entities are their bodies. But that is not, I think, because they are writing about something other than people; it is rather because they take seriously the idea that people are not their bodies. We will have to look at what inclines them to do so.

I will myself, for brevity, often use the word 'person'; but when I do, I mean it to be understood merely as the singular of 'people'. I hope no confusion will result from this practice.

II

I asked what stands in the way of adopting the following simple and attractive view:

Physical Thesis: People are their bodies.

And I suggested that the manner in which death normally comes on us (in bed) does not stand in the way of adopting it. The most familiar of the other objections to it are objections to it by virtue of being objections to something it entails, namely,

Physical Criterion: $x = y$ if and only if x's body = y's body.

(I here and throughout let x, y and z range only over people.)

But before looking at those objections, let us first stop over a point of interest. What I have in mind is that much of the current literature on personal identity focuses on personal *identity*, attending to what we might call personal *ontology*, if at all, only as something of an after-thought.

Physical Thesis is a thesis about personal ontology. It entails a criterion for personal identity: namely, Physical Criterion. But these two theses are not equivalent, since Physical Criterion does not entail Physical Thesis. On the face of it, at any rate, there seems to be no contradiction in supposing that $x = y$ if and only if x's body = y's body and that x is nevertheless not identical with x's body. (For example, let a and b range over sets with one member. Then $a = b$ if and only if a's member = b's member. But a is nevertheless not identical with a's member.) If this is right, then Physical Criterion does not entail Physical Thesis, and the two theses are therefore not equivalent.

I should imagine, however, that anyone who accepts Physical Criterion is very likely to accept Physical Thesis as well; I should imagine, in fact, that anyone who accepts Physical Criterion accepts it precisely because he or she accepts Physical Thesis.

There seems to be no analogue of this intuitively tight connection between identity criterion and ontological thesis in the case of the other identity criteria familiar to us from the literature on this issue. I have in mind in particular the identity criteria that (very roughly) take something mental, or psychological, to be the mark of personal identity. Is there an ontological thesis you are very likely to accept if you accept a psychological identity criterion? Is there an ontological thesis such that you accept a psychological identity criterion precisely because you accept *it*? Not, anyway, the ontological thesis that people are mental substances: that is a very unpopular view nowadays. A contemporary philosopher is not at all likely to accept that people are mental substances on the ground of accepting a psychological identity criterion, and is also not at all likely to accept a psychological identity criterion because of having accepted that people are mental substances.

I do think this point worth taking note of. More generally, when philosophers tell us their views about personal identity, we should keep in mind that there is a further question to be answered: namely, what people *are*. And if the identity criterion a philosopher offers us is such that if that criterion were true, then it is obscure what people could possibly be, then isn't that a count against his or her criterion? Or might it turn out that there's no saying what people are, the best we can do being to find an account of their identity conditions? (Most philosophers think that this is our situation in the case of sets. But then some of them worry about whether there are such things as sets for that very reason.) In any case, the ontological question is waiting there in the wings, whenever a philosopher is on-stage answering the identity question.

III

To return to the question whether there is something else, besides the manner in which death ordinarily comes on us, that stands in the way of adopting the simple and attractive view that people are their bodies.

The most striking kind of objection issues from cases that descend from Locke's case of the prince and the cobbler. Here are two people, Brown and Robinson, and let us give the names 'Brown-body' and 'Robinson-body' to their bodies.[2] If

Physical Criterion: $x = y$ if and only if x's body $= y$'s body

is true, then it is not the case that Robinson $=$ Brown, since it is not the case that Robinson-body $=$ Brown-body, and that is exactly as it should be. If Physical Criterion is true, then, quite generally, $x =$ Brown if and only if x's body $=$ Brown-body. So far, so good. Now for the trouble. We transplant the brain of Brown-body into Robinson-body, destroying the rest of Brown-body. Let us suppose that the operation succeeds, and that the survivor thinks he is Brown, wants much of what Brown wanted, seems to remember a good bit of what Brown experienced, and so on. It strikes many people as intuitively right therefore to say (i) that the survivor = Brown. It also seems intuitively right to say (ii) that it is not the case that the survivor's body = Brown-body. For isn't the survivor's body Robinson-body? Robinson-body with a new brain? (Compare transplanting someone else's liver into your body. Isn't the result your body? Your body with a new liver?) But if we accept (i) and (ii), then we think that Brown has switched bodies, and we must therefore give up Physical Criterion and therefore also Physical Thesis.

But intuitions in this area are merely openings for discussion, not closings. Let us go back to why people are inclined to opt for (i). As I said, the survivor thinks he is Brown, wants much of what Brown wanted, and so on. What if there had been a slip-up in the process of transplanting the brain of Brown-body into Robinson-body? Let us call the original story Brown-Case-One. In what we might call Brown-Case-Two, the drugs we injected into Robinson-body to prevent rejection of the new brain had the effect of altering the new brain in such a way as to make its configuration resemble that of the brain formerly in Robinson-body, so that the survivor thinks he is Robinson, wants much of what Robinson wanted, and so on. *Here* the only reason to think that the survivor is Brown is the fact that the survivor's body's (new) brain was formerly in Brown-body. But is that of interest from the point of view of the question who the survivor is? Is it of any more interest from that point of view than the fact of your getting a new liver is from the point of view of the question who gets off the operating table after the liver transplant? Everyone, I think, would say that the survivor is not Brown in Brown-Case-Two.

But then it seems plausible to think that the role of the brain transplant in Brown-Case-One – the force which its being the brain that was transplanted has on people's intuitions about that case – lies wholly in the fact that the brain is normally, and slip-ups apart, the 'carrier of a person's psychology'. For where we imagine, as in Brown-Case-Two, that the transplanted brain does not carry Brown's psychology, we are not in the slightest inclined to think that the survivor is Brown.

So what if we imagine that we transplant merely Brown's psychology, without transplanting his brain? In Brown-Case-Three we reconfigure the Robinson-body brain: we reprogram it with Brown's psychology and destroy *all* of Brown-body. The survivor thinks he is Brown here too, and no part of Brown-body was transplanted at all. Many people therefore feel inclined to say of the survivor in Brown-Case-Three, as of the survivor in Brown-Case-One, that he is Brown. They think that transplanting Brown's psychology is necessary for Brown to switch bodies (for Brown does not switch bodies in Brown-Case-Two), and that transplanting Brown's psychology is sufficient for Brown to switch bodies (for Brown switches bodies in Brown-Case-Three as well as in Brown-Case-One). On their view, the force which its being the brain that is transplanted in Brown-Case-One has on people's intuitions about that case really does lie wholly in the fact that the brain is normally, slip-ups apart, the carrier of a person's psychology.

But others would deny these things. On their view, the survivor is not Brown in Brown-Case-Three. They think that transplanting Brown's psychology is necessary for Brown to switch bodies (for Brown does not switch bodies in Brown-Case-Two); but they think that transplanting Brown's brain is also necessary for Brown to switch bodies (for Brown switches bodies in Brown-Case-One, but not in Brown-Case-Three) – they think that the transplanting of Brown's psychology must have been caused by the transplanting of his brain. On their view,[3] the force which its being the brain that is transplanted in Brown-Case-One has on people's intuitions about that case does not lie wholly in the fact that the brain is normally, slip-ups apart, the carrier of a person's psychology.

What to make of all this? Let us call the view that transplanting a person's psychology is both necessary and sufficient for that person to shift bodies *the pure psychological criterion for body-switching*. On this view, Brown switches bodies in Brown-Case-Three as well as in Brown-Case-One. Let us call the view according to which transplanting a person's psychology, and doing so by way of transplanting that person's brain, is both necessary and sufficient for that person to switch bodies *the impure psychological criterion for body-switching*. For my own part, I find it hard to get a grip on why anyone would prefer the impure to the pure criterion. Why is it to be thought that body-switching requires that the transplanting of psychology have been caused by transplanting the brain? Suppose a psychology-transplanting was caused by transplanting a liver. (The drugs injected in the donor to anaesthetize him before the operation caused his brain to imprint on his liver in such a way that, when transplanted, the liver caused reprogramming of the recipient's brain.) Was that good enough? So that what is required for body-switching is really that the psychology-transplanting be caused by the transplanting of just any old body-part the transplanting of which *in fact* causes psychology-transplanting? (Why must some transplanted body-part play this causal role?) Or was it not good enough on the ground that transplanting a liver doesn't *normally* cause psychology-transplanting? (Why should that matter?) So I will concentrate on the pure psychological criterion, making occasional comments on the impure psychological criterion only in footnotes.

Those who think Brown switches bodies in both Brown-Case-One and Brown-Case-Three, and therefore accept the pure psychological criterion, think that body-switching is possible, and they therefore reject Physical Criterion. What do they opt for instead? Well, why do they think that the survivor is Brown in those two cases? As I said, the fact that the survivor in those two cases thinks he is Brown, wants much of what Brown wanted, and so on. That is, the fact that the survivor is in some appropriate sense psychologically connected with Brown. They are therefore likely to conclude that psychological connectedness is the mark of personal identity – in some appropriate sense of 'psychological connectedness', and in some appropriate way of being 'the mark of'.

What sense of 'psychological connectedness'? Let us say that y is at t' psychologically connected with x at t if and only if t' is later than t, and y believes at t' a good bit of what x believed at t, y wants at t' a good bit of what x wanted at t, y seems to remember at t' a good bit of what x experienced at t, and so on. If you think that psychological connectedness is the mark of personal identity, you might well think that something like this is the appropriate sense.[4]

What way of being 'the mark of'? Here there are several possibilities, among which is the following:

Psychological Criterion (Connectedness): $x = y$ if and only if there are times t and t' such that y is at t' psychologically connected with x at t.

If you think that Brown switches bodies in Brown-Case-One and Brown-Case-Three, and therefore conclude that psychological connectedness is the mark of personal identity, then you might well opt for Psychological Criterion (Connectedness): for in Brown-Case-One and Brown-Case-Three, the survivor is at the survivor's waking-time psychologically connected with Brown at Brown's becoming-unconscious-time, and that is exactly why, on your view, the survivor *is* Brown in those two cases – by contrast, of course, with the survivor in Brown-Case-Two.

I stress that if you think that psychological connectedness is the mark of personal identity, you probably have a variety of theses in mind, of which Psychological Criterion (Connectedness) is only one possibility. Another is not itself an identity criterion but instead a thesis about people, to the effect that there are no sudden, dramatic alterations across time in a person's psychology. (Very roughly: a person's psychology is connected throughout time.[5]) Indeed, this is a thesis you are very likely to have in mind if you think that psychological connectedness is the mark of personal identity. It is, of course, entirely consistent with Psychological Criterion (Connectedness).

IV

We should stop to take a closer look at what we have so far.

If you think that Brown switches bodies in Brown-Case-One and Brown-Case-Three, what do you think people *are*?[6] You certainly cannot think that Brown switches bodies in those cases compatibly with thinking that people are their bodies.

I said that if you think Brown switches bodies in Brown-Case-One and Brown-Case-Three, you are likely to conclude that psychological connectedness is the mark of personal identity. It is of interest that one *can* accept the latter cluster of ideas compatibly with thinking that people are their bodies. For example, one can accept Psychological Criterion (Connectedness) compatibly with thinking that people are their bodies. How so? Let us call Bloggs's body Bloggs-body. Psychological Criterion (Connectedness) says that Bloggs is Bloggs-body if and only if there are times t and t' such that Bloggs-body is at t' psychologically connected with Bloggs at t; and couldn't that be true? But do *bodies* believe things, want things, and so on? If we think that people do, and that people are their bodies, we will certainly think that bodies do. And why shouldn't we?[7]

I will call the view that psychological connectedness is the mark of personal identity, and that people nevertheless are their bodies, *the hybrid view of personal identity*.

Since hybridists think that people are their bodies, they must deny that Brown switches bodies in Brown-Case-One and Brown-Case-Three. (*A fortiori*, they must reject the pure psychological criterion for body-switching.) What do they say happens to Brown in those cases? Let us for simplicity focus on Brown-Case-Three, in which no body parts are transplanted: we merely do a brain-reprogramming. Hybridists think that psychological connectedness is the mark of personal identity, so they accept (i) that the survivor = Brown. If they also accept (ii) that it is not the case that the survivor's body = Brown-body, then they must give up Physical Criterion. It follows that they must also give up the thesis that people are their bodies. Hybridists must therefore deny (ii): they must say that the survivor's body really is Brown-body.

There is only one way in which they can make this out: they must accept the metaphysic of temporal parts.

Suppose we say that for every physical object O and every time point and time stretch T through which O exists there is an entity E such that E exists only throughout T, and E occupies every place throughout T that O occupies throughout T, and E is part of O – indeed, O is just the fusion of such entities E. Then in particular, a person's body is the fusion of such entities E, which are its temporal parts.

Now I said at the outset of my description of the case of Brown: here are two people, Brown and Robinson, and let us give the names 'Brown-body' and 'Robinson-body' to their bodies. But which bodies exactly are their bodies? There are what the vulgar think are Brown's body and Robinson's body, but the hybridist can say that the vulgar are just mistaken.

Suppose that the brain-reprogramming is performed at t. Then if psychological connectedness is the mark of personal identity, Brown does, at t, what the vulgar would say is body-switching. The hybridist can instead say that Brown's body is *really* the fusion of (a) the beginning-to-t temporal part of what the vulgar would call Brown's body and (b) the t-to-ending temporal part of what the vulgar would call Robinson's body. If that is what Brown's body really is, then Brown does not switch bodies at t: he has the same body throughout. And if 'Brown-body' is the name of Brown's body – Brown's *real* body – then it follows that the survivor's body = Brown-body.

It was not the metaphysic of temporal parts itself that yielded this conclusion about what Brown's real body is: accepting the metaphysic of temporal parts does not by itself commit one to any view at all about personal identity, and *a fortiori* does not by itself commit one to hybridism. If you accept the metaphysic of temporal parts, you believe that every human body is the fusion of its temporal parts; but that leaves open which temporal body-parts you will believe are parts of a given human body – which temporal body-parts you will believe are, as we may put it, co-bodily.

Suppose you accept the metaphysic of temporal parts. If you also accept hybridism, then you think that people are their bodies, so you think that the relation of co-bodiliness and the relation of co-personality are one and the same. Moreover, you think that psychological connectedness is the mark of personal identity, so you think that the relation of co-personality is definable in terms of psychological connectedness. Perhaps you think it definable in three steps, (roughly) as follows. Let A and B range over temporal body-parts. First, you define 'psychological connectedness': B is psychologically connected with A if and only if B believes a good bit of what A believed, wants a good bit of what A wanted, and so on. Second, you define 'psychological continuity': B is psychologically continuous with A if and only if B has the ancestral of psychological connectedness to A. Third, you define 'co-personality': B is co-personal with A if and only if B is psychologically continuous with A. This *is* rough, but the underlying idea is plain enough. And its puzzlingness is also plain enough. Notice in particular that the relation of psychological connectedness that I defined earlier is a four-place relation on people and times, whereas the relation of psychological connectedness defined here is a two-place relation on temporal body-parts, and that makes for trouble. For example, can one really think that point-duration temporal slices of bodies believe things or want things? (Temporal chunks are one thing; temporal slices seem to be quite another.) Again, how is a hybridist to secure that an unconscious or post-death temporal slice or chunk of a body is psychologically connected with a conscious, pre-death temporal slice or chunk of a body? On the other hand, I see no deep theoretical difficulty standing in the way of defining a relation of psychological connectedness on temporal body-parts in a way that bypasses this and other difficulties. And we may assume in any case that a hybridist will so define psychological connectedness, and thereby co-personality, that the *t*-to-ending temporal part of what the vulgar would call Robinson's body is co-personal with the beginning-to-*t* temporal part of what the vulgar would call Brown's body, the fusion of the two being Brown's body.

Should we accept the metaphysic of temporal parts? I think we should not. I will not argue for that here, however; I throughout leave it open.[8]

Many philosophers who write about personal identity help themselves to the terminology of temporal parts in laying out psychological identity criteria; a certain simplicity is gained in this way. But it should be noticed that this terminology can usually be regarded as mere *façon de parler*: it can be translated out. Even if you positively like, or anyway see nothing objectionable in, the metaphysic of temporal parts, you might find it of interest to see at what place in a discussion of personal identity the terminology has to be interpreted literally and not as mere *façon de parler*. (At exactly what place does getting a plausible account of people really require making reference to temporally bounded proper parts of people and their bodies?) One place is here. You need that metaphysic to be a literal truth if you want to have both that psychological connectedness is the mark of personal identity and that people nevertheless are their bodies.

V

The more important question for our purposes is whether we should accept that psychological connectedness is the mark of personal identity. *Is* there good reason to suppose that the survivor in Brown-Case-Three really is Brown? To suppose that the survivor in that case is Brown is to suppose that the reprogramming done on Robinson's brain produced the state of affairs that consists in

The survivor is Brown,

instead of the state of affairs that consists in

The survivor is Robinson,

Robinson being horrendously confused in that he (wrongly) thinks he is Brown. Why should we agree to this?

I drew attention earlier to the fact that if you think that psychological connectedness is the mark of personal identity, you probably have a variety of different things in mind; and I said that among them, very likely, is a thesis about people, to the effect that there are no sudden, dramatic alterations across time in a person's psychology. Thus, where there is such an alteration across time, a new person has replaced the old one.[9] Why should we agree to this? Isn't it really an odd idea that tinkering with someone's brain – or feeding a person a drug – might result in a new person? A new personality, perhaps. A new consciousness, perhaps. (Remember Locke.) But a new man or woman, child or infant? If I just took LSD and the person now sitting at my desk therefore has beliefs, wants and so on that are dramatically different from those I had an hour ago, shouldn't we say, not that here is a new woman, but rather that here is the same old woman, poor Thomson, who has gone off the deep end?

Suppose that the LSD I just took brought about not merely that the person now sitting at my desk has beliefs, wants and so on that are dramatically different from those I had an hour ago, but, more, that those beliefs, wants and so on are very like those Queen Victoria had shortly before her death. (It was a special British LSD, designed to have this effect.) Can anyone really think it within reason to suppose that the person now sitting at my desk is Queen Victoria – or even to wonder whether it is? Maybe Queen Victoria's consciousness is back with us again; but Queen Victoria, the very woman herself, surely isn't.[10] And if she isn't, then psychological connectedness is not the mark of personal identity.

VI

And then there is the unfortunate possibility of duplication. If we can reprogram Robinson's brain with Brown's psychology, we can also concurrently be reprogramming Dickenson's. Suppose we do; let us call this Brown-Case-Four. There are two survivors in Brown-Case-Four, both of whom are, at their waking-time, psychologically connected with Brown at his becoming-unconscious-time. But the two survivors cannot both be Brown since they are not identical with each other.

Two consequences follow. First, the pure psychological criterion for body-switching is false. According to that criterion, transplanting a person's psychology is both necessary and sufficient for that person to switch bodies; according to that view, therefore, Brown has switched to both Robinson's and Dickenson's bodies in Brown-Case-Four. But Brown cannot be both survivors since they are two.[11] Those who think that Brown switched bodies in Brown-Case-One and Brown-Case-Three must therefore find some other way of explaining what marks him as having done so.

Second, Psychological Criterion (Connectedness) is also false, for both survivors being at waking-time psychologically connected with Brown at becoming-unconscious-time, Psychological Criterion (Connectedness) yields that Brown is both. I said in section III that if you think that psychological connectedness is the mark of personal identity, you probably have a variety of different theses in mind, of which Psychological Criterion (Connectedness) is only one possibility. Brown-Case-Four brings out that Psychological Criterion (Connectedness) had better not be among the theses you have in mind.

What to do? Well, the first question to be answered is what happens in Brown-Case-Four. It seems to me of great interest that most (all?) of those who think that psychological connectedness is the mark of personal identity would say that the result of the double reprogramming in Brown-Case-Four is the state of affairs that consists in

Neither survivor is Brown.

It pays to ask why, however, since they do have other options. In particular, they could instead say that the result of the double reprogramming in Brown-Case-Four is the state of affairs that consists in

Either Brown is the survivor who has what was formerly Robinson's body, or Brown is the survivor who has what was formerly Dickenson's body, and it is indeterminate which,

or the state of affairs that consists in

Either Brown is the survivor who has what was formerly Robinson's body, or Brown is the survivor who has what was formerly Dickenson's body, or neither survivor is Brown, and it is indeterminate which.

I cannot think of anyone who chooses one of these indeterminacy options, and we will return in section X to what this shows.

Meanwhile, however, most of those who think that psychological connectedness is the mark of personal identity would say that the result of the double reprogramming in Brown-Case-Four is that neither survivor is Brown. Suppose *we* take that view. Then, if we think that body-switching is possible, we will want to insert what might be called a no-competitors (or no-branching) clause in the pure psychological criterion for body-switching; and we will then say that it is because there is only one survivor in Brown-Case-One and Brown-Case-Three that Brown switches bodies in those cases, the presence of the second (competing) survivor in Brown-Case-Four being why Brown does not switch bodies in that case. If we are hybridists, we think that body-switching is not possible, and we will therefore reject the result of inserting a no-competitors-clause in the pure psychological criterion for body-switching, just as we originally rejected the pure psychological criterion for body-switching itself. But all of us, hybridist or not, will agree on the need to insert a no-competitors-clause in Psychological Criterion (Connectedness). Here is one way of doing so:

> Psychological Criterion (Connectedness without Competitors): $x = y$ if and only if
> (a) there are times t and t' such that y is at t' psychologically connected with x at t, and
> (b) there is no z of which the following is the case: Not-$(z = y)$ and there are times t and t' such that z is at t' psychologically connected with x at t.

And all of us, hybridist or not, will say that, strictly speaking, it is not mere psychological connectedness, but rather *psychological connectedness without competitors* that is the mark of personal identity.

There is a difficulty here which I think has not been adequately appreciated. What I have in mind is the fact that a no-competitors-clause is going to have to contain a non-identity-clause. For example, the no-competitors-clause (b) in Psychological Criterion (Connectedness without Competitors) contains the clause

> Not-$(z = y)$.

But if we are in search of criteria which tell us under what conditions x is identical with y, we should surely not be satisfied with one that requires that we know independently under what conditions z is not identical with y.

How are we to analyse that non-identity-clause out? If we are hybridists, we have room to manoeuvre: we can appeal to bodily non-identity. (I will come back to this in the following section.) If we are not hybridists, however, we have a real problem on our hands.[12] Whichever we are, however, we must take a stand on the matter. Airy hand-waving about the presence or absence of competitors (or branches) just isn't good enough.

A second difficulty here is familiar. One who thinks that psychological connectedness without competitors is the mark of personal identity thinks that a question about personal identity can be settled by appeal to a fact that should surely be irrelevant to it. On this view, neither survivor is Brown if both reprogrammings succeed; but if only one succeeds, then the survivor of that one is Brown. So a small, chance slip-up in the procedures, which fixes that only one reprogramming goes through, fixes that Brown survives. This sounds very implausible.

In short, we have been led by these ideas to some very implausible conclusions: namely, that tinkering with someone's brain, or feeding a person a drug, could result in a new person (section V), and that the question whether it does turns on what should surely be the irrelevant question whether two brains were tinkered with, or two people fed the drug (this section).

VII

I asked in the preceding section what those who think that psychological connectedness is the mark of personal identity are to do in face of the possibility of duplication, as in Brown-Case-Four, for example. And I said that most of them would say that the result in that case is that neither survivor is Brown. I then drew attention to two difficulties which they face. What if they instead say that the result in that case is indeterminacy? Suppose they do. They still face the first of the two difficulties, for they still stand in need of an account of what marks the case as one in which there *are* two survivors; after all, it is only because there are two that the result is indeterminacy. And they face an analogue of the second, for they are committed to the idea that determinateness in surviving, and in who one is, can be settled by appeal to a fact that should surely be irrelevant to it. On their view, indeterminacy results if both reprogrammings succeed; a small, chance slip-up in the procedures, which fixes that only one reprogramming goes through, fixes that Brown determinately survives, and is, determinately, the sole survivor. This sounds very implausible.

As I said in the preceding section, hybridists do not face the first of those difficulties, for they can appeal to bodily non-identity as sufficient for personal non-identity. Let us have a look at what hybridists would say about Brown-Case-Four. Suppose that the double reprogramming in Brown-Case-Four is carried out at *t*, and consider the following three entities:

(a) the beginning-to-*t* temporal part of what the vulgar would call Brown's body,
(b) the *t*-to-ending temporal part of what the vulgar would call Robinson's body,

and

(c) the *t*-to-ending temporal part of what the vulgar would call Dickenson's body.

Hybridists can say that Brown's body, and thus Brown himself, just is (a); if they do, they are saying that Brown goes out of existence at *t*, and *a fortiori* that neither survivor is Brown in Brown-Case-Four.[13] And *they* have no trouble saying what marks the two survivors off from each other, for (b) is one survivor, and (c) is one survivor, and (b) and (c) are physical objects which occupy different places. On the other hand, the second difficulty remains; for on this view a small, chance slip-up in the procedures – which fixes that only one reprogramming goes through, the Robinson reprogramming as it might be – fixes that Brown's body is the fusion of (a) and (b), instead of merely being (a) alone, and thus fixes that Brown survives. This sounds very implausible.

It is worth noticing that hybridists have yet another option in respect of Brown-Case-Four; they can instead say the following. The fusion of (a) and (b) is *a* body, and thus *a* person; call it Brown–Robinson. The fusion of (a) and (c) is *a* body, and thus *a* person; call it Brown–Dickenson. Since (b) is not identical with (c), Brown-Robinson is not identical with Brown-Dickenson. But Brown-Robinson and Brown-Dickenson overlap, for they share (a). Then, although neither survivor is Brown, this is not because Brown goes out of existence at *t*, but rather because there was no (one) person Brown – there always were two people called 'Brown'.[14]

However an analogue of the second difficulty faces this option. One who takes this line is thereby committed to the idea that how many people there are at a given time and place can be settled by appeal to a fact that should surely be irrelevant to it. On this view, there were two people sitting at Brown's desk prior to *t* if both reprogrammings were going to succeed; a small, chance slip-up in the procedures, which fixes that only one reprogramming goes through, fixes that there was only one. This again sounds very implausible.

In short, if you think that the survivor is Brown in Brown-Case-One and Brown-Case-Three, and therefore think that psychological connectedness is the mark of personal identity, then you have no plausible options in respect of Brown-Case-Four.

VIII

So there is serious trouble for those who think that psychological connectedness is the mark of personal identity. On the one hand, they are committed to its being the case that tinkering with someone's brain, or feeding a person a drug, could result in a new person, and that is very implausible (section V). On the other hand, they are committed to its being the case that a question about personal identity (section VI), or about determinacy in personal identity, or about how many people there are at a given time or place (section VII), can turn on a fact that should surely be irrelevant to it. Why, then, do so many philosophers nevertheless think that psychological connectedness *must* be the mark of personal identity – in some appropriate sense of 'psychological connectedness', and in some appropriate way of being 'the mark of'? There seem to be three reasons.

In the first place, it seems to many philosophers that body-switching – or anyway, doing what is body-switching if the metaphysic of temporal parts is false – really must be possible, for they think we can imagine it. Suppose it is possible. What could be thought to mark the person x who now has body A as the person y who formerly had body B, and who has thus switched from body B to body A? All that is available by way of mark that this has happened is the connectedness of x's psychology with y's. So it must be that psychological connectedness really is the mark of personal identity.

Can we imagine body-switching? Many people have described states of affairs in which, as they say, body-switching would really be going on – or perhaps, more modestly, social arrangements in which, as they say, the participants would themselves say that what was going on is body-switching.[15] But I do not think that those descriptions are themselves what bear the weight: I doubt that people would be moved by those descriptions to conclude that body-switching is possible if they did not think they could imagine body-switching from inside, as it were. It is *that*, I think – the idea that one can imagine oneself switching bodies – that bears the weight, and thereby makes the descriptions seem to be more convincing than they would otherwise be.

Can we imagine body-switching from inside? One is initially inclined to think it's easy. I close my eyes, and form a mental picture of Mary's lap as it would look to her if she were looking down at it, and of Mary's hands on the keyboard of her typewriter as they would look if she were looking down on them, and so on; and I think to myself, 'Now I am imagining my having switched to Mary's body.' But how does my having formed that mental picture warrant my saying that what I am imagining is my having switched to Mary's body? There is nothing in the picture itself which could be thought to make it a picture of my having switched to Mary's body: the picture is merely a picture of Mary's body. (Compare a drawing or photograph of Mary's lap and hands.)

With what reason do I describe myself, having formed the picture, as 'imagining my having switched to Mary's body'? Why not instead as 'imagining how things would look to Mary if she were at her typewriter now'? Or as 'imagining myself under a delusion as to how my own lap and hands look'? It cannot be said that I am master of what I am imagining, on pain of making my being able to imagine something be no ground at all for thinking it possible, for if I am master of what I am imagining, then it is up to me whether I am imagining round squares all over my desk. Moreover, if I am master of what I am imagining, then why did I bother to form the mental picture in the first place? It is of interest that my forming a picture of Mary's lap and hands did seem to play a role in making me feel it right to describe myself as 'imagining my having switched to Mary's body'.

But my forming that picture cannot really have played any more of a role than this: the picture shows how my body would now look to me *if* I had switched to Mary's body and were at her typewriter now. If that is right, then the picture does nothing at all to support the possibility of body-switching, for it shows what I take it to show only on the supposition that I have switched to Mary's body. (Compare my drawing a picture of a banana and saying 'This is how tigers would look *if* tigers were bananas'. Have I now imagined tigers being bananas?)

There is a deep and quite general difficulty in the offing here: namely, what is involved in imagining something from inside, for oneself, and I bypass it. Meanwhile, however, I think it clear that the kind of exercise in picture-forming I have drawn attention to does not bear the weight that needs bearing if we are to conclude that body-switching is possible, or even that we can imagine it.

A second reason why it seems to many philosophers that psychological connectedness must be the mark of personal identity is that it seems to them that people could exist without bodies at all. Suppose that is possible. What could be thought to mark a certain bodiless person x as a certain bodiless person *y*? All that seems to be available by way of a mark of this identity is the connectedness of *x*'s psychology with *y*'s. So it must be that psychological connectedness really is the mark of personal identity.

Why do we think that people could exist without bodies at all? Something similar goes on. I close my eyes (it is of interest that we close our eyes in engaging in these exercises), and I attend to my toothache and my general feeling of fatigue. 'There', I think; 'that could exist without any physical objects existing, and *a fortiori* without my body existing. So *I* could exist without my body existing.' Well, these are things I am inclined to think. The thoughts bubble up so naturally that they seem obvious truths. But they are not. The difficulties here are familiar enough, however, and have a long history, so I set this second reason aside.

A third reason is more direct. Here is David Lewis:

> I find that what I mostly want in wanting survival is that my mental life should flow on. My present experiences, thoughts, beliefs, desires, and traits of character should have appropriate future successors. My total present mental state should be but one momentary stage in a continuing succession of mental states.[16]

And he takes his intuitively finding that what he mostly wants is that his mental life flow on to give him a reason for believing, and thus for trying to show, that *its* flowing on fixes that *he* does. I am sure that Lewis is not alone in taking this route to the idea that psychological connectedness is the mark of personal identity.

On the other hand, he grants that if his mental life's flowing on turned out on analysis not to fix that he does, then he would give up his intuitive finding that what he mostly wants in wanting survival is that his mental life flow on. ('Else it would be difficult to believe one's own philosophy!', he says.) People must of course speak for themselves on these matters, but it is surely true for most of us that if we were told that we will die this afternoon, it would be small consolation to be told also that there will be someone else alive tomorrow who will then be psychologically connected with us today. There are, of course, things we want done in future, many of them such that the more likely it is that there will be someone tomorrow who will then be psychologically connected with us today, the more likely it is that the things will actually get done. (I want my cat to be cared for, for example, and who but someone psychologically connected with me could love so scrawny a creature?) But that those things will actually get done would be, for most of us, thin gruel as consolation. Furthermore, there are also things we want done in future that we do not *just* want done: I have in mind things we want done in future by us, among them being things we want done in future only by us. (Someone psychologically connected with me is going to want to wear my wedding-ring, and that prospect is anything but consoling.)

Parfit thinks that the attitude I express here, and attribute to most of us, is irrational. He argues that, given that there will be someone alive tomorrow who will be, tomorrow, psychologically connected with me today, it is irrational for me to care whether that person will be *me*. His argument appeals to duplication, and can be reconstructed as follows. He invites us to accept

(i) The survivor in the single reprogramming Brown-Case-Three is Brown,

and

(ii) Neither survivor in the double reprogramming Brown-Case-Four is Brown.

Given (i), Brown survives single reprogramming: he lives. Given (ii), Brown does not survive double reprogramming: he dies. So, given that there will be at least one reprogramming at t, Brown will live after t if and only if there is no more than one. So if Brown cares about survival, what he is caring about – given that there will be at least one reprogramming – is whether there will be more than one. But Brown can hardly be thought to get less if there is more than one reprogramming than he gets if there is only one: after all, the relation in which he stands to the survivor in the single reprogramming case is the very relation in which he stands to each of the two survivors in the double reprogramming case, but for the sheer fact that double reprogramming is single reprogramming twice over, and hence results in two survivors. It is therefore irrational for Brown to care whether there will be more than one reprogramming. Therefore, given that there will be at least one reprogramming at t, it is irrational for Brown to care whether he himself will survive what happens at t.[17]

Parfit does not spell out how this conclusion about Brown is to be generalized to the rest of us, but I suppose his thought is this. Suppose there will be someone in existence tomorrow who will then be psychologically connected with me today – *whatever* is going to cause this phenomenon. Given analogues of (i) and (ii) for me, I will live tomorrow if and only if there is no more than one. It is irrational for me to care whether there will be more than one. Therefore, given that there will be at least one, it is irrational for me to care whether I survive tomorrow.

The argument rests, of course, on its premises (i) and (ii); should we accept them? Those who believe that psychological connectedness is the mark of personal identity will of course accept (i); but I have been arguing that that idea leads to serious trouble. And that most of us do not in fact accept (i) comes out in this way: if a doctor tells us we will die this afternoon, but that someone else, exactly one, will be alive tomorrow who will then be psychologically connected with us today, most of us do not reply 'You're suffering from metaphysical confusion, for if there'll be exactly one it'll be me', but instead, 'Well, I suppose that isn't nothing, but it isn't much'. Parfit's argument does nothing at all to show that we are mistaken, since accepting its first premiss (i) requires just assuming that we are mistaken.

And what of (ii)? As I said in section VI, most people who think that psychological connectedness is the mark of personal identity do choose to say that neither survivor is Brown in Brown-Case-Four, but I drew attention to the implausibility of saying (ii), having said (i).[18]

In short, accepting Parfit's premises (i) and (ii) requires supposing that psychological connectedness without competitors is both necessary and sufficient for personal identity. To the extent to which we are right to be suspicious of this idea, we are right to remain unmoved by Parfit's argument for the conclusion that, as he puts it, personal identity is not what matters.

IX

Suppose we reject the idea that psychological connectedness is the mark of personal identity. Suppose we accept the simple and attractive idea that people are their bodies, and therefore take bodily identity to be the mark of personal identity – *and* agree with the vulgar about which body is Brown's body or yours or mine. (We can, if we like, also accept the metaphysic of temporal parts, but our views about personal identity do not require us to do so.) Then we conclude that Brown dies in all four of the cases we have looked at. In the single and double reprogramming cases, Brown-Case-Three and Brown-Case-Four, Brown's body is wholly destroyed at the relevant time t, and so, we conclude, is Brown. In the brain transplant cases Brown-Case-One and Brown-Case-Two, Brown's body is not wholly destroyed at t, for his brain is preserved and transplanted into Robinson's head; but while a part of Brown's body, and so of Brown, does therefore survive in those cases, his body does not, and we say the same of Brown himself.

I will call this 'the ordinary view' of people and their identity conditions, because it does seem to be the view that we would take if we had not gone wandering into the clouds of philosophy trailed by the word 'person'.

In particular, the duplication in Brown-Case-Four makes no trouble for the ordinary view. Both survivors think they are Brown in that case; but if we accept the ordinary view, we think they are mistaken , just as we think the one survivor who thinks he is Brown in Brown-Case-One and Brown-Case-Three is mistaken.

What of duplication of another kind? In a fifth case, Brown's body is split down the middle, and the resulting bits of flesh and bone are refashioned into two smaller living bodies. If we accept the ordinary view, we will say that neither survivor is Brown in this case too. Compare, after all, what happens when an amoeba splits: neither of the resulting two amoebae is the original. No matter if both say 'Me, me, I'm the original!' – neither is.

Does our concern for survival shed doubt on the ordinary view? Would I care about survival if I really thought that for me to survive is merely for this mass of flesh and blood to survive? What is so special about *it* that I should want it to survive? The short, and I think entirely adequate, answer is that it *is* me, so that if it does not survive, I do not.

But a longer answer is available. It is not the mere continued existence of this human body that so concerns me. For example, I think at the moment that I would prefer being buried to being cremated after death, but my preference is not a firm one, and I might later decide otherwise. What I want in wanting to survive is not merely that this body should continue to exist, but that it should continue to function in the ways in which living human bodies function. And not merely that it should continue to function in just any of the ways in which living human bodies function, for the prospect of coma ending only in death is no more attractive than death is. (Nancy Cruzan would surely not have welcomed the prospect of being in the condition she is now in.) What I want in wanting to survive is that this body should continue to function in the ways in which living human bodies function when they support consciousness, and, for preference, in which they function when they also support perception and make action of a wide variety of kinds possible. Mere consciousness wouldn't be nothing: I could still ruminate on the nature of the universe. But the enterprise would pall after a while. What I want is to go on leading a more or less full human life, and for that, this more or less well-functioning human body is exactly what I do need. If I could switch to another – a younger and healthier one – that would be splendid. But since I can't, I do need this one.

X

The difficulty that stands in the way of adopting the ordinary view is not anything that supports a psychological criterion for personal identity: quite to the contrary, it stands in the way of adopting psychological criteria too. What I have in mind is what inclines us to think that Descartes must be right, and that people must really be mental substances. What I have in mind, in short, is what inclines us to reject indeterminacy for people.

Let us go back. I drew attention in section VI to the interesting fact that most people who think that psychological connectedness is the mark of personal identity say that when we reprogram both Robinson's and Dickenson's brains, the result is the state of affairs that consists in

Neither survivor is Brown.

They do not say that the result is the state of affairs that consists in

Either Brown is the survivor who has what was formerly Robinson's body, or Brown is the survivor who has what was formerly Dickenson's body, and it is indeterminate which,

or

Either Brown is the survivor who has what was formerly Robinson's body, or Brown is the survivor who has what was formerly Dickenson's body, or neither survivor is Brown, and it is indeterminate which.

Why do they reject the indeterminacy options? Because they are inclined to think that it just cannot be indeterminate which of two people a given person is, or whether a person survives. Why are they inclined to think this?

What Parfit's Psychological Spectrum (p. 231) brings home to us is that even if you reject indeterminacy about which of two people a given person is, you are going to be committed to indeterminacy about whether a person survives – if you accept a criterion of identity whose central piece of conceptual machinery is psychological connectedness. Parfit invites us to imagine a series of possible operations on a person's brain, Green's, let us say. In the first operation, just a little tinkering is done on Green's brain: the survivor wakes having a belief which Green did not have prior to the operation. Here we are all inclined to say that it is Green who wakes, thus that the survivor is Green. In the second operation, a bit more tinkering is done on Green's brain. And so on. In the last operation of the series, massive tinkering is done on Green's brain, and the survivor wakes thinking he is Napoleon. If you think that psychological connectedness is the mark of personal identity, you will of course say that the survivor of the last operation is not Green. But what of operations somewhere in the middle of this series? Is the survivor Green? There's no saying whether he is.[19] Even if you have avoided indeterminacy as to which of the two survivors is Brown in Brown-Case-Four – by fiat, thus by simply declaring that neither survivor is Brown in that case – you will have to allow for indeterminacy as to whether a person survives at all. After all, the central piece of conceptual machinery in your account of personal identity is psychological connectedness, and that relation is vague. But if you must accept indeterminacy about whether a person survives, why not also about which survivor Brown is? I can see no reason to think that indeterminacy about which is worse than indeterminacy about whether.

If you accept Physical Criterion, then you are not committed to indeterminacy as to which of two survivors a person is in the case I mentioned in the preceding section, in which Brown's body is split down the middle and the resulting bits of flesh and bone are refashioned into two smaller living bodies. What of a case in which we successively removed and then replaced parts of (what we took to be) Brown's body, and then someone else constructed a second body out of the parts that we had removed?[20] Is one of the two resulting bodies Brown's? And if so, which? Compare our successively removing and replacing planks in (what we took to be) the ship of Theseus, and then someone else's constructing a second ship out of the planks that we had removed. Is one of the two resulting ships the ship of Theseus? And if so, which? I am inclined to think that 'One is, but it's indeterminate which' is as good an answer as any, for the ship of Theseus, as for Brown's body.

In any case, Parfit's Physical Spectrum (p. 234) brings home to us that anyone who accepts Physical Criterion is going to be committed to indeterminacy as to whether a person survives. Parfit invites us to imagine a series of operations on a person Blue, in which Blue's cells are replaced: in the first operation, one cell of Blue's body is replaced, in the second, two are replaced, . . . , in the last, all cells but one are replaced. If you accept Physical Criterion, you will say that Blue's body, and thus Blue himself, survives the first operation, and does not survive the last; but what of operations in the middle of the series?[21] There is no saying whether Blue's body, and thus Blue himself, survives them. That this outcome confronts those who are attracted by Physical Criterion should be no surprise: it is a familiar enough fact that the question whether what we have before us today is the same body (ship, shoe, computer) as the one we had before us yesterday may have no determinate answer.

But we are inclined to think that there cannot be indeterminacy *either* as to which of two people a given person is *or* as to whether a person survives. If that thought is right, then Physical Criterion, and *a fortiori*, Physical Thesis, must be rejected – along with all psychological criteria in which psychological connectedness supplies the central piece of conceptual machinery. And the thought that there cannot be either kind of indeterminacy is intimately connected with the thought that a person must really be a mental substance – a mental monad, in fact. For if there cannot be either kind of indeterminacy, then doesn't that mean that people have to be indivisible? (If people have parts, as bodies do, then indeterminacy in respect of them would surely be possible.)

Why are we inclined to think that there cannot be either kind of indeterminacy? This inclination is very strong in us,[22] and I think it has not been taken seriously enough in the contemporary literature on personal identity: people do not ask exactly why it has such a grip on us.

Consider Blue, and imagine he has been subjected to a middle-of-the-series operation, so that it is indeterminate whether the resulting body is Blue's. Physical Criterion says that it is indeterminate whether the survivor is Blue. But we think that it just cannot be indeterminate whether Blue survived, and I suggest that this is because we want to ask what Blue is now experiencing if it is supposed to be indeterminate whether he survived, and that nothing we will count as an answer could possibly *be* the answer. We reject 'Either the recovery room or nothing' as not an answer at all. And what we would count as an answer – as it might be, 'A flickering between the recovery room and nothing' – cannot be the answer if (as let us suppose) the survivor is not experiencing a flickering; for if Blue is experiencing a flickering and the survivor is not, then Blue is determinately not the survivor.

Similarly, I think, with indeterminacy as to which person a given person is. Suppose someone were to say that in Brown-Case-Four the result is that Brown determinately survived, but that it is indeterminate which of the two survivors he is. We think it just cannot be indeterminate which of the two survivors Brown is, and I suggest that this is because we want to ask what Brown is now experiencing if it is supposed to be indeterminate which survivor he is, and that nothing we will count as an answer could possibly *be* the answer. Suppose one survivor is looking at Boston, the other at Worcester. We reject 'Either Boston or Worcester' as not an answer at all. And what we would count as an answer – as it might be, 'A flickering between Boston and Worcester' – cannot be the answer if (as let us suppose) neither survivor is experiencing a flickering;

for if Brown is experiencing a flickering, and neither survivor is, then Brown is determinately neither survivor.

But why do we feel that the question what a person is now experiencing *has* to have a non-disjunctive answer? If it can be indeterminate whether a person survives, or which survivor he is, then the question what a person is now experiencing really can lack a non-disjunctive answer. Why do we feel so tempted to proceed from there, not by *modus ponens*, but instead by *modus tollens*? That feeling must surely have some interesting source, and it probably lies in our overestimating what goes on in determinate survival. In any case, I suspect that no account of personal identity will entirely satisfy us in the absence of an understanding of it.[23]

Notes

1 I here follow Vere Chappell, 'Locke on the Ontology of Matter, Living Things and Persons', *Philosophical Studies*, 60/1–2 (Sept.–Oct. 1990), pp. 19–32. Chappell rebuts the attribution of relativized identity to Locke in 'Locke and Relative Identity', *History of Philosophy Quarterly*, 6/1 (Jan. 1989), pp. 69–83.

2 The case I begin with comes from Sydney Shoemaker, *Self-knowledge and Self-identity* (Cornell University Press, Ithaca, NY, 1963).

3 I take this to be Mark Johnston's view. I take him to believe that we cannot switch bodies without the continuing of our 'mental life', and he says that 'we cannot switch bodies without brain transplantation'. See his 'Human Beings', *Journal of Philosophy*, 84/2 (Feb. 1987), pp. 79–80.

4 I adapt this account of psychological connectedness from Derek Parfit, *Reasons and Persons*, pp. 205–6.

5 We could state this thesis more precisely if we introduced a relation 'psychological continuity' – defined in terms of the relation 'psychological connectedness' that I set out in the text above – in the manner of Parfit, pp. 206–7. I will not take space to do so, however, since actually laying out the definition is a rather messier enterprise than is usually thought. (One way of supplying the details may be found in my 'Ruminations on an Account of Personal Identity', in *On Being and Saying, Essays for Richard Cartwright*, ed. J. J. Thomson (MIT Press, Cambridge, Mass., 1987), pp. 215–40.) For it must be remembered that the relation of psychological connectedness that I set out in the text above is a four-place relation on people and times. In section IV we take note of two-place psychological connectedness and continuity relations.

6 It is worth stress that this question is no less pressing if you think that Brown switches bodies only in Brown-Case-One.

7 We do not *say* 'My body believes that today is Thursday' or 'My body wants a banana'; we instead say 'I believe that today is Thursday' or 'I want a

banana'. Does this fact of usage refute Physical Thesis? Anyone who thinks so will have to explain why we also do not say 'My body weighs 250 pounds', preferring instead, 'I weigh 250 pounds', and why, by contrast, 'My body is all over red splotches' and 'I am all over red splotches' are quite on a par. It seems to me an interesting question what lies behind these facts of usage, but I see nothing in them on which to rest a rejection of Physical Thesis.

8 I argue for it in 'Parthood and Identity across Time', *Journal of Philosophy*, 80 (1983), pp. 201–20. See also Sally Haslanger, 'Persistence, Change, and Explanation', *Philosophical Studies*, 56 (1989), pp. 1–28.

9 Some of those who think that psychological connectedness is the mark of personal identity think that even a gradual alteration in a person's psychology may result in a new person, and does result in a new person if the change is sufficiently deep and extensive. Why should we agree to this? If my Uncle Alfred gradually, over the years, comes to suffer from a severe case of Alzheimer's disease, then isn't the outcome just poor Uncle Alfred, the very man himself, who has undergone this terrible change? (Compare Nancy Cruzan.)

10 Suppose that Queen Victoria's brain had been carefully preserved and was just transplanted into my head, and that it was *that* which caused the current beliefs, wants and so on of the person now sitting at my desk to be those of Queen Victoria. Can anyone really think it is Queen Victoria who sits there now?

11 Instead of reprogramming both Robinson's and Dickenson's brains, we could have split Brown's brain, transplanting half into Robinson's body and the other half into Dickenson's. As many people have pointed out, a person can survive with only half a brain, so we might have two survivors here too, both of them psychologically connected with Brown. I characterized the impure psychological view as follows: transplanting a person's psychology, and doing so by way of transplanting that person's brain, is both necessary and sufficient for that person to switch bodies. So those who accept the impure psychological view are safe against the possibility of duplication only if they insist that body-switching requires that the transplanting of psychology be caused by the transplanting of all of the brain (or anyway, of enough of the brain so that transplanting what is left into someone else does not cause a second transplanting of psychology). Is there supposed to be good reason for this further bit of digging in of heels?

12 Consider a pair of identical twins who die shortly after birth, and whose psychologies, we can suppose, never come to differ. We can hardly fancy the idea that only one baby was born, though it had two bodies; we had better allow that two babies were born. It follows that there isn't going to be any *purely* psychological conceptual machinery that will enable non-hybridists to analyse the non-identity-clause out. What else is available to a non-hybridist? (I need hardly add that those twins make quite general trouble for the ideas we are looking at.)

13 A hybridist who chooses this account of what happens in Brown-Case-Four would of course have to adopt a rather more complicated account of co-personality than I pointed at in section IV.

14　This account of what goes on in Brown-Case-Four comes from David Lewis, 'Survival and Identity', in *The Identities of Persons*, ed. Amelie O. Rorty (University of California Press, Berkeley, 1976), pp. 17–40. Lewis says that persons are aggregates of psychologically related person-stages, but does not declare himself on what those things are. If we construe his person-stages as temporal body-parts, then we are construing Lewis as a hybridist.

15　See e.g. Sydney Shoemaker and Richard Swinburne, *Personal Identity* (Blackwell, Oxford, 1984), pp. 108–11.

16　Lewis, 'Survival and Identity', p. 17.

17　This is a reconstruction, not a mere summary, of Parfit's argument, which appears on pp. 255–66, for Parfit's single and double survivor cases there involve half-brain transplants, and not (as I have it here) reprogrammings. But I take the transplants not to be essential to Parfit's argument, and he says, in fact, that for his part, the psychological connectedness between survivor(s) and original could have had any cause at all (p. 262). Indeed, it is hard to see how Parfit's argument could be generalized so as to bear on the rest of us, who will not be undergoing transplantation, if the transplantation really were essential to it.

18　Parfit himself expresses discomfort about (ii): he asks, 'How could a double success be a failure?' (p. 256). He nevertheless goes on to say that 'the best description' of a duplication case is that neither of the survivors is the original (p. 260), and that 'we can best describe the case by saying that neither' is the original (p. 262); that is because he regards 'It's indeterminate' as an unacceptable answer to the question of which survivor is the original.

19　I say there's no saying whether he is, but do not mean to commit myself thereby to any particular way of squaring indeterminacy with logic. Suppose we have a pair of options p and not-p, and it is indeterminate which. On some views, we should conclude that p and not-p lack truth-values. On other views, we should instead conclude that p and not-p do have truth-values, though it is indeterminate which truth-values they have. (For a recent argument for the latter choice, see Paul Horwich, *Truth* (Blackwell, Oxford, 1990), pp. 80–7.) I take no stand on this matter. If psychological connectedness is the mark of personal identity, then it is indeterminate whether the survivor of a middle-of-the-series operation in Psychological Spectrum is Green, just as it is indeterminate whether a colour mid-way between red and orange is red; I leave open whether we should conclude that 'He is Green' and 'It is red' lack truth-values.

20　I am grateful to Barbara Von Eckardt and Joseph Mendola for reminding me of this possibility.

21　Sheer quantity of matter replaced is surely not what counts, however. I imagine that we would be inclined to say 'same body' even if more than half the matter in it had been replaced, so long as the replacement had been made at places not important to the continued functioning of the body. For example, contrast replacing body fat with replacing the head and chest. (An analogous point holds of ships, shoes and computers.)

22　Discussing a case of future fission on himself, Chisholm says: 'I see the following . . . clearly and distinctly to be true . . . that if Lefty and Righty clearly *are* persons, as we are imagining, then the questions "Will I be Lefty?" and "Will I be Righty?" have entirely definite answers.' Determinate answers, I take him to mean. (That 'I will be Lefty' and 'I will be Righty' have truth-values, it being indeterminate which – see n. 19 – would not satisfy him.) Doesn't he here express a feeling we share? See Roderick M. Chisholm, 'Reply to Strawson's Comments', in *Language, Belief, and Metaphysics*, ed. H. E. Kiefer and Milton K. Munitz (State University of New York Press, Albany, NY, 1970).

23 I am indebted to George Boolos and Paul Horwich for comments on an earlier draft of this essay.

11

Reductionism and the First Person

John McDowell

I

Locke's discussion of personal identity centres on the thesis that a person is 'a thinking intelligent being, that has reason and reflection, and can consider itself as itself, the same thinking thing, in different times and places'.[1] What Locke stresses here is that the continuity that constitutes a person's continuing to exist has an 'inner' aspect. Normally this 'inner' aspect is realized in substantive knowledge: what Locke calls 'consciousness' holds together in a single survey some of the specifics of the career, extended in time, of what the subject of this survey conceives as itself, 'the same thinking thing'. But if a person can survive with the details of its past and future blotted out, its being a person requires that it still conceive itself as a self-conscious continuant, capable of an 'inner' angle on its own persistence, but currently deprived of any specificity in what that capacity yields.

Now a core thought in the reductionism that Derek Parfit recommends is that this 'inner' aspect of personal persistence should be understood in terms of relations between psychological states and events that are intelligible independently of personal identity. It is this claim that allows Parfit to play down the importance of personal identity. If the relations that constitute the phenomenon that Locke stresses are independent of personal identity, they must be detachable in thought from the continued existence of persons, even though Locke's idea has to be that they are constitutive of it (as they indeed are in the normal course of things). And what matters for the rationality of the sort of concern with the future that, with our usual unimaginative restriction to the normal case, we conceive as self-interested is Locke's phenomenon; hence, according to Parfit, what matters is those independently intelligible relations, rather than the facts about personal identity that they normally help to constitute.

II

In advance of looking into the particular moves that Parfit makes to supply a reductionist account of Locke's phenomenon, I think we should query the motivation for supposing that a reduction ought to be available.

For many kinds of continuants, what it is for something to continue to exist, one and the same, is best characterized in terms of spatio-temporal continuity under a substance concept. Now there is no reason to understand this claim in such a way that circularity would be an objection to applications of it. The claim frames an understanding of what the relevant substance concepts must be like for our judgements of identity to work as they do, and it can serve that purpose without purporting to be intelligible independently of those judgements.[2] Generally, there seems to be no reason to try to reduce the notion of the career of a continuant to relations between elements in that career that are intelligible independently of the thought that the elements figure in the career of a single thing.

Locke's thesis is that a person is a continuant of a special kind, special in that 'consciousness' gives it an 'inner' perspective on its own persistence. Does this import any reason to press for a reduction? Only on the basis of what seems to me to be a mistaken thought: that there is no alternative to reduction except to commit ourselves to continuants whose persistence through time would consist in nothing but the continuity of 'consciousness' itself. Such continuants would be items whose activity is purely mental: items like the one that Descartes convinced himself he referred to in first-person thought.

Parfit's introduction of his reductionist notion of psychological continuity suggests that he thinks on those lines. He writes:

> Some people believe in a kind of psychological continuity that resembles physical continuity. This involves the continued existence of a purely mental *entity*, or thing – a soul, or spiritual substance. I shall return to this view. But I shall first explain another kind of psychological continuity. This is less like physical continuity, since it does not consist in the continued existence of some entity. But this other kind of psychological continuity involves only facts with which we are familiar. (pp. 204–5)

But there is another possibility, which is conspicuous by its absence from this passage, and, so far as I can tell, from Parfit's thinking altogether.

This is that Locke's phenomenon, the continuity of 'consciousness', does involve the continued existence of an entity; but the entity is not a peculiar Cartesian item, but a person, of whose continued life that continuity is, precisely, an aspect. If Locke's phenomenon had to be understood all by itself, in abstraction from the idea of the continued life of a person (which is the continued life of a human being, in the case that we have to regard as, at the least, central), then we should perhaps be forced to choose between purely spiritual substances and psychological reductionism. Parfit suggests that reductionism has respectably anti-Cartesian credentials by urging (plausibly enough) that reductionism is the better option in that choice. But the fundamental Cartesian mistake is not the postulation of spiritual substances, but rather the assumption, which is preserved in this implicit defence of reductionism, that seems to pose that choice: the assumption that Locke's phenomenon must be understood in isolation.

III

It is a central fact about what Locke calls 'consciousness' that although the temporally separate states and occurrences that it can hold together in a single survey seem to figure within its purview as elements in the career of something that persists as one and the same, the flow of 'consciousness' does not involve applying, or otherwise ensuring conformity with, criteria for the identity through time of an object. In continuity of 'consciousness', there is what appears to be knowledge of an identity, the persistence of the same subject through time, without any need to take care that attention stays fixed on the same thing. Contrast keeping one's thought focused on an ordinary object of perception over a period; this requires a skill, the ability to keep track of something, whose exercise we can conceive as a practical substitute for the explicit application of a criterion of identity. Continuity of 'consciousness' involves no analogue to this: no keeping track of the persisting self that nevertheless seems to figure in its content.[3]

A mainstream Cartesian response would be to retain the idea that continuity of 'consciousness' constitutes awareness of an identity through time; to assume that the content of that awareness must be provided for completely within the flow of 'consciousness'; and to conclude, from the fact that no criteria for persistence through time are in play in the field to which that assumption restricts us, that what continuing to exist consists in for the continuant in question must be peculiarly simple, something that does not go beyond the flow of 'consciousness' itself.[4] In particular, this line of thought rules out the idea that the continuant in question might be a human being. What it is for one and the same human being to continue existing involves just the sort of criteria of persistence whose absence from the restricted field was the starting-point of these reflections. One cannot be entitled to suppose that third-person thought stays focused on the same human being without applying such criteria, or exercising a skill of keeping track; on present assumptions, this rules out taking it that the apparently stable reference, in the first-person thinking that reflects continuity of 'consciousness', is to a human being.[5]

Now one way to avoid the purely spiritual continuants that this line of thought purports to force on us would indeed be to revise our view of the content of the flow of 'consciousness' in a reductionist direction: to conclude that 'consciousness' does not, after all, present the temporally separated states and occurrences over which it plays as belonging to the career of a single continuant, but rather as linked by a conceptually simpler relation of serial co-consciousness, which might subsequently enter into the construction of a derivative notion of a persisting subject if such a notion seems called for.

But it should be clear that there is another way to disown any commitment to purely spiritual continuants. The alternative is to leave in place the idea that continuity of 'consciousness' constitutes awareness of an identity through time, but reject the assumption that this fact needs to be provided for within a self-contained conception of the continuity of 'consciousness'. On the contrary, we can say: continuous 'consciousness' is intelligible (even 'from within') only as a subjective angle on something that has more to it than the subjective angle reveals: namely, the career of an objective continuant with which the subject of the continuous 'consciousness' identifies itself. The subjective angle does not contain within itself any analogue to keeping track of something, but its content can nevertheless intelligibly involve a stable continuing reference, of a first-person kind; this is thanks to its being situated in a wider context, which provides for an understanding that the persisting referent is also a third person, something whose career is a substantially traceable continuity in the objective world.[6]

Once this alternative is clearly in view, it should come to seem doubtful that reductionism deserves respect because it stands opposed to Cartesian philosophy. Purely spiritual substances are indeed not to be countenanced. But what is much more fundamental is the underlying thesis, that what Locke calls 'consciousness' has its content independently of any embedding in a wider objective context. And that utterly Cartesian conception of 'consciousness' as self-contained goes unquestioned in the implicit defence of reductionism that I have been considering. Indeed, we can see a Cartesian structure in Parfit's reductionism itself. According to the view I recommend, a context of facts about the objective continuation of lives helps to make intelligible a face-value construal of what Locke actually says, that continuous 'consciousness' presents an identity through time. This context figures in Parfit's picture only as the 'normal cause' of a less rich content which is supposed to be what Locke really intended to remind us of, something tailor-made to seem entertainable, like the Cartesian *cogito*, without objective presuppositions. A phrase like 'serial co-consciousness' can indeed be understood to fit 'facts with which we are familiar'; but the familiar fact is that a person experiences his life from within as the career of a single objective subject, and it looks like a Cartesian thought that, in order to consider the content of the familiar experience as it really is, we must purify it of involvement with an objective context.[7]

In her reflections on the first-person mode of thought, G. E. M. Anscombe draws attention to a highly instructive anecdote from William James.[8] A subject nicknamed 'Baldy' had fallen out of a carriage; he asked who fell out, and when told that it was Baldy, he responded 'Did Baldy fall out? Poor Baldy!' This episode reflects, as Anscombe puts it, a 'lapse of self-consciousness', because Baldy's thought of the falling 'was one for which he looked for a subject'. Now this formulation points up a contrast between Baldy's need to rely on extraneous information, in this case supplied by other people, to identify a subject of which to predicate the happening of which he found himself possessing a conception, on the one hand, and the absence of any need to establish an identity, which I have stressed as characterizing Lockean 'consciousness' (i.e. self-consciousness), on the other. Anscombe herself concludes that the contents of 'consciousness' should not be understood to include reference to a persisting subject; as far as it goes, this matches the reductionist response to the peculiarity of 'consciousness'. But the conclusion turns on an unwarranted equation: Baldy looked for a subject for his conception of the falling, and Anscombe equates this with the conception's requiring a subject, and concludes that the contents of 'consciousness' must be conceptions of states and occurrences that do not require a subject. Against the background of the position I have sketched, we can see this to be, remarkably enough, a piece of vestigially Cartesian philosophy. Of course, Anscombe has no sympathy with the mainstream Cartesian thesis, that 'consciousness' embodies reference to a purely spiritual substance. But her way of avoiding that thesis, like the implicit defence of reductionism that I have been considering, betrays a continuing adherence to something more fundamentally Cartesian. The fact that 'consciousness' does not look for a subject for its conceptions would show that its contents do not require a subject, and so are not to be understood as predicated of a subject, only on the assumption that the logical character of 'consciousness' must be provided for entirely within 'consciousness' itself; and that assumption is what I am suggesting is the basic Cartesian mistake.

IV

Lichtenberg remarked that in the Cartesian predicament one ought to say, not 'I think', but 'It's thinking', on an analogy with forms of words like 'It's raining'.[9] Parfit reads this aphorism as a straight-faced statement: he takes Lichtenberg to accept that psychological goings-on can be intelligibly reported impersonally – that is, without imposing a subject–predicate structure – and to hold that Descartes needed to exploit this possibility (pp. 224–6). On this understanding, Lichtenberg is fundamentally Cartesian in the sense I have suggested: he accepts that 'consciousness' has its content in a way that requires no context, and merely protests that once we have 'consciousness' in view in its pure form, stripped of all objective context by the Method of Doubt, it is clear that what we have before us does not contain within itself the resources to make sense of attributing its contents to a subject. But it is really quite doubtful that we can conceive thinking as a subjectless occurrence, like a state of the weather, and Lichtenberg's aphorism is much more pointed if we read him as exploiting that fact. In allowing scepticism to generate the supposed predicament in which the *cogito* is to operate, Descartes has indeed thought away conditions that would be necessary for the idea of singling out a subject to make sense. And it is not that Descartes can, even so, stop the rot with a variant on the purely inner certainty that the *cogito* alleges, divergent in that it must be formulated in impersonal terms. The aphorism goes through the motions of expressing that idea, but we cannot be meant to take it simply in our stride. The point of the aphorism, on this different reading, is to question the basic Cartesian conviction that 'consciousness' is self-contained, so that the stripping away of context that the Method of Doubt effects reveals 'consciousness' as it really is; on the contrary, removal of context makes it impossible to keep 'consciousness' itself in view.[10]

V

Generations of commentators, from Butler on, have supposed that Locke meant to convey a thesis about personal identity of a kind that would be undermined by an accusation of circularity. Butler and his followers think this dooms a Lockean approach to personal identity;

Parfit agrees with Butler that circularity would be a killing objection, but follows Sydney Shoemaker in offering Locke conceptual material to escape it.[11] But the Lockean thesis I have cited is so open about simply using the notion of identity ('can consider itself as itself, the same thinking thing, in different times and places') that we ought to pause before we accept Butler's assumption that circularity would be a problem for what Locke intends. It is not just obvious that the task of philosophy is to 'analyse' every concept around which philosophical issues arise. I have tried to cast doubt on one specific motivation for a reductionist 'correction' of Locke's apparent willingness to have the notion of identity figure unanalysed in what he gives as the content of 'consciousness'. And it is not as if Locke's remark would be pointless otherwise: on the contrary, it pin-points, as it stands, the essential 'inner' availability of personal persistence, which Cartesian philosophy rightly stresses but misconceives. I doubt that we do Locke a favour by interpreting away the unashamed 'circularity' in what he actually says.

Admittedly Locke is eager to affirm a difference between what sameness comes to for persons and what it comes to for human beings ('men'); and his point seems to go beyond making room for, say, dolphins or Martians to be persons, something that would pose no problem for the sort of position I am urging. But this is not an area of Locke's discussion that can carry much weight in a recommendation of reductionism.

Locke's account of human identity is an application of his admirable account of the identity of living things. Persistence, for a living thing, is the continuation of an individual life of the appropriate kind, sustained through alterations of matter so long as they preserve the necessary organization. But when Locke applies this idea to human beings, he lets the application be shaped by a broadly Cartesian division of what might otherwise be regarded as the composite life of the human being that a person is, into merely animal functions on the one hand and operations of 'consciousness' on the other. The result is a conception of the identity of human beings in which human life is conceived as what is left over after a Cartesian skimming off of 'cogitation'. According to this conception, what it is for the same human life to be still in progress is a matter of continuity in merely animal functioning: it suffices that the organic basis of walking, eating and so forth persists, in the sense that there is continuity, through exchange of matter with the environment, in the material underpinnings for the relevant potentialities. Thus, when Locke imagines a case in which the bodies of a prince and a cobbler exchange 'consciousnesses', he takes it that the identities of the human beings involved go with the gross bodily continuities: 'The body too goes to the making the man, and would, I guess, to everybody determine the man in this case.'[12]

If we read Locke's claim about the relevance of 'consciousness' to personal identity outside the context of that broadly Cartesian division, it serves not as a sketch of a putatively self-standing sort of continuity, whose subject (if any) would have to be a purely spiritual continuant, but as describing a special feature of what continuation of life comes to for animals of a distinctive kind. The 'thinking intelligent being' that is a person can be, and be aware of itself as, a human being – to fix on the case that we have to take as central. Locke's account of what a person is, in fact, perfectly fits normal human beings.

But this suggests that we should not go Locke's way with the case of the prince and the cobbler. Suppose that we really can imagine the prince (that person) finding himself with the body that used to belong to the cobbler.[13] The person with that body is the prince.[14] That is, his life after the catastrophe is a continuation of the life of that person, the prince. And if we free Locke from the broadly Cartesian division, there is nothing to stop us saying that that continuing life prolongs the life of that human being, the one that the prince was and is. Indeed, we had better say that: surely there are not two lives being led here, the life of the human being, continuing a life that has always been led hereabouts, and the life of the person, proceeding after a spatial discontinuity.[15] The fact that, for instance, the legs that he moves when he walks are different no more makes this something other than a continuation of the same human life (if we make sense of the story at all) than does the fact that a different heart beats in the chest of someone who has received a transplant. Whether it is a continuation of the same human life depends not on the identity of limbs and organs, but on whether it is a prolongation of the career of the self-conscious agent who lives it.

Locke famously claims that 'person' is 'a forensic term'.[16] What underlies this is the thought that the ethical significance of personal agency is connected with self-consciousness. Now one effect of disallowing any help from the continuity of human (or, if you like, dolphin or Martian) life in understanding personal identity, in the move that reflects the Cartesian division, is to encourage an overblown reading of this good thought. No doubt, incurable amnesia about a past action makes it pointless to punish someone for it; the Cartesian framework induces Locke to proceed as if such reasonable thoughts reflected something much more contentious, that actions to which one's 'consciousness' does not extend are no part of one's life as a person. It is this rather unhappy region of Locke's thinking that gives rise to the appearance that he is committed to a self-sufficient 'memory criterion' of personal identity. I think it uncharitable to emphasize this strand, to the detriment of the evidently non-reductive, and in itself quite non-Cartesian, central claim about awareness of self.

The Cartesian division of 'consciousness' from merely animal life that frames Locke's discussion reflects the assumption that 'that thinking thing that is in us' is immaterial.[17] This is what makes it seem that continuity of animal life, even the life of a human being, cannot be constitutively involved in continuity of 'consciousness'. But though Locke allows himself that assumption, he carefully distances himself from Descartes. It is not only that he leaves it open whether the presumed immaterial subject of 'consciousness' is an unchanging substance, as opposed to something which persists through change in what constitutes it, on an analogy with the way in which an embodied living thing persists through change in the matter of which it is composed.[18] He is also agnostic about the background assumption itself,[19] happily embracing the consequence that his thought-experiments – for instance, the case of the prince and the cobbler – may have an absurdity that he and his readers miss only through ignorance. This equanimity is incomprehensible unless we suppose that his main concern is to affirm that persons are self-conscious, and that he is rightly confident that that thesis, to which he can give vivid expression on the assumption that continuity of self-consciousness is separable from any merely animal continuity, would not be undermined if that Cartesian separation could not be effected.

VI

In trying to spell out what Locke means by 'consciousness', it is natural to focus on memory. Memory in some sense must be part, at least, of anything one could mean by 'serial co-consciousness'. For reductionist purposes what is needed is a capacity that retrospectively holds past states and occurrences together within the purview of a single 'consciousness', but in a way that is intelligible other than in terms of the idea that all this belongs to the past life of the subject who engages in the retrospection. I have tried to suggest that the distinctively reductionist element of this thought is neither well motivated nor part of Locke's basic insight: memory can fall into place as simply part of the capacity of 'a thinking intelligent being' to 'consider itself as itself, the same thinking thing, in different times and places'. But even if reductionism lacks a good external motivation, it would surely be of interest if something recognizably close to Locke's phenomenon could be given a non-circular analysis. In any case, we need to consider an ingenious conceptual innovation with which reductionists have tried to provide for the distinctively reductionist element in face of an obvious objection.

Memory of the appropriate sort, as ordinarily conceived, is the capacity to retain knowledge of one's own past. But that formulation simply uses the notion for which we are supposed to be looking for a reduction.[20] The reductionist response is that retrospective 'consciousness' should be conceived rather as quasi-memory.[21] Quasi-memory, like 'experience' memory as ordinarily conceived, is a capacity to recapture actual past states and occurrences 'from within' (i.e. from the point of view of the subject of an experience or the agent of an action), with whatever causal connection to the past states and occurrences is needed for that to be intelligible. The only difference is that there is no requirement that the remembering subject be identical with the subject from whose point of view the past occurrences are recaptured. So ordinary memories are quasi-memories that satisfy that extra condition. But there can be quasi-memories that are not ordinary memories: cases where the quasi-rememberer has been equipped with a capacity to recapture past occurrences from a participant point of view that was not his own, perhaps by transplantation of brain tissue that might, if left in its original skull, have figured in the aetiology of some ordinary remembering. A similar strategy is obviously available for other aspects of 'serial co-consciousness' – for instance, intention. But it will make for simplicity if we focus on memory.

Ordinary memories are quasi-memories: as the concept of quasi-memory has been explained, an ordinary person quasi-remembers those past states and occurrences that are within the reach of his present 'consciousness'. The truth of this claim simply requires one thing less than the more familiar claim that he remembers those past states and occurrences. But in what sense does it follow that one's ordinary belief, when one takes oneself to have 'experience' memory, that one is aware of something in one's own past is 'a separable belief', as Parfit puts it (p. 222)? For reductionist purposes, quasi-memory needs to be a capacity whose exercises intelligibly constitute retention of knowledge of past states and occurrences 'from within', but in such a way that the identity of their subject – in particular, his being one and the same as the quasi-rememberer – is not represented in the content of the retained knowledge. The reductionist claim is that this identity-neutral, though 'from within', hold on the past is the real content of the retrospective component of 'consciousness'; the specification of identity that Locke adds ('consider itself as itself') reflects an extra belief, warranted in the familiar, normal case, but no part of the pure deliverance of retrospective 'consciousness'. But it is a mistake to think that the intelligibility of quasi-memory meets this reductionist requirement.

Consider a case of mere quasi-memory, intelligibly brought about by suitable intervention in its subject's brain.[22] To say that it is mere quasi-memory, as opposed to ordinary memory, is to say that the subject's

belief that the recalled states and occurrences figured in his own life is
false. But that does not show that the content of this identity-involving
belief is separable from the content of the impression, the knowledge
that the subject seems to retain from the past. On the contrary: we have
not been equipped to make sense of mere quasi-memories other than by
supposing that they would present themselves as memories – that is, that
they would embody an impression, which must be illusory, that the
subject of the recalled state or occurrence was oneself. We need to be
careful about the sense in which, when we drop the identity requirement
that distinguishes ordinary memory from mere quasi-memory, we keep
at our disposal whatever causal connection is necessary to make quasi-
memory intelligible. No doubt a science-fiction story about copying or
transplanting memory traces can make it intelligible that a subject might
have memory impressions from someone else's past. But what it cannot
make intelligible is that such impressions might constitute knowledge.
This kind of aetiology enables us to make sense of quasi-memory as
yielding illusions of ordinary memory, not as what reductionists require
it to be: an autonomously intelligible faculty of knowing the past from a
participant's perspective but without commitment to the participant's
having been oneself.[23]

It is true, but irrelevant, that if a subject of mere quasi-memories knew
how those impressions of the past were caused, they would entitle him to
claim knowledge of the past. That does not put quasi-memory on a level,
epistemologically speaking, with memory. Memories are not something
from which one derives knowledge of one's past, on the basis of sur-
rounding information; they simply are knowledge of one's past. How can
that be so? How can something as slight, so to speak, as an impression
have that cognitive status? The answer to this question lies in the very
same appeal to the objective context of 'consciousness' that explains how
it is possible for 'consciousness' to present an identity through time
without itself applying criteria of persistence. The objective context explains how the contents of 'consciousness' can have both their shape and
their cognitive status even though 'consciousness' does not need to draw
on that context, say to supply premises for inferences, in arriving at its
contents and its epistemic entitlements. Quasi-remembering does have
epistemic potential, but it depends on the objective context in a quite
different way: using quasi-memories as a basis for knowledge would
require 'consciousness' to draw explicitly on information extraneous to
its own contents. So the fact that one might know the past on the basis of
quasi-remembering does no damage to the thesis that quasi-memory is
intelligible only derivatively. It is not special to illusions of this kind that
someone who knew enough about their aetiology could derive knowledge from them; that makes no difference to the fact that the concept of

illusion, of whatever kind, is secondary to the concept of what the illusion misrepresents itself as being.

Once one has the notion of mere quasi-memory, made intelligible in terms of suitable abnormal aetiologies for memory impressions, one can entertain the supposition that an apparent memory is a mere quasi-memory, thereby distancing oneself from the belief that it was oneself who lived through the recalled state or occurrence. In that sense the belief is indeed 'separable'. But this does not equip the memory impression with an identity-neutral content: the supposition one would be entertaining is that an impression whose content is not identity-neutral, because it is that of an ordinary memory, is illusory in respect of that aspect of its content. Compare the way one can distance oneself from the belief that one's objective environment is as one's perceptual experience represents it, by entertaining a suitably abnormal aetiology for the experience. This does nothing to show that the content of the experience is anything other than the content of the suspended belief; the effect of envisaging the abnormal aetiology is that one conceives the experiences not as exercises of some autonomously intelligible faculty of quasi-perception, but as illusions of perception.[24]

This parallel bears elaboration. Quasi-memory was introduced by dropping a requirement for ordinary personal memory, and it may seem difficult to reconcile that with the claim that quasi-memory is intelligible only derivatively from ordinary personal memory: surely, we may be tempted to think, the concept with fewer requirements must be simpler and therefore independently graspable. But this should rouse our suspicion as soon as we see that it parallels the thought that is at work in the Argument from Illusion, which has done enormous damage in the epistemology of perception. Start with, say, the notion of seeing that such-and-such is the case. Now introduce a notion explained as applicable in just the same conditions, except that there is no requirement that such-and-such is the case. There is nothing wrong with this second notion, any more than there is anything wrong with the notion of quasi-memory. But it is disastrous to conclude, from the fact that we can arrive at it by dropping a requirement, that what it is for the second notion to be applicable is intelligible other than in terms of an appearance whose content is the dropped requirement: that the distinctive content with which applications of the first notion make play, that such-and-such is the case, is a mere 'separable belief'. That poses an intractable problem over how there can be a justificatory relation between the perceptual experiences in virtue of which the second notion applies and the 'separable belief'. Here, as with quasi-memory, the dropped requirement does not simply disappear: the second notion cannot be understood apart from the idea of an appearance that the dropped requirement is satisfied, that is, in the context of the other requirements, an appearance that the first notion has application.

How can merely dropping a requirement yield a concept that can be understood only in this derivative way? Well, there is no reason to assume that what is left when the requirement is dropped will stand on its own as an adequate explication of a concept, even though the result constitutes necessary and sufficient conditions for the application of that concept. It takes more than an arithmetic of subtracting necessary conditions to guarantee us an autonomously intelligible concept.

VII

So far, I have considered quasi-memory only as the product of special intervention in our world, leaving what is normal unchanged. This may seem objectionably parochial. The objection I have in mind is that, in suggesting that quasi-memory is intelligible only as a kind of illusion, I have illicitly exploited the way ordinary thought lets itself be shaped by the sheer weight of what merely happens to be normal, and thereby kept a genuine conceptual possibility from coming into view. To correct this, we must allow imaginative alteration of the whole background of normality, by considering, say, beings whose normal mode of multiplying is by splitting, like amoebas, but with retrospective 'consciousness' over the life that precedes a split retained by both the self-contained organisms that are extant after a split. Here, surely, it may be said, we have quasi-memory in the form in which reductionists want it, a cognitive hold on past life-experiences, 'from within' but not representing the subject of the past life-experiences as identical with the subject of the retrospective 'consciousness'; the background of normality which I have so far exploited to force that content on the impressions is simply absent from the imagined world. And once we have exploited this thought-experiment, or another to the same purpose, to ensure a proper understanding of quasi-memory, we can bring the concept, thus liberated from the appearance of being intrinsically derivative, back to our world for the original reductionist purpose: characterizing our retrospective 'consciousness' in an identity-neutral way.

All sorts of questions arise if we try to think the thought-experiment through. Are we to conceive these beings as living continuants whose lives include what is within the survey of their retrospective 'consciousness'? If so, since after a split there are two independently living things who can thus claim to have lived through what was apparently a single life before the split, are we to say that there were two lives (at least) being led all along? This makes it hard to imagine what analogue to first-person thinking might express the 'from within' character of 'conscious-ness' of present life-experiences on the part of, as we cannot easily put it, one of these beings, knowing what shape their lives normally take.[25] Should such thought be in the plural? (Compare the man in the Gospel possessed by demons who, when asked his name, replied 'Legion, for we are many'.[26])

We might try equipping these beings with a primary form of self-conscious thought whose reference can be unproblematically singular because it spans only periods between splits. But the retrospective scope of this mode of thought would be carried by something analogous to ordinary memory. And then we risk once more representing quasi-memories that reach back before a split as illusions: these are animals that come into being and cease to exist at splits, like amoebas, but they are self-conscious, and explicably equipped, from the beginning of their careers, with the appearance of having themselves lived the lives of their progenitors.

Well, perhaps not. Perhaps we can leave them capable of singular self-reference, but avoid populating their retrospective 'consciousness' with illusions; perhaps retrospective 'consciousness' in this world would present the past it surveyed as 'mine or ours', with a first-person plural reference to fellow descendants of the subject whose experience or action was being recalled. (The disjunction would be resolved in favour of one of its disjuncts by suitable information, if available, about whether the recalled material pre-dates the latest split.) But this way of filling out the thought-experiment would not support Parfit's suggestion that the content of our 'consciousness' can stand revealed as really identity-neutral, unshaped by its normal objective background, which serves merely as a normal cause. On the contrary, we are here imagining how a different objective context of normality might make intelligible a differ-ent identity-involving content for retrospective 'consciousness'. The thought-experiment in this form does nothing to recommend regarding the normal background within which a retrospective 'consciousness' op-erates as extraneous to its true content, so that our retrospective 'con-sciousness' is really less committal than Locke represents it as being.

It may be said that I am still imposing parochial restrictions on the imagination, in refusing to understand the idea that 'consciousness' rep-resents its objects 'from within' except in terms of something sufficiently close to first-person reference as we know it, which is reference to par-ticular things that live particular lives. The point of this and similar thought-experiments, it may be said, is to encourage an imaginative detachment of the 'from within' character of 'consciousness' from any such context. But here the accusation of excessive respect for mere normality seems to me to lose its power to disturb. Thought-experiments like these can stretch our sense of the possibilities for lives and the particular things that live them. But how could they show that we can really make sense of 'from within' in abstraction from the idea of a continuing life, lived by a subject whose experiences figure in its 'consciousness' as belonging to itself? In some sense, no doubt, we can focus imaginatively on the 'from within' character of 'consciousness' in abstraction from any objective background. But if one supposes that the simplicity of imaginative attention establishes that what is needed for the target of the attention to be intelligible is all present within the scope of the focused attention, one falls into a familiar kind of fundamentally Cartesian illusion.

Parfit in effect glosses the 'from within' character of 'consciousness' in terms of the first-person mode of presentation, which is fine by my lights.[27] But he suggests that contemplating quasi-memory shows that the fact that 'our apparent memories . . . come to us in the first-person mode' can be detached from their purporting to be about ourselves; that is a mere 'separable belief'. I think this reduces the idea of the first-person mode to unintelligibility. It gets things backwards to suppose that the first-person mode of presentation can be understood in terms of an independently intelligible 'interiority' or 'subjectivity' of the flow of experience, with reference to a subject introduced, if at all, only by a subsequent construction.

VIII

Parfit presents reductionism as the required corrective to an error of which postulating purely spiritual substances is just one form: the error is to regard the identity of a person through time as 'a further fact'. Some people think they can have the further fact without further things, but Parfit argues (pp. 239–40) that belief in the further fact is unintelligible without a belief 'that we are separately existing entities, distinct from our brains and bodies'. Cartesian souls are just the most familiar result of trying to spell out what the separately existing entities might be. The point of insisting on the further fact is supposed to be that it putatively underwrites the belief, which according to Parfit is a mere prejudice, that questions of personal identity are always determinate: that if a person exists at some time, then at all later times there must be a definite answer to the question whether that person still exists.

I think this distorts the credentials of psychological reductionism as a positive thesis: the thesis that what continuity of 'consciousness' really is can be understood without presupposing the idea of a person's continued existence. When Parfit depicts opponents of reductionism as committed to the further fact, he proceeds as if they could not possibly be disputing the availability of the conceptual materials for a reduction: an identity-free account of continuous 'consciousness', and perhaps a similarly identity-free account of bodily continuity. Why would they nevertheless insist that personal identity is a further fact, over and above facts that can be stated in such terms? The only plausible reason is that they think the question whether some person still exists has more determinateness than any construction out of such materials could give it.

But the right basis for opposing reductionism is that we have been given no good reason to believe in a substratum of identity-free relations. In particular, there is no genuinely intelligible reductionist substitute for Locke's identity-involving characterization of continuous 'consciousness'. From this point of view, Parfit's account of what is at issue is prejudicial: reductionism is wrong, not because personal identity is a further fact, but because there is no conceptually simpler substratum for personal identity to be further to.

This opposition to reductionism is simply separate from any insistence that personal identity is always determinate. The question whether a given person still exists is the question whether a certain life is still in progress; and it is not peculiar to personal life that one can imagine tamperings with nature after which the only possible response to that question would be to shrug one's shoulders.[28] This affords no support to the claim that is in doubt, that Locke's phenomenon can be genuinely understood in identity-neutral terms.

What about separately existing entities? Persons are living things whose lives, at least in normal cases, include the capacity for self-awareness that Locke stresses. If we refuse to reduce a person's continuing existence to supposedly prior relations that hold the elements of such a life together, that is not to picture a person's continuing existence as separate from the continuation of his life. Nor is it to suppose that a person is, in some objectionable sense, distinct from his brain and his body (Parfit's gloss on 'separately existing'). Not that a person should be identified with his brain and (the rest of) his body, any more than a house should be identified with the bricks, and so forth, of which it is composed; but there is no commitment to some peculiar extra ingredient, which would ensure determinateness of identity, in a person's make-up.[29]

The distorting effect of Parfit's play with the further fact emerges when he dispenses himself (p. 273) from discussing the view of, for instance, David Wiggins.[30] His justification is that Wiggins's account of personal identity, which is in terms of the continuation of a distinctive kind of life, involves no commitment to separately existing entities, or to the general determinateness of identity which the further fact is supposed to underwrite. That is true enough. But Wiggins's picture of personal identity gives no comfort to the positively reductionist reconstrual of Locke's phenomenon on which I have been casting doubt. And without that, there is nothing to supplant concern with one's own future in the structuring of rationality. A position like Wiggins's is a serious threat to the striking practical implications that Parfit attributes to reductionism.

IX

We are living things, and we share with other living things a natural interest in surviving. This aspect of our animal nature emerges in our rationally governed lives as a concern that has a conceptual content: a concern, naturally felt by each of us, that the living thing he or she is should continue to exist. This helps to structure a whole region of practical reason, in which we locate not just the rationality of taking steps to ensure our persistence, but also such things as reasons for making provision for the quality of our future lives. Or so we naturally suppose.

Parfit aims to dislodge this structure as mere prejudice. But in discrediting the supposed simpler conceptual substratum for personal identity, I have discredited the basis for this suggestion. We have not been given a conceptual pathway along which rational concerns could be understood to be carried into the future in a way that underlies the concern with oneself, and should supplant it once we see that they are separable. Why should my interest in the continuation of the life I am leading be supplanted by an interest in lives that embody the illusion of being continuations of my life?

Suppose I am face to face with the end of my life, the life of the individual living thing I am. Perhaps it would be a consolation to learn that the world without me was going to contain someone with a perfect, and explicable, illusion of having lived my life so far – perhaps two, produced from me by fission.[31] The prospect might indeed have unwelcome features. For instance, it would bother my wife to be competed for by two people, each taking himself to be me; and it would be hard to be confident that a quasi-intention to bow out, somehow formed by me now in respect of just one of them, would be acted on, since each would presumably have a replica of my concern for her. But suppose we waive such difficulties, and focus on the consoling power of the thought that someone will exist who cares especially about my less individualistic projects. (With some projects, the more the better.)

None of this shows that the concern for the future whose promised satisfaction accounts for this possible consolation overlaps with, let alone exhausts, the interest in my own future as it fits into the natural conditions of my life. If a prospect might console me in face of the prospect of an end to the individual life I am living, it does not follow that it is 'about as good as ordinary survival'.[32] Perhaps it would be rational to choose fission in preference to death without quasi-continuation; it does not follow that the rationality of an ordinary concern with my own future can be disconnected from the fact that it is the future of the living individual I am. It can be rational to choose fission over death without quasi-continuation, and still not be a prejudice to prefer the continuation of one's individual life to either.[33]

We should not overestimate the significance of the fact that there is reason to value the existence of someone who cares about one's projects. If we focus on outcomes, to the exclusion of a concern with what a deliberator himself is to do, we single out an application of reason whose topic is reasons why such-and-such should take place or be brought about – never mind by whom. All by itself, this could not be a recognizable conception of practical reason; of course, the topic is part of the subject-matter of practical reason, but it is not intelligible that there should be such a topic except in the context of practical reason proper, whose primary concern is action to be undertaken by the subject who deliberates. Parfit aims at a picture of practical reason as in no way shaped by facts about the persistence of individual human beings. But to my eye it seems quite implausible that the concept of agency, and with it the concept of practical reason, can survive outside a context of thought about the activities of individual living things. And the apparatus of reductionism yields no ground for being suspicious of that impression, and perhaps trying to dislodge it as a prejudice.

A deep element in a broadly Cartesian outlook is an inability to conceive 'cogitation' as part of something as 'merely' natural (so this cast of thought will incline us to put it) as the life of an individual animal. This inability is manifested in the Cartesian segregation of 'cogitation' into a special realm of reality. It deserves sympathy, even if we manage not to share it; it reflects powerful pressures on us to conceive the world of nature in a way that resists fitting rationality into it. (Another manifestation is an attraction towards 'naturalistic' reductions of rationality.) Now I have already suggested that the drift of Parfit's position is Cartesian, and I think we can understand his thinking as a reflection of that felt tension between reason, and hence mind, and 'mere' nature. He is anxious to avoid the more blatant expressions of this tendency of thought: notably pure spiritual substances, conceived as problematically related to living animals. But the tendency shows in his refusal to let the space of reasons be structured by the natural continuities of human life. Perhaps it shows also in his eloquently expressed sense of a liberation that reductionism affords from a felt imprisonment in his own individual life and a special concern with his own individual death (p. 281). A familiar concomitant of the inability to take phrases like 'the life of the mind' at face value is a temptation to fantasies of transcending the finiteness of individual life; and I suspect that Parfit's sense of liberation is just another manifestation of that deeply suspect temptation. So, far from freeing practical reason from prejudice, I think Parfit's position belongs in a long series of philosophical distortions imposed on reflection about reason and human life by our having forgotten, intelligibly by all means, how to maintain a firm and integrated conception of ourselves as rational animals.[34]

Notes

1 John Locke, *An Essay Concerning Human Understanding*, II. 27. 9.
2 See David Wiggins, *Sameness and Substance* (Blackwell, Oxford, 1980), esp. chs 2 and 3.
3 See Gareth Evans, *The Varieties of Reference* (Clarendon Press, Oxford, 1982), p. 237. Evans seems to slip when he suggests (ibid.) that the point can be put in terms of 'immunity to error through misidentification': i.e. the circumstance that a judgement's predication is not attached to its subject by way of a judgement of identity. As he points out on p. 236, 'identification-freedom', so explained, is consistent with a judgement's depending on keeping track of its object. (Keeping track serves as it were instead of an 'identification component' in the basis of continuing demonstrative thought about objects of ordinary perception.) The point about the self is a peculiarly strong form of 'identification-freedom'.
4 See P. F. Strawson's brilliantly suggestive reading of Kant's Paralogisms of Pure Reason, in *The Bounds of Sense* (Methuen, London, 1966), pp. 162–70.
5 The Cartesian *cogito* is supposed to reveal self-reference as still feasible even when the Method of Doubt has done its worst, and one is entertaining the possibility that there are no continuants capable of being thought about in a way that would require applying criteria of persistence or employing a substantial empirical skill of keeping track. Part of the point of this, to be applauded even while we leave ourselves room to object on other scores, is that it serves to make vivid the fact that continuity of 'consciousness' involves no keeping track of the subject.
6 As Strawson puts it (*Bounds of Sense*, p. 165), the thought that reflects continuity of 'consciousness' has 'links' with empirical criteria of identity which are 'not severed' by the fact that the criteria are not applied (not even in the form of a purely practical skill of keeping track) within such thought. Evans's treatment of first-person modes of presentation (*Varieties of Reference*, ch. 7) is an elaboration of the way in which thinking about oneself is to be understood as taking place within, and bearing on, objective reality: reality conceived as independent of any particular point of view.

7   In his debate with Richard Swinburne in their co-authored book *Personal Identity* (Blackwell, Oxford, 1984), Sydney Shoemaker espouses psychological reductionism in the context of an ultimately materialist functionalism about the mental. There is certainly no ontological dualism here. This does not deter me from suggesting that reductionism is fundamentally Cartesian; it is superficial to suppose that we can avoid what is basically wrong with Cartesian philosophy by avoiding the dualism that is the most striking feature of its mainstream versions.

8   G. E. M. Anscombe, 'The First Person', in *Mind and Language*, ed. Samuel Guttenplan (Clarendon Press, Oxford, 1975), pp. 45–65; see esp. pp. 64–5.

9   '*Es denkt*, sollte man sagen, so wie man sagt: *es blitzt*' (quoted by Parfit, p. 517, n. 20).

10 The *cogito* is thus more than just a device to make the 'identification-freedom' of self-consciousness vivid (see n. 5 above); it also embodies the mistaken conclusion from that fact, that self-consciousness has its content independently of any objective context. Contrast another way of making 'identification-freedom' vivid, sensory deprivation: see Anscombe, 'First Person', pp. 57–8. One can think of oneself in conditions of sensory deprivation, that is, without having one's bodily presence in the world perceptually borne in on one; this highlights the way self-reference is separated from criteria of persistence. But this case can be understood without any suggestion that self-reference is consistent with the supposed possibility against the background of which the *cogito* is supposed to operate, that there is no objective continuant for one to be.

11 See S. Shoemaker, 'Persons and their Pasts', *American Philosophical Quarterly*, 7 (1970), pp. 269–85.

12 Locke, *Essay*, II. 27. 15.

13 We may need to embellish Locke's bare fairy-tale with science fiction about brain transplantation, to ensure that we are really imagining a migration of 'consciousness', as opposed to a peculiar illusion.

14 Even if, as Locke supposes, he is 'the same cobbler to every one besides himself'. Everyone besides himself is wrong about which person this is.

15 See Wiggins, *Sameness and Substance*, p. 161, n. 16; see also ch. 1.

16 Locke, *Essay*, II. 27. 26.

17 Ibid., II. 27. 27.

18 Ibid., II. 27. 10–14.

19 Ibid., II. 27. 27.

20 I have formulated the objection of circularity so as to avoid the crude errors exposed by Wiggins, *Sameness and Substance*, pp. 152–4.

21 This resource for reductionism was first devised by Shoemaker, 'Persons and their Pasts'; for Parfit's account of it, see pp. 220–2.

22 See Parfit, p. 220.

23 Not that a quasi-memory would be illusion through and through. Someone would really have lived through the quasi-remembered past. (And perhaps that life experience might have, for the quasi-rememberer, the sort of formative significance that elements from one's own past can have in the familiar normal case.) But this leaves untouched the point that a quasi-memory

would embody an illusion in respect of the subject of the remembered state or occurrence.

24 The case I am urging against the claim that quasi-memory serves the purposes of reductionism comes from Evans, *Varieties of Reference*, pp. 241–8. Parfit (alone, so far as I know, among proponents of reductionism) undertakes to respond to Evans (p. 516, n. 15). But his response consists entirely in stressing the irrelevant point that someone who knew the aetiology of a quasi-memory could acquire knowledge of someone else's past from it. (Evans cheerfully grants the point at p. 245, though one would not gather this from Parfit's representation of him.)

25 See Wiggins, *Sameness and Substance*, p. 168.

26 See Anscombe, 'First Person', pp. 58–9.

27 See pp. 221–2.

28 See Parfit's Spectrum arguments, pp. 231–43.

29 Besides Cartesian souls, Parfit mentions a hitherto unrecognized kind of physical entity as a candidate to fill this role: p. 210.

30 For which see Wiggins, *Sameness and Substance*, ch. 6.

31 I have conceded that it need not be illusion through and through.

32 Parfit, p. 261.

33 See David Wiggins, 'The Concern to Survive', *Midwest Studies in Philosophy*, 4 (1979), 417–22.

34 For an excellent introduction to the wider issues here, see Wiggins, *Sameness and Substance*, pp. 179–87.

12

Should Ethics Be More Impersonal?

Robert Merrihew Adams

When Derek Parfit comes to articulate 'one common feature' of most of the manifold conclusions of his book, he says, 'I have argued that, in various ways, our reasons for acting should become *more impersonal*. Greater impersonality may seem threatening. But it would often be better for everyone' (p. 443). As this statement intimates, *Reasons and Persons* is an ambitious book, morally as well as theoretically, by an avowed 'revisionist' in philosophy (p. x). The work is animated by a manifest concern to find rationally warranted changes in our beliefs that will help us to deal in a morally and humanly more satisfactory way with such problems as the inevitability of our own deaths and the impact of our actions on future generations. It is a book that most philosophers in the English-speaking world, and many others with an educated interest in moral and social problems, will want to read – not only because of its boldness and its wealth of ingenious and fascinating examples and puzzles, but also because of the author's architectonic sensibility, which forces us, time and again, to think about issues in a new way.

The present reviewer disagrees strongly with Parfit's case for greater impersonality; and much of this essay will be devoted to criticism of it. This is particularly true of sections I and II, which are about Parfit's claim that common-sense morality 'fails in its own terms', and about the practical implications he draws from his reductionism about personal identity. In section III, I will argue that some of his ethical paradoxes about the further future can be solved in ways that he does not consider. These are among the main topics of Parts 1, 3 and 4, respectively, of *Reasons and Persons*.

First published as a Critical Notice of *Reasons and Persons* in *the Philosophical Reviews*, 98 (1989), pp. 439–84.

The refutation of the Self-interest Theory, S, which is not only the central topic of Part 2, but a major unifying theme that runs through the first three parts of the book, will not receive such extended discussion here; but something must be said about it at the outset. I agree that S is wrong, and have no interest in defending it against Parfit's critique. S is a theory of practical rationality. Its 'central claim' is

(S1)   For each person, there is one supremely rational ultimate aim: that his life go, for him, as well as possible. (p. 4)

By an 'ultimate' (as opposed to an 'instrumental') aim, Parfit means a goal that is sought for its own sake and not merely as a means to some other end.

Parfit argues persuasively (in section 46) for the controversial assumption that ultimate aims, in this sense, can be irrational, or more and less rational. He gives us less help, I think, in seeing whether there are intuitively plausible and interestingly general criteria for assessing the rationality of such aims. His first, and what he entitles 'the best objection to the Self-interest Theory', is so simple an appeal to intuition that he has more recently commented that it 'hardly deserves the name' of 'argument'.[1] It is merely that there are several ultimate aims or desires (e.g. for achievement and the good of other people) that are (as we judge intuitively) 'no less rational than the bias in one's own favour', and in pursuit of them it can be rational to do what is worse for oneself (pp. 131–3, 192). Like other reviewers, I find this argument, simple as it is, convincing, and indeed 'the best' of Parfit's objections to S.

His more elaborate arguments against S, in Part 2, seem to me much less persuasive. They have to do with *time*. The concern for one's own good demanded by S, as Parfit interprets it, is temporally neutral, at least as regards the future. For this reason S condemns as irrational the very common 'bias towards the near', in which one is willing to accept somewhat lesser pleasures, if they will happen sooner, and somewhat greater pains, if they will happen later. Parfit uses this to show that S allows some types of relation but not others to have rational importance, and he argues that S should be rejected because no good argument can be given to justify this asymmetry. Much that is interesting and illuminating emerges in the course of his argument; but I do not see why those who find the Self-interest. Theory intuitively plausible (as Parfit and I do not) should admit that they stand in any special need of argumentative support here for granting to one sort of relation a rational importance that they deny to another. If they did need it, why would Parfit not need an argument (which he does not give) for granting (as he does) a rational importance to one type of sensation (pain) that he would not grant to others (such as, perhaps, the smell of eucalyptus)? Of course, he thinks that the latter asymmetry is obviously right in a way that S's asymmetries are not; but that just carries us back to the appeal to intuition.

I What Must a Moral Theory Do to Succeed?

Part 1 of *Reasons and Persons* is about 'self-defeating theories'. Parfit thinks of moral theories and theories of rationality as 'giving' us 'aims'. For instance, S gives me the aim 'that [my] life go, for [me], as well as possible' (p. 4). He classifies a theory, T, as *self-defeating* if following, or trying to follow, T is not the most effective way of achieving 'T-given aims'. The self-defeat is *direct* if it results from actually doing what T recommends, *indirect* if it results rather from *trying* to follow T, or from a desire or disposition to do so. The self-defeat is *individual* if individuals' T-given aims are frustrated through individual adherence to T, *collective* if everyone's T-given aims would be frustrated if everyone adhered to T. The two most important kinds of self-defeat for our discussion are defined by Parfit as follows. He says T is

> *indirectly individually self-defeating* when it is true that, if someone tries to achieve his T-given aims, these aims will be, on the whole, worse achieved (p. 5);

> *directly collectively self-defeating* when it is certain that, if we all successfully follow T, we will thereby cause the T-given aims *of each* to be worse achieved than they would have been if none of us had successfully followed T (p. 55).

Parfit compares S with consequentialism (C), according to which the 'one ultimate moral aim' is 'that outcomes be as good as possible' (p. 24), and with common-sense morality (M). Each of these three theories, he argues, is self-defeating in at least one of the four possible ways, but only M thereby 'fails in its own terms'. He holds that S is indirectly individually self-defeating, because it is often worse for individuals if they are disposed to be never self-denying, and that probably C is indirectly collectively self-defeating, because everyone's having the dispositions of 'pure do-gooders' would probably have worse results than our having some non-consequentialist dispositions (e.g. 'not to kill, even when we believe that this would make the outcome better' (p. 28)). But S and C do not thereby fail in their own terms, because such failure results only from direct, not from indirect, self-defeat, according to Parfit.

There are cases (e.g. 'Prisoner's Dilemmas') in which S is directly collectively self-defeating. And Parfit contends that there are analogous cases in which common-sense morality (M) is directly collectively self-defeating. Though direct, this sort of self-defeat does not show that S fails in its own terms. For it is of the essence of a Prisoner's Dilemma that I will do better for myself in it by making the self-interested choice, whatever the others do, because it is not my own altruism, but the altruism of others, that would benefit me (p. 89). Here it would be better for me if others did not follow S. But that is no embarrassment for the S theorist, who (like an investment adviser or a coach in a competitive sport) makes no promise that her advice to me will work out better, from my point of view, if *other people* follow it too. For 'S is not a collective code. It is a theory about individual rationality' (p. 92). Parfit argues, however, that M cannot get off the hook in this way, because M, unlike S, is a moral theory, and 'morality is essentially a collective code' (p. 106). Therefore, he holds, M does fail in its own terms, and must be revised, if not rejected.

I shall argue that M has not been shown to be directly collectively self-defeating, and that in any event, such self-defeat would not amount to failure in M's own terms. I shall also argue that indirect self-defeat at the individual level is more damaging to S than Parfit maintains, and that some features which C might need to have in view of its indirect self-defeat at the collective level, and which Parfit thinks acceptable, are really more unacceptable in a moral theory than direct collective self-defeat. I begin with the point about S.

Parfit distinguishes two ways in which a theory, T, could be indirectly individually self-defeating. The first way is by the agent's trying, but failing, to do what T recommends. If T is 'too difficult to follow', my T-given aims might be better achieved if I pursued some other goal instead of trying to achieve them. 'But this is not true of S,' Parfit claims (p. 5).

This claim is not obviously correct. It does seem difficult for most of use to know what will be best for us. It is not difficult to recognize some things that are obviously bad for us, or obviously necessary for us. But S demands much more discrimination than that. Might there not be, say, a moral code (L) that guided us to our own good more reliably than our own judgement would? Perhaps Parfit would reply that in that case we could (and according to S, should) try to do what is best for us *by* following that code. This might be psychologically impossible, however, because there might be circumstances in which it would be psychologically impossible for us to believe that following L would be better for us than doing something else – even though, in fact, in most such circumstances, following L would be better for us. If we have reason to believe that something of this sort is true, this would seem to me to be a potentially serious criticism of S.

The other way in which a theory can be indirectly individually self-defeating is through the agent's dispositions rather than through his or her actions; and Parfit speculates that this is true of S for most people most of the time (p. 7). Suppose I always try to do the action that will be best for me, and always succeed in doing so. I will not make this strenuous attempt unless I have the disposition never to be self-denying; and it is a thesis (S6) of S that this is 'the supremely rational disposition' (p. 8). But having this disposition is likely not to be best for me. It may be incompatible with other desires that would contribute much to my happiness – strong desires for achievement, for example, or for the good of others (p. 6). As Butler remarked. 'that character we call selfish is not the most promising for happiness.'[2] And if I have the disposition to be never self-denying, I am unlikely to be completely successful in concealing this from others, and the consequent loss of their trust may cost me dearly (cf. p. 7). (Given that this disposition is likely not to be best for me, it follows of course, according to S, that it would be rational for me to try not to have it.)

Even though it would be worse for many people if they had the disposition S praises as supremely rational, Parfit argues: 'S does not fail in its own terms.' Why not? '[T]his bad effect', he says, 'is not the result either of their doing what S tells them to do, or of their having a disposition that S tells them to have. Since this is so, S is not failing in its own terms' (p. 11). This seems to imply that a theory T fails in its own terms only if doing what T *tells* one to do leads to frustration of one's T-given aims.

The most obvious difficulty in applying this criterion to S is that S does not explicitly *tell* anyone to do anything. Parfit's formulations of S are statements about what is rational or irrational. And they give criteria of (supreme) rationality not only for actions, but also for aims, desires and dispositions. Taking all those criteria together, it is misleading to say that 'S does *not* tell these people to be never self-denying, and it tells them, if they can, *not* to be' (p. 11). It would be much more accurate to say that S tells us that one would be most rational in *having* the disposition and in *trying* not to have it.

This suggests an argument for the conclusion that S does fail in its own terms. S is a theory of rationality. It tells us (among other things),

(S6)   The supremely rational disposition is that of someone who is never self-denying. (p. 8)

Parfit grants that it would be better for some people if they did not have this disposition. In other words, he grants that there are people whose S-given aims would be worse fulfilled if they are supremely rational according to S (in one of the respects in which it is possible to be supremely rational). And their S-given aims would be worse fulfilled *because of* their S-certified supreme rationality. Why doesn't that show that, as a theory of rationality, S fails in its own terms?

Consider the case in which it is not psychologically possible for these people to cause themselves not to have a never self-denying disposition. This is an important case for S, because it is the one in which these people will have the disposition that is supremely rational according to S even if they act in the most rational way according to S (i.e. even if they try not to have it). Thus they will be as rational as they could be according to S. And precisely because of that, they will achieve their S-given aims less well than they might if they were less rational (with respect to their disposition) according to S. This would seem to tell strongly against S, if leading to failure to achieve theory-given aims matters to the success of a theory.

I suspect Parfit would reply that the success or failure of a theory in its own terms depends exclusively on the consequences of the *actions* it commends. This is a claim that deserves to be controversial. It is not only actions but also (as Parfit recognizes) desires and dispositions that we evaluate as to their rationality and morality; and we cannot safely assume that only the evaluation of actions is of practical importance.

We might ask, for example, why we should care about S or any other theory of rationality. More precisely, why should we care what ultimate aim, if any, is supremely rational? That this is not an idle question can be attested by anyone who can remember attempting, in an existential crisis, to reason themselves into caring about anything at all. But suppose I do in fact care about being rational, and therefore care about the claims of S; and suppose, further, I am persuaded of the truth of S. Now I discover that this commits me to the conclusion that it would be rational to try not to have the most rational sort of disposition. Might this not undermine the aspiration for rationality that led me to be interested in S in the first place? And is that an unimportant failing for S?

Let us turn to Parfit's argument that common-sense morality (M) fails in its own terms. He does not offer any comprehensive formulation of M, presumably because common sense is sensitive to such a variety of independent moral considerations that a complete statement of M would have to be unmanageably complex. What he does say about M is that it tells each of us that we ought to give some priority (though not an absolute priority) to the interests of 'the people to whom we stand in certain relations – such as our children, parents, friends, benefactors, pupils, patients, clients, colleagues, members of our own trade union, those whom we represent, or our fellow-citizens' (p. 95) – our 'M-related people', for short.

Given this feature of M, it is possible to devise analogues of the Prisoner's Dilemma in which the good of each agent's M-related people takes the place of the agent's own good. A good example is Parfit's Fisherman's Dilemma, in which we are poor fishermen and, because of overfishing and declining stocks of fish,

> It is true of each that, if he does not restrict his catch, this will be slightly better for his own children. They will be slightly better fed. This is so whatever others do. But if none of us restricts his catch this will be much worse for all our children than if we all restrict our catches. (p. 100)

The "tragedy of the commons"

In this case, Parfit argues, M is collectively self-defeating; for if all of us follow M, giving priority to the interests of our M-related people, those interests, which are our M-given aims in this situation,[3] will be advanced less well than if we had all followed a different policy. And this self-defeat is direct; for the bad effect results from *actions* in which we successfully follow M. Because the defeat is direct rather than indirect, and because M, as a moral theory, must be 'a collective code', Parfit concludes that M fails in its own terms.

This assumes that a consistent (rational) set of values must never conflict in any contingent situation

He proposes that M should therefore be revised. The most radical revision would convert M into an *agent-neutral* theory. Parfit rightly observes that problems like the Fisherman's Dilemma arise for theories that are *agent-relative*, in the sense that they assign different aims to different agents. N is the agent-neutral theory into which M can be transformed by saying that 'each of us should always try to do what will best achieve everyone's M-given aims' (p. 108) – that is, I take it, the aims that had been assigned to each by M, counted in accordance with a principle of aggregation not mentioned here by Parfit. How oppressively conformist a unanimity of purpose would be required under N, as the price of avoiding competition and conflict, is not spelled out. In any event, Parfit acknowledges that his argument cannot compel believers in M to move all the way to N (pp. 109 f.).

He argues instead that M-believers ought rationally to be converted at least to a more modestly revised theory, R. R holds in effect that we ought to do the more impartially benevolent thing, rather than giving priority to our own M-related people, *if* we are in a situation where at least $k - 1$ others will make the impartial choice if we do, and where everyone's M-related people will be benefited more if at least k of us make the impartial choice than if each gives priority to her own M-related people (pp. 100–3). According to Parfit, this revision moves some way from M towards an agent-neutral consequentialism (C), and C's indirect self-defeat shows that C in turn (without being revised) gives its adherents reason to foster some dispositions that are more characteristic

A social contract?

of M than of C. He concludes that C and M need to be enlarged and revised 'in ways that bring them closer together' (p. 112).

It may be doubted how far Parfit's proposals would move M toward C. Arthur Kuflik, in a fine paper, has argued, in effect, that common-sense morality already includes what R is supposed to add to M. Common-sense morality needs no revision to tell Parfit's fishermen that they certainly ought to make a concerted effort to restrict their catch, if they can; and it tells each of them that it would be unfair, and hence immoral, for him to make his children free-riders by fishing without restraint when enough others are restricting their catch.[4] Parfit now grants this point.[5]

Even if R were a real revision of M, moreover, it would not touch the cases about which M and C disagree most deeply. In the course of arguing for R, Parfit claims that '[t]here are countless cases where, if each gives priority to his M-related people, this would be worse for all these people than if no one gave priority to his M-related people' (p. 102). What are these countless cases? The condition supposedly satisfied in them is a very strong one: that *all* the affected people would be better off under one condition than under the other. This seems to be true in the case of Parfit's fishermen, but is probably not true in most of the cases in which it is morally plausible to give priority to one's M-related people. Where it is true, there is no deep conflict between personal loyalties and impartial benevolence; for when all are benefiting more from general co-operation than they would from unbridled competition, none can reasonably feel betrayed by their special protectors. These facts make it easier to believe that R is already included in M – and harder to see this as bringing M much closer to C.

The difference between moral partiality and impartiality is deeper, more intractable, and of greater importance in those (probably numerous) cases in which, if we all succeed in following M, the result of our giving priority to our M-related people will be that the M-related people of some of us will be better off, and the M-related people of others of us will be worse off, than if we all had successfully followed C or N. In these cases M is *not* directly collectively self-defeating in Parfit's sense. If the results of M in such cases are sufficiently bad from the point of view of fairness or utility or both, that may be reason to revise M; but Parfit's argument is not cast in such a form as to show that M needs revision to deal with such cases.[6]

For these reasons I think that Parfit has not established that M is directly collectively self-defeating. And even if he could establish it, there are at least two grounds on which it may be doubted whether it follows that M fails in its own terms. One is that Parfit's argument may be vitiated by consequentialist presuppositions.[7] Why would bad consequences of acting on a theory tend to show that the theory fails in its own terms? The answer is easy if the theory is consequentialist; but M is pretty clearly not a consequentialist theory. The M-Theorist's obvious response is: 'We always knew that acting on moral principle might cost some "utility".'

Parfit will doubtless reply that he does not conceive of self-defeat in consequentialist terms. He explains self-defeat in terms of non-achievement or inferior achievement of the 'aims' endorsed by a theory. And his description of theories in terms of their aims is explicitly meant to avoid consequentialist presuppositions. His 'use of aim is broad'.

> It can describe moral duties that are concerned, not with moral goals, but with rights, or duties. Suppose that, on some theory, five kinds of act are totally forbidden. This theory gives to each of us the aim that he never acts in these five ways. (p. 3)

And he offers us an analogue of the Fisherman's Dilemma in which I must choose between giving my child some benefit, and enabling you to give your child a greater benefit; and you face a symmetrical choice. Here, Parfit argues, if each has the M-given aim that *he* benefits *his* child, both of us will better achieve our M-given aims if both choose to enable the other (p. 97).[8]   *? or teleological*

This is not enough to escape consequentialist presuppositions. Describing my aim as 'that I benefit my child', or 'that I never act' in a certain way is still describing it as an outcome, and one which you could take as an aim of yours with reference to me. Many non-consequentialists (Kantians, for example) will deem it important to have aims that are not outcomes but actions, describable as 'to benefit my child' and 'not to act' in that certain way. These you could not intelligibly take as aims of yours, with reference to my action.

This may be a verbal difference, but it corresponds conveniently to a difference that is important for moral theory: the difference between acting on a principle and trying to bring about the optimization of one's whole future course of action from the point of view of the principle.[9] We can say that I have been doing the best for my patients as an *action-aim* in so far as I am disposed to do (now) what I think is best for my (present) patients. I have it as an *outcome-aim* in so far as I am disposed to try (now) to bring it about that I do (in the rest of my career) the best for my (present and future) patients.[10] If I have it as an action- but not an outcome-aim, or if the action-aim takes precedence, I will be disposed to do what I think is best for the patient I am treating now even if I foresee that this will prevent me from making the money to buy equipment that would enable me to do even better for other patients in the future. And that is what many non-consequentialists would say I morally ought to do,

Scanlon casts this as the distinction between teleological and non-teleological reasons.

if the stakes are high enough for my present patient. Given that they self-consciously take this sort of stand, why should they think their theory fails in its own terms if following it will not result in the best outcomes on the whole, from their point of view?

(p258) The other ground for doubting whether M must fail on its own terms if it is directly collectively self-defeating is that it is not clear that M is, as Parfit claims, 'a collective code'. What is a collective code? Parfit says, 'Call a theory . . . *collective* if it claims success at the collective level' (p. 92). If this is a definition, it will be analytic that collective theories fail in their own terms if they are directly collectively self-defeating. As usual, however, analyticity comes at a price. Non-consequentialist moral theories need not be collective on this account, if I am right in thinking that they need not claim 'success' at all.

Waiving this point, we may observe that the apparent definition seems tailor-made for theories like Kantianism (p. 92) and rule utilitarianism (RU), which subject policies to the test, 'What if everybody did the same?' Lanning Sowden has made the interesting point that this test does not have the importance for act utilitarianism (AU) that it has for RU. For AU may be seen as requiring 'that an individual maximize social utility subject to several constraints the most important of which is that he regard the strategies of all other agents as given or constant'.[11] Given this feature of AU, one might argue that AU's acceptability does not depend on whether AU's aims would be achieved if everyone always acted in accordance with AU – since there is manifestly no danger that such utilitarian virtue will actually become universal.

Similar considerations apply to M. Parfit says that when deciding on a moral theory, 'we should first consider our Ideal Act Theory', which says 'what we should all ideally do, when we know that we shall all succeed'. Such a theory is 'ideal' rather than 'practical', because it is a fact that '[w]e are often uncertain what the effects of our acts will be' (and often mistaken about such matters, I would add), and 'some of us will act wrongly' (pp. 99f.). In saying that a moral theory 'claims success at the collective level' Parfit seems to mean that the theory is committed to the thesis that its aims would be better achieved by universal following of its ideal act theory than by universal following of any other ideal act theory. This strikes me as an implausibly romantic constraint on moral theories. Why should it be an objection to a moral theory that, if universally followed with perfect success (as it will not be), it would yield somewhat worse results than would be obtained by everyone following with perfect success an alternative theory *that certainly will not and probably could not be so followed by all*? What is the relevance of this impossible alternative?

In discussing why S is 'not a collective code', Parfit says something that suggests a different understanding of 'collective'.

> Suppose that we are choosing what code of conduct will be publicly encouraged, and taught in schools. S would here tell us to vote against itself. If we are choosing a collective code, the self-interested choice would be some version of morality. (p. 92)

If a collective code is simply a code that is meant to be publicly adopted, in the sense of being publicly encouraged, inculcated as part of moral education, and widely practised, then it is plausible to hold that moral theories must be collective codes. So if it could be shown that such public adoption of M would result in a worse outcome, from the point of view of the concerns that support M, than some alternative that really could be adopted in this way, that might be a serious criticism of M. But this could not be established by proving that M is directly collectively self-defeating in Parfit's sense, because the results of public adoption of a moral theory do not coincide with the results of universal perfect compliance with it. (I am enough of a believer in original sin to suspect that they are not even very similar.)

The thesis that a moral theory must be collective in the sense of being meant to be publicly adopted is actually denied by Parfit (though without using the word 'collective') in connection with consequentialism (C), which claims,

(C3) If someone does what he believes will make the outcome worse, he is acting wrongly. (p. 24)

Should consequentialists think that C ought to be publicly adopted? Sidgwick famously inclined to the negative on this question.[12] Parfit inclines to the affirmative, but argues that the tenability of C need not depend on this answer. Consequentialists should prefer to avoid such dependence, because there is at least some reason to think that in view of the indirect self-defeat of C the public adoption of some other code would lead to a better outcome than the public adoption of C.

Parfit calls a theory 'self-effacing' if it implies that one ought to try to bring it about that it is not believed. He notes that on some views, 'a moral theory cannot be self-effacing', but 'must fulfil what Rawls calls "the publicity condition"; it must be a theory that everyone ought to accept, and publicly acknowledge to each other'. Parfit claims, however, that this view is tenable only for those who 'regard morality as a social product'. 'If a moral theory can be quite straightforwardly *true*, it is clear that, if it is self-effacing, this does not show that it cannot be true' (p. 43). Thus he seems to imply that requiring moral theories to satisfy the publicity condition commits one to some sort of subjectivism, or anti-realism. But that is surely wrong.

The publicity condition does connect morality with society; for it says that a moral theory, as such, must be meant to be publicly adopted. By their very meaning, it may be argued, moral claims have implications about how certain social practices ought to be related to the types of behaviour discussed in the claims. Part of what is meant by saying that a certain type of conduct is morally wrong is that it ought in general to be publicly discouraged as wrong.[13] In this, moral claims differ, no doubt, from scientific and mathematical claims. A proposition of nuclear physics or molecular biology can be objectively true even if the danger of abuse is so great that it ought not to be divulged. But that is because the rightness or wrongness of publicizing them is extraneous to the content of scientific statements. If the publicity condition is not extraneous to the content of moral claims, it is hard to see how this compromises their objectivity, since it has not been shown that it cannot be 'straightforwardly true' that a type of conduct ought to be publicly discouraged as wrong.

I shall mention a second point at which Parfit seems to me to offer an unconvincing defence of a feature that consequentialism might need to have in order to avoid bad consequences of consequentialist dispositions (and thus to deal with its indirect self-defeat). This second point has to do with blame and remorse. Parfit holds that consequentialists should think that there are cases in which a morally wrong action should not be an object of blame and remorse because it flows from a disposition that is morally advantageous and hence should not be discouraged. He comments: 'Consequentialism does not in general break the link between the belief that an act is wrong, and blame and remorse. This link is broken only in special cases,' such as 'those in which someone acts on a motive that it would be wrong for him to cause himself to lose' (p. 35).

This apology is not convincing. Morality doubtless allows for mitigation of blame and remorse when a wrong action is done from a good motive. But if we say that an action, for which the agent is fully responsible, ought not to be an object of blame or remorse at all, what can we mean in calling the action 'morally wrong'? The obvious consequentialist answer is that we can mean that from the point of view of achieving the ends that are important to morality, it would have been more advantageous not to have done the action. This answer makes a consequentialist account of moral wrongness true by definition. It is not a plausible definition. There is an important difference between saying that an action was not likely to result in the best outcome from a moral point of the view and saying that it was morally wrong. And no small part of the difference is in what the charge of moral wrongness implies about the appropriateness of blame and remorse.

These are not trivial problems about consequentialism. If C is self-effacing, or if it has the implications Parfit admits it to have regarding blame and remorse, that is a reason for thinking it is not really a theory about *moral* right and wrong. It is a much more serious failure for a proposal in moral theory, in my opinion, than it would be for common-sense morality, to have less than optimal consequences at the level of ideal act theory.

II   The Importance of Personal Identity for Ethics

In Part 3 of *Reasons and Persons* Parfit defends a reductionistic conception of persons and their identity through time. Using a fascinating array of examples (of a predominantly science-fiction character), he tries to show that 'what matters' practically, where we care about our transtemporal identity, is not identity as such, but the relations of psychological connectedness and continuity in which, he thinks, it mainly consists. He argues that this has important implications for morality and practical rationality. It provides a final argument against the Self-interest Theory, whose insistence that rationality requires equal concern for all periods of our future life is 'defeated' by the consideration that our farther future will be much less connected, psychologically, to our present than our nearer future will be. In addition to other possible implications for morality, Parfit claims that reductionism increases the plausibility of views, like utilitarianism, for which distributive considerations have no intrinsic moral importance. His reason for this is that facts of personal identity and non-identity, on which distributive principles 'are often held to be founded', are less 'deep', metaphysically, on the reductionist view, and therefore it 'becomes more plausible to be more concerned about the quality of experiences, and less concerned about whose experiences they are' (p. 346). I shall not enter here into discussion of Parfit's arguments for reductionism,[14] as I prefer to focus on the practical inferences he draws from it.

Let us begin with his claim that if personal identity is less 'deep', it becomes more plausible to care less about it. I think he means it becomes more plausible to think it irrational to care as much as we do about personal identity.[15] This is in some ways a puzzling claim. It is not obvious what it means to say that personal identity is less 'deep' on the reductionist view,[16] or what is the connection between metaphysical depth and practical importance. Perhaps the argument that Parfit proposes is that our valuing personal identity as most of us do rests on a belief about its nature that is mistaken if reductionism is right.

That would not be a very good argument if it means that we explicitly infer the value of personal identity from non-reductionist beliefs about its nature. For (with the possible exception of a few philosophers) who does that? And who needs to? We care *who* does what, and what happens to *whom*, because we care in a special way about ourselves and about people we love. And who needs reasons for that? Parfit agrees that love need not be based on reasons.[17] Few would suppose that our special concern for ourselves and our own future needs reasons any more than our love for other individuals does.

Can anything be said in defence of the rationality of the way we ordinarily care about personal identity? Here we do well 'to consider the way in which our identification of and concern for ourselves and each other as *persons* essentially contributes to, if you'll pardon the expression, our form of life', as Susan Wolf urges in a richly rewarding essay about this aspect of Parfit's work.[18] I take this remark not as an appeal to a peculiarly Wittgensteinian philosophy of language, but as a claim that the way we care about persons is, and should be, affected by the deep embedding of the concept of personal identity in a complex web of social practices.

One of these practices is child-rearing. According to Parfit, it would be rational to care less about one's own farther future if it will be only weakly connected, psychologically, to one's present, because such connectedness is a major part of 'what matters' in personal identity. If this applies to self-interest, it would seem to apply also to one's concern for the futures of people one loves. But small children, as Wolf points out, are only weakly connected, psychologically, to the adults they will become. So if we cared little about the farther, weakly connected futures of people we love, she argues, love would not motivate parents to discipline children for the sake of their adult development. 'Why should a parent reduce the happiness of the child she loves so much for the sake of an adult she loves so little?'[19] In fact, however, it is a normal part of our practice of child-rearing that one takes the whole life of one's child as a project[20] about which one cares greatly.

I regard my own life in that way too. No doubt I learned that from my parents, whose project it was before it was mine. Had I been neglected as a child, I might have found it natural to live more 'for the moment', and might never have learned to 'postpone gratification'. Having adopted my own (whole) life as a project, however, I have access to further projects and practices that would otherwise be inaccessible to me. I can enter into long-term commitments, such as marriage. I can apply for a thirty-year mortgage. I can undertake a scholarly project that will take twenty years to complete. I can care about the moral significance and consistency of my life as a whole. I can aspire to grow and change in ways that I cannot fully foresee, but that will surely involve some loss of psychological connectedness. I am committed to my future without regard to variations of connectedness within the range that normally occurs in human life, though a sufficiently radical loss of connectedness might place a possible future outside the bounds of my project altogether.[21]

Much of what we care most about in human lives cannot, of its very nature, be found in an experience or a short period of life. Should reductionists care more about experiences, and less about persons? 'If the reason we care about persons is that persons are able to live interesting, admirable, and rewarding lives,' Wolf argues, 'we may answer that time slices of persons, much less experiences of time slices, are incapable of living lives at all.[22] For this reason, indeed, I think that most of our caring about the quality of experiences, except perhaps those that we are having right now, is due to our caring about the people to whom they belong. Many of Parfit's arguments seem to presuppose that our concern for the quality of experiences would, or rationally should, continue undiminished if we became less interested in whole lives as such; this seems to me very questionable.

Another way in which our conception of personal identity is woven into our form of life is that it marks the boundaries of the past and the future that *belong* to me. My life belongs to me retrospectively, in the sense that I am responsible for it; prospectively, in the sense that it is, in a special way, mine to shape. This belonging has a subjective and voluntary aspect: I *take* responsibility for my past (and in a different way for my future); I have *intentions* for my future. It has a social and voluntary aspect which is at least as important: I am *held* responsible for my past. 'It's your life,' others say with regard to many decisions I make or can make about my future. There is also a normative aspect to this belonging: I have a *right* to a certain control over my future; I *ought* to be held responsible, and accept responsibility, for certain things.

The rationality of caring about personal identity in this complex network of ways, which I have only begun to sketch, is established, *within a* form of life to which they belong, by our finding that they *make sense*. The concepts involved in these projects 'work'. We are able to interpret our lives in terms of them. Using them, we can commonly make plausible judgements, which often enough seem to us illuminating. There is nothing we care more about than some of the projects that are inextricably intertwined with our conception of personal identity. We can commonly pursue these projects with some hope of success, but it would hardly make sense to pursue them at all if we did not care about our lives as wholes in the way we normally do. These considerations do not

show that it would be *ir*rational to adopt a radically different form of
life in which we would not think about our lives in this way, if we
could do so (or even imagine doing so, in any detail). But they establish
a strong presumption that we are not irrational in continuing to treat
the whole lives of particular individuals as specially important projects,
and to regard our pasts and futures as belonging to us in a special
ways.[23]

None of this implies that there are not imaginable circumstances in
which it would become irrational (cease to make sense) to care about
personal identity in these accustomed ways. To draw on Parfit's examples, it is imaginable that incidents of fusion and fission of persons (or at
any rate, events empirically indistinguishable from such) would often
happen. In that context it might well not make sense to regard pasts and
futures as belonging to us in the way that we now do. If we value our
present form of life (as most of us do), we have reason to prevent such
incidents if we can. Parfit sometimes seems to be arguing on the assumption that if we care about identity in our actual circumstances in a way
that we would not if certain science fictions became reality, we ought to
have a quite general and theoretically interesting rationale for the difference. In view of the subtle complexity of human forms of life, I think it
is quite unrealistic to expect that we should have such a rationale for the
differences in what concerns would seem reasonable to us in vastly
different physical, and especially social, environments.[24]

So the value we set on personal identity needs no justification from
non-reductionist arguments. But Parfit may think it rests on non-
reductionist beliefs in a less explicit way. He might argue that if
we became reductionists, and reflected adequately on the significance
of reductionism, we would find that personal identity no longer seemed
so important to us. He testifies that something like that has happened
to him since he became a reductionist; and he thinks it is a good
thing. Because facts of personal identity and non-identity seem less
important, 'I am less concerned about the rest of my own life, and more
concerned about the lives of others', and 'my death seems to me less bad'
(p. 281).[25]

Not all who become reductionists will react in this way, however. Wolf
does not, for one. 'Parfit has convinced me of reductionism with respect
to persons,' she says. 'But I find that this conviction does not lessen the
degree of my interest in persons a bit.'[26] If Parfit charges that Wolf's
caring about personal identity rests on a belief in non-reductionism, she
will reply that she does not hold that belief. He could argue that if she
had reflected adequately on reductionism, she would no longer care as
much about personal identity, and that therefore the degree of her caring
about it still rests on the non-reductionism she no longer holds. But that

(handwritten margin note:) If true circumstances in which our concepts make sense change radically, we would change our concepts. That doesn't mean we should change now true or m Parfit (as Parfit thinks.)

kind of attack on opposing intuitions would not settle anything, as it is a game that any number can play.

This does not show that Parfit could not reasonably have a deep conviction that reductionism warrants diminished concern for facts of personal identity and non-identity. It might be a religious conviction. Parfit calls attention to the fact that Buddha was a reductionist about persons and their identity (p. 273). And Buddhist texts do use reductionistic metaphysical arguments about identity in an effort to weaken such attitudes as self-centredness and anxiety about death.[27] But that is not the only possible broadly religious response to reductionistic conclusions. I doubt that Kierkegaard was committed to metaphysical reductionism about personal identity. But he certainly agreed with Parfit that being the same self over time in a way that is morally and humanly significant requires psychological connectedness. In fact, he thought it requires repentant taking of responsibility for one's past, followed by constantly repeated affirmation of (the same) ethical or religious commitment. The persistence of significant selfhood is assured not by ontology but by will-power.[28] But this certainly did not lead Kierkegaard to think personal identity less important. On the contrary, it was for him the most precious of all achievements. It would be hard to think of anyone who cared more about it.[29]

Besides claiming that the lesser metaphysical 'depth' ascribed to personal identity by reductionism makes it more plausible to care less to *whom* things happen, Parfit offers arguments for other theses about morality, of which the most important, perhaps, are about *desert* and *guilt* and about *compensation*. Parfit views with increasing favour arguments for the Extreme Claims 'that, if the Reductionist View is true, we cannot deserve to be punished for our crimes', and cannot be compensated at any time for anything that happens at another time. In *Reasons and Persons* he wrote that both the Extreme Claims and their denials are defensible (pp. 324 f., 342 f.); in more recent 'Comments' he doubts that they can be defensibly denied.[30]

I will discuss first the argument he suggests in the book for the Extreme Claim about desert and guilt. The argument for the Extreme Claim about compensation (pp. 342 f.) is similar, and my response to it would be similar. The arguments are based on a case of 'my imagined division', in which my brain has been divided into left and right halves, which are transplanted into the bodies of my two brothers, resulting in two persons, Lefty and Righty, somewhat similar, physically, to each other and to me as I was, and strongly connected, psychologically, with my pre-surgical state. In this case, Parfit claims, non-reductionists must say it will be true either that I am Lefty, or that I am Righty, or that I am neither.

Suppose I am Righty. On that assumption, Parfit thinks a non-reductionist could defensibly deny that Lefty would 'deserve to be punished for the crimes that I committed before the division. . . . How can he deserve to be punished for crimes that someone else committed, at a time when he himself did not exist? Only the deep further fact of personal identity [as the non-reductionist believes it to be] carries with it responsibility for past crimes.' From this he infers that a non-reductionist, if converted to reductionism (and hence any reductionist as well), can defensibly deny that we ever have desert or guilt, since (according to reductionism) the 'deep further fact' is never present (pp. 324 f.).

Non sequitur. For the fact of personal identity, whether deep or not, is assuredly present in the cases in which we ordinarily assign desert and guilt. Suppose it is true that when we think that personal identity requires something more than physical and psychological continuity, it seems reasonable to deny desert and guilt where that something more is not present. How can that fact show that it is defensible to deny desert and guilt where only (unduplicated) physical and psychological continuity are present, when we think that is all that is required for personal identity?

Parfit seems to be assuming that whether we count a condition as sufficient for personal identity cannot affect whether it is reasonable to regard it as sufficient for assigning desert and guilt. This assumption disregards the role of the concept of personal identity in our form of life. An important part of the concept's role is juridical (a point that is implicit in Locke's pioneering discussion of personal identity[31]). Part of what we decide when we decide that a certain condition is sufficient for personal identity is that it will be sufficient for a past and/or future to *belong* to me in a way that is linked with such concepts as those of responsibility, desert, guilt and compensation.[32] So when we shift from thinking physical and/or psychological continuity insufficient for personal identity to thinking it sufficient for personal identity, why should we not be expected also to shift from regarding it as insufficient to regarding it as sufficient for desert and guilt?

To be sure, Parfit has argued in sections 90–1 that identity is not 'what matters when I divide'. But this arguments there are not clearly relevant to questions about desert and guilt. The question mainly addressed there is whether a development that preserves relation R (as he calls psychological continuity and connectedness) but not personal identity would be (as Parfit claims) 'about as good as ordinary survival' (p. 264). And he answers that for reductionists, 'what fundamentally matters is whether I shall be R-related to at least one future person' (p. 268). Let us grant him, for the sake of argument, that he has described imaginable cases of division in which relation R would be preserved but identity would not; and that such division, if not as good as ordinary survival, would at least be much better than annihilation. This gives him a way in which identity, as such, matters much less than relation R. But it certainly does not follow that personal identity does not matter much for questions of desert and guilt, which are quite different from questions about the satisfactoriness of alternatives to straightforward survival.

It is also part of Parfit's argument in sections 90–1 that all that keeps identity from being preserved in cases of my division, on a reductionist view, is the fact that there is a plurality of fairly equally matched contenders for the status of being me. He argues that this fact is too *trivial*, and too *extrinsic* to the relation between successive person-stages, to determine 'what matters'. In relation to juridical issues, however, it is not a trivial fact at all. Our practices of assigning rights and responsibilities to persons rest on the assumption that personal pasts and futures will have at most one 'owner' at any time. Since some of these rights and responsibilities are not easily or conveniently divisible, the existence of two evenly matched claimants is decidedly an important fact. Similarly, if we are using the concept of personal identity to give shape to decisions about such matters as desert and guilt, it is hard to see how a reasonable objection could arise from the fact that identity involves a uniqueness condition that is 'extrinsic' to the relation between successive person-stages. These juridical issues are undeniably social; why should they not depend on relations between persons as well as between person-stages?

Parfit's arguments for the Extreme Claims in his more recent 'Comments' are in one way harder to dismiss, because he begins not with what it may plausibly be claimed we *would* say if we were non-reductionists, but with what we *are* intuitively inclined to say about another of his examples. Again I will discuss the argument for the Extreme Claim about desert and guilt; but the argument for the Extreme Claim about compensation[33] is similar, using the same example, and my response to it would be similar. In teletransportation my brain and body are destroyed here on Earth, while 'the exact state of all my cells' is recorded and beamed by radio to Mars, where the replicator 'create[s], out of new matter, a brain and body exactly like mine' (p. 199). Relation R is perfectly preserved in teletransportation. The branch-line case is a variant of teletransportation in which, for reasons too complicated to explain here, the scanner on Earth does not destroy my body but damages it, so that it will die of cardiac failure within a few days. Though Parfit thinks we might reasonably decide to say that in simple teletransportation *I* get

to Mars, he believes we clearly must describe the branch-line-case as one
in which I remain on Earth, doomed to early death, while a replica of me
('Backup') begins a more promising life on the red planet (pp. 201 f.).

'Suppose that, in the Branch Line Case, I had earlier committed some
crime.' Could Backup justly be punished for it? 'Most of us', Parfit
claims, would say no. We would hold that because Backup would not be
me, he would not be guilty, or even responsible, for my crime, even
though Backup would be as strongly connected and continuous, psychologically, with my earlier history as we normally are with ourselves
from day to day. On the reductionist view, Parfit claims:

> Backup is not me only because . . . these [psychological] connections do
> not have their normal cause: the continued existence of my brain. Is it the
> absence of this normal cause which makes Backup innocent? Most of us
> would answer no. We would think him innocent because he is not me.

Parfit goes on to argue that '[t]his reply would show that we are not
Reductionists' and believe that only the non-reductionistic 'further fact'
of identity 'carries with it desert and guilt', and that therefore if we
become reductionists, we ought to conclude that '[n]o one ever deserves
to be punished for anything they did'.[34]

This is an outrageous argument. When we say that Backup is innocent
because he is not me, we are not committing ourselves to any metaphysical view about the nature or grounds of the non-identity; we are simply
saying that it is the non-identity, and not its grounds, whatever they may
be, that is the ground of the innocence. If asked whether it is because of
the metaphysical irreducibility of personal identity that I am guilty of my
own offences, 'most of us', I think, would equally answer no – that I am
guilty of them simply because I am still myself.

Moreover it is extremely plausible to think that normality of the
causal basis of action is relevant to questions of moral responsibility.
Philosophical discussions of free will have emphasized this point. If I act
under the influence of drugs, hypnosis, electrodes in my brain or even
insanity, my responsibility for the action is diminished or eliminated. We
often explain this by saying that 'I was not myself' when I did it. We are
concerned with quite a different sort of abnormality in Parfit's science-
fiction examples, of course; but there is no clear reason why it should not
'matter' for moral responsibility, especially when it supports a judgement
of non-identity.[35]

Both versions of Parfit's arguments for the Extreme Claims fail,
at bottom, for the same reason. He argues that the non-reductionist
'deep further fact' of identity is intuitively required for moral responsibility and for the possibility of compensation. But all that his examples

will support is that personal identity, whatever its metaphysical basis may be, is required. He begins with intuitions that I think draw their power (though he might deny it) from the difference between these examples and normal, clear cases of personal identity, and then tries to use these intuitions to talk us into assimilating the normal to the abnormal case. But we cannot pull ourselves up by our own intuitive bootstraps.

Positive arguments also can be offered against the Extreme Claims. The analogy between the nature of persons and the nature of nations, to which Parfit appeals, not only fails to help his argument for the unimportance of personal identity,[36] but actually tells against the Extreme Claims about desert, guilt and compensation. For hardly anyone holds a non-reductionist view about nations or other institutions, but most of us think that they can be deserving, guilty and compensated. Our legal system reflects this belief. Perhaps it is erroneous; but if so, the error cannot be explained by (mistaken) belief in a non-reductionist theory of nations or institutions, for we hold no such belief. This consideration adds to the implausibility of holding that it would be unreasonable for reductionists to believe that persons can be deserving, guilty or compensated.

But might not we hold inconsistent beliefs?

There may also be a reasonable *ad hominem* objection to the Extreme Claim about compensation, at least as it applies to benefits received *after* the burden is borne. It is plausible to suppose that *I* can be personally compensated for present burdens by a benefit enjoyed by someone existing at a future time *t* if the existence of that person at *t* will be about as good, for *me*, as my surviving to *t*. But then, since Parfit claims that the existence at *t* of someone R-related to my present person-stage is about as good, for me, as surviving to *t* (pp. 263 f.), he must also grant that I can be compensated by benefits to such a person.

Parfit says an Extreme Claim about *commitments*, that 'we can never be bound by past commitments' if reductionism is true, can be defended by arguments similar to those offered for the other Extreme Claims (p. 326). He also argues that one might become so weakly connected, psychologically, to one's earlier self as to be unable to release another person from a commitment made to that earlier self. He builds this argument on an example that involves no science fiction, 'The Nineteenth-Century Russian'. A young nobleman of socialist ideals plans to give to his peasants the vast estates he will inherit in several years. Knowing that he might lose his ideals, however, he 'signs a legal document, which will automatically give away the land, and which can be revoked only with his wife's consent'. And he obtains from her a promise that she will never give her consent, even if he changes his mind and asks for it. He says:

E.g.

I regard my ideals as essential to me. If I lose these ideals, I want you to think that I cease to exist. I want you to regard your husband then, not as me, the man who asks you for this promise, but only as his corrupted later self. Promise me that you would not do what he asks.

'This plea', as Parfit says, 'seems both understandable and natural.' He also claims that if the Russian nobleman in middle age did ask his wife 'to revoke the document, she might plausibly regard herself as not released from her commitment' (p. 327).

I agree that she might plausibly think she had some sort of obligation not to sign the revocation, but I am not convinced by Parfit's analysis in terms of a commitment from which she cannot be released because the 'self' to whom she made it no longer exists. The example turns on at least two factors extraneous to Parfit's theories: the moral value of the contemplated actions and the wife's judgement of their value. A pair of variations on the story may help us to see the importance of this point.

Case A: Suppose the direction of change reversed, and suppose the wife to change with the husband. That is, suppose that when young they are arch-conservatives, and hear with horror and disgust of other land-owners freeing their serfs and giving land to them. The husband there-fore executes a document that would require his wife's signature for any gift of land, and gets her to promise that if he should ever be corrupted by the spread of liberalism and wish to give land to his peasants, she will refuse to sign. In this connection he says things about selfhood similar to those that Parfit's young liberal landowner says. Some years later, how-ever, both the landowner and his wife have been won over to a more liberal persuasion, and wish to give land to the peasants. Will she, or should she, feel that she must not sign because she is bound by a promise to her husband's earlier self that his present self cannot revoke? No; I think she probably will not, and certainly should not, feel that. If this is right, it shows that if in Parfit's case there is some obligation from which the husband cannot now release the wife, it is not because an earlier self no longer exists. For there is as much reason in Case A to think the husband no longer the same self, but in Case A either there is no obligation, or the husband is still able to release his wife from it.

There are two alternative explanations for this reaction to Case A, by which Parfit might try to defend himself against my argument. (i) He might claim that even in Case A the husband cannot release his wife from a promise made to an earlier self, but that the wife rightly regards the promise as void because it was an evil promise. (ii) Alternatively, he might claim that in Case A the husband cannot release from the promise made to his earlier self, but that the wife is not bound by it because she too is changed and cannot be bound by a promise made by her earlier self. I can respond to both of these replies with a single variation on my counter-example.

Case B is like Case A except that the wife's promise (not to consent to a gift of land to the peasants) was made not to her husband, but to her late father-in-law, a generous man to his family and friends, but extremely conservative politically, who bequeathed the land to his son. In this case, it seems to me, she probably would, and should, feel the force of an obligation from which her husband cannot release her – especially if she feels that her father-in-law is someone who deserves their gratitude. It may be that, having become more liberal, she would, and should, conclude that the moral desirability of giving the land to the peasants is great enough to override this obligation. But at least there seems to be something to override – whereas my intuition about Case A, in which the promise was to her husband (or her husband's earlier self), is that there is no obligation there to be overridden, once her husband has made his present preference clear. This tells against both the replies I suggested for Parfit; for (i) the original promise was as bad in Case B as in Case A, and (ii) the wife is as changed in Case B as in Case A, but there is an obligation remaining in Case B as there is not in Case A.

This suggests to me a different view of Parfit's example. I think our sympathy with his verdict on it depends heavily on our sympathy (and the wife's continuing sympathy) with the husband's earlier ideals. The consideration that does, and perhaps should, hold her back from signing the paper, in Parfit's case, is less like ordinary promise-keeping than like a solemn vow. The appropriate reason for her refusing to sign, and for her thinking that her husband cannot release her from her commitment, is not that he is not the same person, but that signing would be playing false to something that is important to the significance of her and his individual and shared lives – more important than her respecting his wishes now. I doubt that reductionism about personal identity has any implications for the morally binding character of commitments.

III Future Generations

The fourth and final part of *Reasons and Persons* seems likely to provide, for some years to come, one of the main frameworks for discussion of ethical issues about future generations. It is linked, somewhat loosely, to the rest of the book by the fact that it begins with a point about personal identity. No child not conceived by my parents within a month of my actual conception would have been me (p. 352). (Whether any such child *could*, metaphysically, have been me, is another and more controversial question.) Any public policy or feature of collective behaviour sufficient to have a globally significant effect on the environment in which future human generations will live will have a pervasive impact on who conceives children with whom, and when. After at most three centuries, Parfit (p. 361) suggests – after much less time, I would guess – there will be no one living who would have existed if our policy or practice were significantly different. If none of them is so miserable that it would be better for them if they had never existed, it follows that after that period of time there will be no one living for whom it would have been better if we had followed a different policy or practice – no one who will have been harmed, on the whole, by what we have actually done.

Should we conclude that we have no moral obligation to restrain, for example, our consumption of natural resources, for the benefit of such distant generations (so long as we can be confident that their lives will be at least minimally worth living[37])? Such a permissive conclusion, as Parfit heartily agrees, seems obviously wrong. But what sort of ethical theory will provide a home for our rejection of it? Our need to answer this sort of question Parfit calls 'the Non-Identity Problem' (p. 363).

This problem shows, as Parfit argues, that our obligations regarding future generations cannot be adequately accounted for by his first attempt at formulating a 'person-affecting' ethical principle of beneficence (V): 'It is bad if people are affected for the worse' (p. 370). At the end of a very interesting and clarifying discussion, he is able to formulate principles of beneficence that are recognizably person-affecting (concerned with benefits or harms to individual persons as such) and that do solve the non-identity problem, on the assumption[38] that a person can be benefited by being caused to exist (section 136). But there is little practical difference between these principles and more impersonally stated principles about the sum, or average level, of human well-being.

It is worth noting, because Parfit singles it out as a main contribution of Part 4 to the impersonality theme of the book, that he also argues that we should not invoke principle V, even when it could apply, when we are thinking about beneficence that will have its effect in the near future. He proposes the example of two medical programmes. One would screen pregnant women for condition J. By curing J, doctors could prevent the children to be born from having handicap H (which impairs life but leaves it well worth living). The other programme would screen for condition K in women intending to conceive. By waiting to conceive until condition K has disappeared, after two months, women can avoid having children with handicap H. It is true of the first programme, but not of the second, that identifiable individuals will be worse off if it is not adopted, because the children who would be born healthy because of it would be the same persons as children who would otherwise have had handicap H.

Is that a morally good reason for favouring the first programme, if only one of them can be funded? Parfit thinks that intuitively it is not.

I am not sure that I agree with him about that. But if we do, this shows at most that our intuitions about beneficence to persons yet unborn are not person-affecting.[39] I doubt that many of us will have similar intuitions about beneficence to persons already clearly recognizable as part of our moral community. Varying the example, let us suppose that handicap H does not become evident until after puberty, and that condition J is not a condition of the pregnant mother, but a disease of prepubescent children, which, if untreated, causes them later to have handicap H, but which has no harmful effects if treated by the age of eleven. I think most of us would feel that a program of testing eleven-year-olds for condition J should be preferred to the programme of testing intending mothers for condition K, unless the latter would be *much* more efficient than the former.

Parfit also argues that our obligations regarding future people cannot be accounted for entirely in terms of *rights*. I think this conclusion is probably right; but I will not discuss here his arguments for it, which are only partly based on the non-identity problem.[40] Parfit concludes that we need a theory of beneficence to deal with this area of ethics. Indeed, he thinks 'we need a new theory about beneficence' (p. 443), which he has not yet found, if we are to solve all of the problems and paradoxes that set the agenda for Part 4 of his book. All the accounts of beneficence he discusses contain or presuppose the principle: 'If other things are equal, it is wrong knowingly to make some choice that would make the outcome worse' (pp. 394, 396). They differ from one another chiefly in what they say about what would make an outcome better or worse. They presuppose that (at least in many cases) alternative futures for the world, in which entirely different individual persons, and vastly different numbers of them, would live under widely diverse physical and social conditions, can be compared as globally better or worse, either impersonally, or for the people who would live in them, considered collectively.

This presupposition seems to me very questionable, though I will not launch a systematic attack on it here.[41] I believe a better basis for ethical theory in this area can be found in a quite different direction – in a commitment to the future of humanity as a vast project, or network of overlapping projects, that is generally shared by the human race. The aspiration for a better society – more just, more rewarding and more peaceful – is a part of this project. So are the potentially endless quests for scientific knowledge and philosophical understanding, and the development of artistic and other cultural traditions. This includes the particular cultural traditions to which we belong, in all their accidental historical and ethnic diversity. It also includes our interest in the lives of our children and grandchildren, and the hope that they will be able, in turn, to have the lives of their children and grandchildren as projects. To the extent that a policy or practice seems likely to be favourable or unfavourable to the carrying out of this complex of projects in the nearer or further future, we have reason to pursue or avoid it.

The concept of 'quality of life', which dominates Parfit's discussion of the evaluation of alternative futures, may have some role to play in thinking about what is 'favourable or unfavourable' here. But it is too abstract to represent adequately the concrete concerns that are bound up in our commitment to the human project. And it focuses attention too much on the quality of experience at particular moments in the future, as opposed to how we get there. Continuity is as important to our commitment to the project of the future of humanity as it is to our commitment to the projects of our own personal futures. Just as the shape of my whole life, and its connection with my present and past, have an interest that goes beyond that of any isolated experience, so, too, the shape of human history over an extended period of the future, and its connection with the human present and past, have an interest that goes beyond that of the (total or average) quality of life of a population-at-a-time, considered in isolation from how it got that way.

We owe, I think, some loyalty to this project of the human future. We also owe it a respect that we would owe it even if we were not of the human race ourselves, but beings from another planet who had some understanding of it. But this is not the place to enter into a discussion of why it is not morally optional to care about this project.[42] For in what follows I will mostly not follow my own preferred line, but will discuss Parfit's paradoxes in his own terms of global outcome and quality of life. I think that even in those terms something can be done toward realizing his hope of more adequate solutions than those discussed in his book.

One test he proposes, to be passed by an acceptable theory, is that it should avoid

> *The Repugnant Conclusion*: For any possible population of at least ten billion people, all with a very high quality of life, there must be some much larger imaginable population whose existence, if other things are equal, would be better, even though its members have lives that are barely worth living. (p. 388)

This absurdity clearly is implied by both impersonal and person-affecting forms of the Total Principle, which measures the value of outcomes by summing the net quantities that different persons enjoy in them of 'whatever makes life worth living' (p. 387). This view allows the value of an outcome to be improved by the addition of sheer numbers of persons, so long as their lives are at least minimally worth living.

The most-discussed alternative to the Total Principle for evaluation outcomes in terms of quality of life has been the Average Principle, which awards the prize to the outcome in which the average quality of life is highest. The Average Principle does indeed avoid the Repugnant Conclusion, for it awards no points for the addition of happy people, unless they are average-raisers. But Parfit quite rightly dismisses the Average Principle as implausible, because it has such consequences as that the addition to the world of a person who will have a very good life can make the outcome worse just because other people have lives that are even better (pp. 420–2).

Another view considered by Parfit is that '[t]he value of quantity has an upper limit, and in the world today this limit has been reached' (p. 403). (By 'quantity' here is meant the quantity of good that can be increased by increasing the sheer number of people, so long as their lives are worth living.) This view is plausible – though I think it would be even more plausible to think of the limit as a size of population rather than a sum of good. If the human race numbered only a few tens of thousands, we should probably think it a good thing to increase our numbers, so long as the newcomers would have lives worth living. Now that we number four billion, it is hard to see that it would make a better outcome to have more people just to be vessels for additional happiness – and I think that would be true even if the addition would not be burdensome to the rest of us.

Parfit argues, however, that this view is not tenable, and no limit can be set to the value of 'quantity'. His argument begins with the intuition (which I share) that a hell containing ten million innocent people would be a worse outcome than a hell containing just ten innocent people, even if the average level of misery were a little worse in the smaller than in the larger hell. From this he infers that '[i]n the case of suffering, there is no upper limit to the disvalue of quantity' (p. 406). But, he argues, if we still maintain that there is an upper limit to the positive value of the sum total of good enjoyed, we will be led to absurdly incongruous conclusions.

Imagine a population of many billions, living on a number of planets. Almost all of them have a much higher quality of life than is enjoyed by most of even the more fortunate people on Earth today. There is one in ten billion, however, who 'through sheer bad luck' suffers so much as to have a life 'not worth living'. Now imagine another state of affairs, in which there is a population several times as large, living on proportionately more planets, with the same very high prevailing quality of life, and the same proportion of unfortunates. Since there is no upper limit to the disvalue of quantity of suffering, Parfit argues, the second state of affairs will be worse than the first if there is an upper limit to the positive value of quantity of good lives.

> And, if this population was sufficiently large, its bad feature would out-weigh its good features. Badness that could be unlimited must be able to outweigh limited goodness. If this population was sufficiently large, its existence would be intrinsically bad. It would be better if, during this period, no one existed. (p. 410)

I agree with Parfit that these consequences are implausible. But they do not show that there must be no upper limit to the value of 'quantity'. He has not canvassed enough possibilities. Consider the following principles:

> *Positive Threshold Principle*: If the number of people living at any time is at least N, the existence of a larger number of people with the same (or worse) average levels and distribution of happiness, suffer-ing and other goods and evils would not be better.

> *Negative Threshold Principle*: If the average levels and distribution of happiness, suffering and other goods and evils among the people living at any time are *not too bad*, the existence of a larger number of people with the same average levels and distribution of happiness, suffering and other goods and evils would not be worse.

In other words, there is a *quantitative* threshold beyond which mere quantity of good does not count, and a *qualitative* threshold beyond (better than) which mere quantity of suffering does not count in deter-mining the overall value of states of affairs. These principles both seem plausible to me (if we are going to assign values to these global outcomes at all). Similar principles can be added, if necessary, to deal with other problems. It would probably be fruitless to try to quantity 'not too bad' in the Negative Threshold Principle, but for present purposes we do not need to. The average levels in Parfit's two hells obviously are too bad, as would be the case in any population that had, on average, a life not worth living (and perhaps in some other sorts of situation too). The average levels and distribution in Parfit's imagined populations with one wretched person in ten billion are clearly not too bad, in his judgement. Thus, adopting these Threshold Principles would enable Parfit to avoid both the paradoxes that have driven him to abandon an upper limit on the value of 'quantity'.

This view also has the virtue of accounting for the asymmetry (section 132) between the cases of the 'Happy Child' and the 'Wretched Child'.

The addition of the happy child would merely increase the quantity of happiness beyond the quantitative threshold, and so would not result in a better state of affairs. (Other good effects, on other people, or on the *average* quality of life, are assumed not to be in view in this example.) But the addition of the wretched child would either make the average quality of life, and its distribution, worse; or, if the situation is already very bad, would increase the quantity of suffering in a population that is below the qualitative threshold, and so would result in a worse state of affairs.

Parfit sees another obstacle in his path as he seeks to avoid the Repugnant Conclusion. In the Mere Addition Paradox we start with possible state of affairs A: a large population, all with an extremely high quality of life. 'The quality of life in B [with a population twice as large] is about four-fifths as high as the quality of life in A' (p. 419). Parfit shares the intuition that 'B is worse than A', because of the lower (average and maximum) quality of life, although the total quantity of human good enjoyed is about 60 per cent greater in B than in A.

A can be compared, however, with another state of affairs, A+, in which, in addition to the A-people, enjoying their A-quality of life, there are 'the extra people'. There are as many of them as of the A-people, and their quality of life is only about half as high, but their lives are worth living. No issue of social injustice arises here, and the two groups do not harm each other, because they live on different continents (or it could be different planets), and do not even know of each other's existence (section 142). Parfit argues that A+ is not worse than A. The 'mere addition' of happy people does not make the outcome worse, even though it lowers the average quality of life and introduces (without social injustice) an inequality (section 144). This point may be debated, but I will grant it.

The plot thickens as we turn to another possible state of affairs. In Divided B, as in B and A+, there are twice as many people as in A. As in B, their quality of life is roughly uniform, and about four-fifths as high as in A. But as in A+ (and unlike B), Divided B's people live in two groups of roughly equal size that do not know of each other's existence and have no influence on each other. Parfit argues that Divided B is better than A+ on several counts. In Divided B the average quality of life is higher, there is less inequality, and the worse off are better off. 'In a change from A+ to Divided B, the worse-off half would gain more than the better-off half would lose' (pp. 425–6).

One more premiss is needed to generate the paradox. 'Clearly', Parfit states, 'B is as good as Divided B' (p. 425). Given that 'Divided B is better than A+', then, '[s]ince B is as good as Divided B, B is better than A+'. But Parfit has argued that 'A+ is not worse than A. We now believe that B is better than A+. These beliefs together imply that B is not worse than A' – contrary to our initial intuition (p. 426).

They might be thought to imply something worse – namely, the Repugnant Conclusion. 'It may seem that, if B would be better than A+, which is not worse than A, B must be better than A' (p. 430). If so, the argument can be iterated, showing that C, which has twice as large a population as B, with a quality of life about 80 per cent as high, is better than B, and hence better than A – and so forth until we reach the vast population of the Repugnant Conclusion, whose lives are marginally worth living, proving by this sorites that this state of affairs is better than A.

But this extension of the argument rests on a mistake, according to Parfit. So long as we claim no more for A+ than that it is *not worse than* A, we do not have to agree that if B is better than A+, then B is better than A. He suggests that A+ might be thought only roughly comparable to A; and '[w]hen there is only rough comparability, *not worse than* is not a transitive relation', and does not imply *at least as good as*. Because it does not imply *at least as good as*, we can hold that A+ is not worse than A, B is better than A+, and still B is not better than A, but only not worse than A. Because *not worse than* is not transitive, we can hold that B is not worse than A, and C is not worse than B, but none the less C is worse than A; and thus the argument will not carry us to even a 'not worse than' version of the Repugnant Conclusion (section 146).

This point about *not worse than* seems correct to me, and it can be used to solve the Mere Addition Paradox by attacking the premiss 'Clearly B is as good as Divided B'. 'Is as good as' in this context must be intended by Parfit to express a transitive relation. Otherwise the argument, 'We would thus believe that Divided B is better than A+. Since B is as good as Divided B, B is better than A+,' would be fallacious. Thus the argument presupposes that B and Divided B are comparable, not only roughly, but with some precision.

Why would there be only rough comparability between A and A+? The most obvious reason is that in evaluation A we are evaluating a situation for a single population, whereas in evaluating A+ we are evaluating a situation in which there are two separate populations with no morally interesting relation between them. These are two quite different kinds of evaluation.

But there is exactly the same reason for thinking that there is only rough comparability between B and Divided B as there is for thinking that A and A+ are only roughly comparable. In evaluating B, we are evaluating a situation for a single population, whereas in evaluating Divided B, we are evaluating a situation in which there are two separate populations with no morally interesting relation between them. So why should we assume that 'B is [at least] as good as Divided B' in a sense intended to be transitive? It was not the difference in welfare levels between A and A+, but their mutual isolation, that kept us from making a more precise value comparison between them. Without the isolation, I take it, Parfit would agree that it is initially most plausible to say that A+ is worse than A. That being so, he is not entitled to the assumption that simply eliminating the welfare disparity makes precise comparison possible between B and Divided B.

This conclusion can be reinforced by reflecting on the ways in which A+ might change into B or Divided B. In trying to persuade us that Divided B is better than A+, Parfit helps himself to evaluations of processes, explicitly envisaging a change from A+ to Divided B as a gradual change over two centuries, as 'the result of natural events, affecting the environment' (p. 425). I think we may fairly infer that he envisages it as *not* involving any change in the mutual isolation. But how would A+ evolve into B? This might happen by one population discovering the other, and the richer population then voluntarily making some sacrifice to effect a larger improvement in the welfare of the other. This would be a morally attractive history; and we might want to say that if B developed in that way, it would indeed be a better state of affairs than A+ (and *at least* as good as Divided B). But if we stick with Parfit's assumption of no interaction between the two populations, then the only way A+ could evolve into B would be by one population developing into B and the other dying out.[43]

Suppose it is the richer population that develops into B. Considered in itself, this is equivalent to the development of B from A, which Parfit admits would be most plausibly regarded as a change for the worse. And it's hard to see how he could think of the dying out of the other population as a good thing, even if it happened relatively painlessly (perhaps through universal but voluntary adoption of celibacy). So B would hardly be an improvement on A+ if it developed in this way. In fact, it would be plausible to think of this development as a deterioration in the situation. Perhaps this would be a judgement mainly on the process of change, and would not give a clear verdict on the comparative merits of the initial and terminal states as distinct from the process. But then I think we are likely to be left unsure how to make the latter comparison. We have (as well as need) much clearer intuitions about the value of possible *changes* than about the comparative value of states of affairs considered in abstraction from any possible story about how one would get to them.

Suppose it is the poorer population that develops into B (certainly an improvement) while the richer dies out. It is very hard to say whether this would be a change for the better (or, more cautiously, a good change), because it is so hard to evaluate the dying out of either population. The main upshot of all these considerations about how A+ could change into B, in my opinion, is that, after reflecting on them, we are not likely to have confidence in any precise assessment of the comparative value of A+ and B as such, independently of how they would have arisen. In other words, these considerations strongly confirm the judgement that A+ and B are no more than roughly comparable. And if we grant that Divided B can be judged more precisely to be superior to A+ (on the assumption that there has never been any contact between the populations), the judgement that B and Divided B are only roughly comparable is also confirmed.

The most plausible comparative evaluation of B and Divided B, therefore, is that *neither is worse than* the other, and that this relationship is *not* transitive. But now (the first version of) the Mere Addition Paradox collapses. We have the following relationships:

(i)   A+ is not worse than A.
(ii) Divided B is better than A+.
(iii) B is not worse than Divided B.

'Is better than' is a tight enough relationship so that from (i) and (ii) we can infer

(iv) Divided B is not worse than A.

But from (iii) and (iv) we *cannot* infer

(v) B is not worse than A,

because transitivity fails.

Parfit presents a second version of the paradox, which is more threatening, inasmuch as it does lead, in his opinion, to the Repugnant Conclusion (section 148). We begin with the two separate populations of A+; but in this version 'even the worse-off group have an *extremely* high quality of life' (p. 434). There are ten billion people in each group, and they live on different planets. In all the other states of affairs that we will consider as alternatives to A+, there are a vast number of inhabited planets, each with a population of ten billion persons; as in A+, none has knowledge of the people on other planets. In New A the people on two of the planets enjoy a quality of life even higher than that of the better-off group in A+; but the people on the remaining planets (the overwhelming majority of New A's total population) 'are not much above the Bad Level' (the quality of life below which 'it would in itself have been better if they had never existed').

Parfit argues that New A is better than A+. 'There is at least one way in which New A is better than A+. In New A there are twenty billion people, all of whom have a higher quality of life than [any of the twenty billion people] in A+.' And the inequality in New A is not worse than that in A+, because inequality 'produced by Mere Addition . . . does not make the outcome worse' (p. 434).[44]

Now consider New B, which is like New A except that the people on four, rather than two, of the planets are better off than the others. The forty billion fortunates in New B all enjoy a quality of life about four-fifths as good as that of the twenty billion privileged in New A. The people on the remaining planets still subsist just above the Bad Level. Parfit argues that 'New B is better [than New A] on any plausible principle of beneficence'. For '[i]f there was a change from New A to New B, worse-off groups would gain *very much more* than better-off groups would lose' (p. 435).

'Better than' is a transitive relationship. So if New B is better than New A, and New A is better than A+, then New B is better than A+. The path of sorites to the Repugnant Conclusion is clear. We will arrive eventually at a state of affairs in which there are very many tens of billions of people, none of them much elevated above the Bad Level, but which must be judged a better state of affairs than A+, in which all of the twenty billion people enjoy an extremely high quality of life.

I believe that this argument is unsound, and in particular that there is as much reason to think A+ is better than New A as to think New B is better than New A. For consider the morally relevant differences between New A and New B. New A has the advantage that the quality of life that is ever achieved by a significant number of people is significantly higher there than in New B. On the other hand, in New B there is (i) double the number, and (ii) a (perhaps significantly) higher proportion, of people enjoying a very high quality of life; and there is (iii) a (perhaps significantly) higher average quality of life for the aggregate of populations, and (iv) the overall distribution of quality of life is somewhat more egalitarian.

Reflection on this comparison might lead us in more than one direction. The first point to which I wish to call attention is that, except for (i), all the advantages of New B over New A are also advantages that A+ enjoys over New A[45] – and (i) is a very dubious advantage, since the total population in all these cases is above the threshold beyond which it is implausible to think that mere quantity matters. So if it is clear to us that New B is better than New A, why should we not also conclude that A+ is definitely better than New A, contrary to Parfit's claims?

But perhaps New B is not better than New A. If all the people in New A and New B were socially related to each other (in a broad sense), the advantages of New B over New A would be morally decisive. But since they are not so related, the comparison is not so clear. It is not clear, for example, that a more egalitarian distribution between socially unrelated populations is a moral advantage. Nor is it clear that averages of quality of life across socially unrelated populations are morally important. These considerations might lead us to conclude that New B and New A are only roughly comparable, and neither is worse than the other. This relation, being intransitive, will not lead to any version of the Repugnant Conclusion.

Parfit's argument largely ignores these considerations, and relies heavily on one-to-one matchings of the welfare of the isolated subgroups, which causes the comparison between New A and A+ to come out quite differently from that between New A and New B, because of the much smaller number of subgroups in A+. There is much potentiality for misleading argument here. Parfit says, for example, that in New B, in comparison with New A, 'it would be true that, though the better-off group would lose, a worse-off group would gain *several times as much*' (p. 435). The same could be said about A+ in comparison with New A, if the worse-off subgroup in A+ were identified with one of the worst-off subgroups in New A. When making his comparison arguments, Parfit speaks as if the two subgroups in A+ are assumed to be identical with the two best-off groups in New A; but officially, as far as I can see, the identity of the subgroups is not supposed to play a part in the argument.

Suppose it is meant to play a part, however, and that A+ is composed of the two best-off groups of New A. Then we are certainly entitled to consider also A*, which is just like A+ except that the less well-off group in A* is identical with one of the worst-off groups in New A. Now if New B is better than New A, A* must surely be better than New A with respect to this pair of groups. And if mere quantity does not matter in these cases, so that its additional populated planets are not a countervailing advantage of New A over A*, we seem to be led to the conclusion that A* is better on the whole than New A. But since A+ and A* are qualitatively identical, it is hard to deny that they have exactly the same value, and that if A* is better than New A, so is A+.

By judicious choice of perspective, now one, now the other of many such pairs of 'outcomes' can be made to seem the better. I think the wisest conclusion to draw is that it is a very dubious enterprise to assign comparative values to outcomes in abstraction from our moral assessment of processes by which they might arise. But even if we insist on pursuing that enterprise, I do not see how the Mere Addition Paradox can be made to stick, or to lead to the Repugnant Conclusion.[46]

Notes

1 Derek Parfit, 'Comments', *Ethics, 96 (1986)*, p. 843n.
2 Joseph Butler, *Fifteen Sermons Preached at the Rolls Chapel*, ed. T. A. Roberts (SPCK, London, 1970), p. 102 (sermon 11, par. 9).
3 It is an oversimplification to treat these, as Parfit does, as our only M-given aims in the situation, a simplification made inevitable, perhaps, by the (inevitably) incomplete presentation of M. One complication, neglected in Parfit's discussion, which might affect the soundness of his argument, is that an aim may owe its status as M-given to another aim more fundamentally given by M. Thus if I am a lawyer, M gives me the interests of my client as an aim that is specially mine; but that is largely because M gives me more fundamentally the aim of keeping faith with my client. M also gives me such aims as respecting my client's autonomy. It is therefore far from obvious that my M-given aims regarding my client will always be better achieved if my client's interests are better advanced, or even if they are better advanced *by me*. The achievement of my M-given aims may well depend on *how* I advance my client's interests.
4 Arthur Kuflik, 'A Defense of Common Sense Morality', *Ethics*, 96 (1986), pp. 784–803, esp. pp. 801 f.
5 Parfit, 'Comments', pp. 852 f.
6 As he acknowledges, in effect, in sect. 40, where he pulls back from arguing for N.
7 As Lanning Sowden suggests in his review of *Reasons and Persons, Philosophical Quarterly*, 36 (1986), pp. 514–35; see p. 527.
8 Cf. ibid., pp. 527 ff.
9 I am much indebted to John Giuliano for help in understanding this distinction.
10 I do not know whether this distinction has anything in common with Parfit's distinction between 'formal' and 'substantive' aims (p. 3).
11 Sowden, review, p. 526. Sowden goes on to say: 'Roughly, RU tells me to select an action on the assumption that we all perform that action, whereas AU does not. Thus RU, but not AU, is a collective code in Parfit's sense.' This may be too swift. I imagine Parfit would reply that while AU often commends individual 'strategies' (Sowden's term) that would not be successful if they were followed (as they will not be) by everyone, AU's one fundamental principle of maximizing utility would (necessarily) be successful if universally followed. Even so, as I argue in the text, it is hard to see why this collective success would matter to the tenability of AU. It is interesting also to note that Parfit himself distinguishes consequentialism as a moral theory that is '*individualistic* and concerned with *actual* effects', from what he calls 'collective consequentialism', which 'is both *collective* and concerned with *ideal* effects' (p. 30).
12 Henry Sidgwick, *The Methods of Ethics*, 7th edn (Macmillan, London, 1907), p. 490, cited by Parfit, p. 41.

13 This is not to say that the opinion that it is *occasionally* right, in special circumstances, to lie about moral principles is logically inadmissible. To affirm a principle of conduct, however, while denying that it ought *in general* to be inculcated, is not to affirm it as a moral principle.

14 They are the subject of Sydney Shoemaker's illuminating review of *Reasons and Persons* in *Mind*, 94 (1985), pp. 443–53; reproduced here as ch. 7.

15 More recently he has claimed to have argued that our 'car[ing] a great deal about personal identity . . . is irrational' (Parfit, 'Comments', p. 833).

16 Parfit has conceded (ibid., p. 838) the justice of a charge of vagueness at this point, made by Bart Schultz, 'Persons, Selves, and Utilitarianism', *Ethics*, 96 (1986), pp. 721–45, p. 732.

17 Parfit, 'Comments', p. 834, responding to Susan Wolf, who was making essentially the same point as I am making here.

18 Susan Wolf, 'Self-Interest and Interest in Selves', *Ethics*, 96 (1986), pp. 704–20, p. 708.

19 Ibid., p. 711.

20 In this use of 'project' I am mindful of, but probably not in complete conformity with, John Perry's use of it in 'The Importance of Being Identical', in *The Identities of Persons*, ed. A. O. Rorty (University of California Press, Berkeley, 1976), pp. 67–90.

21 Parfit considers a position like this on the practical importance of psychological connectedness, but rejects it in favour of the belief that such connectedness is one of those 'relations which can be rationally believed to be less important when they hold to reduced degrees'. He states without argument that this belief '*cannot be defensibly denied*' (p. 314). I think common sense would suppose that I have as much reason from the connectedness between my present state and my state a week hence to care about what will happen to me then as I have from the even greater connectedness that obtains from day to day to care about what will happen to me tomorrow. I do not really wish, however, to dispute Parfit's rejection of S's contention that it would be *irrational* to be less concerned about my more distant, and less connected, future. What I want to say is that I *can* reasonably have my life as a project in which my level of concern for my future does not vary with any normally expected variation in psychological connectedness.

22 Wolf, 'Self-Interest', p. 709. Thus we have a *reason* for caring about persons that does not apply to experiences. Parfit alludes to this argument in a footnote ('Comments', p. 833), but does not respond to it. He focuses on Wolf's claim that the reason for caring about persons as such 'is that life, or, if one prefers, the world, is better that way' (Wolf, 'Self-Interest', p. 713). His main response is that 'if some desire has good effects, this fact cannot show that this desire is rational; it can at most show that we have a reason to try to have, or to keep, this desire'. 'Whatever the effects', for example, 'it would be irrational not to care about future Tuesdays' (Parfit, 'Comments', pp. 832 f.). With this rejoinder in mind, I am trying, in the text, to address the issue of rationality (though I believe the relation between the salutariness of a motivational pattern and its rationality is probably quite complex).

23 This is only a presumption. I have not proved that it could not be overridden. If we came to believe, for example, that there is no causal influence, direct or indirect, of earlier on later stages of the same person, then, perhaps, it would be irrational for us to care as we do about personal identity. The point of invoking a presumption in this context is that we are considering whether Parfit can support his position by arguing that the value we are accustomed to set on personal identity must be justified by appeal to non-reductionist beliefs. And the answer to this question is: 'No, we need no such non-reductionist justification', if the sort of presumption I have described favours the belief that our valuation is rational.

24 One might try to construct a different sort of argument from Parfit's cases of fission and fusion, using them first to try (as Parfit does) to establish that it is psychological connectedness and continuity, rather than personal identity, that it would be reasonable for us to care about in these cases where they may be supposed to diverge. This is turn might be taken as some reason to think that in ordinary cases, where (according to this argument) they coincide, it is the connectedness and continuity, rather than personal identity as such, that matters to us. This argument, however, proposes a reinterpretation rather than a revision of our interest in our lives. It is crucial to Parfit's revisionist project that he sees the interest in continuity and connectedness as diverging in the actual case too from the interest in identity as such, inasmuch as connectedness, unlike identity, comes in degrees. What I argue in the text is that science-fiction examples provide dubious support, at best, for the revisionist project, because there is little reason to suppose that what it is rational to care about under actual circumstances must be the same as what we think it would be reasonable for us to care about under the very different imaginary circumstances.

25 Parfit might not want to rely on this argument. He reports that he is still 'much more concerned' about his own future than he 'would be about the future of a mere stranger'. And he thinks that this would be generally true of reductionists. In saying this, however, he distinguishes sharply between the questions of whether reductionists would have this attitude and whether it would be rationally justified (p. 308). This suggests that the claims he discusses as to what it would be rational for Reductionists to care about are not meant to depend on what reductionists would in fact care about.

26 Wolf, 'Self-Interest', p. 705.

27 This is far from the whole story about Buddhism, of course. The third of its Four Noble Truths is that cessation of suffering comes from cessation of craving; and the craving that must cease is 'the craving for sensual pleasure', the concern about the quality of present experience, paradigmatically rational for Parfit, that seeks 'satisfaction now here now there', just as much as 'the craving for continuing existence'. And this cessation is promised as the fruit, not of mere philosophical reflection, but of persistent following of the Noble Eightfold Path of moral and spiritual discipline, at the end of which one may hope for an *enlightenment* that seems to be held out as something rather more interesting and enticing than merely coming not to care so much about one's own inevitable death. I quote from

Majjhima-nikaya, iii. 248–52, as translated in Sarvepalli Radhakrishnan and Charles Moore (eds), *A Source Book in Indian Philosophy* (Princeton University Press, Princeton, 1957), pp. 276f. An alternative translation can be found in Edward Conze's collection of *Buddhist Scriptures* (Penguin, London, 1959), pp. 186f.

28 At this point Parfit (p. 446) may come close to Kierkegaard.

29 See Søren Kierkegaard, *Concluding Unscientific Postscript*, tr. David F. Swenson and Walter Lowrie (Princeton University Press, Princeton, 1941), e.g., pp. 152–8, 276–82; and *Either/Or*, vol. 2, tr. Walter Lowrie, rev. Howard A. Johnson (Doubleday Anchor, Garden City, NJ, 1959). Much of the discussion of 'existence' in the *Postscript* should be classified by analytic philosophers as being about personal identity through time.

30 Parfit, 'Comments', p. 843, n. 26.

31 John Locke, *An Essay Concerning Human Understanding*, II. xxvii. 18–19, 26.

32 Perhaps the link between the concept of personal identity and these other concepts could be broken by a sufficiently radical change in our beliefs about causality. This would entail a significant change in our form of life, and I am not sure how well the concept of personal identity would retain its own identity through the change. But I cannot see that a compelling reason has been given for thinking that the conceptual link would be broken by a change from a non-reductionist to a reductionist theory of personal identity. Indeed, the view I am sketching in the text is particularly well adapted to reductionism, inasmuch as the juridical role of the concept of personal identity can be seen as a constraint on the form of an acceptable reduction or construction of the concept.

33 Parfit, 'Comments', pp. 839–42.

34 Ibid., pp. 838f.

35 Parfit argues that 'we cannot rationally . . . claim that [it] matters much' whether relation R has its normal cause. But in saying this, he seems to be thinking mainly about what matters for the question whether teletransportation is as bad as annihilation. And I cannot see much more in his argument than a bare appeal to the intuition that '[i]t is the *effect* which matters' here (p. 286).

36 As Parfit concedes to Wolf in his 'Comments', p. 837, n. 14.

37 In practice, this is a major proviso which could not be ignored. But assuming that it is satisfied will help us to focus on the issue that Parfit wishes to discuss.

38 Which seems defensible to Parfit, and obviously correct to me.

39 Perhaps Parfit did not mean to show more than this. But his claim of 'very wide theoretical implications, of an impersonal kind' for this argument (p. 447) suggests that he did.

40 James Woodward argues for according a larger role to *rights* of future people, in a fine paper on 'The Non-Identity Problem', *Ethics*, 96 (1986), pp. 804–31. He criticizes my use of a similar problem, in papers about the problem of evil, as well as Parfit's use of the non-identity problem. I am not convinced that the concepts of rights, fairness and wronging people can be

given the larger scope that Woodward claims for them in these matters. But I am persuaded by his examples that room must none the less be found in intergenerational ethics for such a rights-related conception as that of compensation owed to a person for harm arising from an action without which her (worthwhile) life would never have begun.

41 Some of the arguments of James Woodward ('Non-Identity Problem', pp. 828–31), and of Philippa Foot, 'Utilitarianism and the Virtues', *Proceedings and Addresses of the American Philosophical Association*, 57 (1983), pp. 273–83, are relevant here.

42 Considerations that I think highly relevant to this issue are developed in my paper, 'Common Projects and Moral Virtue', *Midwest Studies in Philosophy*, 13 (1988), pp. 297–307. Religious considerations are likely also to bear on it. Jonathan Bennett, in one of the best essays I have read on this subject, appeals to much the same sort of commitment to a project or 'great adventure' as I have been discussing, but quite explicitly does not regard it as a matter of moral obligation; see his paper, 'On Maximizing Happiness', in *Obligations to Future Generations*, ed. R. I. Sikora and Brian Barry (Temple University Press, Philadelphia, 1978), pp. 61–73.

43 I ignore here the possibility that B might evolve out of A+ by way of Divided B, the two populations discovering each other, meeting and mingling *after* they had come to the same quality of life in Divided B. This may be the scenario in which it is most plausible to think that B is precisely as good as Divided B. But throwing it into the hopper as yet another alternative only underlines the impossibility of getting a plausible precise comparison of the value of these states of affairs independently of the history by which they would arise.

44 Parfit tries to score an extra point here by arguing that the inequality in New A is actually *better* than in A+, on the ground that '[t]here is no longer inequality between the two best-off groups'. This is a bad argument. It depends on Parfit's thinking of the best-off groups in New A as the two groups from A+, and the many worse-off groups in New A as the 'mere additions'. But at this point in his argument, the identities of people are supposed to make no difference to the comparative values of outcomes. This type of flaw in his argument will be discussed more fully below, in another connection.

45 Indeed, they also seem to be advantages that A+ enjoys over New B, but I will not develop that point here.

46 I wish to thank Marilyn McCord Adams for discussion of ideas for this essay, and Warren Quinn and the editors of the *Philosophical Review* for comments on drafts of it.

13

Rethinking the Good, Moral Ideals and the Nature of Practical Reasoning

Larry S. Temkin

Introduction

In Part 4, 'Future Generations', Derek Parfit raises many perplexing questions. Unfortunately, some find Parfit's ingenious arguments more irksome than illuminating, while others think them little more than delightful puzzles. Alas, it is not uncommon for Parfit's harshest critics to ask dismissively, 'What do *boxes* have to do with ethics?' – as if Parfit's results are mainly clever artefacts stemming from a peculiar use of abstract diagrams. On the other hand, even among those regarding Part 4 as genuinely insightful, 'Future Generations' is often regarded as the book's least significant part, relevant mainly to consequentialists concerned with determining the best principle of beneficence – Parfit's Theory X – and to those (few) environmentalists and others seriously worried about future generations.

Such reactions to Part 4 are thoroughly misguided. Parfit's arguments are original, and strike at the core of some of our deepest beliefs. Indeed, I believe Part 4 is one of the richest, most profound works in contemporary philosophy. My reasons for this will become clear as the essay progresses. It is divided into two main parts. In part I, I discuss the Repugnant Conclusion, in part II the Mere Addition Paradox. I will argue that the Repugnant Conclusion forces us to reject the most common view of utility and its relation to our all-things-considered judgements, to develop a new way of understanding the role that moral ideals play in relation to each other, and to recognize that certain moral ideals may have to share certain formal or structural features in ways that have significant and previously unrecognized implications. Next, I will argue that the Mere Addition Paradox raises profound questions about the nature of moral ideals, questions that ultimately challenge the consistency and intelligibility of some fundamental assumptions about moral and practical reasoning. If the arguments I present here are right, Part 4 will alter our understanding of the nature of moral ideals and their role in our all-things-considered judgements in ways that have far-reaching practical and theoretical implications.

First, a few preliminary comments. The reader will notice that I have little to say about future generations. This is no accident. I believe Part 4 is misleadingly titled. Though Parfit is surely right that we can now affect the course of future generations as never before, and that therefore consideration of future generations must now play a prominent role in our moral reflections, I think his arguments' implications about future generations are secondary in importance to their fundamental implications for moral theory itself. Correspondingly, I focus on the latter rather than the former.

Analogously, at some points the reader may wonder whether I have been faithful to Parfit's views. I believe I have, but I confess I am much less concerned about assessing Parfit's arguments as *he* presents them than about critically assessing what we can *learn* from those arguments. This is one reason why, for the most part, I ignore Parfit's errors. It is his insights that I am interested in.

This essay is long, but in many respects it is not long enough. Besides leaving many questions open, I ignore many important arguments. So, for example, time and space considerations prevent me from addressing the Non-Identity Problem, the Absurd Conclusion, the Asymmetry and Hell Three, among others. These are rich arguments that would amply repay careful study.[1] Moreover, there are interesting connections between these arguments and those presented here. Unfortunately, I cannot pursue these issues in this essay.

Part I. The Repugnant Conclusion

A. In chapter 17 of *Reasons and Persons* Parfit presents

> *The Repugnant Conclusion*: For any possible population of at least ten billion people, all with a very high quality of life, there must be some much larger imaginable population whose existence, if other things are equal, would be better, even though its members have lives that are barely worth living. (p. 388)

Figure 13.1 helps to illustrate the Repugnant Conclusion. According to the Repugnant Conclusion, if only there are *enough* people in Z, Z will

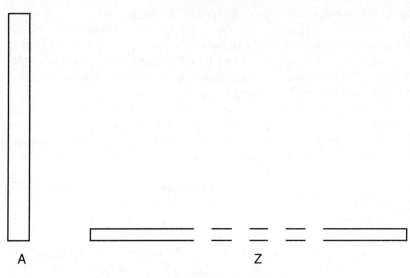

Figure 13.1

be better than A, and this is so no matter how large A is, and even if those in A are *very* well off while those in Z have lives barely worth living. As Parfit writes, 'this conclusion [is] very hard to accept' (p. 388).

The Repugnant Conclusion has significant implications. In supporting this claim, I shall argue that the Repugnant Conclusion challenges what is perhaps the standard, or naïve, way of thinking about utility and its relation to our all-things-considered judgements. I shall then indicate how rethinking our views about utility suggests a new model for understanding moral ideals. Finally, I shall illustrate that, depending on their role in relation to our all-things-considered judgements, some ideals must share certain formal, or structural, features, and that this has important, though largely unrecognized, implications.

My discussion assumes, with Parfit, that the Repugnant Conclusion is *genuinely* repugnant and should be rejected. Also, throughout this essay I shall assume that there are only four principles, or ideals, relevant to comparing Parfit's alternatives: utility (U), equality (E), maximin $(M)^2$ and perfectionism (P).[3] So, for example, I assume there is nothing to choose between Parfit's alternatives in terms of other moral factors such as virtue, duty, liberty or rights. This assumption is, of course, controversial, both for what it includes and what it excludes, but it greatly facilitates my presentation and does not affect my central results.

B. I believe that many implicitly accept four basic assumptions:

1   Utility is intrinsically valuable, even if it is not the only thing that is.
2   In so far as one cares about utility, one should care about total utility.
3   How good a situation is regarding utility is a simple additive function of how much utility sentient beings have in that situation.
4   How good a situation is, all things considered, is an additive function of how good it is regarding each ideal; so, in so far as a situation gets better regarding utility, it will, to that extent, be getting better, all things considered.

Not everyone accepts (1)–(4). Average utilitarians reject (2), strict Kantians reject (1) and (4), and an increasing number reject (3)'s and (4)'s additive assumptions. Nevertheless, (1)–(4) have great appeal. In fact, though rarely explicitly formulated, I believe that they represent perhaps the most natural and prevalent way of thinking about utility and its connection to our all-things-considered judgements.

Together (1)–(4) support the Repugnant Conclusion. After all, given (1)–(3), the addition of lives worth living *will* make an outcome better regarding utility. But then, if adding an extra person improves a situation *at all* – even in only one respect, and even if, because the person's life is barely worth living, it is just a tiny bit – (3) and (4) imply that if only there are *enough* people in Z, it would be better than A. That is, if only Z is large enough, its all-things-considered score will be higher than A's, as its score for utility will be sufficiently higher than A's to outweigh the extent to which it has lower scores for perfectionism and maximin.[4]

The preceding argument makes two assumptions. First, it assumes that Z's scores for maximin and perfectionism are not inversely related to Z's size: that is, that merely increasing Z's population does not *worsen* Z regarding M and P. Second, it assumes the possibility of something like a numerical model for judging outcomes, according to which each outcome will merit a (rough numerical) 'score' representing how good that situation is, all things considered, where *that* score will be an additive function of other (rough) 'scores' for each relevant factor or ideal (i.e. U, E, M and P). Though I think the second assumption's details are enormously complicated, I think both assumptions are intuitively plausible, and likely to be granted by most advocates of (1)–(4).

The foregoing results are important. They reveal that, to avoid the Repugnant Conclusion, we need an alternative model to (1)–(4) for understanding utility and the role it plays in our all-things-considered judgements. Let us next consider one such model.

C. Reflecting on the Repugnant Conclusion, most of us are reminded that we are not strict utilitarians. While utility matters a lot, it is not all that matters. But we also learn a further, deeper lesson. We learn that mere increases in the quantity of utility are not sufficient (or so we think) to outweigh significant losses regarding other ideals. This is why Z is worse than A. Though better regarding utility, it is not better regarding equality, and it is much worse regarding other ideals, like perfectionism and maximin.

The importance of the further lesson cannot be exaggerated. It suggests that there may be an upper limit to how good a situation can be regarding utility. Moreover, if this is so for utility, it is probably also so for the other ideals, and hence there may also be an upper limit to how good a situation can be, all things considered.

Consider an analogy from sports. In a gymnastics competition the best all-round gymnast is decided by adding together each person's score in each event. For women, there are four events, each with a maximum score of ten; so the maximum total score one can attain is 40. While theoretically one can approach, and even attain, a perfect performance, one can never exceed the maximum score. So, to be the best all-round gymnast, it is not enough to near, or even attain, perfection in the floor exercises. One must also excel on the balance beam, the vault, and the uneven parallel bars.

On reflection, it seems that something like this may also hold for our all-things-considered judgements. Perhaps in comparing situations, all things considered, we must compare them in terms of each ideal, where there is a maximum score they can get for each ideal, determined by how much the ideals matter *vis-à-vis* each other. Suppose, for example, that in assessing outcomes, U, E, M and P were equally important and all we cared about. Then we might assign numbers to situations such that the highest score a situation could get for each ideal would be, say, 100, and the 'perfect' situation would score 400. Similarly, to note a more complicated example, if we thought that P was twice as important as E and M, and half again as important as U, then we might assign numbers to situations such that the highest score a situation could get would be, say, 150 for P, 100 for U, and 75 each for E and M. Clearly, the highest score for each ideal sets an upper limit to the score that situations can receive for that ideal. Situations will receive the highest score for an ideal if they are perfect regarding that ideal; to the extent they are less than perfect, they will receive appropriately lower scores.

Let us call such a position the *gymnastics model* for moral ideals. The gymnastics model expresses the views, noted previously, that there is an upper limit to how good situations can be regarding each ideal, and also an upper limit to how good situations can be, all things considered.

Now a 'perfect' situation regarding U – one that could not be improved on and would merit the highest possible score for U – would have infinite utility. Correspondingly, no finite world will be perfect regarding utility. So, on the gymnastics model, a finite world may approach the maximum score for utility, but it can never attain that score or go beyond it. Note that, on the gymnastics model, there is no limit to how *much* utility can be added to a situation. In addition, for any finite situation, it will always be possible to improve that situation regarding utility, even if only slightly. However, as there is an upper limit on how good a situation can be regarding utility, there is also an upper limit on how much a situation can be improved – that is, be made normatively *better* – regarding utility. So, after a point, mere increases in the *amount* of utility will not substantially increase the *value* of a situation, even regarding utility.[5] It follows that, on the gymnastics model, mere increases in utility alone, however great, will not always be sufficient to outweigh significant losses in other respects.[6]

To illustrate this position, let us again make the simplifying assumption that each ideal matters equally, and let us (arbitrarily) assign scores to A and Z of up to 100 for U, E, M and P. A is perfect regarding E, and (by hypothesis) very good for U, M and P. So let us suppose that $E = 100$, $U = 80$, $M = 80$ and $P = 80$. A would then have an all-things-considered score of 340. Z is perfect regarding E, and, we may suppose, nearly perfect[7] regarding U, but it is much worse regarding M and P. For Z, then, let us suppose $E = 100$ and $U = 99$, but $M = 20$, and $P = 20$. Z would then have an all-things-considered score of 239 – 100 points lower than A's on a scale of only 400! One can see, then, how such a model can account for the genuine repugnancy of the Repugnant Conclusion. Of course, the extent of the repugnancy will depend on how A and Z in fact compare for U, M and P – or any other relevant ideals – as well as how much those ideals matter to our all-things-considered judgements.

There is a logical limit to how much one can reduce a situation's inequality, but no logical limit to how *much* utility obtains. Because of this, it is natural to suppose that there is a limit to how much one can improve a situation regarding equality, but none regarding utility. Nevertheless, this supposition seems mistaken. *However much more we may care about one ideal relative to another, they play similar roles in our all-things-considered judgements.* Thus, on reflection, most believe that, other things equal, transforming a situation into one perfect, or nearly perfect, regarding E, U or P would not be better *all things considered* if it involved significant losses regarding U and P, M and P, or E and M, respectively.

Let us contrast the gymnastics model for moral ideals with the 'standard' model noted in section B. In terms of (1)–(4), the gymnastics model can capture (2) – in so far as one cares about utility, one should care about total utility. It can also capture (4) – how good a situation is, all things considered, is an additive function of how good it is regarding each ideal; so, in so far as a situation gets better regarding utility, it will, to that extent, be getting better, all things considered. But it denies (3) – how good a situation is regarding utility is a simple additive function of how much utility sentient beings have in that situation. Thus, while it grants that doubling the *amount* of utility in a situation improves it regarding utility, it denies that it necessarily does this by a factor of two. Correspondingly, it denies (1) – utility is intrinsically valuable – *in the sense* that each unit of utility has intrinsic value of a constant amount which increases a situation's objective value in direct proportion to that amount. On the other hand, the model *is* compatible with utility being intrinsically valuable *in the sense* that it can regard utility as a significant factor in all-things-considered judgements beyond the extent it promotes other ideals.

Faced with paradoxes involving future generations, and hoping to avoid the Repugnant Conclusion, Parfit and others have suggested that there may be *no* respect in which the 'mere addition' of extra people to an already large and well-off population improves the situation.[8] However, many find this position implausible. They think that the addition of extra people with lives worth living must always improve utility. The gymnastics model captures this belief, while avoiding the unpalatable conclusion that sheer increases in a situation's *amount* of utility must always significantly improve it regarding utility and (hence) all things considered.[9] To be sure, from the subjective perspective, each extra life worth living will be as important to its possessor as every other. But from the objective perspective, though each extra life will matter *some*, after a point, it will matter less and less.[10]

There are problems with the gymnastics model, which I cannot pursue here. For example, while it may seem plausible to think that there is an upper limit to how good a situation can be regarding utility or equality, it seems much less plausible to think that there can be a lower limit to how bad a situation can be regarding utility or equality – as if, after a point, it does not really matter (much) any more whether extra people are excruciatingly tortured, or the gaps between the haves and have-nots increase still further.[11] Yet, as Parfit has demonstrated in chapter 18, it is not clear that one can have upper limits without lower limits, at least without facing serious problems of coherence and consistency.[12] Similarly, as we shall see in part II, if one adopts a gymnastics model, and combines it with what I call the *intrinsic aspect* view of moral ideals, one may have to accept the 'absurd' conclusion of Parfit's 'How Only France Survives', according to which it might be *better* if everyone but the best-

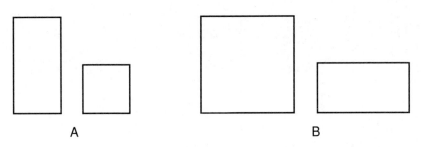

A   B

Figure 13.2

off died, even if all those who died had lives *well* worth living, and even if the lives of the best-off were worsened as a result. On the other hand, if, to avoid such implications, one combines the gymnastics model with what I have called the *essentially comparative* view of moral ideals, then, as we shall also see in part II, the threat of intransitivity looms for our all-things-considered judgements.

I mention the foregoing because I do not want to minimize the difficulties facing a gymnastics model for moral ideals. Still, the gymnastics model is hardly alone in facing grave difficulties, and, reflecting on the Repugnant Conclusion, it seems clear that what is perhaps the most natural and prevalent way of thinking about utility and its relation to our all-things-considered judgements must be rejected. Whether we should ultimately accept the gymnastics model, a variation of it (e.g. one that rejects (4)'s additive assumption as well as (3)'s), or pursue an entirely new alternative to (1)–(4), I must leave open for now.

In sum, the Repugnant Conclusion forces us to rethink the nature and role of our moral ideals in relation to each other and our all-things-considered judgements. I have suggested one direction our rethinking might go.

D. I have claimed that however much more we may care about one ideal relative to another, they play similar roles in our all-things-considered judgements. So, for example, just as there is an upper limit to how good a situation can be regarding equality, there may have to be an upper limit to how good a situation can be regarding utility. Let me next suggest further reason to hold that a plausible and coherent account of the role that moral ideals play in relation to each other and our all-things-considered judgements may require some ideals to share certain formal or structural features. Specifically, I shall argue that if numbers count regarding utility, they may also have to count regarding equality.

Consider figure 13.2. As drawn, A's and B's better- and worse-off

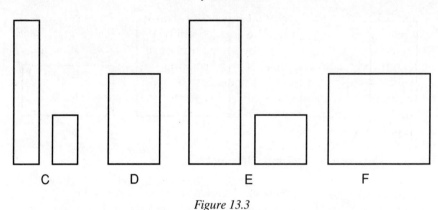

Figure 13.3

groups are at the same levels, but B's groups are twice as large as A's. Regarding *inequality*, many would judge A and B equivalent. As they might put it, since the *pattern* of inequality is identical in A and B, there is nothing to choose between them; the 'mere' fact that B is larger than A is irrelevant to how they compare regarding inequality.

The judgement that A and B are equivalent expresses the following view:

PV: Proportional variations in the number of better- and worse-off do not affect inequality.

According to PV, size is not *itself* relevant to inequality. Size variations will only matter in so far as they affect inequality's *pattern* – for example, by altering the better- and worse-off's levels or the ratios between them.

PV is widely accepted, and has great plausibility. It is, for example, implied by each of the economists' statistical measures of inequality,[13] and they have not, to my knowledge, been criticized for that feature. Yet, despite its appeal, and the fact that numerous considerations can be offered supporting it, ultimately PV may be incompatible with our views about other ideals and the role they play in our all-things-considered judgements.

Consider figure 13.3. As drawn, C represents an unequal society, D a perfectly equal society with less total utility. E and F are just like C and D, respectively, except they are twice as large. Looking at C and D, many would judge that D is better than C, all things considered. They would judge the (slight) loss of utility in moving from C to D regrettable, but outweighed by the (substantial) gain in equality. Similarly, looking at E and F, many would judge that F is better than E, all things considered. Again, they would judge the loss of utility in moving from E to F regrettable, but outweighed by the gain in equality. More importantly, few, if any, would approve a redistribution between the better- and worse-off in C so as to bring about D, yet oppose a redistribution between the better- and worse-off in E so as to bring about F. That is, most would agree that *if* moving from C to D were desirable, then moving from E to F would *also* be desirable.

The foregoing claims may seem obvious and uninteresting, but they have important implications. Depending on how one thinks that moral ideals combine to yield all-things-considered judgements, they imply that if numbers count for utility, they must also count for equality.[14]

Consider. Suppose one thinks that the move from C to D is only a *slight* improvement, all things considered, because the gain in equality is just *barely* enough to outweigh the attendant loss in utility. Then it looks as if F would be *worse* than E if numbers count for utility but not for equality. After all, E and F are twice as large as C and D. This means that the loss in utility in moving from E to F will be twice the loss in utility in moving from C to D, and hence, on the view in question, that the move from E to F will be worse than the move from C to D regarding utility. Yet, if numbers don't count for equality, or, more specifically, if we accept PV, the view that proportional increases do not affect inequality, then the gain in equality in moving from F to E will be *exactly* the same as the gain in equality in moving from D to C. But then it looks as if the gain in equality in moving from F to E *won't* be sufficient to outweigh the attendant loss in utility, since, by hypothesis, the gain in question is *barely* enough to outweigh a loss in utility which is only *half* as large. In sum, if moving from E to F is significantly worse than moving from C to D regarding utility, and no better regarding equality, then it is easy to see that, all things considered, moving from E to F could be undesirable even if moving from C to D were desirable. But this, of course, is contrary to the 'obvious and uninteresting' view noted earlier.[15]

The foregoing result may be surprising. But, on reflection, it is not, I think, perplexing or disturbing. Suffice it to say, I accept the view that if moving from C to D were desirable, so too would be moving from E to F. I also accept the view that in an important sense the latter move would be worse than the former regarding utility. This leads me to believe that there is an important sense in which the latter move would be better than the former regarding equality. But, of course, this implies that E is worse than C regarding inequality, which in turn implies that there is reason to reject PV.[16]

Some will insist that inequality is not bad in the same way disutility is. More generally, they will insist that equality and utility are different *kinds* of moral ideals, and that the two ideals must be treated differently. So, for example, some will insist that while utility is essentially additive, equality is essentially distributive – that is, that while utilitarians are essentially concerned with how much there is, egalitarians are essentially concerned *not* with how much there is, but with the way, or *pattern*, in which what there is, is distributed. On this view, the fact that numbers count regarding utility should be completely irrelevant to whether numbers count regarding equality.

Such thinking is powerfully seductive, but as we have seen, it is not clear that our moral ideals can be fully and adequately characterized in isolation from each other. Specifically, a plausible and coherent account of the role that moral ideals play in relation to each other and our all-things-considered judgements may require at least some ideals to share certain formal or structural features. Thus, as the Repugnant Conclusion reveals, there may be a limit to how much improvement regarding one ideal can offset significant losses regarding other ideals, and this in turn suggests that, just as there may be an upper limit regarding how good a situation can be regarding equality, so there may be an upper limit regarding how good a situation can be regarding each of our moral ideals. So, too, if one holds that numbers count regarding utility, one may also have to hold that numbers count regarding equality.[17]

Part II.   The Mere Addition Paradox

A. Arguably, 'The Mere Addition Paradox' is both the most ingenious and the most error-filled chapter in *Reasons and Persons*. Between them, the versions of the Mere Addition Paradox and the two examples, 'How Only France Survives' and 'Hell Three', raise a host of intriguing questions. Yet many of Parfit's claims and arguments are at best controversial, and at worst mistaken. For example, against Parfit, it could be argued that in the second version of the Mere Addition Paradox, New A's inequality *is* much worse than A+'s (see p. 434), and Parfit is surely wrong in contending that 'all of the plausible views [of inequality] would agree that the inequality in New B is less bad than the inequality in New A' (p. 435).[18] Moreover, regarding the first version of the Mere Addition Paradox, I think Parfit is wrong in claiming that if one accepts that A+ is better than A, and B is better than A+, one 'cannot avoid the Repugnant Conclusion' (p. 430); and that he is also wrong in making similar claims regarding the second and third versions of the paradox (see pp. 436–7 and 441). The conclusions in question *can* be avoided if, for example, one adopts something like the gymnastics model for moral ideals suggested in part I.[19] In addition, I think that sometimes Parfit's reason-

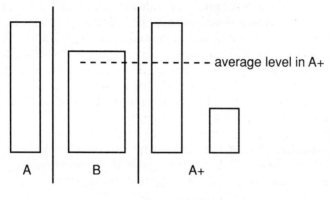

Figure 13.4

ing is inconsistent, implicitly adopting one view of moral ideals in support of certain conclusions, but another, incompatible view of moral ideals in support of other conclusions.

I level the above charges, but shall not pursue them. This is not because I think Parfit's mistakes – if they *are* mistakes – are uninteresting. To the contrary, in almost every case much can be gleaned from carefully considering where, and why, Parfit has gone wrong. Still, the shortcomings of Parfit's arguments are insignificant compared to the importance of their insights and implications. So in the space remaining I shall focus on the latter.

Sadly, many have regarded the Mere Addition Paradox as an arcane esoteric puzzle involving hypothetical future generations and having little to do with the central problems of moral philosophy. Nothing could be further from the truth. Unfortunately, to do full justice to the issues raised by the Mere Addition Paradox would require at least a book. So my remarks must be sketchy, programmatic and open-ended. Still, I can perhaps give the reader some sense of why I think the Mere Addition Paradox is one of the most profound, though least well-understood, arguments in contemporary moral philosophy.

B. Though in some ways Parfit's second and (especially) third versions of the paradox are more interesting and compelling, for our purposes it will be sufficient to consider a slightly simplified form of Parfit's first version of the Mere Addition Paradox.[20] Consider figure 13.4. Parfit claims that, all things considered, most would judge that B is worse than A. After all, by hypothesis, A is already a large population (say, ten billion), and *everyone* in A is better off than *everyone* in B. Parfit also argues that, all things considered, most would judge that B is better than A+. Though B is worse than A+ regarding perfectionism, it is better regarding maximin, equality and utility;[21] so though élitists might deny that B is better than A+, most would not. Finally, Parfit contends that, all things considered, most would judge that A+ is not worse than A. Parfit's lengthy argument for this (pp. 419–26) will be discussed below, but the key point is that A+ involves Mere Addition, where, according to Parfit, there is

> Mere Addition when, in one of two outcomes, there exist extra people (1) who have lives worth living, (2) who affect no one else, and (3) whose existence does not involve social injustice. (p. 420)

As Parfit puts it in a passage from 'Future Generations: Further Problems[3]:

> Let us compare A with A+. The only difference is that A+ contains an extra group, who have lives worth living, and who affect no one else . . . it seems [hard] . . . to believe that A+ is *worse* than A. This implies that it would have been better if the extra group had never existed. If their lives are worth living, and they affect no one else, why is it bad that these people are alive?[22]

According to Parfit, then, most believe that A+ is not worse than A and that B is better than A+. 'These beliefs together imply that B is not worse than A. B cannot be worse than A if it is better than something – A+ – which is not worse than A' (p. 426). But most also believe that 'B *is* worse than A. [Hence] we have three beliefs that are inconsistent, and imply contradictions . . . this [is] the *Mere Addition Paradox*' (p. 426).

Parfit insists that the Mere Addition Paradox does *not* merely illustrate a tension between different moral principles, which may often conflict and cloud our all-things-considered judgements. Such cases need not reflect any inconsistency. 'In the Mere Addition Paradox', Parfit claims, 'things are different. We are here inclined to believe, *all things considered*, that B is worse than A, though B is better than A+, which is not worse than A. These three judgements cannot all be consistently believed, since they imply contradictions. One of these beliefs must go' (p. 427).

In sum, Parfit believes that rationality requires us to give up one of the three claims, and the paradox is that, considered alone, each claim seems (far) more plausible than its denial.

C. Unfortunately, Parfit's discussion of the Mere Addition Paradox is misleading. Believing that the Mere Addition Paradox would be dissolved if one of Parfit's three main claims were rejected, many spend time questioning whether B really *is* worse than A, all things considered, and whether the judgement that B is better than A commits one to the Repugnant Conclusion. (It doesn't.[23]) Similarly, people often wonder if B really is better than A+, and whether one could deny this without being an élitist. (One can.[24]) As it happens, I think Parfit is right – though his arguments are not conclusive – regarding the most plausible pairwise judgements of A, A+ and B. But even if Parfit is wrong, and we should reject the claim that A is better than B, or that B is better than A+, the most fundamental insights and implications of Parfit's argument would remain unaffected. The *crucial* question Parfit raises is whether the fact that A+ involves Mere Addition is relevant to our assessment of outcomes. As we shall see, the answer to this question has profound implications about the nature of moral ideals, implications that may alter our very conception of practical and moral reasoning – perhaps of rationality itself.

Consider the move from A to A+. One natural response to the Mere Addition Paradox is to claim that A+ is worse than A (in part) because it is worse regarding inequality. Against such a response one might reason as follows. Typically, when we say that one situation's inequality is worse than another's, the same people exist in both situations, and the worse-off fare worse in one situation than the other. This, we may agree, is bad. However, comparing A+ to A, the choice is *not* between a situation where the worse-off fare poorly relative to the better-off and one where they fare better; rather, it is between one where they exist – with lives worth living – and one where they do not. Here, it may seem, the inequality is not morally regrettable.

Parfit explicitly adopts this line. His argument is lengthy, but worth giving in some detail. He writes:

> Whether inequality makes [an] outcome worse depends on how it comes about. It might be true either ... that some existing people are worse off than others, or ... that there are extra people living who, though their lives are worth living, are worse off than some existing people. Only [the former] makes the outcome worse.... When inequality is produced by Mere Addition, it does not make the outcome worse.... It would not be better if there was no inequality because the extra people do not exist. It would be better only if the extra people do exist and are as well off as everyone else. Since the inequality in A+ is produced by Mere Addition, this inequality does not make A+ worse than A. We cannot plausibly claim that the extra people should never have existed, *merely because, unknown to them, there are other people who are even better off.* (p. 425)

Parfit is *not* denying the obvious fact that A is perfectly equal while A+ is not, nor that A+'s inequality is morally regrettable *when compared with B's*. Parfit's contention is that A+'s inequality is not regrettable *if the alternative is A.* As we shall see next, it is hard to overstate the importance of this view.

D. On Parfit's view, *equality is essentially comparative* (EEC), not merely in the ordinary sense – that it involves judgements about how some fare relative to others – but in the sense that our judgement about a situation's inequality depends on the alternative to which it is being compared. The advocate of EEC believes that inequality is not objectionable when it is brought about by the mere addition of extra people all of whom have lives worth living and who affect no one else, and where the alternative is a situation not where those people are better off, but where they don't exist at all. This underlies his view that the inequality in A+ *is* morally regrettable when A+ is compared to B, but not when it is compared to A. So, on EEC, the relevant and significant factors for comparing A+ and A regarding inequality differ from the relevant and significant factors for comparing A+ and B in a sense connected with inequality's being essentially (pairwise) comparative.

More generally, though still roughly, let us say that:

A principle (or moral ideal), *f*, is *essentially comparative* if the *relevant and significant* factors for comparing two alternatives regarding *f* may vary depending on the alternatives being compared; and, more specifically, *f* is *essentially pairwise comparative* if one must directly compare two alternatives in order to determine their relative ranking regarding *f*.

Two key points regarding essentially (pairwise) comparative principles: first, on an essentially (pairwise) comparative view, how good or bad a situation is regarding *f* depends partly on factors that are not (solely) *internal* to the situation. Hence, there is no *fact of the matter* as to how good or bad a situation *really* is regarding *f*, considered just by itself. How good or bad it is depends on the alternative to which it is compared. Thus, for example, on EEC, there is no fact of the matter as to how bad the inequality in A+ *really* is considered just by itself.[25] How bad it is depends on the alternative compared to it. Compared to B's, A+'s inequality is bad; compared to A's, it isn't. Second, on an essentially (pairwise) comparative view, there may be no fact of the matter as to how two situations compare considered 'purely' abstractly. One may need to know who their 'members' are or how they have come about. For example, suppose half of the people in A were lowered to the level of the worse-off in A+, and then the entire population doubled. A world like A+ would result, and it seems clear that, brought about *this* way, A+'s inequality *would* be worse than A's.[26] Hence, on EEC, to even make the kind of static judgements that Parfit and we are interested in, it is not sufficient to consider abstract diagrams like A and A+. In addition, we need to know the relation, if any, between them. Thus, if Parfit is right, it makes a difference whether A+ involves Mere Addition.

The above result may initially seem puzzling, but it has a straightforward explanation. On EEC, how good a situation is regarding inequality will depend on which alternative it is being compared with. But, in terms of the relevant and significant factors for applying EEC, which alternative it is being compared with may itself partly depend on the members involved or how the alternative has come about. In other words, despite their abstract structural similarities, A and A+ are *different* pairs of alternatives in the cases imagined. This explains why our judgements can vary about those cases.

We are now in a position to see why Parfit's arguments are so interesting and important. If, in fact, we should accept EEC – that is, if the nature of equality is essentially (pairwise) comparative – then many patterns of inference generally regarded as valid for all concepts will in fact be invalid for inequality, with the result that 'all-things-considered better than' will *not* be a transitive relation.

Consider. Most people accept what I have elsewhere called

The Principle of Substitution for Equivalence: Given any concept *c*, for all *x*, *y* and *z* to which *c* is appropriately applied, then *regarding c*, if *x* is equivalent to *y*, however *x* compares to *z*, that is how *y* compares to *z*.

Clearly, on EEC, the Principle of Substitution for Equivalence is not valid. After all, in the Mere Addition Paradox A and B are equivalent regarding equality – both are perfect – and B is better than A+; yet, on EEC, A is *not* better than A+, as A+ is not worse than A. Thus, on EEC, knowing how two situations compare to a third will not necessarily be helpful in determining how *they* compare. More generally, where a concept is essentially comparative, it can be true that even *precise* comparisons between A and B, and B and C, do not reflect how A and C compare.

The foregoing results are important, and may initially seem startling; but on reflection they are not surprising. If A is a better tennis-player than B, and B a better bridge-player than C, *nothing* follows about how A and C compare either as tennis-players or as bridge-players. The simple reason for this is that the factors that are relevant and significant for comparing tennis-players are *different* from those that are relevant and significant for comparing bridge-players. By the same token, if a moral principle *f is* essentially comparative, then, by hypothesis, the relevant and significant factors for comparing A and B regarding f may be different from the relevant and significant factors for comparing B and C, or A and C, regarding f. Consequently, knowing how A and B, and B and C, compare regarding f by itself tells us nothing about how A and C compare regarding f.

Notice that, in an important sense, the advocate of EEC could insist that the nature and extent of her concern regarding equality remain the same in each comparison. It is not as if she cares about equality when comparing A+ and B, but not when comparing A+ with A. Nor is it that she really cares about equality$_1$ when comparing A+ and A, but an entirely different equality$_2$ when comparing A+ and B. She has an unchanging commitment to a single principle of equality, EEC, but its impact on her judgement varies with the alternatives being compared. To be sure, at one level the relevant and significant factors appealed to by EEC change with the alternatives being compared, but there need not be anything inconstant or inconsistent about this. Instead, the advocate of EEC could contend, this merely expresses what we really are (and should be) concerned about regarding inequality – including the conditions under which that concern is properly evoked.

Following terminology introduced elsewhere, let us say that a concept is *deeply intransitive* if the Principle of Substitution for Equivalence does not hold for that concept.[27] Then it is easy to see that if f is a moral principle which plays an important role in our all-things-considered judgements, the deep intransitivity of f may carry over into our all-things-considered judgements.

Suppose, for example, that although f is not all we care about, or even perhaps what we most care about, it is *one* important element in our all-things-considered judgements. This means that how situations compare regarding f may determine how they compare, all things considered, if 'other things are equal' or at least 'equal enough' in terms of the *other* principles or ideals about which we care. But then, if f is deeply intransitive, it seems that there are bound to be *some* situations which are equivalent, or nearly equivalent, in terms of the other ideals we care about, such that the deep intransitivity of f will carry over into our all-things-considered judgements. And, of course, this will be so for any principle f which is deeply intransitive. Indeed, the point is generalizable. If an important aspect of a complex notion is deeply intransitive, the notion itself will be deeply intransitive.

Again, the foregoing result may initially be shocking, but on reflection it is not surprising. If an important principle in our all-things-considered judgements is essentially comparative, then the relevant and significant factors for comparing alternatives, all things considered, will, to at least some extent, depend on the alternatives being compared. Correspondingly, there is no reason to expect transitivity to hold. After all, how any two situations compare, *all things considered*, will presumably depend on how they compare in terms of each of the relevant and significant factors for making that comparison. But then, where *different* factors are relevant and significant for comparing different alternatives, it can be true that even if A is better than B, and B is better than C, in terms of the relevant and significant factors for comparing *those* alternatives, A may *not* be better than C in terms of the relevant and significant factors for making *that* comparison. Hence, it appears that in *some* cases at least, and perhaps many, 'all-things-considered better than' would not be a transitive relation.

In sum, *if* Parfit is right regarding the nature of inequality – if the fact that A+ involves Mere Addition is, in an important sense, morally relevant and significant in assessing A+ when the alternative is A but not when the alternative is B – then we are faced with a far graver problem than how to reject one of the particular judgements that A is better than B, that B is better than A+, or that A+ is not worse than A. We are faced with rejecting the transitivity of 'all-things-considered better than'. And this has enormous implications extending far beyond the topic of future generations.

E. Most react strongly to the suggestion that our all-things-considered judgements might be intransitive. Some believe that, if true, it threatens to undermine large parts of not only morality, but practical reasoning. Clearly, if 'all-things-considered better than' is not transitive, then knowing that A is better than B, and B better than C, will not be sufficient reason to prefer A to C, since C might still be better than A, all things considered. Less clearly, but just as importantly, if 'all-things-considered better than' is not transitive, then presumably, even knowing that A is better than B, all things considered, will not be sufficient reason to prefer A to B, or to remove B from further consideration, if there might be some third alternative which is both worse than B yet better than A. The practical implications of such consequences are enormous, some of which are noted later.

Some believe that the very concept of rationality is intimately bound up with the notion that all-things-considered judgements *must* be transitive. Similarly, some believe that the suggestion that our all-things-considered judgements might be intransitive borders on the self-contradictory. Even in this Quinean era, the reaction of many able philosophers is that it is virtually part of the *meanings* of the words that 'all-things-considered better than' is transitive – that they would not understand what someone meant who claimed that, *all things considered*, A was better than B, and *all things considered*, B was better than C, but *all things considered*, C was better than A. To even make such a claim is, on this view, sufficient to establish that the words 'all-things-considered better than' are being used non-standardly.

Finally, some believe that even if the suggestion is not self-contradictory, or a major threat to practical reasoning, it is wildly implausible. More particularly, they believe that no matter how plausible the arguments leading to such a conclusion *may* have appeared, their denial is more plausible than the alternative of accepting that 'all-things-considered better than' is intransitive.

In sum, most firmly believe that 'better than' and 'all-things-considered better than' are *not*, and perhaps *cannot* be, intransitive. Thus, if forced to choose between the latter beliefs and those entailing their rejection, I suspect most would, at least initially, opt for the latter beliefs.

It should now be clear why I think that, whatever its shortcomings, the Mere Addition Paradox strikes at the core of some deep beliefs. Let us next consider how best to respond to Mere Addition, and the threat that EEC poses to transitivity.

F. There are several ways of responding to Mere Addition and the arguments supporting EEC. The most general, and the one I want to focus on, denies the claim that different factors can be relevant and significant for comparing different alternatives. On this view, different factors *may*, perhaps, be relevant and significant for the question of what we ought to *do*, and if this is so, then 'ought to do' may be intransitive. But this, it might be claimed, is not particularly troubling. What *cannot* be the case, according to this view, is for different factors to be relevant and significant for the question of what ought to *be*, or which *outcome* would be best. That is, *whatever* factors are relevant and significant for determining whether one outcome is better than another, all things considered, those *very same* factors must be relevant and significant in the exact same way and to the exact same extent for determining which of any other pair of outcomes is better, all things considered.

The preceding is rough and abstract, but its point should be fairly clear. It seems that the best way to avoid intransitivity in our all-things-considered judgements will be to deny that the relevant and significant factors for determining how two situations compare can vary depending on the situations considered – that is, to deny that *any* essentially comparative principles or ideals are relevant to our all-things-considered judgements.

Let us be clear about what such a position involves. Basically, it involves rejecting the essentially comparative view of moral principles in favour of *an intrinsic aspect view* (IA) where, roughly, how good or bad a situation is regarding some principle, *f*, will be an *intrinsic* feature of that situation. That is, it will *not* depend on the alternative that situation is compared with, but solely on features *internal* to the situation.

On IA, how a situation has come about, or who its members are, will be *irrelevant* to the abstract impersonal judgement about how it fares regarding *f*.[28]

Intuitively, perhaps the most natural way of understanding IA is in terms of a numerical model of the sort suggested in part I. On such a model – or at least, a simplified version sufficient for our purposes – for any principle *f*, one can assign a number to represent how good a situation is regarding *f*.[29] The number assigned will depend solely on internal features of the situation relevant of *f*. Thus, alternatives with the same internal features will be assigned the same number *whatever their origins or comparative alternatives*.

As should be clear, on the numerical model of IA, 'better than regarding *f*' will be transitive. This is because if A is better than B, A will be assigned a higher number than B. Correspondingly, if, regarding some morally relevant principle like equality or utility, A is better than B, and B is better than C, then A would have to be better than C, since if one number is higher than a second, which in turn is higher than a third, the first must be higher than the third. ('Being a higher number than' *is* a transitive relation.)

Clearly, the numerical model for IA could be applied to the notion of 'all-things-considered better than', as well as notions like equality or utility. Indeed, it is natural to apply the same reasoning to the former notion as to the latter ones, and to see them as intimately connected. That is, it is natural to suppose that how good a situation, S, is, all things considered, is solely a function of how good it is regarding *each* principle about which we care. But, on IA, how good S is regarding any principle *f* – at least, any principle relevant to our abstract impersonal all-things-considered judgements – depends only on S's internal features. Hence, how good S is, all things considered, must itself depend only on S's internal features.

Roughly, then, on the numerical model for IA each situation merits a 'score' – a number based on the situation's internal features – for each principle relevant to how good that situation is, all things considered. Correspondingly, each situation will merit a score representing how good that situation is, all things considered, where *that* score will be a function of the other scores, such that each principle is given its appropriate weight. On this model, then, each situation will merit an all-things-considered score such that, we may suppose, if one situation is better than another, all things considered, it will merit a higher number. It follows that on this model 'all-things-considered better than' *will* be transitive; for if, *all things considered*, A is better than B, and B better than C, then A *must* be better than C, for, as noted previously, 'being a higher number than' *is* a transitive relation.

One can see, then, how the numerical model for IA would support the view that both 'better than with respect to f' and 'all-things-considered better than' must be transitive. For the purpose of later discussion, let me add that I believe this position, or something close to it, also lies at the heart of another deeply held belief.

Arrow's Impossibility Theorem invokes an *Independence of Irrelevant Alternatives Principle* which has been the subject of much scrutiny and criticism.[30] Whatever the merits of the principle as Arrow presents it, one version of such a principle seems almost overwhelmingly compelling. It might be put as follows. For any two situations, A and B, to know how A compares to B, all things considered, it is, at least in principle, sufficient to compare them directly in terms of each of the principles about which we care. More particularly, if one accurately knew how A compared to B in terms of each principle relevant to our all-things-considered judgements, and if one granted each principle its due weight, then one would be in a position to know how A compared to B, all things considered. In such circumstances, knowing how A or B compared to some third alternative, C, either regarding some particular principle, like equality or utility, or all things considered, would be unnecessary, and indeed *completely irrelevant* to knowing how A and B compared.

Understood in such a way, the Independence of Irrelevant Alternatives Principle has great plausibility. But the core of the position is, I think, IA. The point is that *any* alternative will be irrelevant to how A and B compare, because how they compare will depend solely on how good *they* are, all things considered, and on IA this will depend solely on A and B's internal features.[31]

So far, I have been merely explicating what is involved in rejecting the view that concepts can be essentially comparative in the manner of EEC. It follows from what has been said that, on IA, we are mistaken if, in considering the Mere Addition Paradox, we allow our comparative judgments about A, A+ and B to be influence by Parfit's claims about what would be involved in moving from one to another. What Parfit, and we, are presumably interested in is our abstract, impartial, static judgements about how such situations compare, all things considered. But, on IA, *those* judgements can only be based on the situation's internal features.

Consider, for example, figure 13.5. Assuming that those in A and B are equally deserving, and that B is no better than A regarding principles like freedom, virtue or rights, A would be better than B, all things

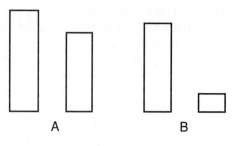

Figure 13.5

considered, as it is better regarding U, E, P and M. Of course, if one's mother would be in A's worse-off group, but B's better-off group, this might give one reason to prefer B to A, perhaps even a duty to promote B rather than A, depending on one's agent-relative duties, if any. But this would not make B better than A from the standpoint Parfit is interested in. Similarly, if the only way to bring about A would be to lie. or cheat, that might be relevant to what ought to be *done*, and even to whether A *together with its history* would be better than B together with its history. But it would not be relevant to how A and B *themselves* compare, and it is *such* judgements Parfit asks us to make regarding the Mere Addition Paradox.

Thus, *if we accept IA*, we make a grave mistake in so far as we allow our judgement about A and A+ to be influenced – as most of us surely did – by Parfit's claim, indeed emphasis, that the move from A to A+ involves Mere Addition.[32] On IA we must close our ears to such information, which may be relevant to the permissibility of such a move, but not to how A and A+ themselves compare.

G. Suppose we accept IA. What effect, if any, would that have on our understanding of the Mere Addition Paradox? I believe that if one accepts IA, the Mere Addition Paradox then loses much of its air of intractability, and that in so far as it remains problematic, it illustrates familiar problems, rather than new ones previously unrecognized.

On the essentially comparative view of moral ideals, it would be extremely implausible to give up any of the three judgements comprising the Mere Addition Paradox.[33] However, as we have seen, on the essentially comparative view of moral ideals, 'all-things-considered better than' would *not* be a transitive relation, hence there would be no paradox in maintaining all three judgements. On IA, matters are considerably different. As we have seen, 'all-things-considered better than' *would* be transitive; so, as Parfit first thought, one could not consistently maintain that, all things considered, A+ is not worse than A, though it is worse than B, which is worse than A. On the other hand, once one accepts IA, it seems there would be much less difficulty giving up one of the judgements. In particular, while accepting IA probably would not affect our judgement about A+ and B, it could easily cause revision of one of the other judgements.

Consider, for example, the judgement that A+ is not worse than A. Presumably, A+ is neither better nor worse than A regarding perfectionism (P). However, on IA, A+ would be worse than A regarding equality (E), and also worse regarding maximin (M). Now admittedly, A+ would be better than A regarding utility (U). Still, one can see how IA leaves plenty of room for the judgement that A+ is worse than A. This would be so if the extent to which A+ is better than A regarding U is outweighed by the extent to which it is worse regarding E and M.

Similarly, IA leaves room for the judgement that B is better than A. After all, on IA, though B would only be the same as A regarding E, and worse regarding P and M, it would be better regarding U. Hence, one could judge B better than A, all things considered, if one thought the extent to which it was better regarding U outweighed the extent to which it was worse regarding P and M.[34]

Although IA rules out the consistency of the three judgements in the Mere Addition Paradox, it is misleading to think that it *forces* us, by logic alone as it were, to give up one of three judgements we find deeply plausible. To the contrary, someone who accepts IA will no longer find all three judgements deeply plausible.

Consider, for example, someone who accepts IA, but retains the view that A+ is not worse than A. Unless she grants no weight to equality or maximin, she probably thinks A+ is better than A regarding utility. And, since it is unlikely that the extent to which A+ is better than A regarding U will be exactly equal to the extent to which it is worse regarding E and M, such a person may well believe the former outweighs the latter, so that A+ is actually better than A. In other words, on reflection, someone who accepts IA may well come to believe that, all things considered, it is *good* that the extra people are alive, rather than merely being not bad. (This assumption corresponds to many people's actual reactions to A+ and A.) But if she finds this plausible, why should she find it implausible that B is better than A? Why should she not believe that the extent to which B is better than A regarding U outweighs the extent to which it is worse regarding P and M? Indeed, given that there is even more utility in B than in A+, and that B is better than A+ regarding both equality and maximin, it would be plausible to suppose that B was worse than A only if one thought that the extent to which B was worse than A (and A+) regarding perfectionism outweighed the extent to which B was better

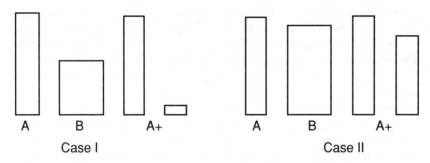

Figure 13.6

than A+ regarding U, E and M. But, of course, if one thought this, there would be no paradox, as it would not seem that B was better than A+.

I believe, then, that if one accepts IA, the Mere Addition Paradox should lose its air of intractability. No longer must it seem deeply implausible to give up one of the three judgements. To the contrary, on IA, the very factors convincing one of the plausibility of two of the judgements will serve to convince one of the implausibility of the third.

These considerations fit well with reactions that many have to variations of the Mere Addition Paradox. Consider figure 13.6, where in each case A+ involves, relative to A, the existence of extra people all of whom have lives worth living and who affect no one else, and B stands to A+ in the manner Parfit described. The difference between Parfit's original case and the above variations is that the worse-off in A+ fare much worse in case I than they do in Parfit's case, while they fare best in case II. Similarly for the B group.

Examining case I, I think most would agree that A is better than B. And many, though not all, would judge B better than A+. However, on IA, there is good reason to reject the claim that A+ is not worse than A. A+ is better than A regarding U, but not by much. On the other hand, A+ is *much* worse than A regarding E and M. So, unless one believes that utility matters *so* much more than equality and maximin that even small increases in the one can outweigh large decreases in both of the others – in which case one would not only have to, but want to, revise one of the other judgements – the judgement that A+ is not worse than A will be implausible.

In case II, I think many, though not all, would continue to judge that B is better than A+. But I also think that many would alter their other two judgements. Unlike case I, the extra people in A+ are *very* well off, almost as well off as the very best-off. That may seem like a significant improvement regarding U. On the other hand, while A+ is worse than A regarding E and M, it is not much worse, especially on the view that equality and maximin matter more at low levels than at high levels. Thus, in case II, it seems quite plausible that, all things considered, A+ is better than A. Similarly, it no longer seems implausible that B is better than A. To the contrary, it seems that the small difference between A and B regarding P and M would be outweighed by there being twice as many in B, all of whom are *almost* as well off as those in A.

Cases I and II suggest the following. IA provides a way of avoiding the Mere Addition Paradox because, on IA, there is always a way of rejecting one of the three judgements comprising the paradox. But this does not mean that in all cases of the sort Parfit has imagined the same judgement must be rejected. Which judgement should be rejected will depend on how the situations actually compare regarding the ideals we value, together with how much these ideals matter in relation to each other. This, of course, is precisely as it should be.

Now in some cases, like I and II perhaps, it may be obvious which judgements should be rejected. However, in other cases it may not be possible simply to look at a diagram and 'read off' which judgement(s) should be rejected. Perhaps by drawing his diagram the way he did, Parfit, in essence, presented such a case. That is, even accepting IA, it may not be evident for Parfit's case which of the three judgements should be given up. But on IA there need be nothing surprising about this, much less deeply inconsistent. Rather, what Parfit would have given us, despite his protestations to the contrary, is an illustration of a case where our different moral principles so conflict that our all-things-considered view is clouded. More specifically, Parfit's case would simply be one in which we are unsure of how the situations actually compare regarding U, E, P or M, or of how much these matter in relation to each other.

There are, of course, many problems in deciding how situations compare regarding ideals, and how to weigh ideals against one another. Moreover, some of these may strike at the very intelligibility of IA. But these problems are not new with the Mere Addition Paradox. They can arise in comparing just two situations.

I believe that we face a genuine *paradox* – like the Liar Paradox – when the conditions that would make a position true are the very conditions that would make it false. More weakly, I believe a position is *paradoxical* if it involves two or more incompatible views, each of which seems, even on reflection, intuitively obvious, certain or (virtually) undeniable. Parfit thought the Mere Addition Paradox was paradoxical, because he thought it would be extremely difficult to deny any of the three judgements that A is better than B, that B is better than A+, or that A+ is not worse than A, and he thought that, together, these three judgements were incompatible, given the intuitively 'obvious' view that 'all-things-considered better than' is a transitive relation. *If* one accepts an essentially comparative view of moral principles, Parfit's three judgements regarding A, A+ and B may well be undeniable, but they will no longer be incompatible, since, as we have seen, given essentially comparative moral principles, 'all-things-considered better than' will not be transitive. On the other hand, *if* one accepts the intrinsic aspect view of moral principles, the transitivity of 'all-things-considered better than' will be undeniable, but it will no longer seem intuitively obvious, certain or (virtually) undeniable that A is better than B, B is better than A+, and A+ is not worse than A. To the contrary, once one accepts IA, it will be clear that various reasons oppose each judgement, and the question of which should ultimately be rejected will be a matter of determining how Parfit's situations actually compare regarding our ideals, together with how much weight each ideal should be given. Now my own view is that, once one accepts IA, one is likely to feel little difficulty deciding these issues, at least sufficiently to resolve the 'paradox'. However, even if this is not the case, and one is unsure which judgement to give up, this need not reflect inconsistency in one's thinking. More likely, it will merely reflect the deep difficulties involved in measuring and balancing the things that matter. This is an important, but familiar, issue: one which might make Parfit's example problematic, but not a paradox, or even paradoxical.

I have suggested that *if* one accepts an essentially comparative view of moral ideals, then the Mere Addition Paradox will no longer be paradoxical. In addition, I have suggested that *if* one accepts an intrinsic aspect view of moral ideals, then the Mere Addition Paradox may be problematic, but not paradoxical. Assuming that one or other of these views of moral ideals is (roughly) right, then it may appear that the Mere Addition Paradox is not, in fact, paradoxical. After all, if one assumes that A or B must be true, and A and B both imply C, then does one not know that C is true, even if one does not know which of A or B is true?

Should we conclude that the 'Mere Addition Paradox' was misnamed? Was Parfit mistaken in describing his results as paradoxical? Not necessarily. As we have seen, many believe that 'all-things-considered better than' must be a transitive relation. Believing this, they may find it (virtually) undeniable that something like the intrinsic aspect view must be right. By the same token, many may find it deeply implausible that they should ignore the fact that the move from A to A+ involves Mere Addition. More generally, it may seem intuitively clear that we cannot simply 'close our ears' to considerations of the sort Parfit has adduced, that our judgements about different outcomes do, and should, depend on such considerations. Thus, on reflection, it may seem (virtually) undeniable that certain moral principles are essentially comparative. If the Mere Addition Paradox seems genuinely paradoxical, herein lies its source. It is not that we cannot decide between three seemingly incompatible judgements regarding A, A+ and B; rather, it is that the Mere Addition Paradox compels us towards a view of moral principles which is incompatible with a view to which many seem[35] committed.

The Mere Addition Paradox should lose its air of paradox when, and if, there are compelling reasons to both accept an intrinsic aspect view of moral principles and reject essentially comparative views, or vice versa. But, until then, the Mere Addition Paradox will be paradoxical, for many.

H. *Should* we accept the intrinsic aspect view of moral principles, and reject the essentially comparative view? Do we in fact make a grave mistake in allowing our judgement about A and A+ to be influenced by the fact that A+ involves Mere Addition? It may seem that the answers to these questions must surely be 'Yes!' As we have seen, adopting IA would give us a way of rejecting the Mere Addition Paradox, and, more important, it would enable us to avoid intransitivity in our all-things-considered judgements. Moreover, in addition to the unwanted implications of its denial, the intrinsic aspect view has great appeal in its own right. Nevertheless, for many, adopting the intrinsic aspect view may not be easy. This is because, on reflection, I think that many of the principles people attach most value to in arriving at their all-things-considered judgements are essentially comparative in nature. Let me next present some considerations supporting this view, and note some of the responses and problems such a view generates. Again, let me remind the reader that my remarks are, perforce, incomplete, as a full exploration of these issues lies well beyond the scope of this essay.

Consider first a principle of justice like the following:

> maximin: The best outcome is the one in which the worst-off people are best off.

Many people believe that maximin, or something like it, represents a fundamentally important moral principle relevant to the assessment of outcomes.[36] But, as with equality, Parfit has offered powerful reasons to reject an intrinsic aspect view of maximin.

Consider again A and A+, where A+ involves Mere Addition. On IA, A+ would be worse than A regarding maximin, since A is the outcome in which the worst-off group is best off. Parfit denies this. Parfit distinguishes two ways in which, in one of two outcomes, the worst-off group might be better off, and contends that only one of these ways

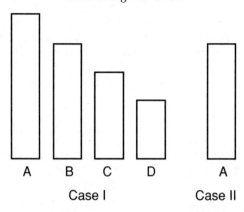

Figure 13.7

makes an outcome better. So, for Parfit, while A+ *is* worse than B regarding maximin, A+ is *not* worse than A regarding maximin, despite A's worst-off group being better off than both B and A+'s. In particular, Parfit points out that the only reason that A's worst-off group is better off than A+'s is because in A the extra people who exist in A+ and have lives worth living *do not exist*. This, Parfit insists, does not make A's outcome better than A+'s *even regarding maximin*.

Parfit's argument in support of his position is confusing,[37] and in some respects both misleading and mistaken (see below). But his crucial insight – though he does not put it in these terms – is that maximin is essentially comparative. This insight is right on the mark. IA is *not* plausible for a principle like maximin.

Consider figure 13.7, which represents a variation of Parfit's 'How Only France Survives' (p. 421). On IA, II would be better than I regarding maximin since, considering solely their abstract internal features, II's worst-off are better off than I's. But suppose II resulted from I via groups B, C and D dying off from old age and the lives of the A group being adversely affected. Parfit contends that it would be *absurd* to say that II was better than I, even regarding maximin. He writes, 'How can it be better if all . . . [groups but one] cease to exist, with the result that the survivors would be *much worse off?*' (p. 424). Even if the position is not *absurd*, it seems deeply mistaken. *Maximin reflects our special concern for those worst-off*, and this concern is not alleviated by the prospect of the worst-off *dying* (at least if their lives are worth living).

Next, consider figure 13.8. III is better than IV regarding maximin.[38] Next suppose that V resulted from IV by the *mere addition* of the extra groups A, B and C. This would not, I think, improve IV regarding

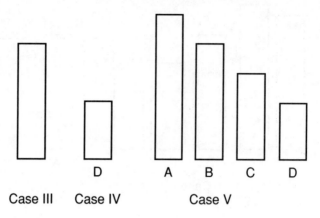

Figure 13.8

maximin. Just as our concern for the worst-off is not alleviated by the worst-off dying, so it is not alleviated by bringing into existence *other* people who are better off than they. But then, if III is better than IV regarding maximin, it seems that III will also be better than V, if V results from IV in the manner suggested.

Now, from the purely abstract perspective, we see that in comparing figures 13.7 and 13.8 II is the same as III, and I is the same as V. So, if IA were appropriate for maximin, we should think that III compared to V as II compared to I. But we don't think this. This is because maximin expresses a concern for the worst-off which is not – and *cannot* be – fully reflected in a situation's abstract internal features.

Parfit employs an example like figure 13.7 to argue that maximin is not appropriately applied in different number cases. As indicated, this entails the crucial insight that maximin is essentially comparative. But I think the issue about numbers is a red herring. Consider figure 13.9. If VI and VII have the same number of people, most would agree that VII is better than VI regarding maximin, *if* VII and VI have entirely different populations, or if VII has resulted from VI by redistribution. But suppose that VII resulted from VI as follows: first, VI was transformed into a situation like II (fig. 13.7) via B, C and D dying off and A being made worse off, then extra people were added so that the population was transformed into VII. Brought about *this* way, VII would not be better than VI regarding maximin, for reasons similar to those presented above. Thus, even where the same numbers are involved, judgements about maximin will not depend solely on the situation's abstract internal features.

By the same token, suppose that we could bring about a future state

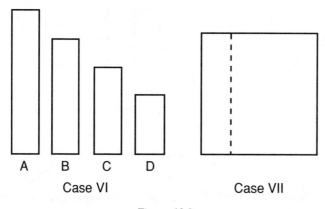

Case VI   Case VII

Figure 13.9

with eight billion people or one with ten billion people in which the worst-off group would be significantly better off. I think that the second situation might be better than the first regarding maximin, and that that would be *one* reason to prefer it. I think, then, that the manner and extent to which maximin applies to two alternatives depends not on their numbers, but on how they are related. But whether I am right about this particular point, or Parfit is, it seems undeniable that the most plausible version of maximin will be essentially comparative. Thus, those valuing maximin cannot avoid the threat of intransitivity by simply adopting IA.

Consider next

> *the person-affecting view* (PAV): where, roughly, how good or bad an outcome is, is a function of the extent to which it *affects people* for better or worse.[39]

As Parfit demonstrates, PAV is subject to various interpretations.[40] However, PAV is perhaps most naturally interpreted in a way that supports a kind of Pareto principle with respect to individual good.[41] Specifically, on PAV, one situation is better than another if there is *someone* for whom it is better and *no one* for whom it is worse. Analogously, on PAV, one situation is worse than another if there is *someone* for whom it is worse and *no one* for whom it is better.[42]

Many believe that PAV expresses a deep and important truth, and those endorsing it span a broad range of positions. Indeed, many think that PAV expresses the *essence* of morality, or at least that portion of morality concerned with outcomes. Even if this is too strong, it is hard to

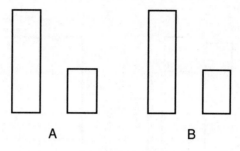

Figure 13.10

deny that PAV is an extremely plausible principle that is at least relevant, if not dominant, in our assessment of (many) outcomes.

Accepting the relevance and significance of PAV has important implications. PAV is essentially pairwise comparative. Its content cannot be captured by an intrinsic aspect view.

Consider figure 13.10. If the people in A were completely different from those in B, then PAV would yield no reason to prefer A or B. However, suppose that the *same* people would be in A's better-off group and B's worse-off group, while *different* people would be in the other two groups. On PAV, A would then be better than B, since A (unlike B) would then be better for some and worse for no one.[43] On the other hand, if the same people would be in A's worse-off group and B's better-off group, while different people would be in the other two groups, then B would be better than A, on PAV. Clearly, then, on PAV our judgement about how A and B compare will depend crucially on the identities of the people involved. Correspondingly, A's and B's desirability will not depend, in the relevant sense required by IA, solely on their internal features, but on both the alternatives they represent and the ones with which they are compared.[44]

Next consider figure 13.11. A, B and C represent three possible outcomes. Each outcome would contain two of the following groups: the p-group, the q-group and the r-group. The members of each group remain the same in each alternative in which the group exists. So, for example, the very same people would exist in the p-group in both A and B, though *they* wouldn't exist in C.

On PAV, A would be better than B, as the coming about of A, rather than B, would be better for some (the p-group) and worse for no one. Analogously, B would be better than C. But A is *not* better than C on PAV. To the contrary, C is better than A, as the coming about of C, rather than A, would be better for some (the q-group) and worse for no one. Clearly, then, 'better than' is not transitive on PAV. This in turn

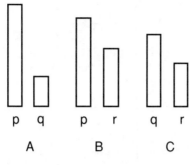

Figure 13.11

threatens the transitivity of 'all-things-considered better than', and this is so even if we regard PAV as only *one* important element in our all-things-considered judgements. After all, as observed earlier, if one important aspect of a complex notion is deeply intransitive, the notion itself will be deeply intransitive.

In sum, PAV expresses an important, widely accepted view, whose nature is essentially pairwise comparative. Thus, as with maximin, it appears that advocates of PAV must look beyond IA to plausibly avoid the threat of intransitivity.

Let us next consider the view that

> *utility is essentially comparative* (UEC): where, roughly, the only way to improve a situation regarding utility is to increase the utility of some of those already living in that situation.

Jan Narveson defends UEC, though he does not call it that, and does not consider its implications for transitivity. According to Narveson, 'Morality has to do with how we treat whatever people there are. . . . [We] do not . . . think that happiness is intrinsically good. We are in favor of making people happy, but neutral about making happy people.'[45] UEC maintains an essential connection between the ideal of utility and our concern with how people fare. On UEC it isn't important that there merely *be* lots of utility but, rather, that people have as much utility as possible. Thus, on UEC, one does *not* improve a situation regarding utility by merely adding new people;[46] nor can one make up for losses in utility to those who exist by merely adding new people.

On reflection, many are attracted to Narveson's position. This is not surprising in light of our previous remarks. UEC is a *person-affecting* version of utility, according to which 'the principle of utility requires that

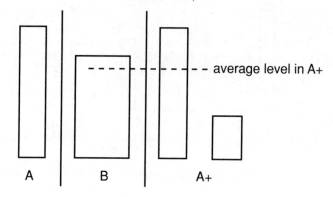

Figure 13.12

before we have a moral reason for doing something, it must be because of a change in the happiness [or utility] of some of the affected persons'.[47] Thus, UEC is able to accommodate people's concern for utility in a way consistent with their more general, and perhaps fundamental, concern about the extent to which people are affected for better or worse.

In the end, UEC may not *fully* capture our views about utility. For example, in Parfit's Non-Identity Problem, UEC may need to be supplemented, or another principle invoked, to accommodate our beliefs. Nevertheless, it seems that for many cases UEC accurately expresses people's concerns regarding utility, and hence will play a significant role in their all-things-considered judgements.

But now it is easy to see that UEC will generate intransitivities. Consider a version of the Mere Addition Paradox where the A people would also exist as A+'s better-off group, and where the same people (including the A people) would exist in both A+ and B (fig. 13.12). On UEC, A will be better than B, because loss in people's utility cannot be made up for merely by adding more people. And B will be better than A+, because loss in some people's utility *can* be made up for by sufficient increases in the utility of others who *already* exist. But on UEC, A is *not* better than A+, as it would have to be if UEC were transitive. This is because, in the example, the mere addition of extra people does *not* lower the level of those who already exist.

One can see, then, that in so far as one is attracted to UEC, and many are, utility will be intransitive. Hence, for reasons noted earlier, 'all-things-considered better than' will also be intransitive.

It should now be clear why, at the beginning of this section, I claimed that, for many, adopting the intrinsic aspect view may not be easy.

Adopting the intrinsic aspect view not only forces us to reject Parfit's forceful considerations for the view that equality is essentially comparative; it also forces us to reject what many will regard as the most plausible versions of maximin, the person-affecting principle and utility. Given the nature of these notions and the prominent role they play in our assessment of outcomes, it is far from clear that this is a viable option, much less a desirable one.

I. My main concern in this part is with general principles and largely theoretical considerations relevant to the assessment of outcomes. However, before considering various responses to the foregoing arguments, it is perhaps worth adding that when one moves from abstract cases to more concrete ones, it may seem there are many cases where the spirit of IA must be rejected – that is, where certain relevant and significant principles for comparing situations are essentially comparative.

For example, consider the following position regarding affirmative action. Some believe that for certain positions in the United States a significant, but not overwhelming, preference should be given to African-Americans over Whites; that is, the preference should do more than break the mythical tie between otherwise 'equally deserving candidates', though a White should still be selected if his qualifications are 'sufficiently' greater than an African-American's. However, preference should not be given to African-Americans over Mexican-Americans, or to Mexican-Americans over Whites. According to this position, what *justifies* affirmative action regarding African-Americans *vis-à-vis* whites is *the particular nature of the historical relationship between African-Americans and Whites* in American society, and, put crudely, Mexican-Americans didn't enslave African-Americans, nor were they enslaved by Whites.

Whether such a position is ultimately defensible, many believe that *something* like it is, or at least might have been, correct. But on this view, it could be better, all things considered, that A be hired before B, that B be hired before C, yet that C be hired before A. This might be so if A were White, B were Mexican-American, and C were African-American; for then, a factor which was relevant and significant when comparing A with C – that is, the peculiar historical relationship between African-Americans and Whites – and which might give C the edge over A, would not apply when comparing A with B, or B with C.

Some people may be uncomfortable with the example of affirmative action. So let me note another example. Many societies have thought that parents should be given preference over their offspring in certain situations. This seems plausible, especially on the view that such preferences should be significant, but not overwhelming. But then, if C were the parent of A, and B were a stranger, it could be better, all things considered, if A were selected rather than B, and B were selected rather than C, yet C were selected rather than A. After all, a relevant and significant factor which might give C the edge over A would not apply when comparing A with B, or B with C.[48]

These examples could be multiplied endlessly. Many special relationships give rise to factors that seem to (rightly) influence our all-things-considered judgements; were the relationships different, we would make different judgements. But then, in comparing alternatives affecting different groups, between whom different relationships obtain, the relevant and significant factors may vary with the alternatives being considered. Correspondingly, the spirit of IA must be rejected, and for such cases there is no reason to expect transitivity to hold. After all, as noted earlier, how any two situations compare, all things considered, will presumably depend on how they compare in terms of the relevant and significant factors for making that comparison. Thus, where different factors are relevant and significant for comparing different alternatives, it can be true that even if A is better than B, and B is better than C in terms of the relevant and significant factors for comparing *those* alternatives, A may *not* be better than C in terms of the relevant and significant factors for making *that* comparison.

Some think that examples of the above sort cast doubt on the transitivity of 'ought to be done rather than', but not on the transitivity of 'better than regarding outcomes'. My own view is that in some cases, though not all, intransitivity in judgements of the former sort, regarding what we ought to do, will carry over into judgements of the latter sort, regarding what ought to be the case. This is because I regard right and wrong acts as relevant to, though not determinant of, the goodness of outcomes.

Either way, I find such examples troubling. Perhaps if it is better to do A than B, B than C, and C than A, we should rest content in the knowledge that any of the three acts would be (equally) right. However, to me, such cases have the feel of the so-called moral blind alleys about which many philosophers deeply – and rightly, I think – worry. In such a case each of the acts may seem seriously wrong, since to choose one would be to choose an act which, by hypothesis, seems morally worse than another available to us.

Since the relevant status of such intransitivities for our central concerns is controversial, I mention, but shall not pursue, them. Instead, let us return to the main argument, and consider next how, if at all, one might respond to the alleged intransitivities associated with the moral ideals of equality, maximin, the person-affecting principle and utility.

J. Some people might try to avoid deep intransitivity in our moral ideals by restricting the scope of those ideals. For example, one might attempt to avoid intransitivity in the notion of PAV by only allowing it to influence our judgements in cases where exactly the same people are involved. Likewise, one might claim that maximin is only plausible when comparing situations which do not involve future generations or when comparing situations involving the same people. (Rawls, himself, seems to have adopted something like the former position when confronted with problems involving future generations.) And similar moves might be adopted for EEC and UEC.

Now, ultimately, I am not sure whether such restrictions are plausible. Nor am I sure that they will succeed in avoiding intransitivities in the notions in question. But none of this really matters. The important point is that such moves will at most win a few battles, but are doomed to lose the war. Specifically, even if such moves preserve the transitivity of our individual moral ideals, they do not preserve – indeed, they directly threaten – the transitivity of our all-things-considered judgements.

For example, suppose that one successfully defends restricting PAV's scope, and that A, B and C are three alternatives such that, given its restricted scope, PAV is relevant only in comparing A and C. It could then be the case that, all things considered – that is, in terms of *all* the relevant and significant principles for making *each* comparison – A is better than B, and B is better than C, yet C is better than A. After all, even if C is worse than A in terms of the principles relevant for comparing A with B, and B with C, the extent to which this is so might be outweighed by the extent to which C is better than A regarding PAV.

The above point is generalizable, *extremely* significant, and to my knowledge *never before noted or taken account of in discussions of moral value*. If the scope of a moral principle or ideal is restricted, such that it applies when comparing some situations but not others, then different principles may be relevant and significant in comparing alternative situations. If this is so, then our all-things-considered judgements may be deeply intransitive *even if none of the aspects underlying those judgements are themselves deeply intransitive*. Thus, restricting the scope of a significant moral ideal opens up the possibility – indeed, virtually guarantees – that the notion of 'all-things-considered better than' will be intransitive even if none of its aspects are.

It is striking that this feature of morality has not been noticed. For example, in *A Theory of Justice* Rawls makes it plain that his two principles of justice are restricted in scope in the sense that 'there are surely circumstances in which they fail'.[49] More specifically, in his early work Rawls contends that his principles of justice apply only in situations in which civilization is 'sufficiently' advanced;[50] while in his later work

Rawls limits their scope even further, contending that they (may) only apply to situations analogous to modern Western-style democracies. Moreover, as noted previously, Rawls (as well as his critics and followers) have suggested that maximin may not be applicable to cases involving future generations, particularly where change in population size may be involved. These limitations in the scope of Rawls's principles have been the subject of much discussion and criticism, yet, as indicated above, to my knowledge, no one has noticed their profound implications for transitivity. After all, if maximin really is relevant and significant in comparing some outcomes, but not relevant and significant in comparing others, then there is no reason to expect transitivity in our all-things-considered judgements.

Maximin is hardly the only principle which has been widely regarded as limited in scope. Indeed, a common view is that there are *no* 'universal' principles – that is, that *every* moral principle is limited in scope, in the sense that it will be relevant and significant for comparing some, but not all, possible outcomes. Unless one wants to conclude that outcomes are non-comparable *whenever* different principles are relevant to assessing them – a view I find too strong and implausible, as it is likely to result in a *severely* incomplete (partial) ordering of all-things-considered judgements – one must look elsewhere to avoid the threat of intransitivity.

K. Convinced that 'all-things-considered better than' *cannot* be intransitive, some philosophers, economists and logicians suggest a technical solution to the arguments which Parfit and I have presented. Roughly, the 'solution' is to offer a finer-grained individuation of outcomes than our discussions suggest. For example, on this view the outcome depicted by A+ in the Mere Addition Paradox *is a different outcome* when its alternative is A than when its alternative is B. Hence, what Parfit has really shown is *not* that A is better than B, B better than A+, and A+ not worse than A; but that A is better than B, B better than A+, and A+' not worse than A – and of course there is nothing intransitive about the latter ordering.[51]

I have grave reservations about the metaphysical and ontological implications of such a solution for the individuation of outcomes. How is it, for example, that one outcome A+ becomes another, *different* outcome, A+', merely because a new alternative is compared with it, one which may or may not even be realizable, let alone realized? Would a similar view be plausible regarding the individuation of *persons*? Surely not. I mention these worries, but shall not pursue them. My main claim is that such a 'solution' is best regarded as a logical trick. Though such a move may succeed technically – that is, formally – it fails substantively. Let me explain.

Formally, one can always preserve transitivity by invoking a sufficiently fine-grained method for individuating outcomes. But doing so loses sight of the *point* of transitivity: that is, of the *reasons* why transitivity seems so desirable. One reason why transitivity is desirable is because it is supposed to help us *choose* between alternatives. Knowing that A is better than B, and B better than A+, I know I can safely choose A over A+. On the view in question, such an inference is misleading and unhelpful. Knowing that A is better than B, and B better than A+, I may know I can safely make the *vacuous* choice of A over A+. But, of course, by hypothesis, my choice will not be between A and A+; rather it will be between A and A+'. Hence my previous knowledge about the relative merits of A and B, and B and A+, will be of no help in deciding what to do. I still won't know which outcome should be chosen.

In part, transitivity is desirable for decision-making precisely because it helps as us to choose between options: it does this by eliminating some of them. Correspondingly, a method which preserves transitivity by *adding* a viable option at each point where we might have wanted and expected to invoke transitivity is not a satisfying *solution* to the threat of intransitivity. In sum, it is one thing to be told that A+ cannot be worse than A if A is better than B, and B is better than A+. It is entirely different – and unhelpful – to be told that since 'better than' *must* be transitive, it is really A+' that is not worse than A if A is better than B, and B better than A+.

The point here might be put in terms of the famous 'money pump'. One reason why economists and others have thought intransitive preferences irrational is that a person with intransitive preferences might spend all their money moving from one preferred outcome to another, and end up exactly where they began. For example, if I *genuinely* prefer an apple to a pear, a pear to an orange, and an orange to an apple, I might rationally trade you my apple and a nickel for your orange, my orange and a nickel for your pear, and my pear and a nickel for your – that is, my original – apple. I have then lost fifteen cents to end up exactly where I started off, and if the exchanges are only repeated often enough, I will end up broke with only my original – now well-worn – apple to show for it. But notice, on the suggested view I might similarly be 'money pumped', though *technically* I would have a perfectly transitive set of preferences. Preferring A to B, and B to A+, and regarding A+' as not worse than A, I might rationally pay a nickel to move from A+ to B, another nickel to move from B to A, and then be indifferent about moving from A to A+' – indeed, I would presumably favour such a move if you paid me a nickel to do so. This money pump would be a bit slower than the previous one, but the end result would be the same. With my 'perfectly transitive' preferences, generated by individuating outcomes in terms of their alternatives, I might be induced to 'rationally' go broke only to end up where I initially started.

Naturally, everything I have just said about A+ and A+' might have been said, *mutatis mutandis*, about A and A', or B and B'. So, for example, knowing that A is better than B, all things considered, won't help me decide between A and B', where B' *is just like* B, except that it is better than A+', which is better than A. More specifically, I will know that while I should prefer A to B. I should also prefer B' to A, since, by transitivity, B' is better than A. Given that B' and B are just like each other, such knowledge will hardly illuminate my decision; nor will the knowledge that, by transitivity, B' *must* be better than B![52]

I shall not pursue the 'technical' solution further. Suffice it to say, I think we must continue to look elsewhere if we hope to find a positive substantive response to the problems in question.

L. Can one avoid intransitivity in one's all-things-considered judgements if one accepts that certain relevant and significant principles for comparing alternatives are essentially comparative? Perhaps one could avoid intransitivity via a set of second-order dominance principles telling us which principles dominate over others when intransitivity threatens. For instance, we might give lexical priority to certain principles, at least for certain cases. I leave this avenue for others to pursue. There are many well-known difficulties with lexical orderings, and I do not see how a set of second-order dominance principles can be arrived at which (a) will not be *ad hoc*, (b) will plausibly respond to the theoretical difficulties raised by essentially comparative principles, and (c) will not themselves be subject to intransitivity (thus requiring a set of third-order dominance principles, which in turn may be intransitive, etc.).

There is another way in which one might respond to the threat of intransitivity. Let me present it with an analogy from sports. In baseball, it is perfectly possible that the first-place team consistently beats the second-place team, which consistently beats the third-place team, which consistently beats the first-place team. Still, most do not think that 'better than' is intransitive regarding baseball teams. Indeed, most think that the better of two teams is the one that wins the most games against *all* the other teams during the season. Thus, for baseball teams, 'all-things-considered better than' remains transitive, notwithstanding the intransitivity of 'consistently beats'; for if A has more total wins than B, and B more than C, A will have more than C, regardless of their records against each other.

One might apply a similar model to the judgements we have been discussing. On such a model, how two situations compare, all things considered, will be a function of both how they compare to each other *and* how they compare to other situations.

On this model, then, one can grant that there are essentially comparative principles, and hence that, in terms of the relevant principles for making each *particular* comparison, A is better than B, B better than C, and C better than A, yet deny that these particular judgements are 'all things considered', and hence deny that 'all-things-considered better than' is intransitive.

The position sketched has obvious attractions. But is the analogy with baseball ultimately plausible? In baseball, there is a small, fixed, conventionally agreed-upon set of alternatives with which each team is to be compared – namely, the other teams currently in the league. The situation is different regarding most questions of 'all-things-considered better than', and this raises both practical and theoretical problems.

Consider a simple case, where n people have applied for a job. On the old, standard way of judging candidates, if the first candidate was better than the second, considering each of the factors relevant to comparing them directly, the first would be regarded as better, all things considered, and the second could be removed from further consideration. Proceeding in this way, one would theoretically need to make only $n - 1$ judgements to determine the best candidate.

On the baseball analogy, to know how two candidates compare, all things considered, it is not sufficient to know how they compare directly; one must also know how they compare to each of the other candidates. So, to determine the best candidate each must be compared to every other. One can easily calculate that this would require $(n \div 2) \times (n - 1)$ judgements.

Consider. On the old way, when a philosophy search committee is swamped with 200 applications for a single job, a 'mere' 199 separate comparisons are required to determine the best candidate. But to compare each of 200 candidates with every other would require 19,900 separate comparisons. The practical impossibility of this will be evident to everyone who has ever served on a search committee.

There is a further problem exacerbating the one just noted. It may be illustrated as follows. Suppose that three baseball teams are up for sale. In assessing which to buy, one would definitely *not* restrict one's attention to how the available teams fared against each other in direct competition. (It *might* be that while A consistently lost to B and C, A was the very best team, while B and C were the two worst.) Instead, one would take into consideration how each team fared against *all* the other teams, *including all the teams that were not on the market*. The point has obvious and important implications for the suggestion in question.

Consider again the apparently simple case of job candidates. On the standard way of thinking, it is sufficient to compare the credentials of the applicants *themselves* to determine the best applicant. On the baseball analogy this is no longer plausible. To the contrary, one would need to compare each applicant not only with the other applicants, but also with those who have not applied! This, of course, would be impossible.

One might alter the baseball analogy to try to address the problems it faces. Or one might pursue yet another way of reconciling essentially comparative principles with the transitivity of 'all-things-considered better than'. However, either way, I think one faces an unavoidable problem of which the shortcomings of the baseball analogy are symptomatic.

I suspect IA lies at the core of both the transitivity of 'all-things-considered better than' and the Independence of Irrelevant Alternatives Principle in perhaps its most plausible form. So, if we reject IA, we should reject them both. Nevertheless, both positions have enormous appeal, and we continue to find them compelling even if we reject IA. Still, once one accepts essentially comparative principles, as it seems we may have to, at least one of these positions must be rejected. This is because on the view that certain principles are essentially comparative, A can be better than B, B better than C, and C better than A, in terms of the relevant and significant principles for making each comparison. It follows that if, in accordance with the Independence of Irrelevant Alternatives Principle, how two situations compare, all things considered, depends solely on how *they* compare in terms of each of the relevant and significant principles for making *that* comparison, then the judgements in question will be all things considered, and 'all-things-considered better than' will be intransitive. On the other hand, if 'all-things-considered better than' *is* transitive, then the judgements in question are not all things considered, contrary to what is implied by the Independence of Irrelevant Alternatives Principle. Thus, once one rejects IA, while both of the positions in question may be false, they cannot both be true.

M. The main reason for rejecting IA, and giving up one or both of the positions in question, is simply that it seems almost undeniable that *certain* special relationships and concerns give rise to essentially comparative principles. A second reason is that *if* one accepts something like the gymnastics model for moral ideals sketched in part I – as it seems one must in order to avoid the Repugnant Conclusion – then it seems that one must reject IA to avoid the absurd conclusion of 'How Only France Survives'. To illustrate this, consider figure 13.13, and let us once again make the simplifying assumption that on the gymnastics model the top 'score' one could receive regarding each ideal is 100. As noted earlier, Parfit contends that it would be absurd to rank II better than I, all things

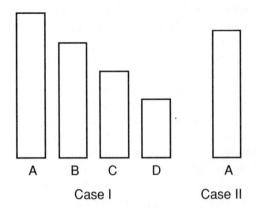

Figure 13.13

considered, if II resulted from I via groups B, C and D dying, with A being adversely affected – though in this case only slightly. But surely if the A group is *very* large, and very well off, in some cases II would be better than I if IA is combined with a gymnastics model. For example, arbitrarily assigning numbers for the sake of illustration, on IA II's scores might be U = 90, P = 90, E = 100 and M = 90 for an all-things-considered score of 370, while I's scores might be U = 98, P = 98, E = 20 and M = 20 for an all-things-considered score of 236, 134 points lower on a scale of 400. The problem, of course, is that on a gymnastics model I may be only slightly better than II regarding utility and perfectionism, while on IA it is almost certain to be *much* worse regarding equality and maximin. Hence II will be better than I, all things considered.

In sum, if, with Parfit, one wants to avoid both the Repugnant Conclusion and the absurd conclusion of 'How Only France Survives', one may have to reject IA. Moreover, reflecting on figure 13.13, one is reminded of the plausibility of the essentially comparative view. After all, there is nothing absurd about the idea that an outcome like II might be better than an outcome like I – for example, if they represent two different futures with entirely distinct populations. What seems absurd is thinking that II would be better than I if it were brought about in the manner described. In other words, our ranking of I and II seems to depend crucially on who their members are, or how they have been brought about, exactly as EC permits and IA forbids.

A further reason for rejecting IA is that, besides providing a response to esoteric problems like the Mere Addition Paradox and 'How Only France Survives', it provides a response to many common cases of apparent inconsistency. For example, many seemingly rational people express views like the following. Given the choice between tennis and softball, they prefer softball; between softball and opera, they prefer opera; and between opera and tennis, they prefer tennis. Or, given the choice between a small expensive house in the city and a large cheap house on the outskirts, they prefer the latter; between a large cheap house on the outskirts and an even larger, more expensive house further out, they prefer the latter; but between the small expensive house in the city and the larger more expensive house further out, they prefer the former. In the past, many philosophers and others have felt compelled to insist – lamely and implausibly? – that, all appearances to the contrary, such preferences were necessarily misinformed, muddle-headed, inconsistent and/or irrational.[53] However, if one rejects IA, many apparently inconsistent orderings may be perfectly understandable and rational, since the relevant and significant principles for comparing certain alternatives (e.g. two athletic events, or two houses both of which would involve commuting) may differ from those for comparing others (e.g. an athletic activity with a non-athletic one, or a house that would require commuting with one that would not).

There is another advantage to rejecting IA. Many philosophers and economists have been deeply troubled by Arrow's Impossibility Theorem according to which, roughly, there can be no decision procedure for arriving at a social ordering among alternatives which simultaneously satisfies certain very plausible assumptions. But Arrow's Theorem, and many of its offshoots, invoke the Independence of Irrelevant Alternatives Principle, which, as we have seen, there is good reason to reject if one rejects IA. Hence, by rejecting IA, one is in a position to reject Arrow's Theorem and its corollaries.

To be sure, rejecting IA and the Independence of Irrelevant Alternatives Principle raises new and significant problems regarding decision procedures for both individual and social orderings and, correspondingly, for both individual and collective rationality. But at least it opens up the possibility of there being a decision procedure for arriving at social orderings. And at least the issues, insights and methods applicable to the individual realm need no longer seem so distinct, much less necessarily irrelevant, to those of the social, or collective, realm.

In sum, in addition to the independent reasons for rejecting IA, there are certain theoretical advantages to rejecting the transitivity of 'all-things-considered better than' and/or the Independence of Irrelevant Alternatives Principle. Still, as should be clear, there are also enormous problems with such a move. As our discussion of the baseball analogy suggests, giving up the Independence of Irrelevant Alternatives Principle raises substantial practical and theoretical difficulties concerning the alternatives which must be considered to determine how two situations compare, all things considered. So, too, does giving up the transitivity of 'all-things-considered better than', since, as we have noted, knowing that A is better than B, all things considered, would no longer be sufficient to prefer A over B, or to remove B from further consideration, if there might be some third alternative which is both worse than B and better than A. Moreover, for most, there seems to be an extremely deep, almost conceptual, link between the notion of 'all-things-considered better than' and *both* the notion of transitivity *and* the Independence of Irrelevant Alternatives Principle.

N. I have contended that, despite IA's advantages, it is extremely difficult to reject the view that at least *some* principles are essentially comparative, and have suggested a fundamental incompatibility between that view, the view that 'all-things-considered better than' *must* be transitive, and the view that how two alternatives compare, all things considered, depends solely on how *they* compare in terms of the relevant and significant factors for making *that* comparison, and not on how one or both compare to some other, independent alternative(s).

Not everyone will be troubled by my results. Those caring only about total utility, or perfectionism, might simply deny the moral relevance of essentially comparative principles. However narrow and implausible, such positions could at least avoid the deep practical and theoretical problems associated with rejecting either the transitivity of 'all-things-considered better than' or the Independence of Irrelevant Alternatives Principle.

Others might accept the view that certain notions are essentially comparative, and not be bothered by its implications. In fact, some Aristotelians and Kantians might relish insuperable difficulties with ranking outcomes. Already convinced that the question 'What ought to be the case?' receives too much attention, they might welcome its relegation to the scrap-heap of the unanswerable, enabling the 'genuinely' important questions – such as 'How ought one *to be*?' or 'What ought one *to do*?' – to receive more consideration in the domain of practical reasoning.

This position cannot be taken lightly. Though it is not a position I readily endorse, perhaps my arguments are best interpreted as a frontal assault on the very intelligibility of consequentialist reasoning about morality and rationality. While it has always *seemed* that one should be able to compare two outcomes directly, and decide which would be better considered just by itself – that is, independently of who its members are, or how it has come about – that notion may be illusory. The question of whether one outcome is better than another *simpliciter* may be unintelligible. Contrary to what most have assumed, in the end there may be no way of separating the question of whether one outcome is better than another from the question of whether one outcome *together with its history* is better than another outcome together with *its* history. For that matter, these questions may be inseparable from the question of whether one outcome together with its history *and its future* is better than another outcome together with its history and *its* future. But of course there may be no limit to how far back, or forward, we would have to go before we could finally arrive at our all-things-considered judgements. This would be contextualism with a vengeance, and to the extent that such worries have force, they must surely make us wonder whether consequentialist reasoning – which depends on our being able to arrive at a meaningful ranking of outcomes – must ultimately be jettisoned altogether.

Unfortunately, I do not see how plausibly to reject the view that certain morally relevant principles are essentially comparative. Nor am I able to happily embrace the deep difficulties involved in rejecting the transitivity of 'all-things-considered better than' or the Independence of Irrelevant Alternatives Principle. To the contrary, as important, and perhaps even primary, as the Aristotelian and Kantian concerns are, it seems that there are countless moral and practical situations in which one either needs or wants to determine which of several outcomes would be best, all things considered. To simply dispense with consequentialist reasoning *tout court* is not, I think, an option. In sum, I am in the disturbing position of failing to see how to reconcile the three views noted above, but am loath to give up any of them. And I believe that, on reflection, many others will also find themselves in this position.

If, in the end, at least one of the three views must be given up, which one(s) should go? I do not know. Much more work needs to be done to answer that question. However, I am confident that, for many, to give up *any* of the three views would require a major shift in their practical and moral reasoning. In fact, I suspect that it would fundamentally alter their very conception of practical and moral reasoning – perhaps of rationality itself.[54]

Conclusion

This has been a long essay. Let me give it a brief conclusion. The Repugnant Conclusion challenges the standard way of regarding utility and its role in our all-things-considered judgements. It forces us to develop a new model for understanding our moral ideals, one which recognizes that however much more we may care about one ideal relative to another, they play fundamentally similar roles in our all-things-considered judgements. In suggesting such a model – the gymnastics model – I have argued that there may be an upper limit to how good a situation can be regarding any particular ideal and, correspondingly, all things considered. Moreover, I have argued that, depending on their role in relation to our all-things-considered judgements, some ideals must share certain formal, or structural, features. Specifically, I suggested that if numbers count regarding utility, they may also have to count regarding equality.

The Mere Addition Paradox forces us to come to grips with the very nature of our moral ideals and two central tenets of practical reasoning. If we accept the view that moral ideals can be essentially comparative – as the Mere Addition Paradox implies – or if we simply accept that moral ideals may be limited in scope – as Rawls and others insist – we must forsake either the transitivity of 'all-things-considered better than' or the Independence of Irrelevant Alternatives Principle in its most plausible form. Either move would have devastating practical consequences. On the other hand, if we reject the view that moral ideals can be essentially comparative, and accept an intrinsic aspect view, we must forsake what many would regard as the most – and perhaps only – plausible versions of some of our deepest moral ideals, including maximin, the person-affecting principle and utility, as well as, if Parfit is right, equality. We would also have to reject the common-sense agent-relative view that special relationships can give rise to relevant factors that rightly influence our all-things-considered judgements. These implications too would have devastating practical consequences. Moreover, on IA we may have to accept the absurd conclusion of 'How Only France Survives', if we are to avoid the Repugnant Conclusion.

Where do we go from here? As already indicated, I do not know. But I do know that we cannot remain complacent in the face of these arguments. Ultimately these arguments may challenge the very intelligibility of a fundamental approach to practical reasoning. Minimally, they challenge us to rethink our views about the good, the nature and structure of moral ideals, and some of our deepest assumptions about practical reasoning. Perhaps our taking up the challenge will be Parfit's greatest legacy to future generations.

Notes

1 For a discussion of the Non-Identity Problem's lessons see my 'Harmful Goods, Harmless Bads', in *Value, Welfare and Morality*, ed. R. G. Frey and Christopher Morris (Cambridge University Press, Cambridge, 1993), pp. 290–324, and *Inequality* (Oxford University Press, Oxford, 1993), ch. 9. See also 'Weighing Goods: Some Questions and Comments', *Philosophy and Public Affairs*, 23–4 (1994), pp. 350–80; pt. 3.

2 Roughly, maximin is a principle whose aim is to 'maximize . . . the long-term prospects of the least advantaged' (John Rawls, *A Theory of Justice* (Harvard University Press, Cambridge, Mass., 1971), p. 157). It ranks alternatives or outcomes according to the expectations of a representative member of the worst-off group, so that if the worst-off group would fare better under A than B, A would be ranked better than B according to maximin. (As we will see, this characterization eventually needs refinement, or careful interpretation, but it is suitable as an initial statement of maximin.)

3 As with our other ideals, characterizing perfectionism is not a simple matter. For our purposes, let me loosely describe perfectionism as an ideal that ranks outcomes in terms of what is 'best' or 'highest' in human (or global?) achievement. On different views the best outcome might be the one with the 'greatest' achievements in social, political, moral, cultural, intellectual or individual development. In what follows, I shall assume that such achievements are directly correlated with how well off the best-off are. That is, for the purposes of discussion I assume – and it is *only* a simplifying assumption – that improvements in the best-off group's level are directly correlated with improvements regarding perfectionism. (I realize that perfectionists need not be elitists, but there may be cases where their views overlap, and my assumption is not only useful but plausible.)

4 Since, in Parfit's example, A and Z are both perfect regarding equality, they will receive the same, perfect scores for equality.

5 Does the gymnastics model entail the controversial claim that there is a diminishing marginal utility of utility? No, at least not in a way that is obviously objectionable. Unfortunately, there is an ambiguity in the usage of 'utility', an ambiguity fostered by a rich philosophical tradition. 'Utility' is often used interchangeably with such notions as 'happiness', 'welfare' and 'quality of life'. Moreover, given the influence of classical utilitarianism and its followers – according to which something is valuable to the extent, and only to the extent, that it promotes increases in happiness, welfare or quality of life – 'utility' is also often used interchangeably with the notion of 'value'. The gymnastics model does *not* imply that there is a diminishing marginal utility (happiness) of utility (happiness) – i.e. that the better off someone is, the less their happiness would be increased by each extra unit of happiness. I share the view that such a position is unintelligible. However, the gymnastics model does imply that there is a diminishing marginal utility (value) of utility (happiness) – i.e. that the objective *value* of increasing a situation's happiness by a certain amount is less if the situation already has a lot of happiness than if it does not. Such a position is not unintelligible; it merely requires that one break the particular, intimate connection between value and happiness prescribed by utilitarianism. (The difference between the subjective and the objective perspective of these matters is important, as noted briefly later.)

6 The preceding paragraphs only present the gymnastics model; they do not defend it. In fact, as will be clear soon, in this section my concern is not to argue for the gymnastics model, but to illustrate a possible alternative to our usual way of thinking about moral ideals.

7   As Parfit originally presents the Repugnant Conclusion, there is no reason to suppose that Z is 'nearly perfect' regarding U, only that it is better than A. But on the position we are now discussing, there will be some population size such that if Z were that size, it would be nearly perfect regarding U. Though we could make our point using the 'weaker' assumption that Z is (merely) better than A regarding U, the assumption that Z is 'nearly perfect' strengthens our example's force, and better illustrates our position.

8   More specifically, Parfit has suggested that this may be so for 'lives whose quality is below a certain level' (p. 412). See his discussion of the Valueless Level in sect. 139, pp. 412–13.

9   Another way of capturing the view that the addition of extra people with lives worth living must always improve a situation, while still avoiding the Repugnant Conclusion, is given by Parfit in his discussion of the 'Lexical View'. See sect. 140, pp. 413–14. Note that, on the gymnastics model, the addition of extra lives worth living might worsen a situation, all things considered, if, for example, it only slightly improved the situation's utility, while significantly worsening its inequality. This has important but controversial implications for Parfit's Mere Addition Paradox, the Absurd Conclusion, and 'How Only France Survives'.

10 This parallels a similar claim suggested by Parfit's distinction between *personal* and *moral* value (pp. 408–9).

11 This may correlate with our psychological response to such situations; but on reflection, our considered moral judgements may resist the deadening effect which prolonged exposure to grave evils sometimes has on our intuitive sensibilities.

12 I believe this is an extremely interesting and important point, but I cannot pursue it here. The point is one that Parfit and I have both developed during discussions over the years. Parfit's discussion of this point is the main focus of ch. 18, esp. sect. 138.

13 These include the range, the relative mean deviation, the variance, the coefficient of variation, the standard deviation of the logarithm and the Gini coefficient. A useful discussion of these measures is contained in Amartya Sen, *On Economic Inequality* (Clarendon Press, Oxford, 1973). See also my *Inequality*, sects 5.1, 5.2, 6.8 and 7.11.

14 Not everyone accepts the view that numbers count in the moral realm. But most do. And I think they are right in doing so (even though I also think that, for reasons implied by the previous section, numbers probably do not count in the *simple* additive way that most have implicitly assumed). John Taurek explicitly denies that numbers should count in his rich and widely discussed article 'Should the Numbers Count?', *Philosophy and Public Affairs*, 6/4 (1977), pp. 293–316. Other authors who raise serious questions about whether numbers count in all cases include Bernard Williams and Elizabeth Anscombe. See the concluding comments of '2. The structure of consequentialism', in Williams's 'A Critique of Utilitarianism', in *Utilitarianism For and Against*, ed. J. J. C. Smart and B. A. O. Williams (Cambridge University Press, Cambridge, 1973), and also G. E. M. Anscombe, 'Modern Moral Philosophy', *Philosophy*, 33 (1958), pp. 1–19.

Shelly Kagan challenges a number of widely held assumptions about additivity in a fascinating article entitled 'The Additive Fallacy', *Ethics*, 99/1 (1988), pp. 5–31. Other reasons to worry about simple additivity are contained, implicitly, in my 'Intransitivity and the Mere Addition Paradox', *Philosophy and Public Affairs*, 16/2 (1987), pp. 138–87, and, explicitly, in *Inequality*. It is perhaps worth emphasizing that *some* reasons why people are drawn to the view that numbers don't count, or that additivity should be rejected, are in fact compatible with an additive model for moral ideals, but not with a *simple* additive model. There may be good reason to retain the view that two pains or deaths are worse than one, that three are worse than two, and so on, and yet to reject the view that two pains or deaths are necessarily *twice* as bad as one, that three are three times as bad, and so on. Thus, for example, while I think that, strictly speaking, utilitarians and others are right to insist that massacring seven million and one is worse than massacring seven million, I suspect that Anscombe and Williams may be correct in thinking that the objective difference between those cases may not be nearly as great as the objective difference between murdering two people and murdering one, and may, in fact, be (virtually?) insignificant. I raise these issues only to leave them aside. Though deep and important, they are not central to our current concerns.

15 This argument is powerful, but not conclusive. David Aman and John Broome have pointed out, in personal correspondence, that one could avoid its implications by adopting a multiplicative function for moral ideals rather than an additive one. For example, instead of adding together numbers representing how good situations are regarding utility and equality in order to arrive at one's all-things-considered judgement, one might multiply the relevant numbers. Such a function would enable one to maintain that while moving from E to F is significantly worse than moving from C to D regarding utility, and *no* better regarding equality, the move from E to F will be desirable if the move from C to D is. Though such a move accommodates what many people would (at least initially) want to say about the particular situations in question, I am not sure that it can be independently motivated or ultimately defended. Prima facie, at least, it strikes me as odd, implausible and (hence) *ad hoc* to contend that how good a situation is, all things considered, will depend on, among other things, how good it is regarding utility *times* how good it is regarding equality. (Are there any *other* moral ideals that might be related in a *multiplicative* manner?) Still, I think the suggestion is worth pursuing, since there are serious difficulties with the more natural and intuitively appealing additive approach. (See n. 14. I take it that Kagan might be quite sympathetic to Aman and Broome's suggestion. I am less so, since the difficulties I see with the additive approach, though significant, do *not* undermine the argument I have presented.)

16 The argument presented here is in fact only one of several supporting the conclusion that PV should be rejected. Others are presented in my article 'Intergenerational Inequality', in *Philosophy, Politics, and Society*, 6th ser., ed. Peter Laslett and James Fishkin (Yale University Press, New Haven, 1992), pp. 169–205, as well as my book *Inequality*.

17 Tyler Cowen has an interesting discussion of the Repugnant Conclusion in his article 'What Do We Learn from the Repugnant Conclusion?', *Ethics*, 106/4 (1996), pp. 754–75. Unfortunately, Cowen's article appeared after this essay's completion.

18 Parfit's claims regarding New A and A+ are defensible if one assumes, as most have, that mere (proportional) increases in population size do not themselves worsen inequality. But, though various considerations support this assumption, ultimately, it is highly questionable, and should probably be rejected. Given that New A is a *much* larger population than A+ and, correspondingly, that in New A there are *far* more people who are much worse off than others through no fault of their own than there are in A+, there are good grounds for claiming that New A's inequality is much worse than A+'s. See *Inequality*, ch. 7, where I defend this view at length. In addition, see ibid., chs 2 and 3 for other considerations relevant to assessing Parfit's claims regarding inequality. Finally, Parfit's claim regarding New A and New B seems to rely on the Pigou–Dalton condition, according to which any transfer from better- to worse-off lessens inequality. However, as I show in *Inequality*, ch. 3, the Pigou–Dalton condition is supported by 'all of the plausible views' of inequality only in cases involving 'even' transfers – i.e. in cases where the worse-off gain one unit for each unit that the better-off lose. On many plausible views of inequality the Pigou–Dalton condition must be rejected for certain cases of 'efficient transfers – including the case Parfit describes regarding New A and New B – where the worse-off gain more than the better-off lose. Thus, in fact, on many plausible views of inequality New B's inequality would be worse than New A's. (See *Inequality*, sects 3.4–3.6, for detailed arguments supporting these claims.)

19 See n. 23 for further considerations relevant to these claims.

20 In what follows I omit Parfit's 'Divided B', as it does not affect my argument.

21 Parfit puts his discussion in terms of beneficence; for simplicity, I have recast it in terms of utility. The shift in terminology does not affect my arguments.

22 Parfit, 'Future Generations: Further Problems', *Philosophy and Public Affairs*, 11/2 (1982), pp. 158–9.

23 Some people do not find the Mere Addition Paradox problematic; what they find problematic is iterations of the paradox which seemingly lead to the Repugnant Conclusion. So, while they have little difficulty accepting the initial moves from A to A+, to B, to B+, they are confident that *somewhere* between A and Z the line should be drawn, even if they are not sure exactly where.

   I believe this line is defensible, and not merely because, as Parfit suggests in section 146, 'not worse than' is not a transitive relation. Parfit writes: 'it is true that, by the same reasoning [underlying the paradox], C cannot be worse than B, D cannot be worse than C, and so on. But since *not worse than* is not transitive, we can claim that, while C is not worse than B, which is not worse than A, C *is* worse than A' (p. 432). Suppose, however, we think A+ is *better* than A, and B better than A+, then since, according to Parfit, 'better than' *is* a transitive relation, B would be better than A, and it *looks* as if iterations of the paradox would entail the Repugnant Conclusion. After all, 'by the same reasoning', C would be better than B, D would be better than C, and so on. Hence, given 'better than's' transitivity, C would be better than A, and Z would be best.

Such reasoning is appealing, but can, I think, be resisted. Specifically, it is not clear that 'the same reasoning' which underlies our judgements regarding A, A+ and B would apply to situations closer to Z. For example, even if A+ is better than A, and B+ is better than B, F+ might be worse than F. This might be so if, as many believe, inequality matters more at low levels than at high levels, or if, analogously, maximin matters more at low levels. (Since maximin expresses our special concern for how the worst-off fare, this concern may be heightened, the worse off the worst-off are.) On such views the move from F to F+ may be worse regarding E or M than the move from A to A+. Similarly, if one adopts something like part I's gymnastics model for understanding utility, then the extent to which F+ is greater than F regarding U may be less than the extent to which A+ is better than A. Any of these factors alone could prevent the slide from A to Z. Combined, they make it quite plausible that F+ could be worse than F, even if A+ is better than A.

In sum, critics of the Mere Addition Paradox could not only reject the claim that B is worse than A; they could insist that A+ is better than A, B is better than A+, and B better than A without accepting the Repugnant Conclusion. This position corresponds to some people's actual reactions to the Mere Addition Paradox and iterations of it, and has important implications in its own right.

24 Parfit questions whether one could deny that B is better than A+ without being an elitist. He writes, 'can we honestly claim to believe that a change from A+ to B would not be a change for the better? If we claim [this] . . . , we would be saying that what matters most is the quality of life of the best-off people. . . . Call this the *Elitist View*. On this view, what happens to the best-off people matters *more* than what happens to the worst-off people' (p. 427). Parfit's remarks here are misleading.

Consider two variations of A+ and B (fig. 13.14). Suppose that in I, even A+'s worse-off fare very well, while in II the B group fares well, but A+'s worse-off fare poorly. Suppose, further, that the difference in quality of life between II's B group, I's B group and A+'s better-off group in I and II is due to the quality of artistic works in the different situations. Specifically, suppose that in II's B there are many fine artistic works, in I's B some very good works as well, and in A+, a few, rare works of genuine genius, in addition to many others of lesser quality. It is plausible to hold that in so far as one cares about perfectionism, the loss of a few works of true genius would matter much more than the loss of many works that are merely very good. So, regarding perfectionism, the difference between A+ and B in I might be much more significant than the difference between I's B and II's B. Correspondingly, regarding perfectionism, the difference between A+ and B in I might be quite significant, and almost as significant as the difference between A+ and B in II. By the same token, since A+'s worse-off group fares much worse in II than I, both in absolute terms and relative to the

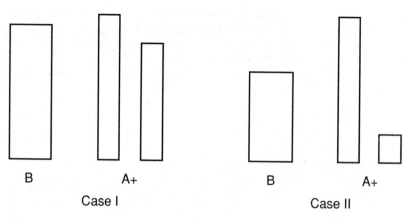

B   A+   B   A+

Case I   Case II

Figure 13.4

better-off group, and since it is plausible to hold that inequality and maximin matter more at low levels than at high levels (see previous note), one might hold that, regarding equality and maximin, A+ is much worse than B in II, but not significantly worse than B in I. It follows that, all things considered, B might be better than A+ in II, but worse than A+ in I. Specifically, in I, the significant loss regarding perfectionism in moving from A+ to B might outweigh the relatively slight gains regarding equality, maximin and utility; but in II, the significant loss regarding perfectionism in moving from A+ to B might be outweighed by the significant gains regarding equality and maximin, together with the relatively slight gain regarding utility.

The preceding suggests that one need not be an elitist to deny that B is better than A+. The key question is whether one believes that the relation between B and A+ resembles I or II. Parfit may have been implicitly assuming that in the Mere Addition Paradox the relation between B and A+ resembles II, and, as drawn (p. 419), his B and A+ certainly *look* more like II than I. Moreover, since the example is his, Parfit can hardly be faulted for making such an assumption, and given such an assumption, it is not unreasonable to claim that only an elitist would deny that B is better than A+. Nevertheless, Parfit's presentation does not dictate such an assumption, hence there is nothing to preclude someone from assuming that in the relevant respects the relation between B and A+ resembles I more than II. Correspondingly, some might claim that B is worse than A, because they think that in this particular case a relatively significant loss regarding one ideal outweighs relatively minor gains regarding other ideals. Clearly, such people need not be elitists; indeed, they might vehemently deny that 'what matters most is the quality of life of the best-off people', or that 'what happens to the best-off people matters *more* than what happens to the worst-off people'.

25   The issue here is not one of objectivity versus subjectivity. On EEC there

may be a fact of the matter regarding how bad the inequality in A+ *really* is when compared to A, and also when compared to B. But there are no facts about how good or bad situations are regarding inequality outside the context of essentially pairwise comparisons.

26 All the economists' measures of inequality would support this claim, as would my own work on inequality. See part I for some relevant considerations.

27 My reasons for using this particular terminology need not detain us here. The interested reader is referred to my 'Intransitivity and the Mere Addition Paradox'.

28 In some ways my terminology is misleading. For example, in one sense the identities of a situation's members are clearly an internal feature of that situation. However, on the intrinsic aspect view, identity *per se* should play no role in our evaluation of a situation. So, on IA, if two situations are exactly alike in all other respects, except that they involve different people, then for any factor *f* relevant to the ranking of outcomes, the two situations must be equally good regarding *f*. Likewise, if the identity of a situation's members affects our evaluation of the situation in a way that depends on whether alternatives would involve the same people, then, in ranking outcomes, we would not be focusing solely on features internal to the outcomes in the relevant way required by IA. Unfortunately, a precise characterization of the intrinsic aspect view is difficult to give, but the basic idea should be fairly clear.

29 In reality, of course, we might never be able to assign a precise number that would meaningfully reflect exactly how good a situation is regarding *f*. At best one could assign a rough range of numbers that would give us a partial, rather than complete, ordering of outcomes regarding *f*. For simplicity, my discussion ignores such complications. Though important in some contexts, they do not affect my central claims.

30 Arrow's revolutionary Impossibility Theorem is presented in K. J. Arrow, *Social Choice and Individual Values* (John Wiley and Sons, New York, 1951; rev. edn 1963).

31 To avoid confusion, let me emphasize that this is *not* Arrow's view. Arrow believed that all meaningful rankings of alternatives must be relative, or essentially pairwise comparative. He would have denied that a meaningful comparison between A and B could be achieved by combining evaluations of A and B arrived at independently of each other. Of course, Arrow also thought comparisons with other alternatives would be irrelevant to the comparison between A and B. Hence, for Arrow, to know how A compared to B, it was both necessary, in an essentially pairwise comparative sense, and sufficient to compare them directly. My claim is that there is a version of the Independence of Irrelevant Alternatives Principle, different from Arrow's, that has great plausibility and is based on IA.

32 It does not follow that Parfit was mistaken in emphasizing Mere Addition, since his argument, in essence, challenges IA. But if, on reflection, one accepts IA, one cannot be influenced by such information.

33 I give a detailed argument in support of this claim in part I of 'Intransitivity and the Mere Addition Paradox'.

34 Recall that someone who judges B better than A need not necessarily be committed to the Repugnant Conclusion. As one moves from A toward Z, conditions may change sufficiently to block iteration of one's judgements regarding A, A+ and B. So, for example, it might be the case that, all things considered, B is better than A, and C is better than B, but G is not better than F. See n. 23.

35 This qualification is important. Some people may be committed to an intrinsic aspect view only in so far as that seems necessary to preserve the transitivity of 'all-things-considered better than', and, as we will see, there is a way of reconciling an essentially comparative view of moral principles with the transitivity of 'all-things-considered better than'. But, as we will also see, the move in question involves significant costs of its own.

36 Rawls's own version of maximin differs from the version given here in important respects (see following note). But many people are attracted to the one given here, and, importantly for our purposes, it is probably the version of maximin most naturally adopted on IA. I directly argue for the essentially comparative nature of Rawls's version of maximin in 'Intransitivity and the Mere Addition Paradox', and say more about Rawls's own view of maximin and its relevance to our concerns below.

37 The argument is given in sect. 144; see esp. pp. 423–4. Parfit himself now regards the argument in question as 'opaque'.

38 Recall that the version of maximin under discussion is not Rawls's. Rawls's maximin principle does *not* directly assess outcomes in terms of the worst-off groups' levels; rather, it assesses the *justness* of a society's principles and institutions in terms of the effect that they have on the expectations of a representative member of the worst-off group (see *Theory of Justice*, pp. 78–9). On Rawls's view, we can not say yet how III and IV compare regarding maximin. Indeed, for all we know, IV might be better than III regarding maximin, as IV might be a perfectly just society, and III an unjust one. This feature of Rawls's view is often overlooked. It has important implications, some of which are discussed in my 'Intransitivity and the Mere Addition Paradox'.

39 This is a generalized version of Parfit's Person-Affecting View, V (p. 370). It is, I think, sufficiently within the spirit of the Person-Affecting View as Parfit has developed it over the years to warrant using the same name, and I trust that my doing so will not be a source of confusion.

40 Parfit distinguishes various versions of person-affecting views, including a *narrow* view, a *wide total* view, and a *wide average* view (pp. 393–401). Though interesting in their own right, these distinctions need not concern us here.

41 John Broome advocates a principle of this sort, which he calls 'the principle of personal good', and notes the ways in which it differs from the 'classic' Pareto principle. Broome is aware of his principle's shortcomings, and qualifies it accordingly. But he does not discuss the controversial implications for

transitivity of the qualifications he makes. (See his *Weighing Goods* (Blackwell, Oxford, 1991), and also my 'Weighing Goods'.)

42 There is an intimate connection between PAV and the view I have else-where called the 'Slogan' – the view that one situation *cannot* be worse (or better) than another if there is *no one* for whom it *is* worse (or better). However, PAV is not equivalent to the Slogan; nor does it entail the Slogan. The Slogan represents an all-things-considered position, while PAV is compatible with a plurality of principles, some of which may conflict with the Slogan. I discuss the Slogan in 'Harmful Goods, Harmless Bads' and in *Inequality*, ch. 9.

43 It would be worse for no one for the reasons Parfit presents in discussing the Non-Identity Problem (pp. 351–79).

44 I am not denying the obvious fact that there is a straightforward sense in which people's identities can be regarded as intrinsic, or internal, features of situations. But on IA people's identities cannot be relevant to how good or bad a situation is regarding such ideals as equality, utility, maximin or perfectionism – at least, not if IA is to avoid the intransitivities arising from essentially comparative views. Moreover, though I did not argue this, I take it that the whole *point* of IA is to deny that identity *per se* is (or could be) relevant to our abstract, impartial, static judgements about how good situations *themselves* are. Of course, identities would be (indirectly) relevant to such moral factors as duty or desert, but this is not relevant to our claims.

45 Jan Narveson, 'Moral Problems of Population', *Monist* 57/1 (1973), pp. 73 and 80.

46 This position assumes that bringing people into existence with lives worth living does not, itself, benefit the people in question. I, myself, believe this is the most plausible position on the question of whether causing someone to exist can benefit that person, though in appendix G Parfit argues that the contrary position is also plausible. Regardless, UEC involves the position in question, which is all that matters for our present concern.

47 This quotation is from Narveson's pioneering work 'Utilitarianism and New Generations', *Mind*, 76 (1967), p. 67.

48 I owe this parent–offspring example to an unpublished note which Ronald Dworkin sent to Parfit, and which Parfit showed me after reading an early draft of this essay. Frances Myrna Kamm presents two similar examples in 'Supererogation and Obligation', *Journal of Philosophy*, 82/3 (1985), p. 137.

49 Rawls, *Theory of Justice*, p. 63.

50 See e.g. ibid. sects 11 and 26.

51 This move has been suggested to me in correspondence by both Warren Quinn and John Broome, and it has been raised in discussion at various universities where I have lectured, though Broome readily recognized and admitted the substantive – as opposed to the purely formal – shortcomings of such a 'solution'.

52 This point is similar to the previously noted fact that, once one rejects the transitivity of 'all-things-considered better than', knowing that A is better than B, all things considered, will not be sufficient to prefer A to B, or to remove B from further consideration. Basically, if one preserves transitivity

by adding options in the manner suggested by the technical solution, knowing that A is better than B, all things considered, will not be sufficient to remove B' from consideration where, from an abstract perspective, B' is just like B.

53 Not everyone has felt this way. Some have claimed that purported instances of intransitive preferences are more apparent than real. Others have suggested that, given the actual conditions of choice under uncertainty, it might be useful, and therefore rational, to adopt 'simplification procedures... which approximate one's "true preference" very well', and hence which *usually* serve one in good stead, but occasionally lead to intransitivities. (The quote is from Amos Tversky's classic article, 'Intransitivity of Preferences', *Psychological Review*, 76 (1969), pp. 31–48.) My suggestion is different from these, in supposing that one might rationally hold three genuinely intransitive preferences, *not* simply as a result of relying on a simplified approximation method which is usually helpful but occasionally steers us wrong.

54 For further discussion and another kind of argument for intransitivity see my 'A Continuum Argument for Intransitivity', *Philosophy and Public Affairs*, 25/3 (1996), pp. 175–210. See also my 'Weighing Goods', pt 4, and my contribution to *Well-Being and Morality: Essays in Honour of James Griffin*, ed. Roger Crisp and Brad Hooker (Oxford University Press, Oxford, forthcoming).

Notes on Contributors

Robert Merrihew Adams is Clark Professor of Moral Philosophy and Metaphysics at Yale University. Educated in philosophy and theology at Princeton, Oxford and Cornell, he has also taught philosophy at the University of Michigan and UCLA. He is the author of *The Virtue of Faith* (Oxford Univeristy Press, 1987) and *Leibniz: Determinist, Theist, Idealist* (Oxford University Press, 1994), as well as numerous papers in the philosophy of religion, ethics, metaphysics and the history of modern philosophy.

Simon Blackburn is Edna J. Koury Professor of Philosophy at the University of North Carolina, Chapel Hill. Educated at Cambridge, he held a Research Fellowship at Churchill College before becoming Tutor in philosophy at Pembroke College, Oxford, where he taught from 1970 to 1990. From 1984 to 1990 he was editor of the journal *Mind*. His books include *Spreading the Word* (Oxford University Press, 1984), *Essays in Quasi Realism* (Oxford University Press, 1993), and the *Oxford Dictionary of Philosophy* (Oxford University Press, 1994).

David O. Brink is Professor of Philosophy at the University of California, San Diego. His research interests are in ethical theory, history of ethics, political philosophy and philosophy of law. He is the author of *Moral Realism and the Foundations of Ethics* (Cambridge University Press, 1989). He is currently working on historical and systematic conceptions of practical reason and morality and on issues in constitutional jurisprudence about the role of judicial review within a constitutional democracy.

Jonathan Dancy taught at the University of Keele before becoming Professor of Philosophy at the University of Reading, UK, in 1996. He was Visiting Professor at the University of Pittsburgh in 1988–9 and Visiting Fellow of All Souls College, Oxford, in 1993–4. His books include *An Introduction to Contemporary Epistemology* (Blackwell, 1985) and *Moral Reasons* (Blackwell, 1993).

David Gauthier is Distinguished Service Professor of Philosophy at the University of Pittsburgh. His most recent books are *Morals by Agreement* (Oxford University Press, 1986) and a collection of his essays, *Moral Dealing: Contract, Ethics, and Reason*. In addition to moral, political and legal contractarianism, and their founder Thomas Hobbes, his principal philosophical interests include the theory of rational deliberation and the relation between social thought and autobiography in the writings of Jean-Jacques Rousseau.

Frank Jackson has taught at La Trobe University and Monash University, and is currently Professor of Philosophy in the Research School of Social Sciences at the Australian National University. He is the author of *Perception* (Cambridge University Press, 1977), *Conditionals* (Blackwell, 1987), and, with David Braddon-Mitchell, *The Philosophy of Mind and Cognition* (Blackwell, 1996). He was Senior Humanities Council Fellow at Princeton University in 1990, and John Locke Lecturer at Oxford University in 1995.

Mark Johnston is Professor of Philosophy at Princeton University, and is the author of many widely discussed papers on philosophy of mind, metaphysics and moral psychology.

John McDowell was a Fellow of University College, Oxford, until 1986, when he moved to the University of Pittsburgh, where he is now a University Professor. He translated Plato's *Theaetetus* for the Clarendon Plato series (Clarendon Press, 1973); co-edited *Truth and Meaning* (Oxford University Press, 1976) with Gareth Evans, and *Subject, Thought, and Context* (Oxford University Press, 1986) with Philip Pettit; and prepared Evans's *The Varieties of Reference* for publication (Oxford University Press, 1982). He is the author of *Mind and World* (Harvard University Press, 1994) and of numerous articles. He is a Fellow of the British Academy and of the American Academy of Arts and Sciences.

Philip Pettit is Professor of Social and Political Theory at the Australian National University and a Professor of Philosophy, on a visiting basis, at Columbia University. Before that he was Professor of Philosophy at the University of Bradford, UK. He is the author of a number of books and articles, including, most recently, *The Common Mind: An Essay on Psychology, Society and Politics* (Oxford University Press, 1993) and *Republicanism: A Theory of Freedom and Government* (Oxford University Press, 1997).

Sydney Shoemaker is Susan Linn Sage Professor of Philosophy at Cornell University. He was born in Boise, Idaho, in 1931, received his BA from Reed College in 1953, and his Ph.D. from Cornell University in 1958. He is the author of *Self-Knowledge and Self-Identity* (Cornell University Press, 1963), *Identity, Cause, and Mind* (Cambridge University Press, 1984), *Personal Identity* (coauthored with Richard Swinburne) (Blackwell, 1984), and *The First Person Perspective and Other Essays* (Cambridge University Press, 1996).

Michael Smith is Senior Fellow in the Philosophy Program at the Research School of Social Sciences, Australian National University. He taught previously at Oxford University, Princeton University and Monash University. He is the author of *The Moral Problem* (Blackwell, 1994) and the editor of *Meta-Ethics* (Dartmouth, 1995), and has published articles in the areas of ethics, moral psychology and philosophy of mind.

Michael Stocker is Professor of Philosophy at Syracuse University, NY. He developed an abiding interest in ethics during graduate work at Harvard in the early 1960s – at that time, mainly in theories of act evaluation. His present philosophical concerns are more with people, their motives, purposes and emotions, and as givers and receivers of attention, affection and value. He is the author of *Plural and Conflicting Values* (Oxford University Press, 1990), and with Elizabeth Hegeman, *Valuing Emotions* (Cambridge University Press, 1996).

Larry S. Temkin is Professor of Philosophy at Rice University in Houston. He received his Ph.D. from Princeton University, and studied for awhile at the University of Oxford. He was Visiting Professor at the University of Pittsburgh in 1986, and has received numerous honours and awards including the Danforth Fellowship, the Andrew Mellon Fellowship, the National Humanities Center Fellowship, and Harvard University's Program in Ethics and the Professions Fellowship. He is the author of *Inequality* (Oxford University Press, 1993). His main philosophical interests lie in normative ethics, meta-ethics and social and political philosophy, with a special emphasis on practical rationality.

Judith Jarvis Thomson is Professor of Philosophy at MIT. She works primarily in ethics and metaphysics, and is the author of *Rights, Restitution and Risk* (Harvard University Press, 1986) and *The Realm of Rights* (Harvard University Press, 1990); her most recent book, written jointly with Gilbert Harman, is *Moral Relativism and Moral Objectivity* (Blackwell, 1996).

Index of Names

Anscombe, G. E. M., 197, 234–5,
 249n, 337n
Aristotle, 56, 65–6, 132n, 133n
Arrow, K. J., 310, 332, 342n

Bayesianism, 77, 78–9
Bennett, J., 289n
Berkeley, G., 180, 183, 196
Boonin-Vail, D., 21
Brandt, R., 79
Broad, C. D., 99, 109, 189
Broome, J., 343n
Buddha, Buddhism, 267, 287n
Butler, J., 116, 235–6, 255

Cassam, Q., 199n, 200n
Chappell, V., 226n
Chisholm, R. M., 228n
Crozan, N., 203, 222

Descartes, R., 231–48

Elster, J., 80
Evans, G., 248n, 250n

Gauthier, D., 79
Gillett, G., 199n

Hume, D., 80, 100, 103, 116, 130n,
 138–9, 183–91

Jeffrey, R. C., 79
Johnston, M., 226n

Kagan, S., 338n
Kant, I., 55, 67, 182–99
Kierkegaard, S., 267
Korsgaard, C., 177n, 191
Kuflik, A., 258

Lewis, D., 133n, 179n, 181, 219, 228n
Lichtenburg, G. C., 138, 235
Locke, J., 116, 142, 203, 205, 230–48,
 268

McTaggart, J. M. E., 156, 177n
Mill, J. S., 23n, 56, 120
Moore, G. E., 151

Nagel, T., 92, 99, 102, 110, 130n, 140,
 178n
Narveson, J., 321
Nozick, R., 178n

Perry, J., 139, 144, 286n
Prior, A. N., 155

Quine, W. V. O., 171

Rawls, J., 79, 80, 325–6, 335, 343n
Reagan, R., 153
Rovane, C., 194–5
Russell, B. A. W., 139

Shoemaker, S., 169, 226n, 249n
Sidgwick, H., 79, 89, 91, 96, 98–9,
 101–12, 116, 131n, 261

Sosa, E., 179n
Strawson, P. F., 183, 187–91, 248n
Sowden, L., 260, 285n

Taurek, J., 337n

Wiggins, D., 136, 245–6
Williams, B. A. O., 131n, 136–7, 186,
  196–7, 200n, 337n
Wolf, S., 171, 264–6, 286n
Woodward, J., 288–9n

Index of Examples, Positions, Theories etc., Originally From *Reasons and Persons*

Appeal to Full Relativity, 72, 89–93, 98–102, 111, 252–3

Average Principle, 277

Backup, 270

Cartesian ego, 140–3, 153–4, 156, 159, 184, 244

Clare, 13–16

Combined Spectrum, 136, 159, 172–5, 178n

Common-Sense Morality (M), 194, 253, 256–63, 285n

Consequentialism (C), 2–4, 11–21, 45–52, 253–63

continuity, connectedness, 10, 116–21, 124, 126–8, 132n, 133n, 135–47, 162–75, 185, 208–26, 231, 268–73, 286n

Critical Present-aim Theory, (CP), 54, 71–2, 82–89, 129n, 130n, 147; CPM and CPS, 83, 87–8, 194

desert breakdown, 4, 20–1, 26–34

Elitist View, 340n

Extreme Claim (about what matters), 132n, 145, 162

Extreme Claim (about desert and punishment), 267–73

featureless Cartesian view, 142

Fisherman's Dilemma, 257–9

fission, 117, 123–6, 137–8, 159–72, 178n, 179n, 181, 246–7, 287n

formal/substantive theories, 11, 24–8, 31–5, 40n

further fact, 116, 145–6, 153–76, 177n, 244–5, 268

Future Tuesdays, 55, 82, 88, 286n

Garbo, G., 137

Happy Child, 278–9

Hell Three, 300

How I end My Slavery, 38–40

How Only France Survives, 296, 300, 317, 330, 331

Japanese woman, 141

Kate, 7–11, 19–21

Lefty/Righty, 160, 168, 178n, 229n, 267–8

Lexical View, 337n

Medical Programmes, 274

Mere Addition Paradox, 279–84, 300–35

Moderate Claim, 145, 162–76, 263

My Moral Corruption, 13–14

Neutral (Common-Sense) Morality (N), 71, 83, 99–102, 257

Nineteenth-Century Russian, 271–3

Non-Identity Problem, 274–5, 322

Overdetermination case one, 42–52; case two, 46–7; case three, 46–7

Person-Affecting View, 274–5, 319–21, 343n
Physical Spectrum, 137, 224
Preference-Hedonism, 57
Present-aim Theory (P), 71–2, 80–93, 99–101, 194
Psychological Spectrum, 136, 223

quasi-memory, 130n, 183–4, 239–44, 249n

Reductionism, 110, 116–29, 135–47, 149–76, 231–48, 263–73
Relation R, 116–29, 133n, 162, 268–73
Repugnant Conclusion, 276–84, 291–335
Revised (Common-Sense) Morality (R), 257–63

Schelling's answer to armed robbery, 5–7, 10, 37–8
Second Mistake, 43–5, 52
self-defeating theories, 1–2, 24–40, 253–63
self-effacing theories, 261–2
Self-interest Theory (S), 1–11, 16–21, 24–40, 71, 81–93, 96, 99, 101–29, 146–7, 194, 200n, 252–63
Share-of-the-Total View, 51, 52n
subjective/objective rationality, rightness, 2–4, 17, 49–52, 53n, 81, 106
Success Theory, 57

Teletransportation, 162–76, 178n, 269
Timeless, 54
Total Principle, 276
Two Hells, 277–8; see Hell Three

Valueless Level, 337n

Wretched Child, 278–9